許斐　剛

Kal becomes a raccoon!

—Takeshi Konomi, 2000

About Takeshi Konomi

Takeshi Konomi exploded onto the manga scene with the incredible **THE PRINCE OF TENNIS**. His refined art style and sleek character designs proved popular with **Weekly Shonen Jump** readers and **THE PRINCE OF TENNIS** became the No. 1 sports manga in Japan almost overnight. Its cast of attractive male tennis players attracted legions of female readers even though it was originally intended to be a boy's comic. The manga is a continuing success in Japan. A hit anime series was created, as well as several video games and mountains of merchandise.

THE PRINCE OF TENNIS
VOL. 4
The SHONEN JUMP Manga Edition

STORY AND ART BY
TAKESHI KONOMI

English Adaptation/Gerard Jones
Translation/Joe Yamazaki
Touch-up Art & Lettering/James Gaubatz
Graphics & Cover Design/Sean Lee
Editor/Michelle Pangilinan

Editor in Chief, Books/Alvin Lu
Editor in Chief, Magazines/Marc Weidenbaum
VP of Publishing Licensing/Rika Inouye
VP of Sales/Gonzalo Ferreyra
Sr. VP of Marketing/Liza Coppola
Publisher/Hyoe Narita

Printed in the U.S.A.

Published by VIZ Media, LLC
P.O. Box 77010
San Francisco, CA 94107

SHONEN JUMP Manga Edition
10 9 8 7 6 5 4 3
First printing, October 2004
Third printing, October 2007

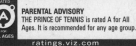

www.viz.com

THE WORLD'S
MOST POPULAR MANGA

www.shonenjump.com

SHONEN JUMP Manga

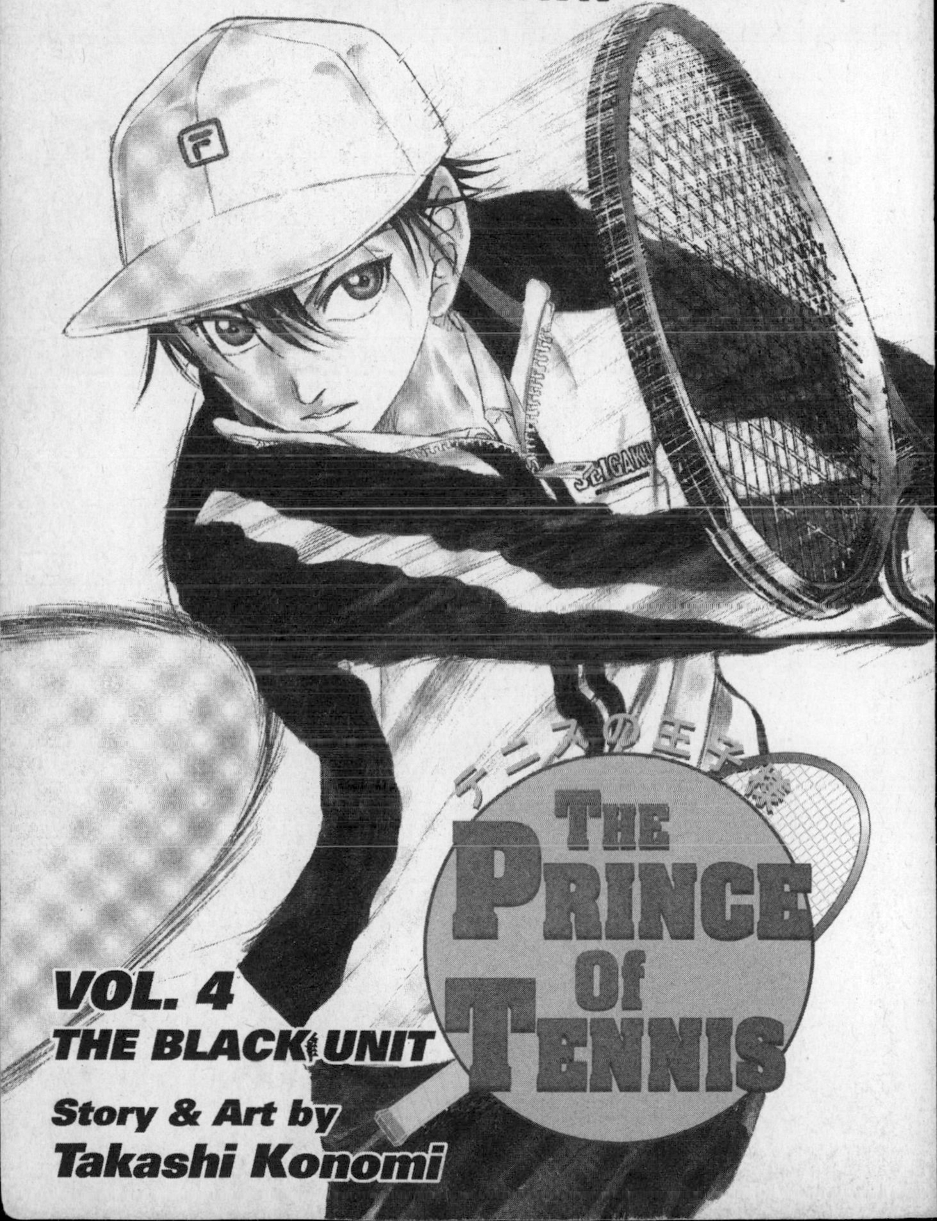

THE PRINCE OF TENNIS

VOL. 4
THE BLACK UNIT

Story & Art by
Takashi Konomi

THE PRINCE OF TENNIS

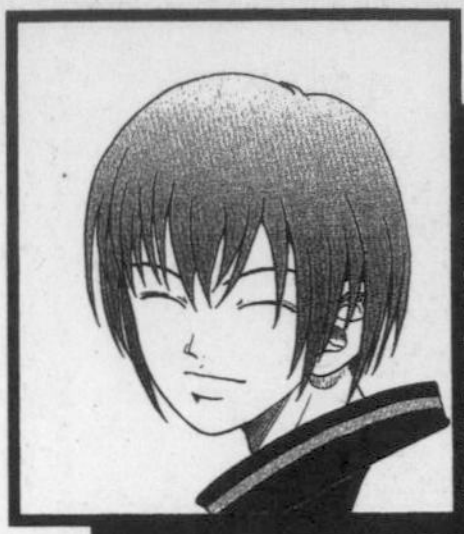

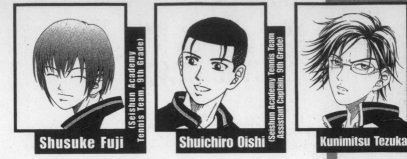

Shusuke Fuji (Seishun Academy Tennis Team, 9th Grade)

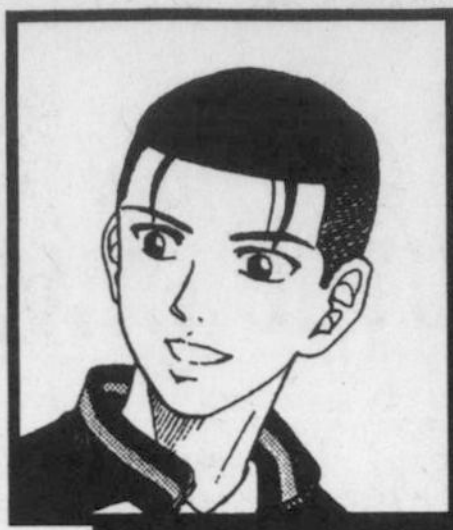

Shuichiro Oishi (Seishun Academy Tennis Team Assistant Captain, 9th Grade)

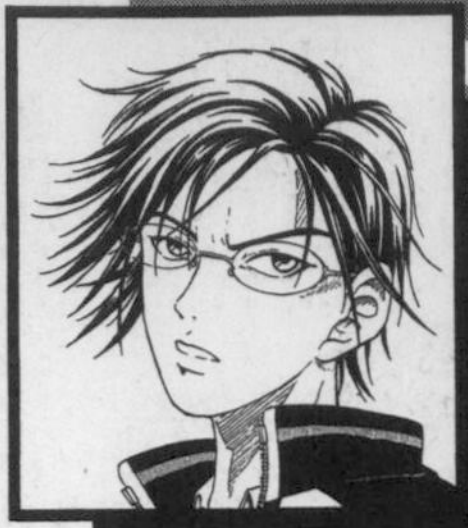

Kunimitsu Tezuka (Seishun Academy Tennis Team Captain, 9th Grade)

STORY & CHARACTERS

VOLUME 1 ▶ 4

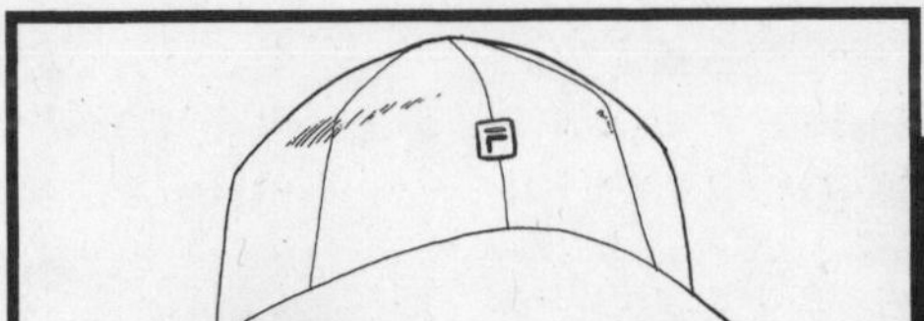

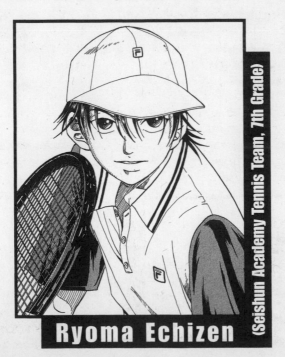

Ryoma Echizen (Seishun Academy Tennis Team, 7th Grade)

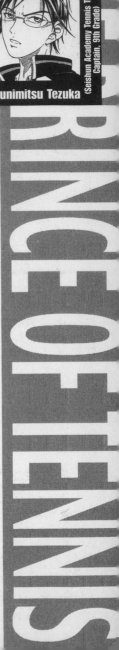

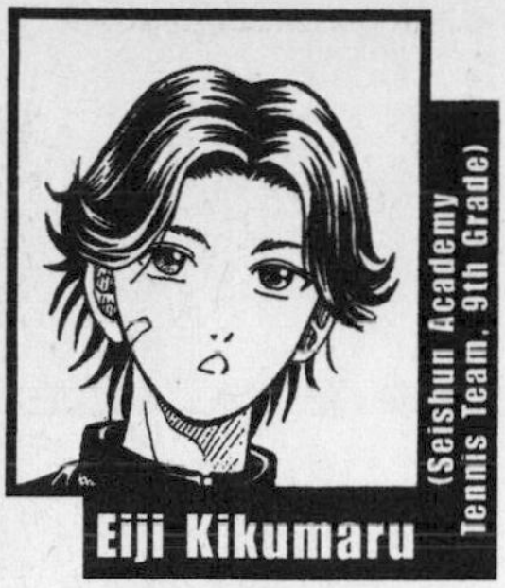
Eiji Kikumaru
(Seishun Academy Tennis Team, 9th Grade)

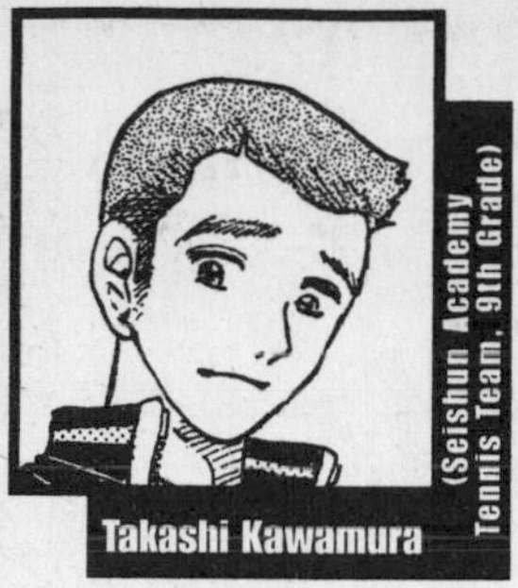
Takashi Kawamura
(Seishun Academy Tennis Team, 9th Grade)

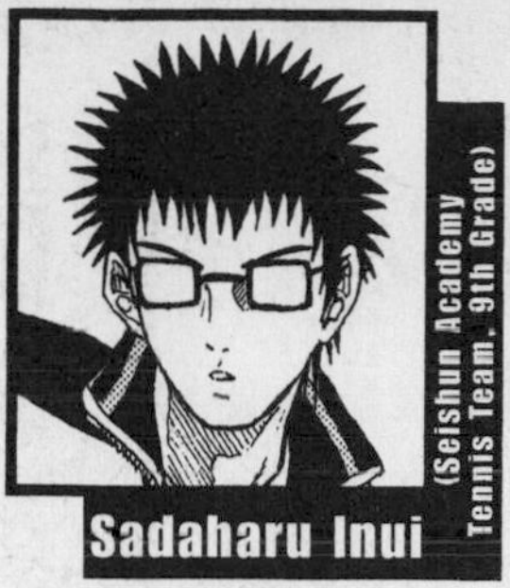
Sadaharu Inui
(Seishun Academy Tennis Team, 9th Grade)

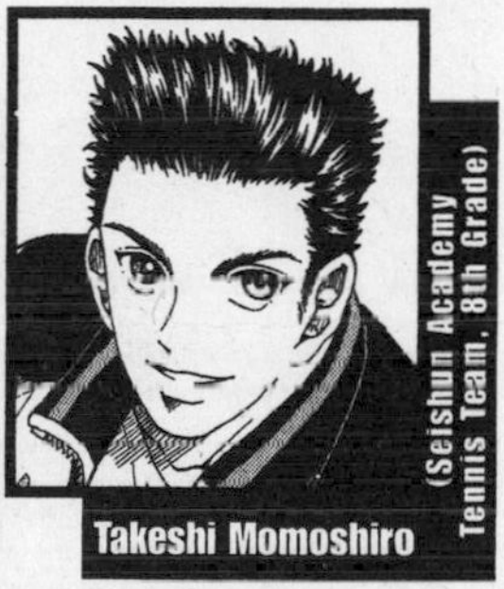
Takeshi Momoshiro
(Seishun Academy Tennis Team, 8th Grade)

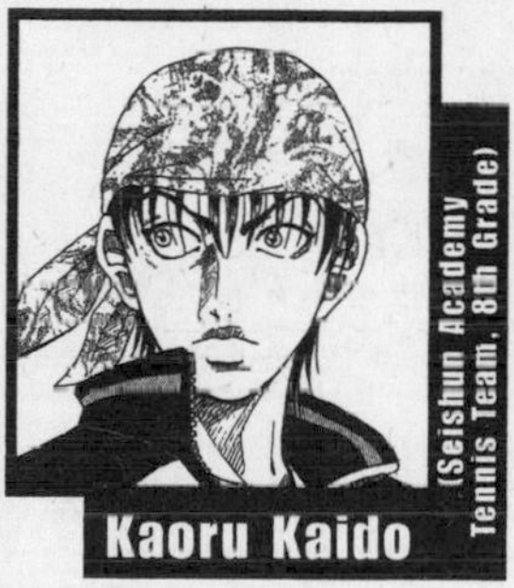
Kaoru Kaido
(Seishun Academy Tennis Team, 8th Grade)

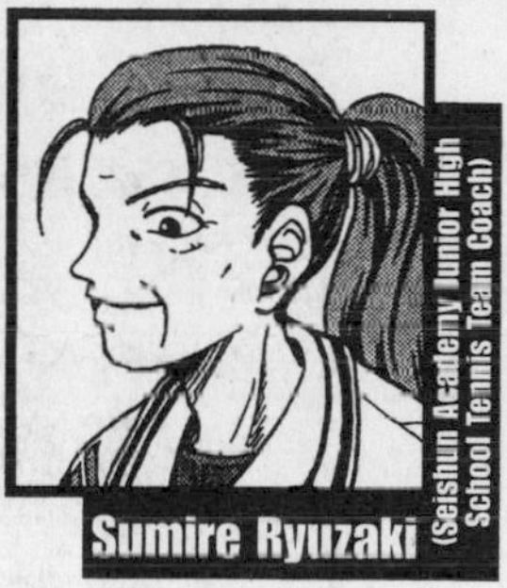
Sumire Ryuzaki
(Seishun Academy Junior High School Tennis Team Coach)

Ryoma Echizen, a tennis prodigy and winner of four consecutive U.S. Junior tournaments, has returned to Japan and enrolled at Seishun Academy Junior High. He is the first Seishun student to become a starter in 7th grade, and now he's in the District Preliminaries!

Predominantly a singles player, he unexpectedly finds himself as the other half of a competitive doubles pair along with Momoshiro. This last-minute "Odd Couple" pairing—after one hard day of practice—wins its first match as Seishun Academy sweeps Gyokurin. Seishun easily wins its semifinal matches and moves into the finals, but...

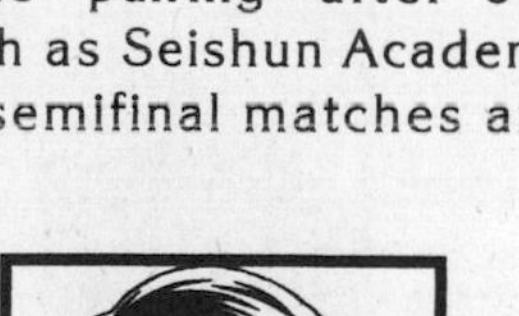
Sakuno Ryuzaki
(Seishun Academy Tennis Team, 7th Grade)

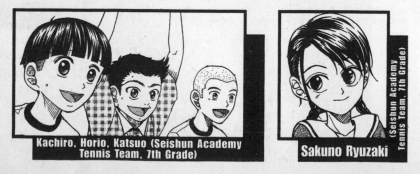

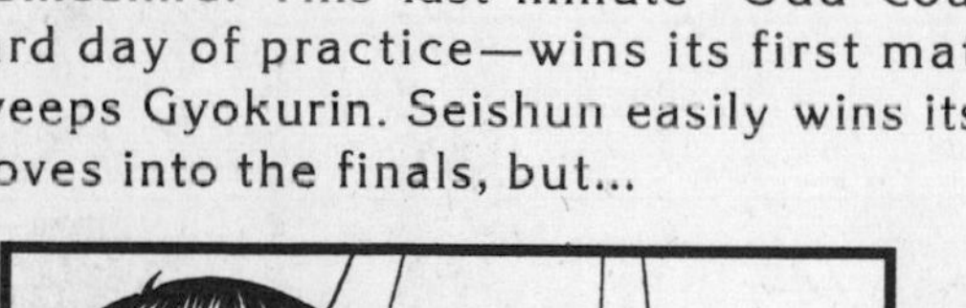
Kachiro, Horio, Katsuo (Seishun Academy Tennis Team, 7th Grade)

CONTENTS

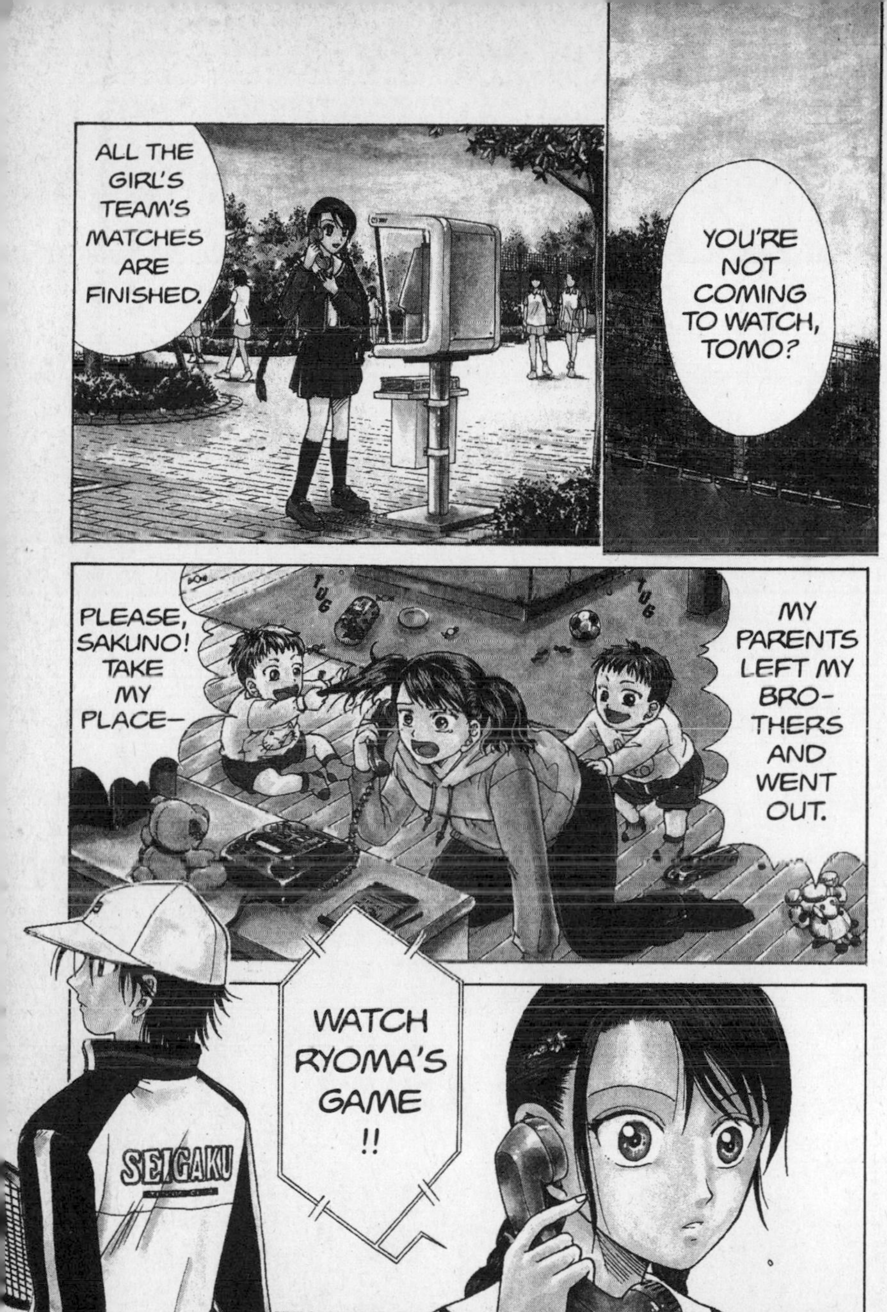
YOU'RE NOT COMING TO WATCH, TOMO?
ALL THE GIRL'S TEAM'S MATCHES ARE FINISHED.
TUG
TUG
MY PARENTS LEFT MY BRO-THERS AND WENT OUT.
PLEASE, SAKUNO! TAKE MY PLACE—
WATCH RYOMA'S GAME !!
SEIGAKU

Genius 26: THE BLACK UNIT—FUDOMINE

Genius 26:

THE BLACK UNIT—FUDOMINE

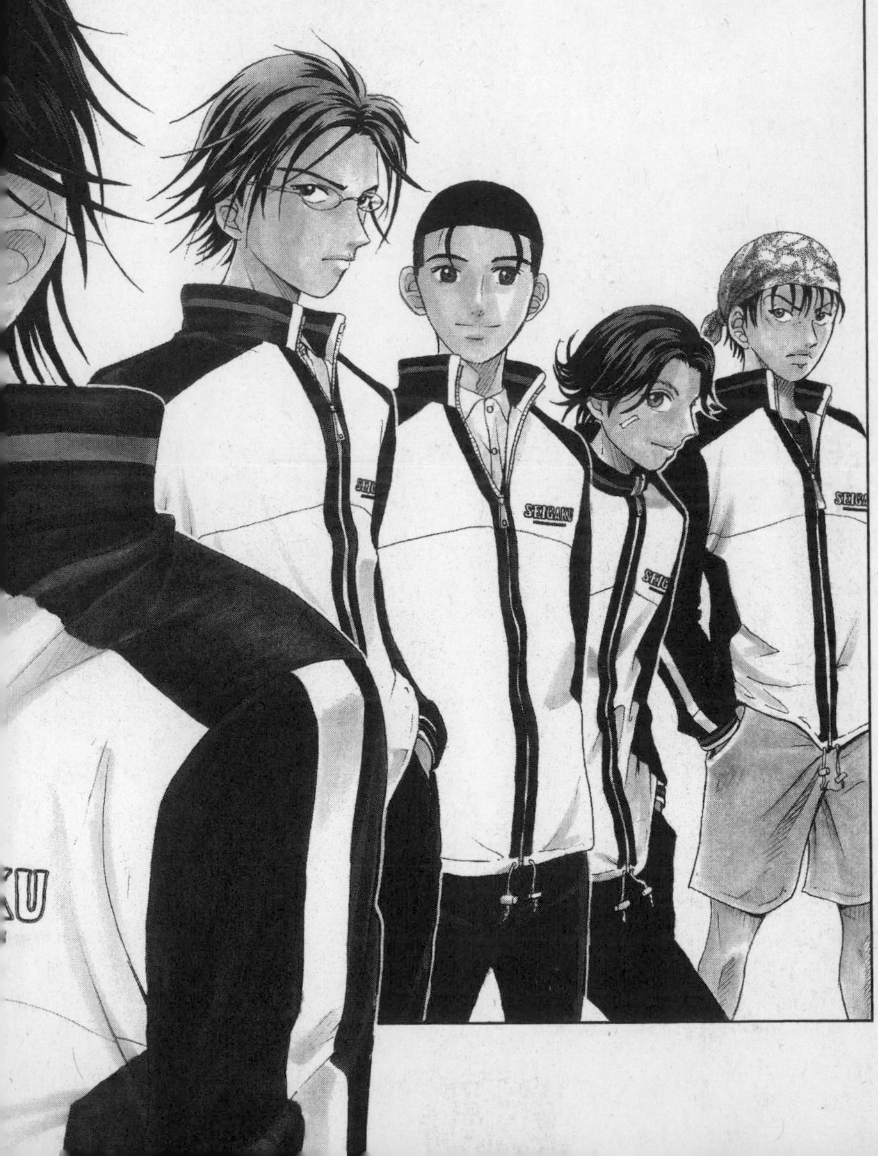
SEIGAKU

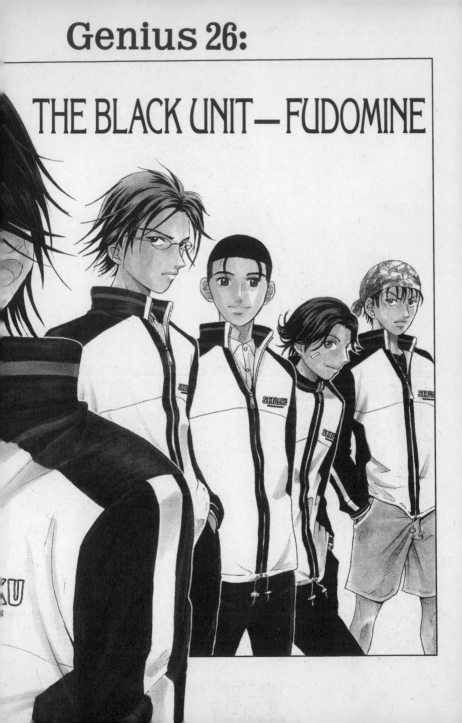

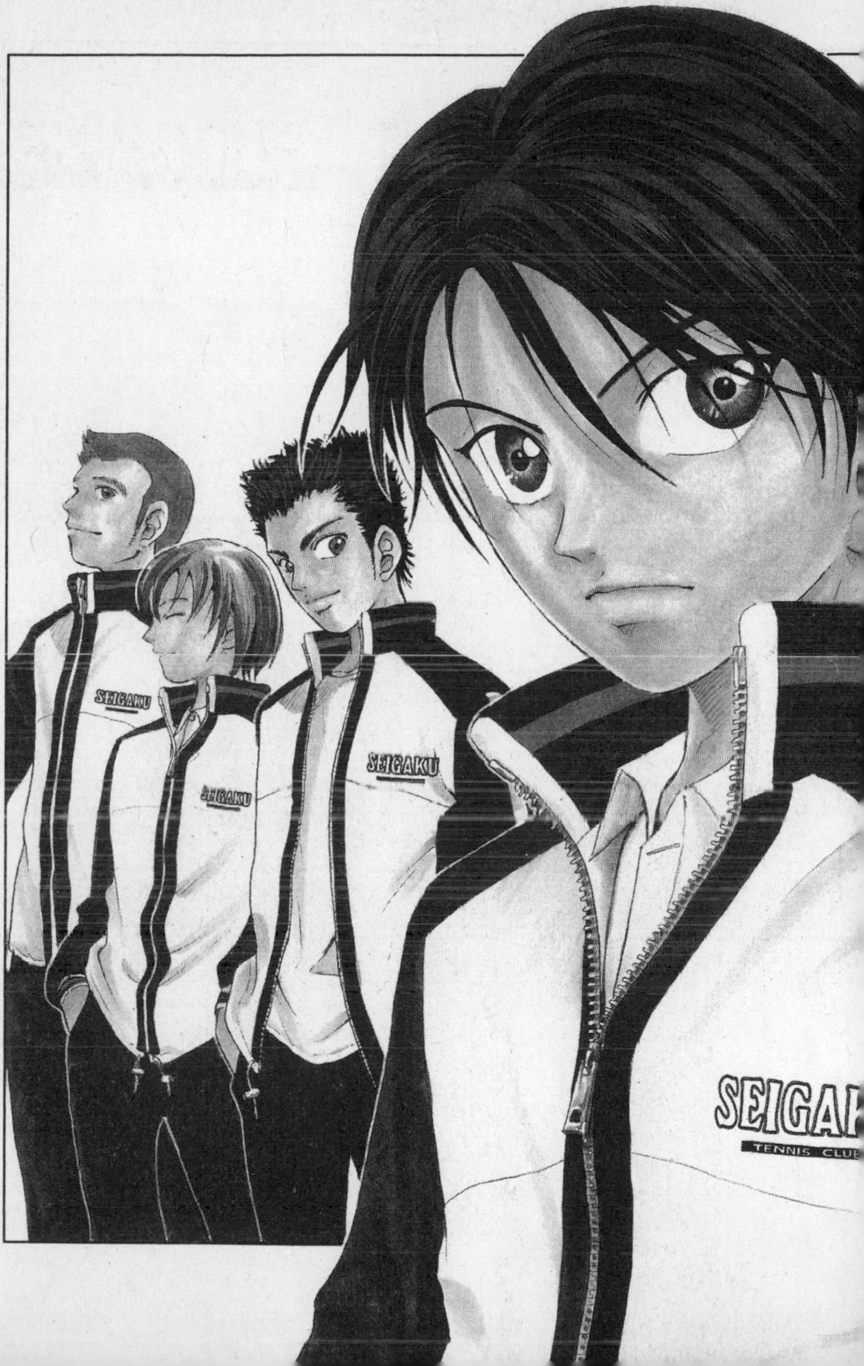
SEIGAKU
SEIGAKU
SEIGAKU
SEIGAK
TENNIS CLUB

The Prince of Tennis

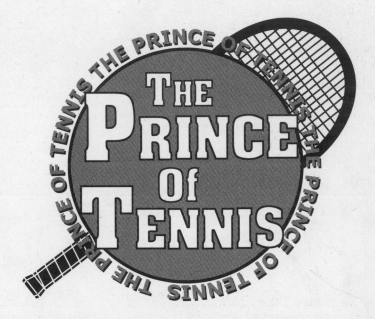

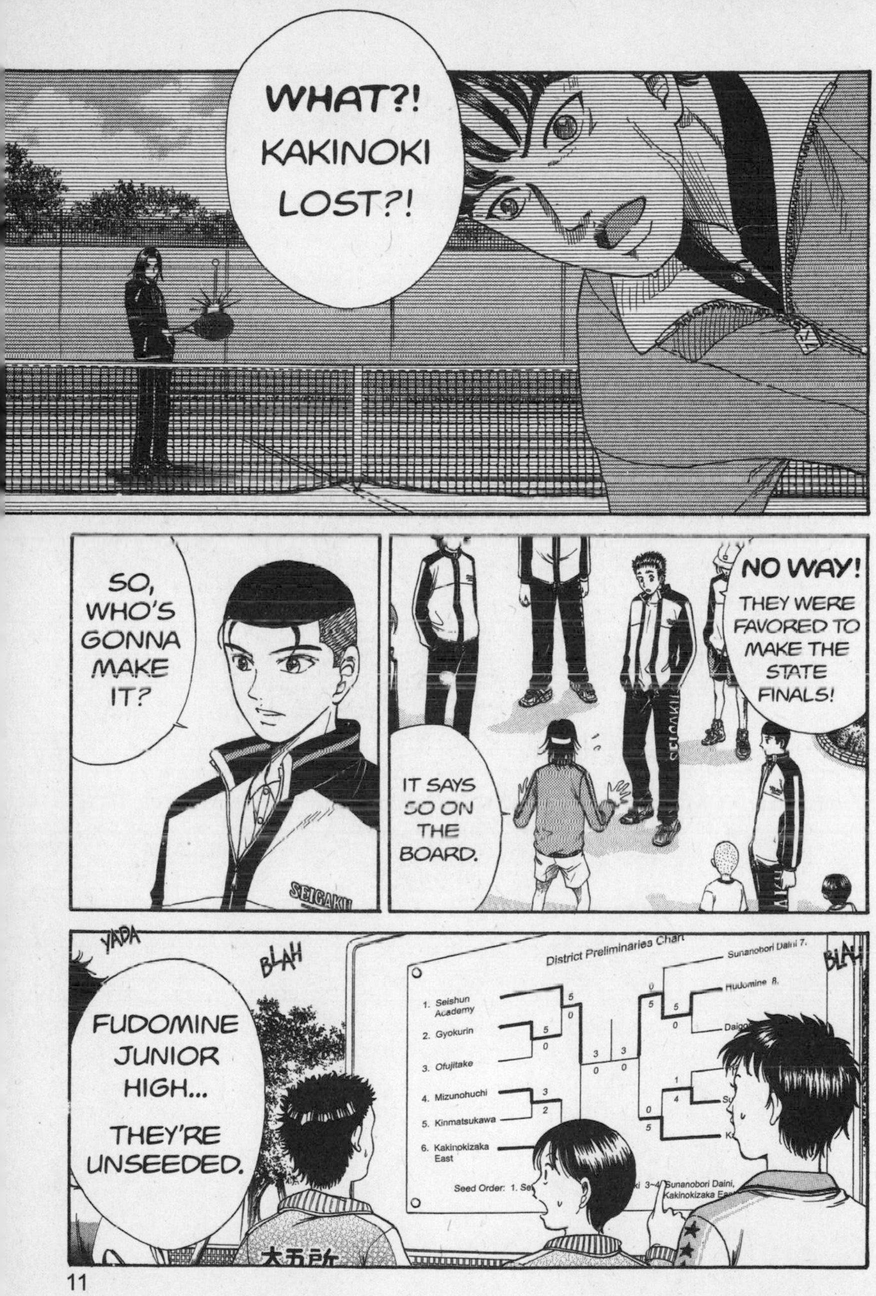
WHAT?! KAKINOKI LOST?!
NO WAY! THEY WERE FAVORED TO MAKE THE STATE FINALS!
IT SAYS SO ON THE BOARD.
SO, WHO'S GONNA MAKE IT?
BLAH
BLAH
YADA
District Preliminaries Chart
1. Seishun Academy
2. Gyokurin
3. Ofujitake
4. Mizunohuchi
5. Kinmatsukawa
6. Kakinokizaka East
Sunanobori Daini 7.
Hudomine 8.
FUDOMINE JUNIOR HIGH...
THEY'RE UNSEEDED.

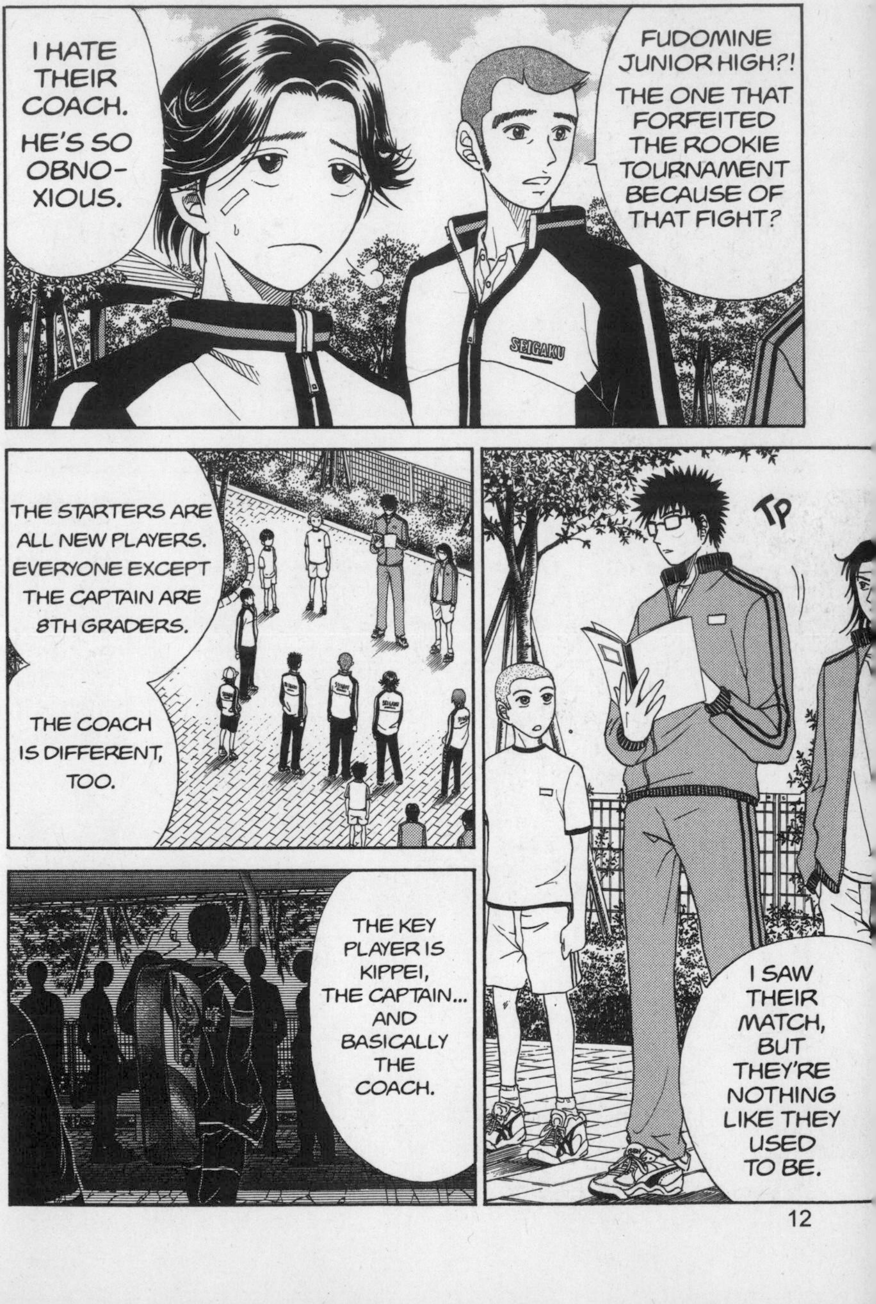
FUDOMINE JUNIOR HIGH?! THE ONE THAT FORFEITED THE ROOKIE TOURNAMENT BECAUSE OF THAT FIGHT?
I HATE THEIR COACH. HE'S SO OBNOXIOUS.
SEIGAKU
TP
I SAW THEIR MATCH, BUT THEY'RE NOTHING LIKE THEY USED TO BE.
THE STARTERS ARE ALL NEW PLAYERS. EVERYONE EXCEPT THE CAPTAIN ARE 8TH GRADERS.
THE COACH IS DIFFERENT, TOO.
THE KEY PLAYER IS KIPPEI, THE CAPTAIN... AND BASICALLY THE COACH.

READ THIS WAY

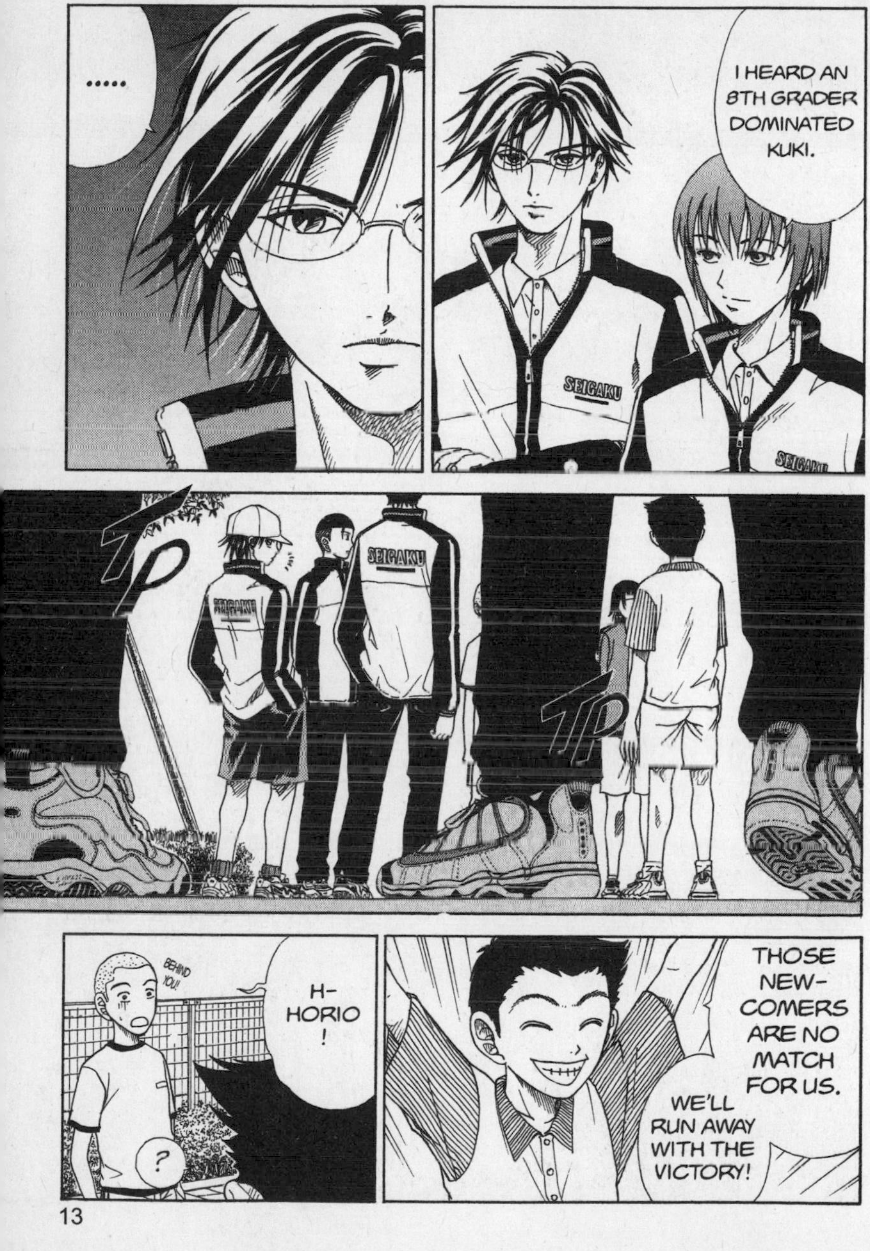
I HEARD AN 8TH GRADER DOMINATED KUKI.
.....
TP
TP
THOSE NEW-COMERS ARE NO MATCH FOR US.
WE'LL RUN AWAY WITH THE VICTORY!
H-HORIO!
BEHIND YOU!
?

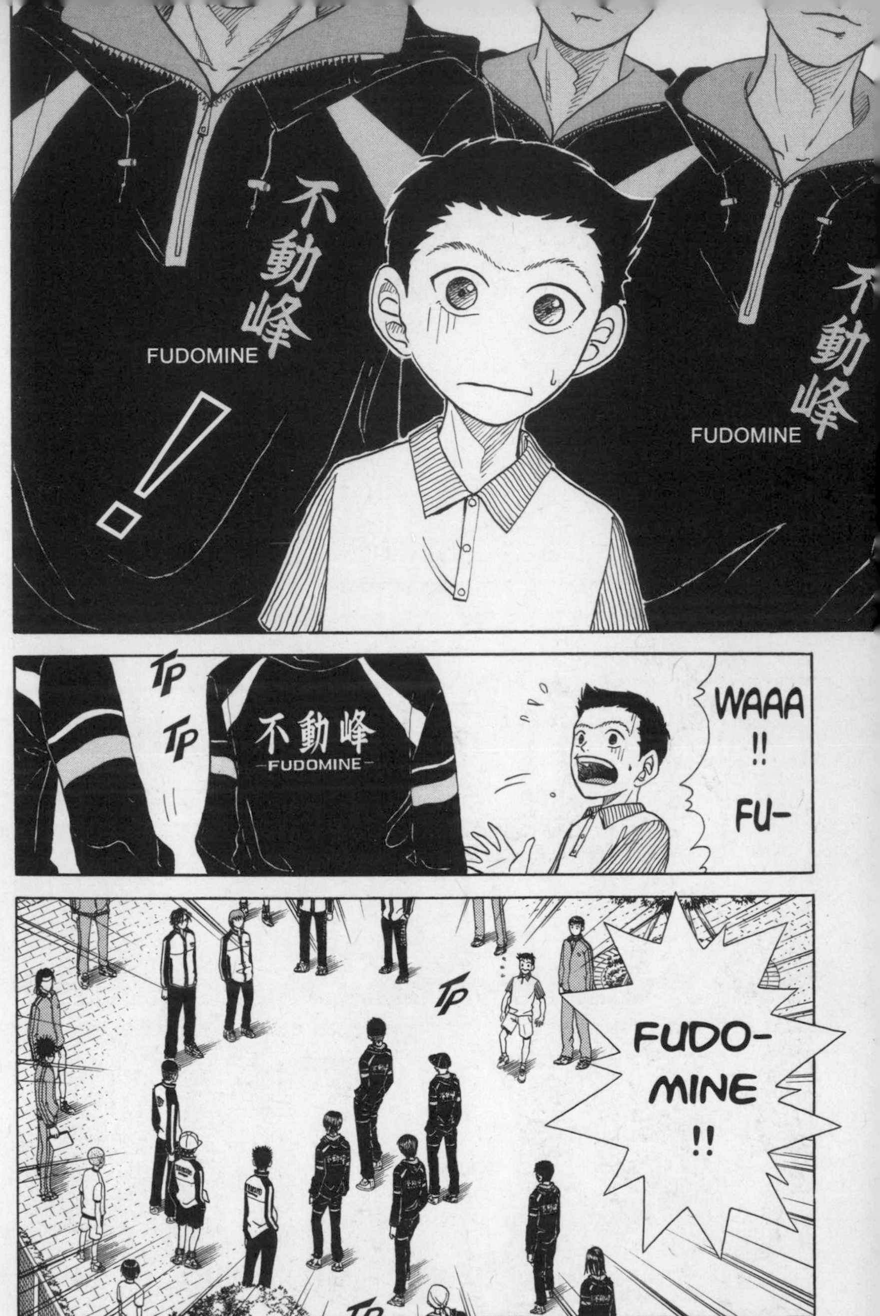
不動峰
FUDOMINE
不動峰
FUDOMINE
!
WAAA !! FU-
不動峰
-FUDOMINE-
TP
TP
FUDO-MINE !!
TP
TP

READ THIS WAY

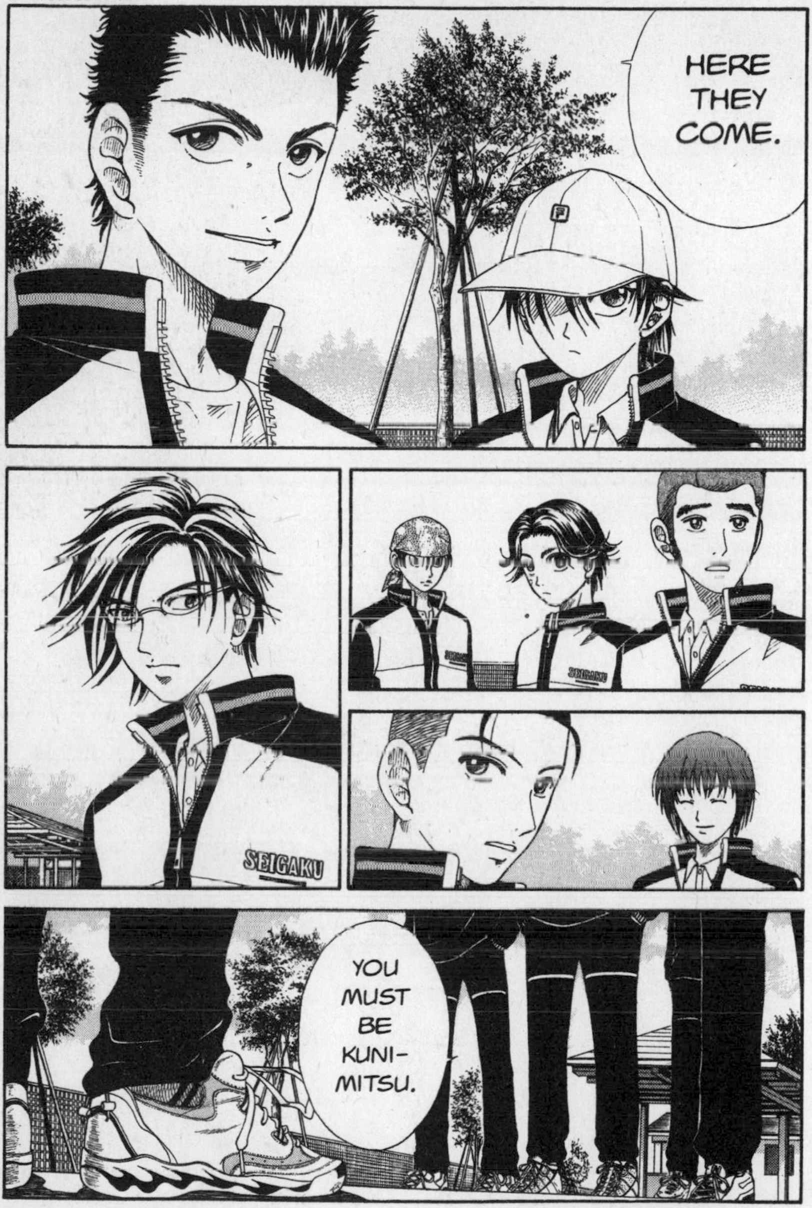
HERE THEY COME.
SEIGAKU
SEIGAKU
SEIGAKU
YOU MUST BE KUNI-MITSU.

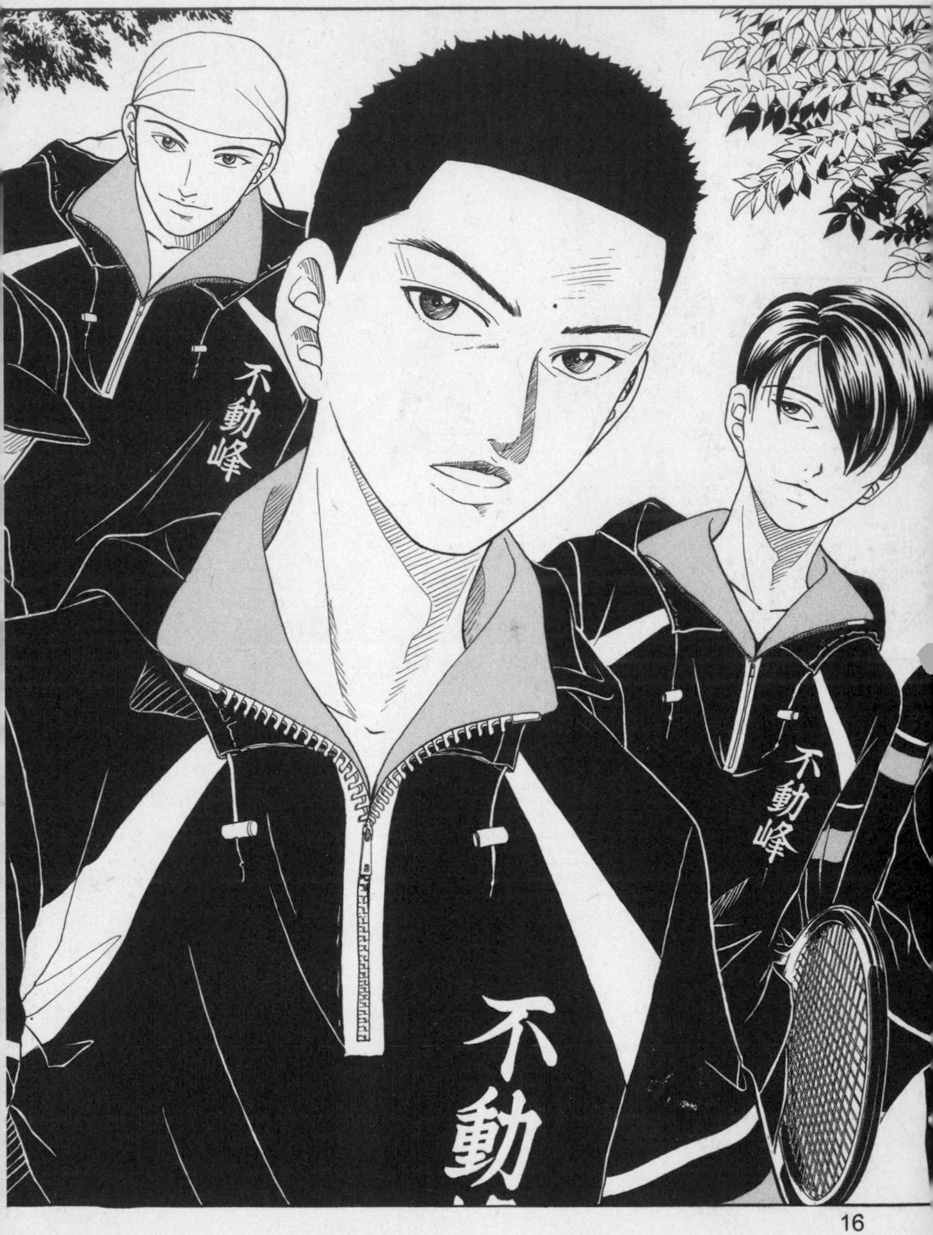
不動
不動峰
不動峰

READ THIS WAY

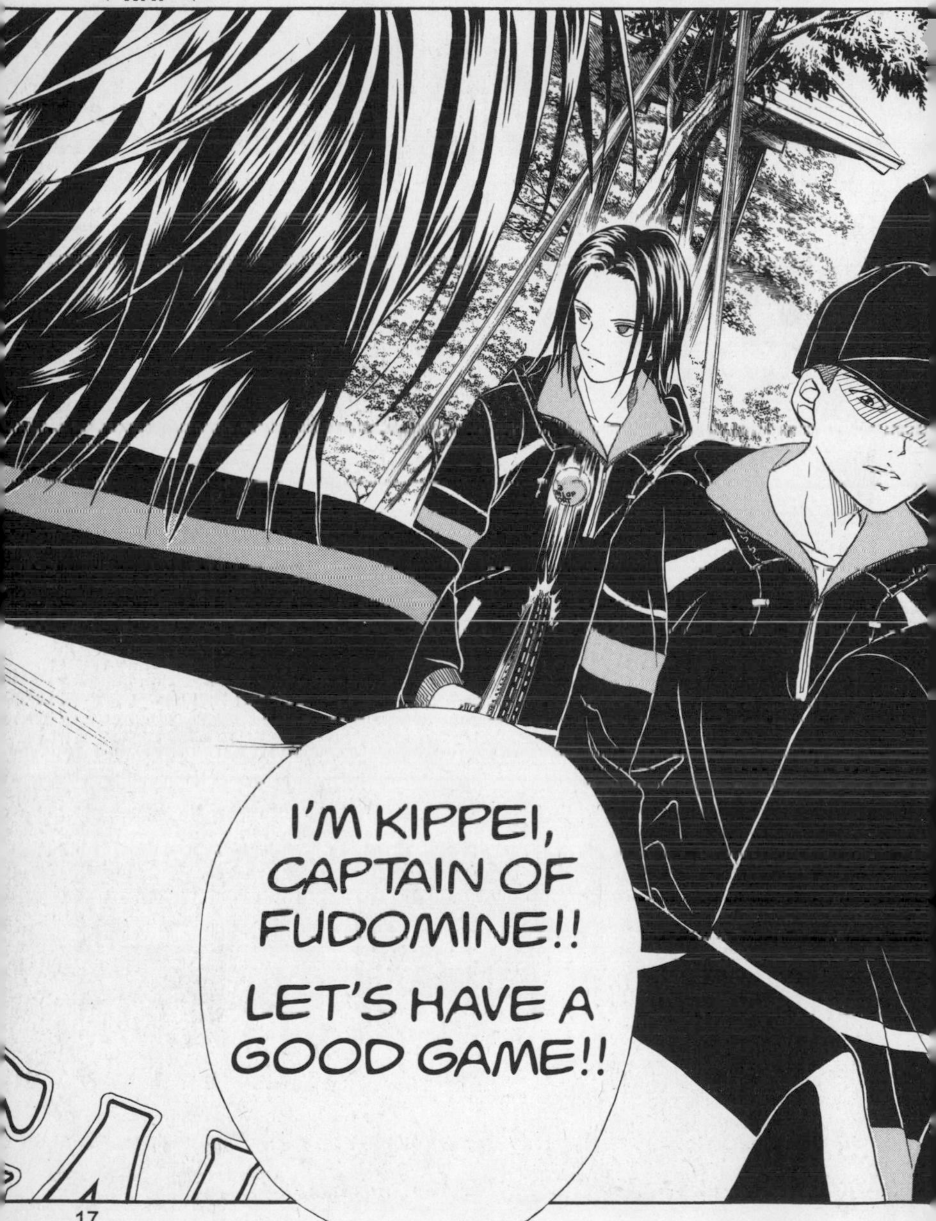
I'M KIPPEI, CAPTAIN OF FUDOMINE!! LET'S HAVE A GOOD GAME!!

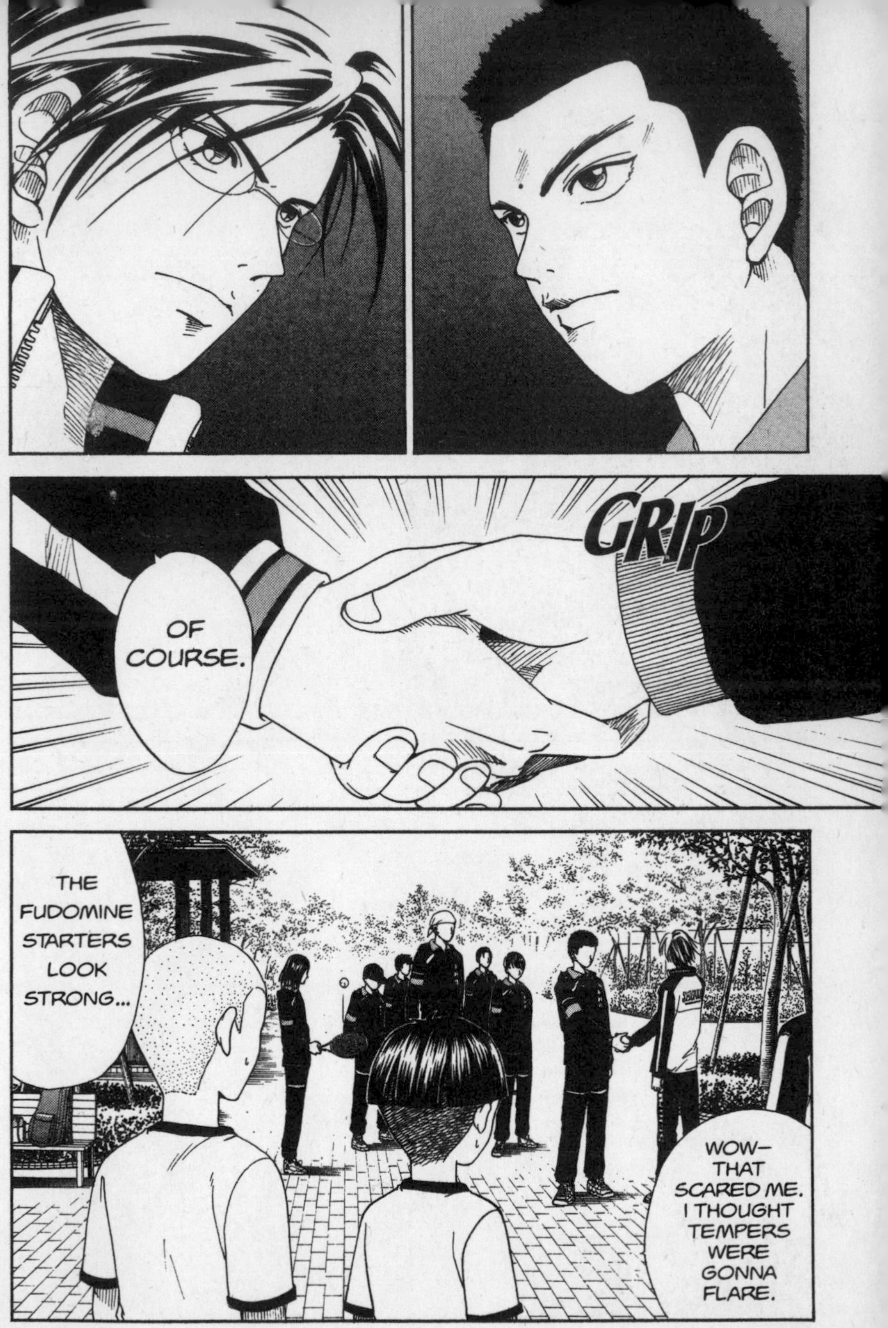
GRIP
OF COURSE.
WOW— THAT SCARED ME. I THOUGHT TEMPERS WERE GONNA FLARE.
THE FUDOMINE STARTERS LOOK STRONG...

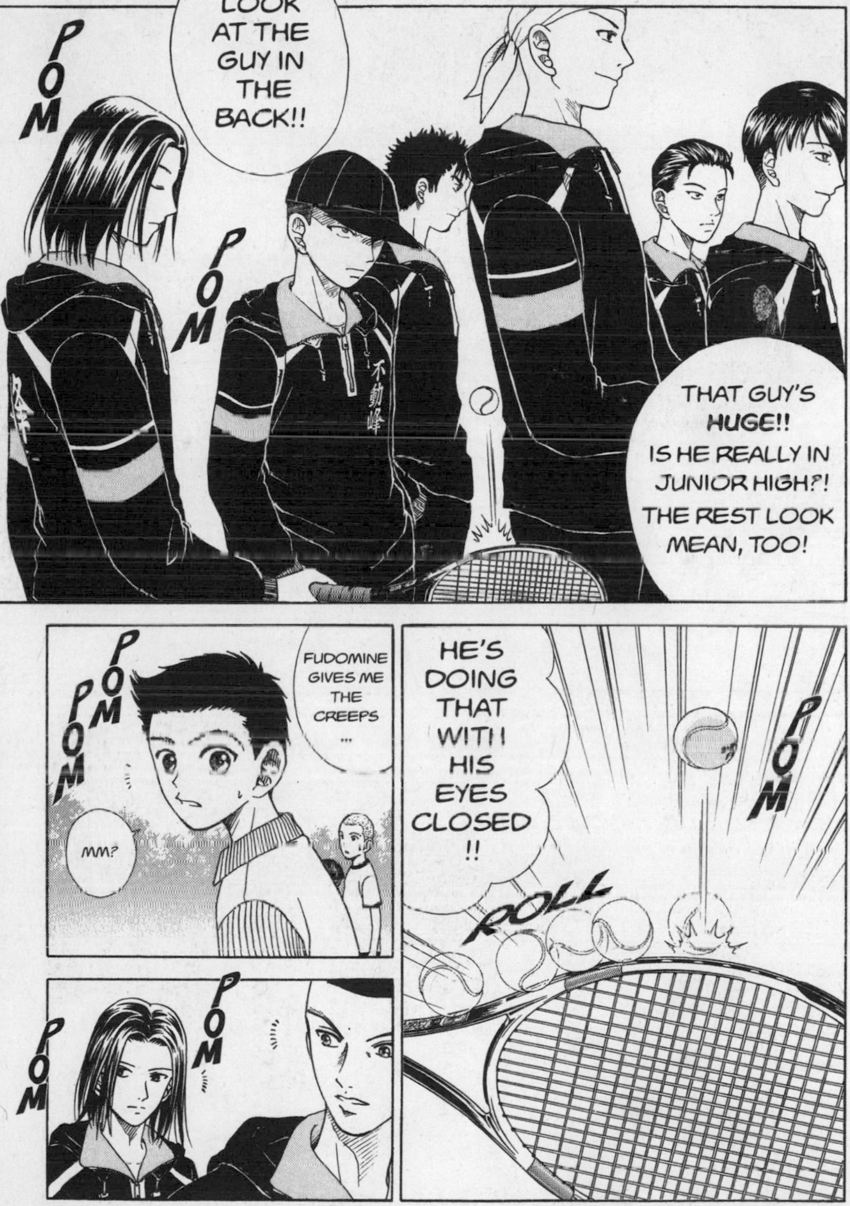
LOOK AT THE GUY IN THE BACK!!
POM
POM
POM
POM
不動峰
THAT GUY'S **HUGE!!** IS HE REALLY IN JUNIOR HIGH?! THE REST LOOK MEAN, TOO!
POM
POM
HE'S DOING THAT WITH HIS EYES CLOSED !!
ROLL
FUDOMINE GIVES ME THE CREEPS ...
POM
POM
MM?
POM
POM
POM
POM

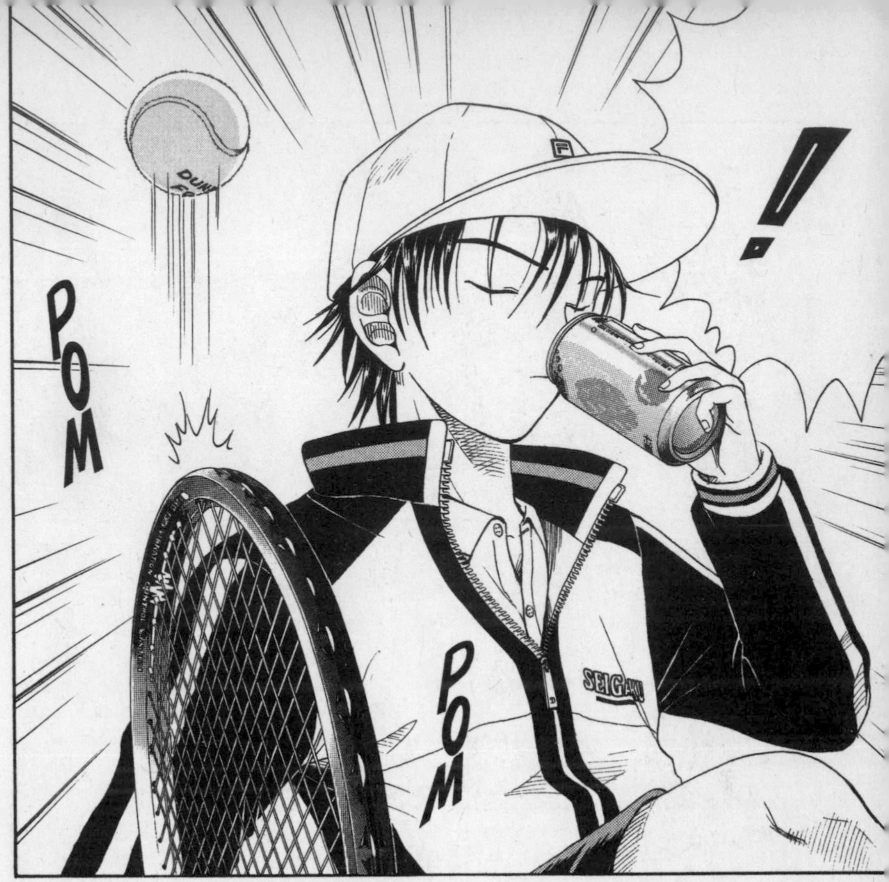
POM
!
POM

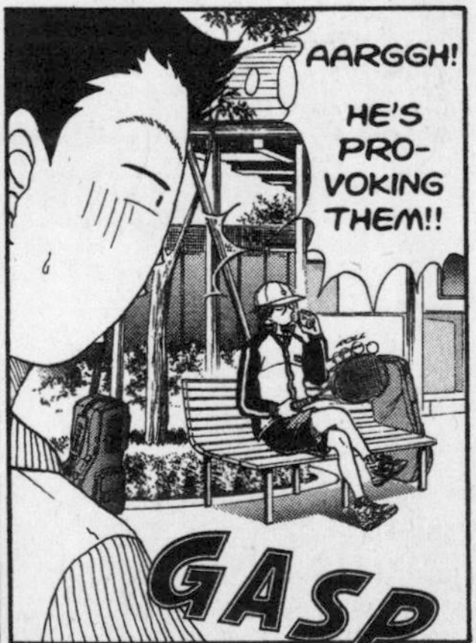
AARGGH!
HE'S PRO-VOKING THEM!!
GASP

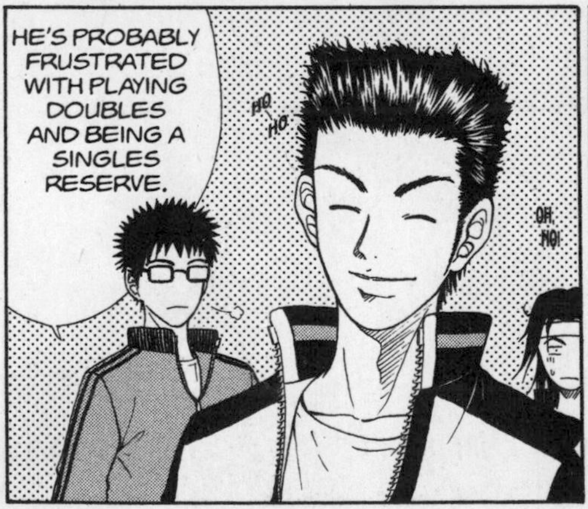
HE'S PROBABLY FRUSTRATED WITH PLAYING DOUBLES AND BEING A SINGLES RESERVE.
HO HO.
OH, NO!

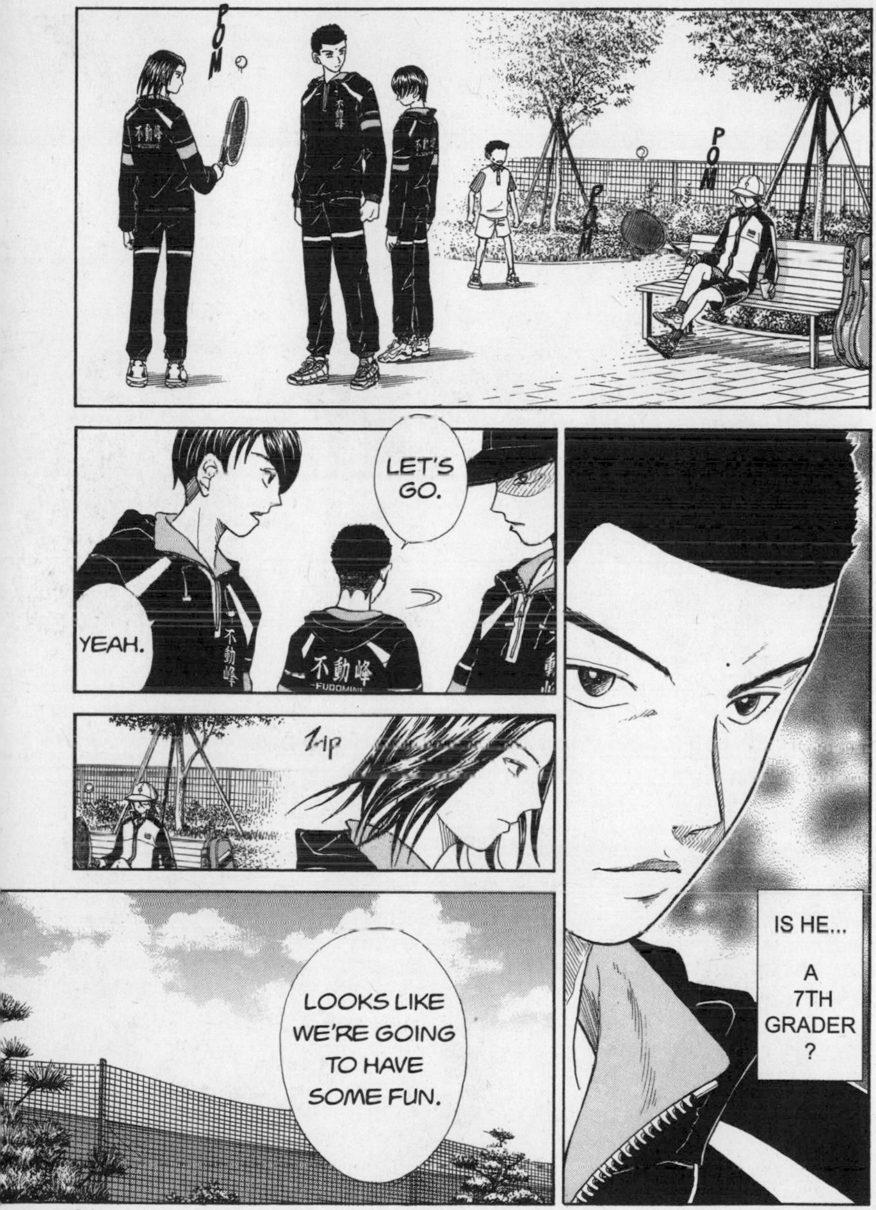
POM
POM
IS HE... A 7TH GRADER?
LET'S GO.
YEAH.
Zip
LOOKS LIKE WE'RE GOING TO HAVE SOME FUN.

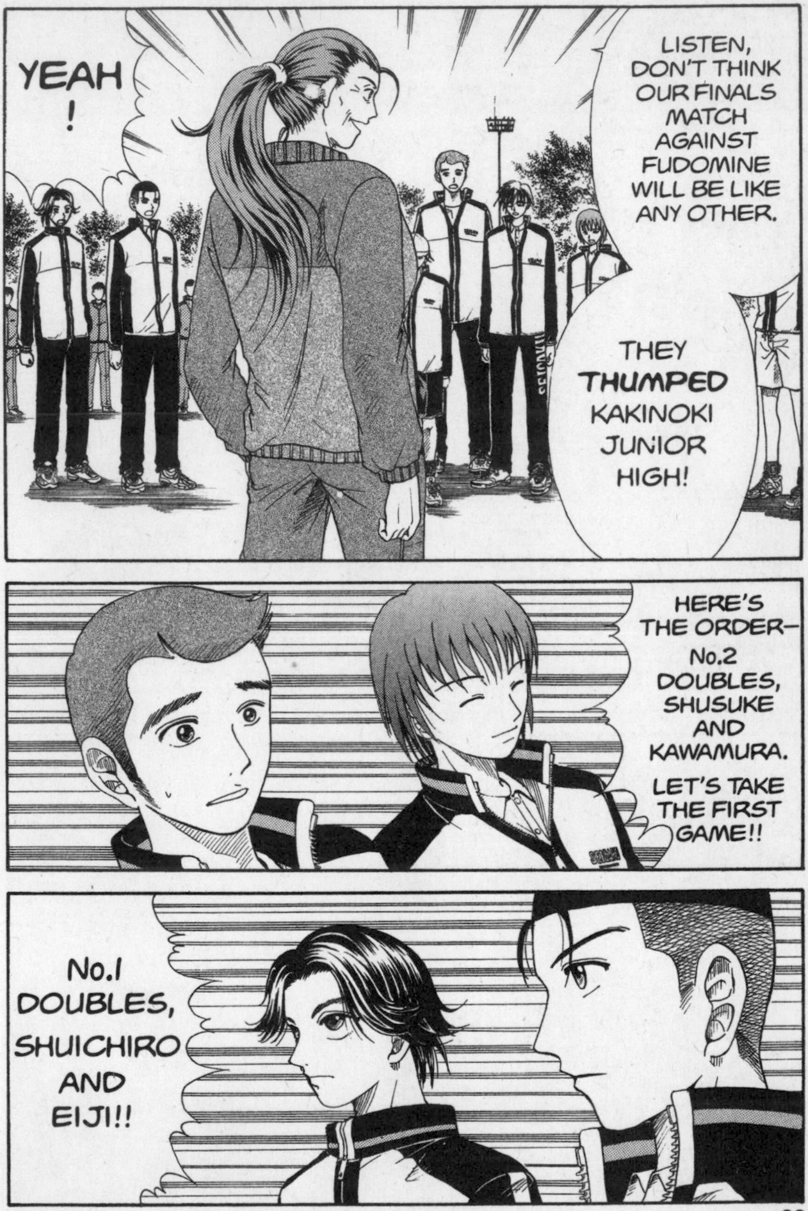
LISTEN, DON'T THINK OUR FINALS MATCH AGAINST FUDOMINE WILL BE LIKE ANY OTHER.
THEY THUMPED KAKINOKI JUNIOR HIGH!
YEAH!
HERE'S THE ORDER— No.2 DOUBLES, SHUSUKE AND KAWAMURA.
LET'S TAKE THE FIRST GAME!!
No.1 DOUBLES, SHUICHIRO AND EIJI!!

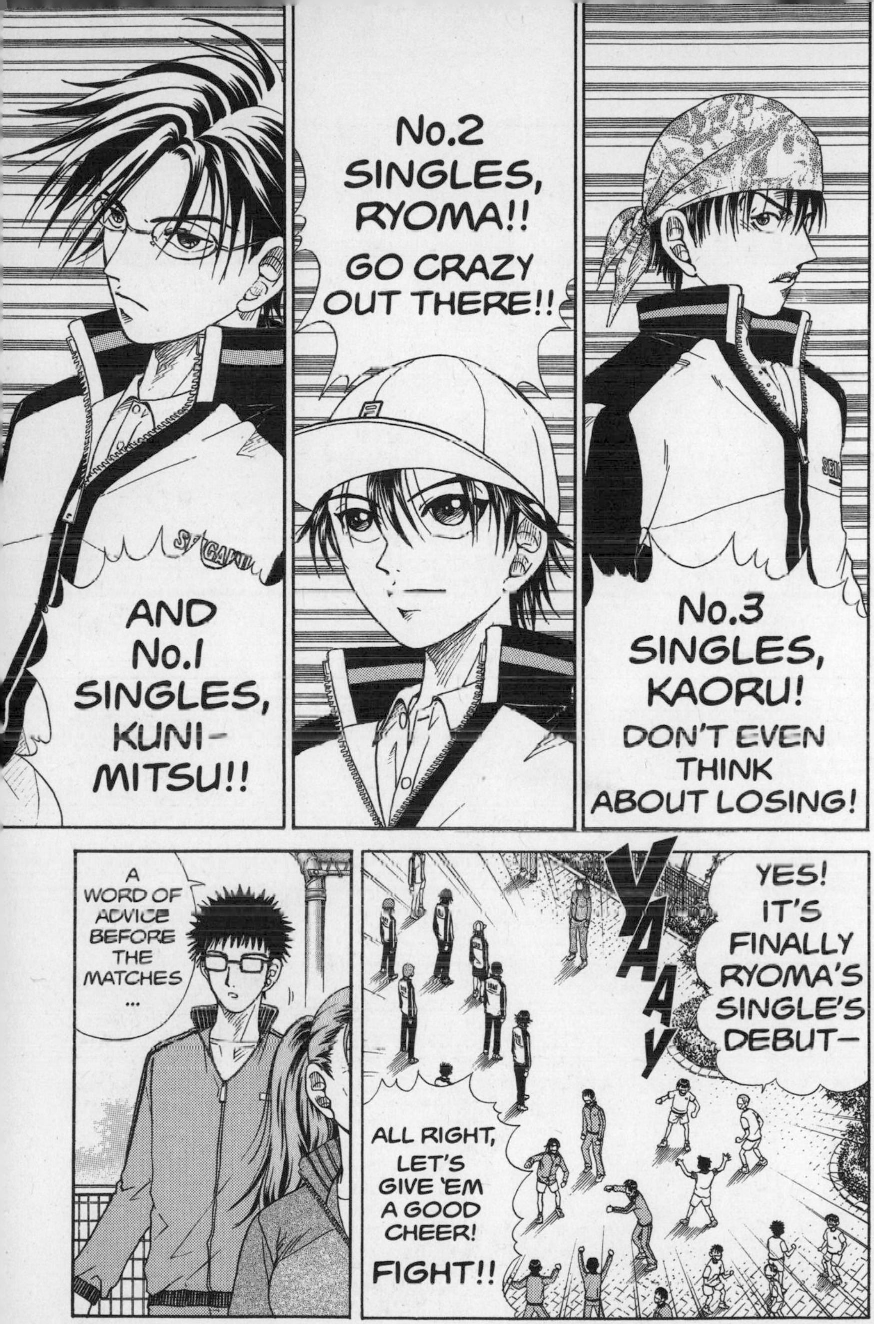

No.3 SINGLES, KAORU!
DON'T EVEN THINK ABOUT LOSING!
No.2 SINGLES, RYOMA!!
GO CRAZY OUT THERE!!
AND No.1 SINGLES, KUNI-MITSU!!
YES! IT'S FINALLY RYOMA'S SINGLE'S DEBUT—
YAAY
ALL RIGHT, LET'S GIVE 'EM A GOOD CHEER!
FIGHT!!
A WORD OF ADVICE BEFORE THE MATCHES ...

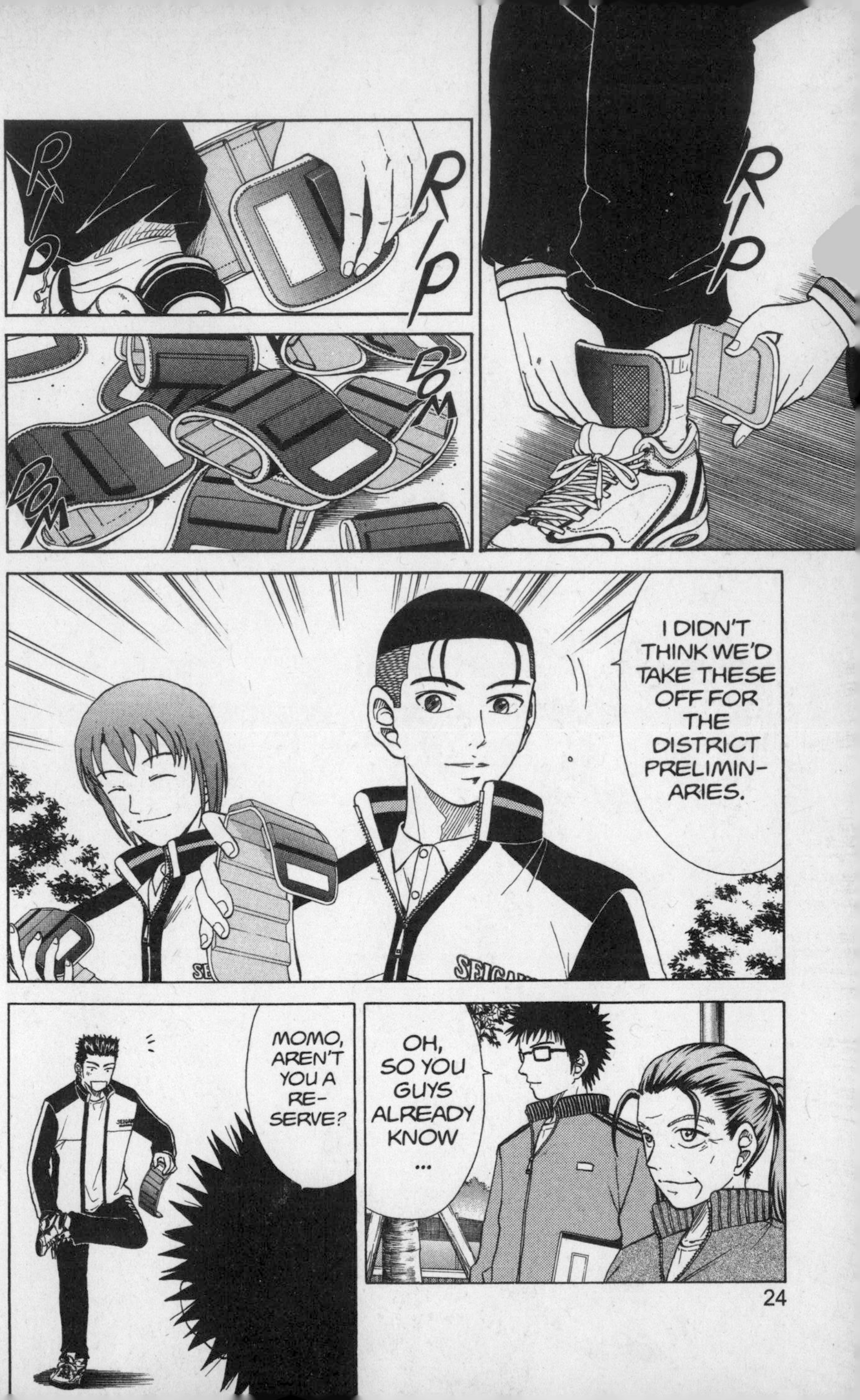
RIP
RIP
RIP
RIP
DOM
DOM
I DIDN'T THINK WE'D TAKE THESE OFF FOR THE DISTRICT PRELIMIN-ARIES.
OH, SO YOU GUYS ALREADY KNOW ...
MOMO, AREN'T YOU A RE-SERVE?

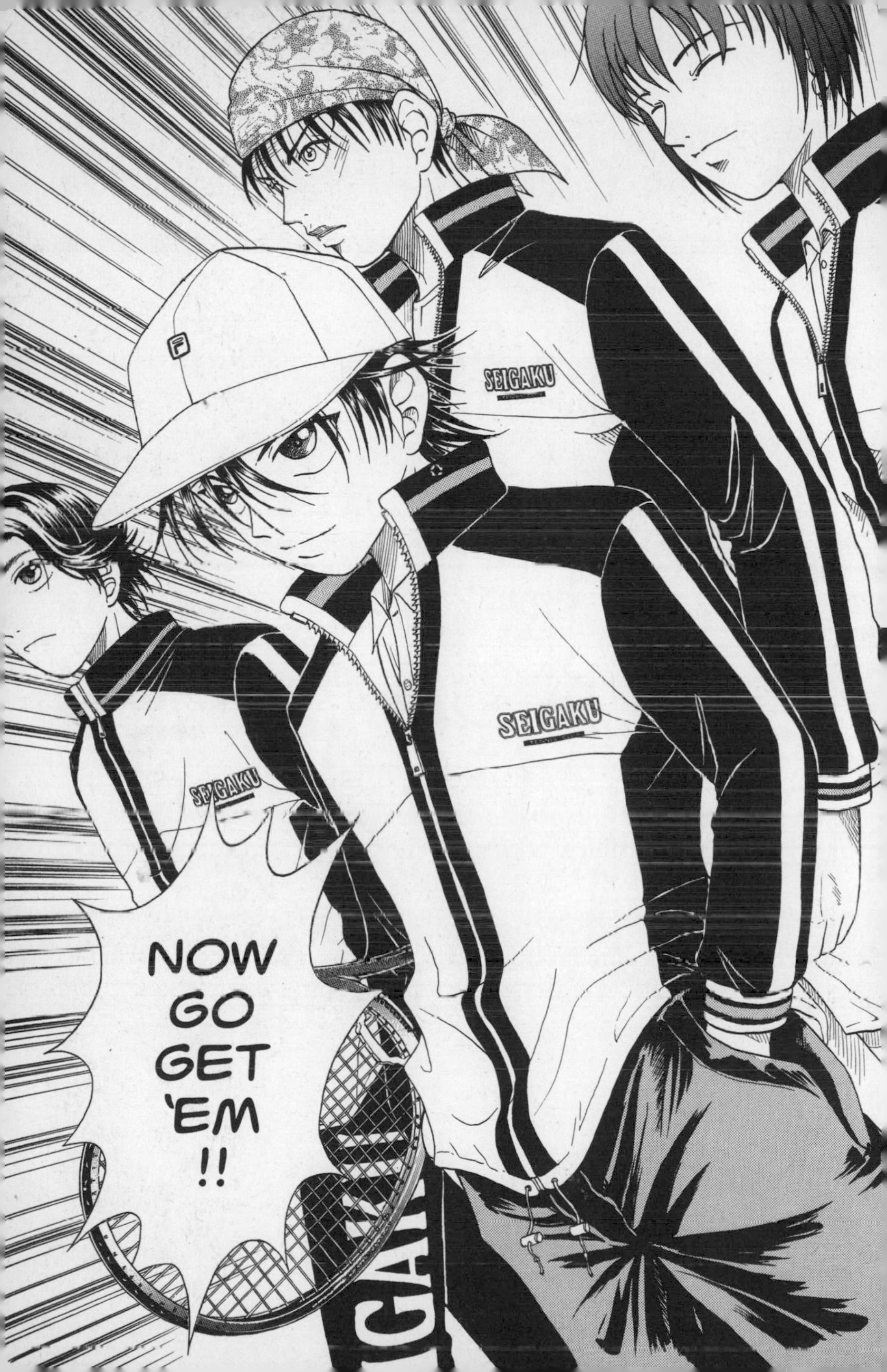
SEIGAKU
SEIGAKU
SEIGAKU
NOW GO GET 'EM !!

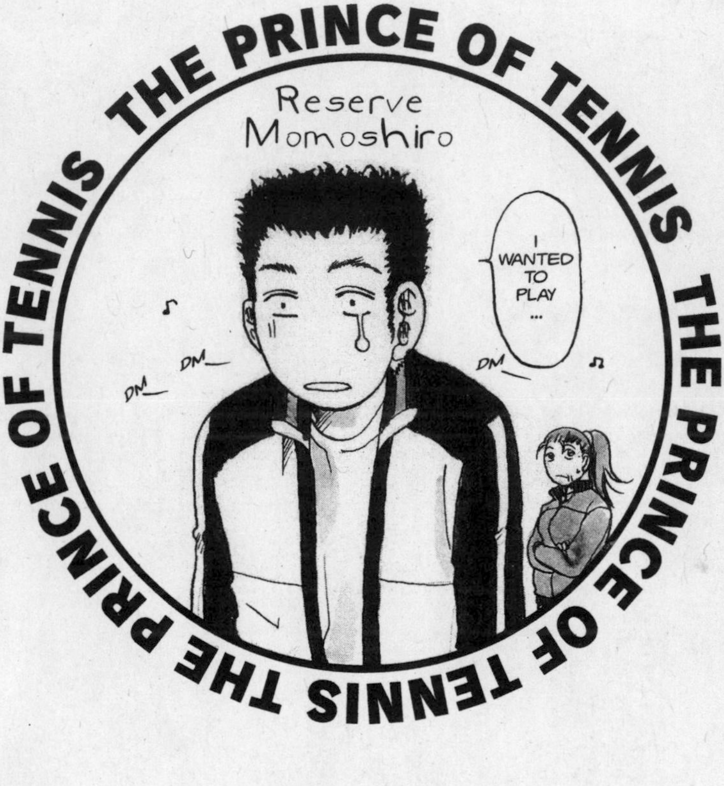
THE PRINCE OF TENNIS THE PRINCE OF TENNIS THE PRINCE OF TENNIS
Reserve Momoshiro
I WANTED TO PLAY ...
DM_
DM_
DM_

Fifth Match No. 1 Singles	Forth Match No. 2 Singles	Third Match No. 3 Singles	Second Match—No. 1 Doubles		First Match—No. 2 Doubles	
Kunimitsu Tezuka (9th Grade) Blood Type O	Ryoma Echizen (7th Grade) Blood Type O	Kaoru Kaido (8th Grade) Blood Type B	Shuichiro Oishi (9th Grade) Blood Type O	Eiji Kikumaru (9th Grade) Blood Type A	Shusuke Fuji (9th Grade) Blood Type B	Takashi Kawamura (9th Grade) Blood Type A

Genius 27:

SEISHUN VS. FUDOMINE

Kippei Tachibana (9th Grade) Blood Type O	Shinji Ibu (8th Grade) Blood Type AB	Akira Kamio (8th Grade) Blood Type A	Kyosuke Uchimura (8th Grade) Blood Type B	Tatsunori Mori (8th Grade) Blood Type A	Tetsu Ishida (8th Grade) Blood Type O	Masaya Sakurai (8th Grade) Blood Type O

* The Finals for the District Preliminaries is a one-set match.
The first team to win three matches wins the round.

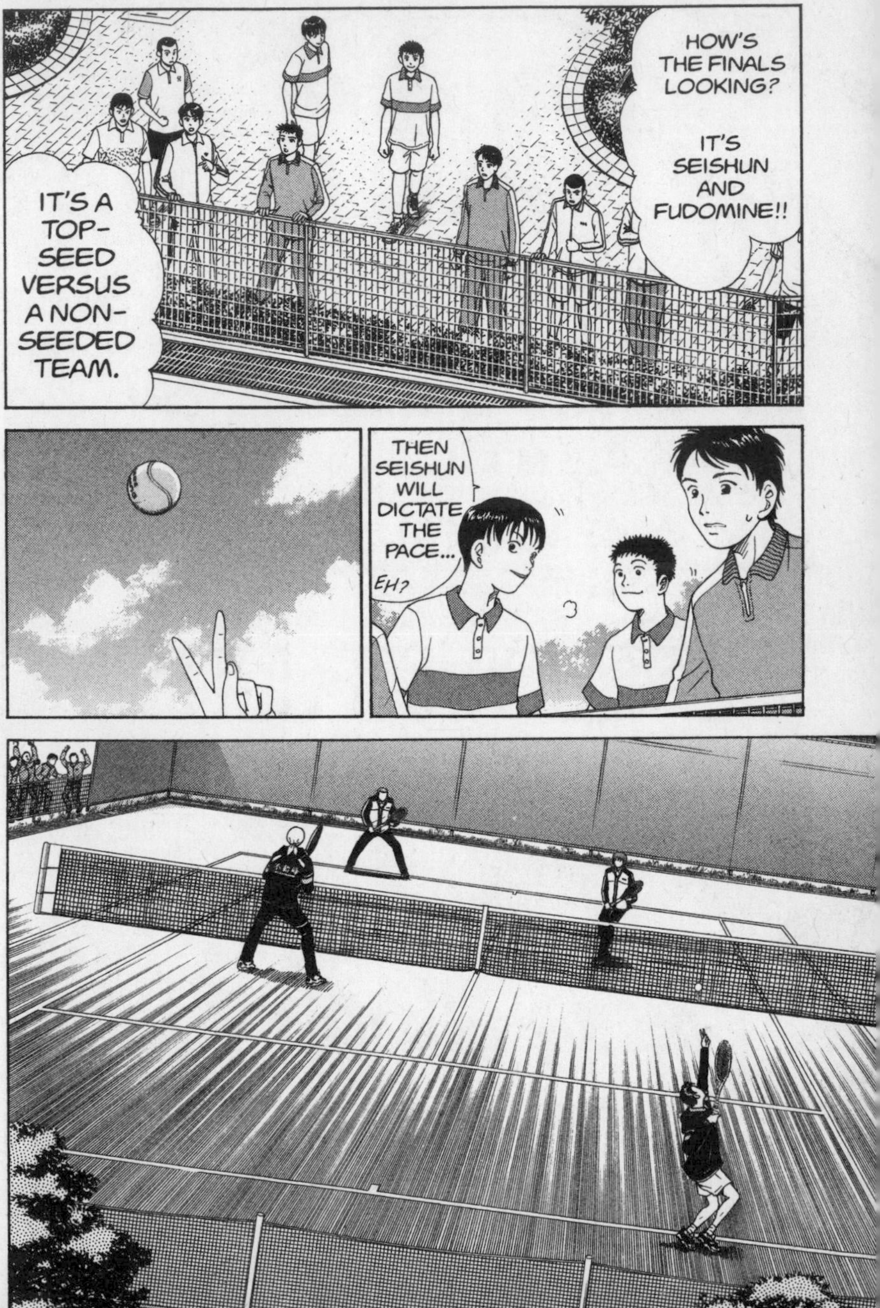
HOW'S THE FINALS LOOKING?
IT'S SEISHUN AND FUDOMINE!!
IT'S A TOP-SEED VERSUS A NON-SEEDED TEAM.
THEN SEISHUN WILL DICTATE THE PACE...
EH?

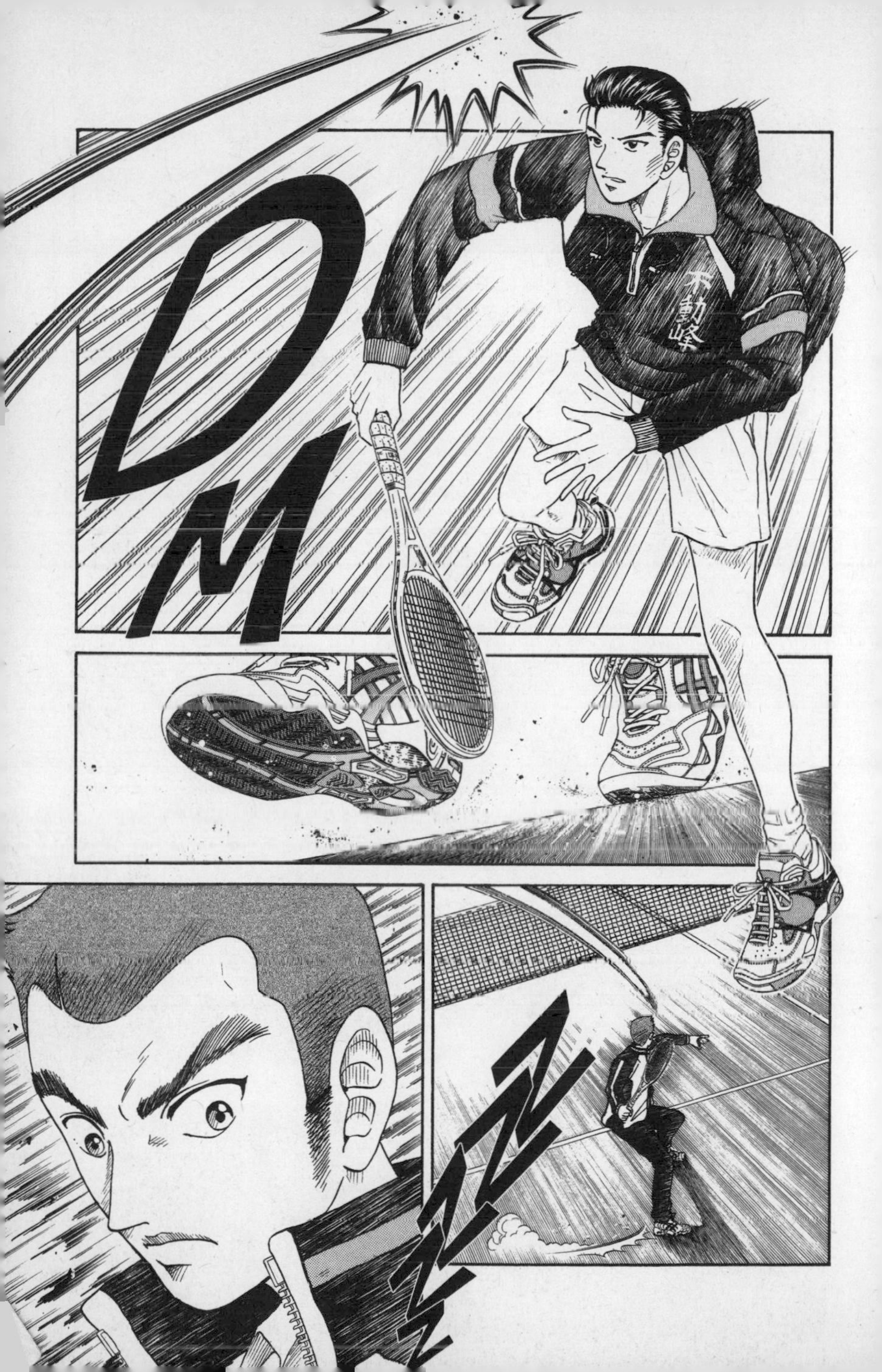
不動峰
DM
ZZZ

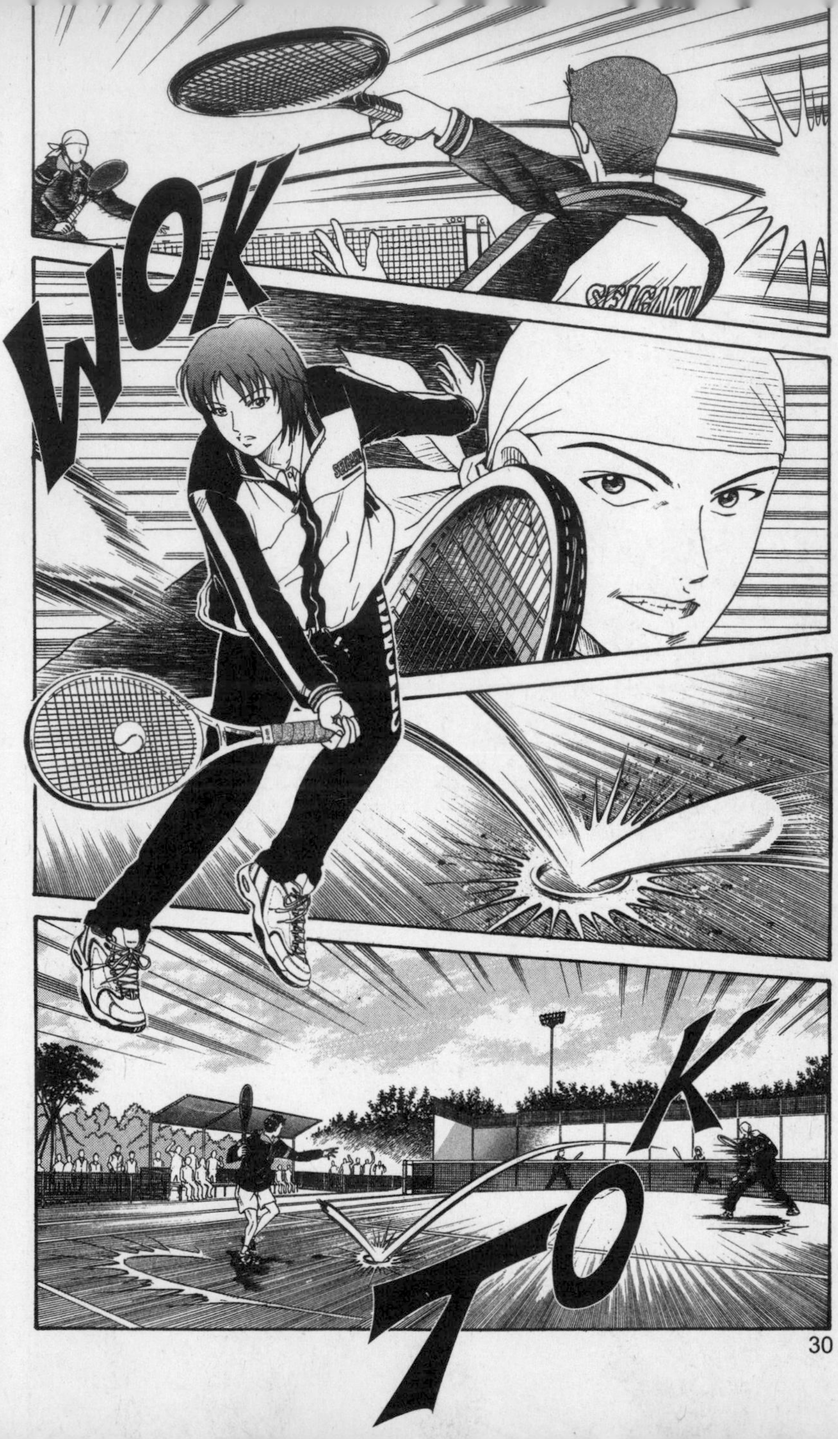
WOK
SEIGAKU
TOK

READ THIS WAY

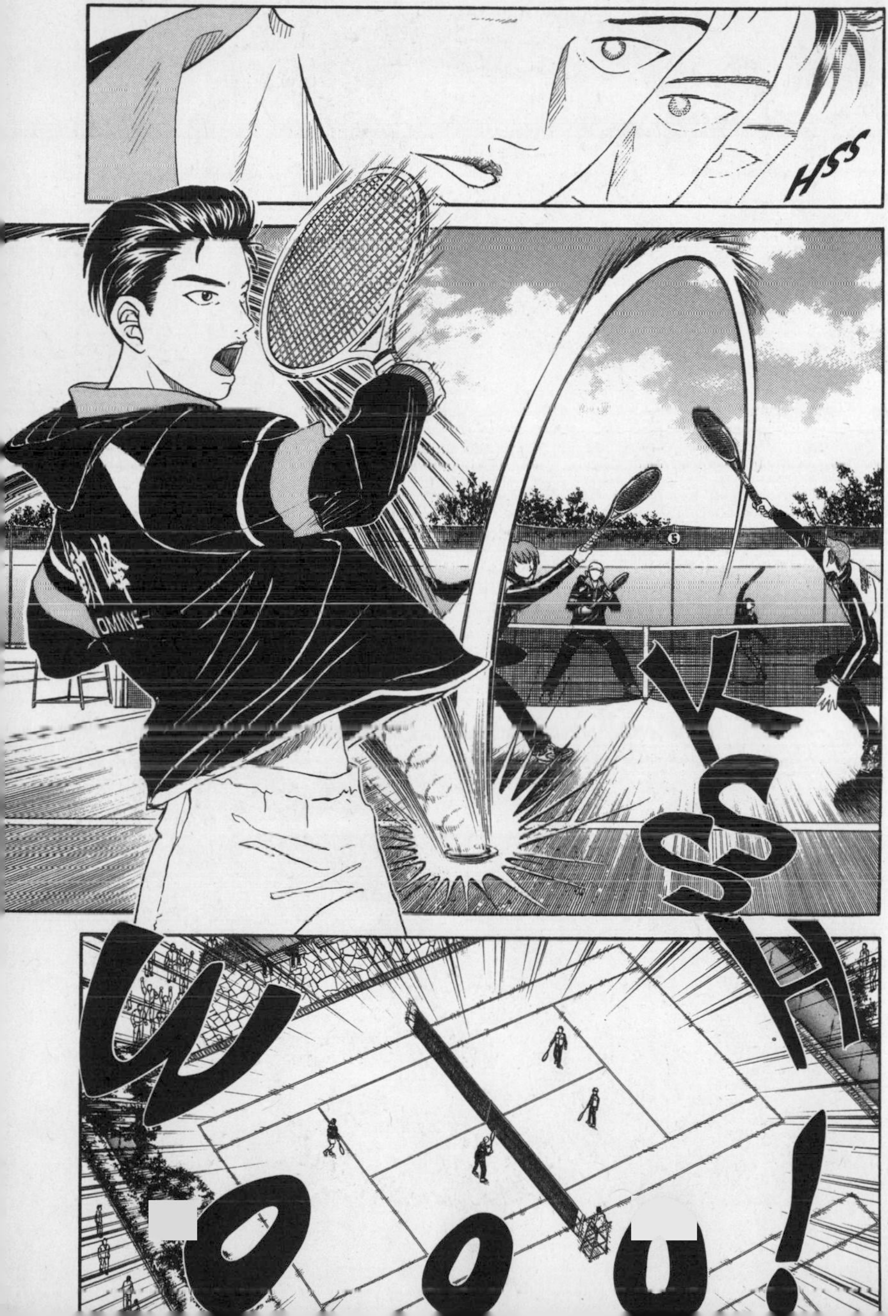
HSS

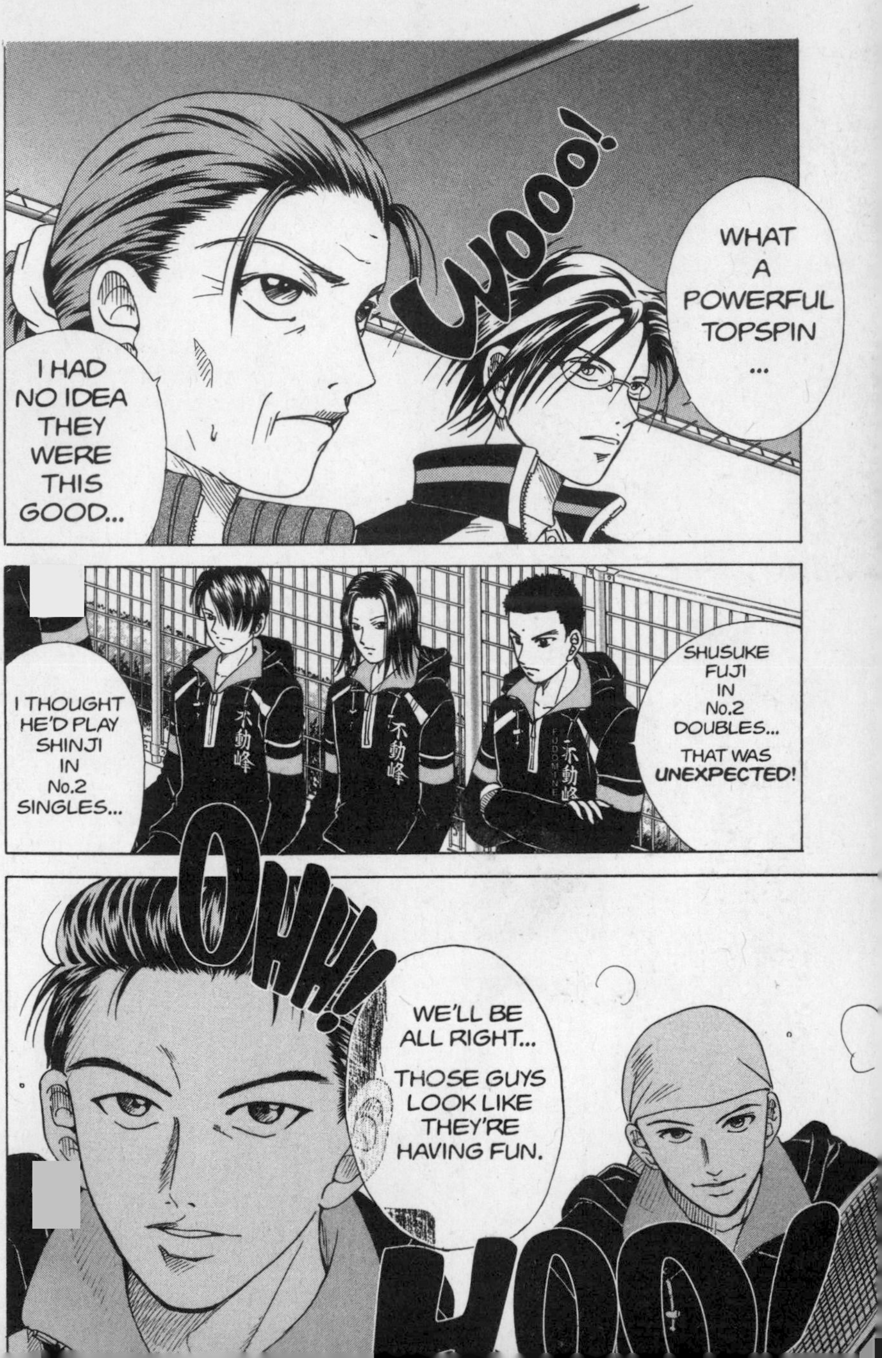
WHAT A POWERFUL TOPSPIN ...
WOOO!
I HAD NO IDEA THEY WERE THIS GOOD...
SHUSUKE FUJI IN No.2 DOUBLES... THAT WAS UNEXPECTED!
I THOUGHT HE'D PLAY SHINJI IN No.2 SINGLES...
不動峰
FUDOMINE
OHH!!
WE'LL BE ALL RIGHT... THOSE GUYS LOOK LIKE THEY'RE HAVING FUN.

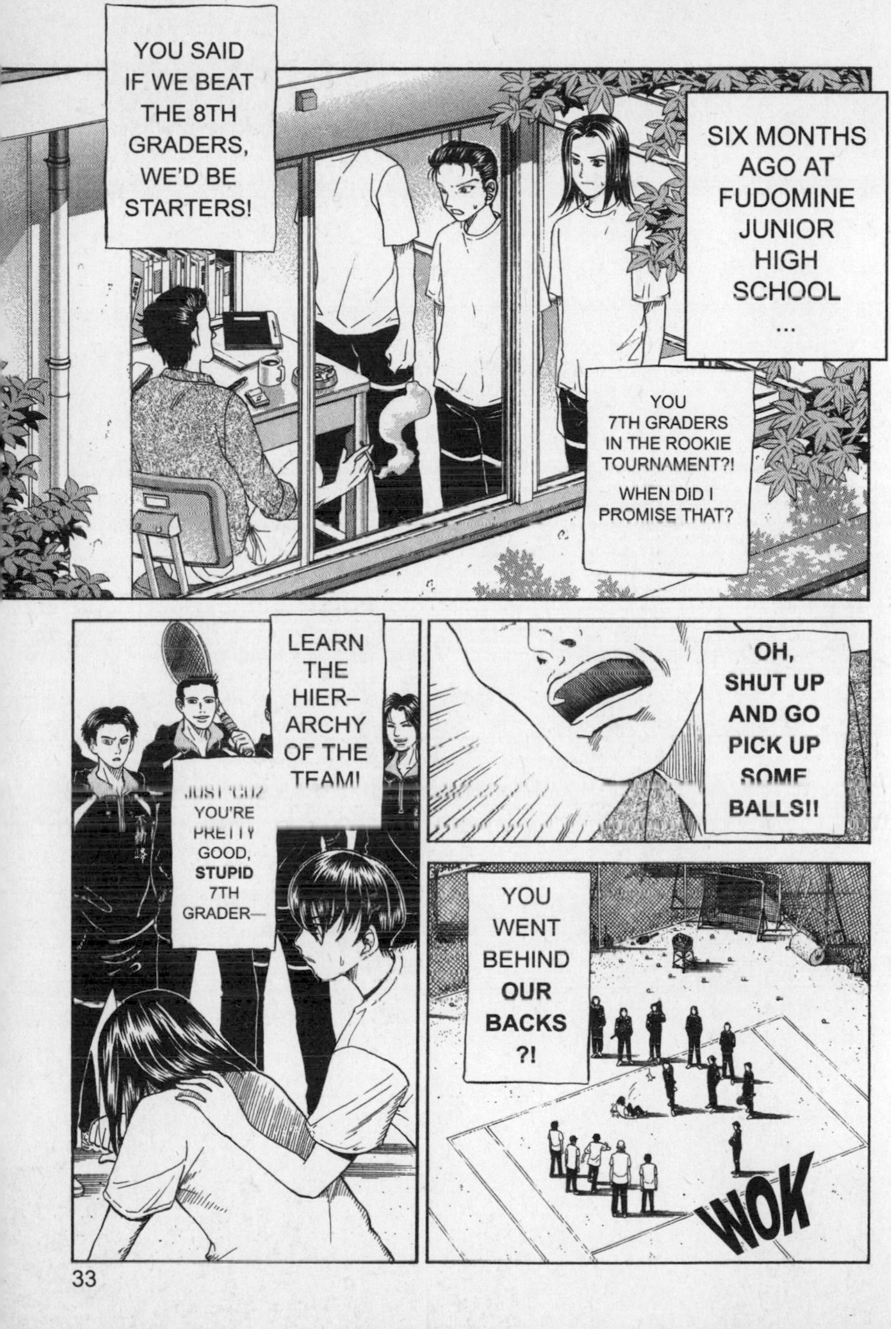
SIX MONTHS AGO AT FUDOMINE JUNIOR HIGH SCHOOL ...
YOU SAID IF WE BEAT THE 8TH GRADERS, WE'D BE STARTERS!
YOU 7TH GRADERS IN THE ROOKIE TOURNAMENT?!
WHEN DID I PROMISE THAT?
OH, SHUT UP AND GO PICK UP SOME BALLS!!
YOU WENT BEHIND OUR BACKS?!
WOK
LEARN THE HIER–ARCHY OF THE TEAM!
JUST 'CUZ YOU'RE PRETTY GOOD, STUPID 7TH GRADER—

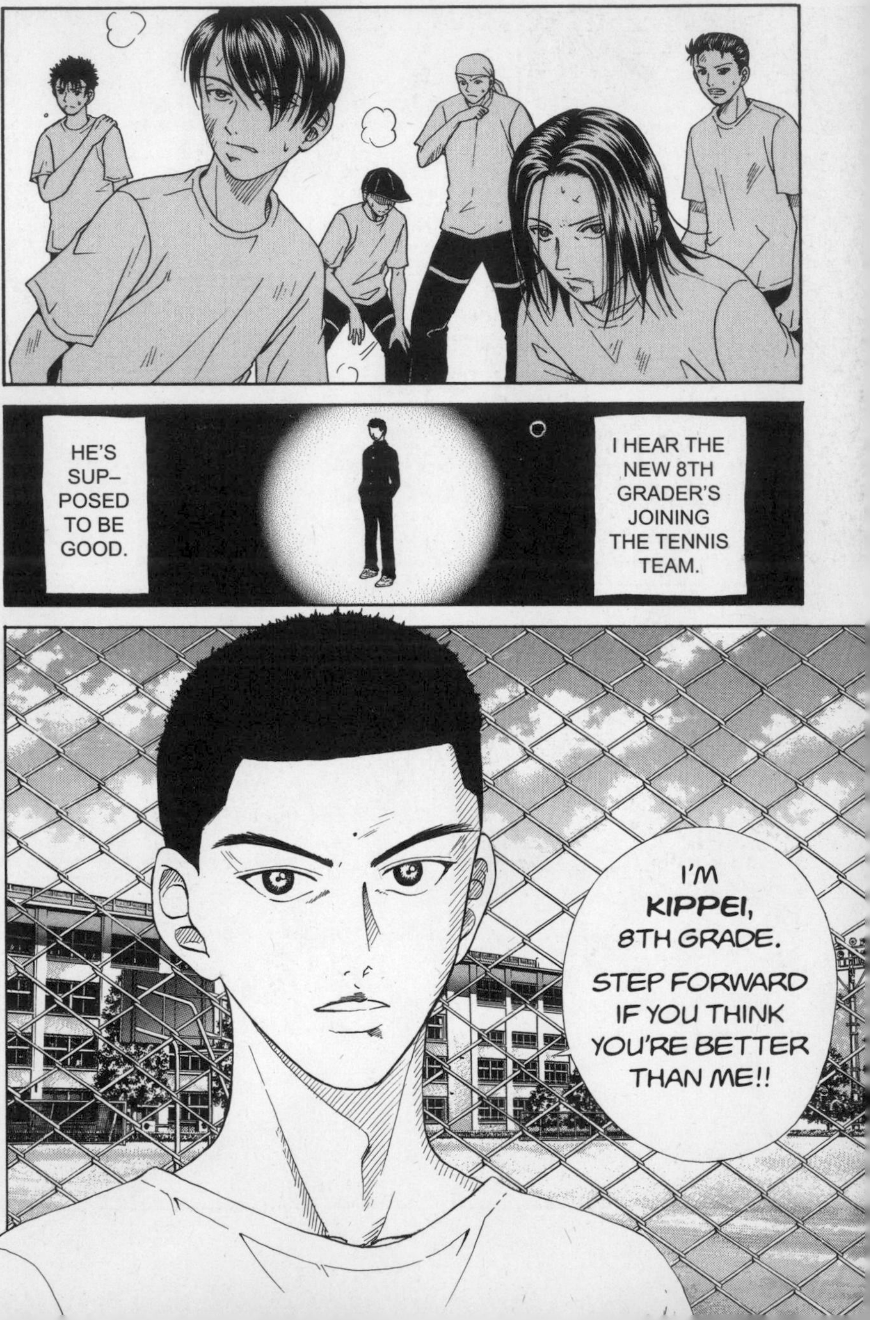
I HEAR THE NEW 8TH GRADER'S JOINING THE TENNIS TEAM.
HE'S SUP–POSED TO BE GOOD.
I'M KIPPEI, 8TH GRADE.
STEP FORWARD IF YOU THINK YOU'RE BETTER THAN ME!!

READ THIS WAY

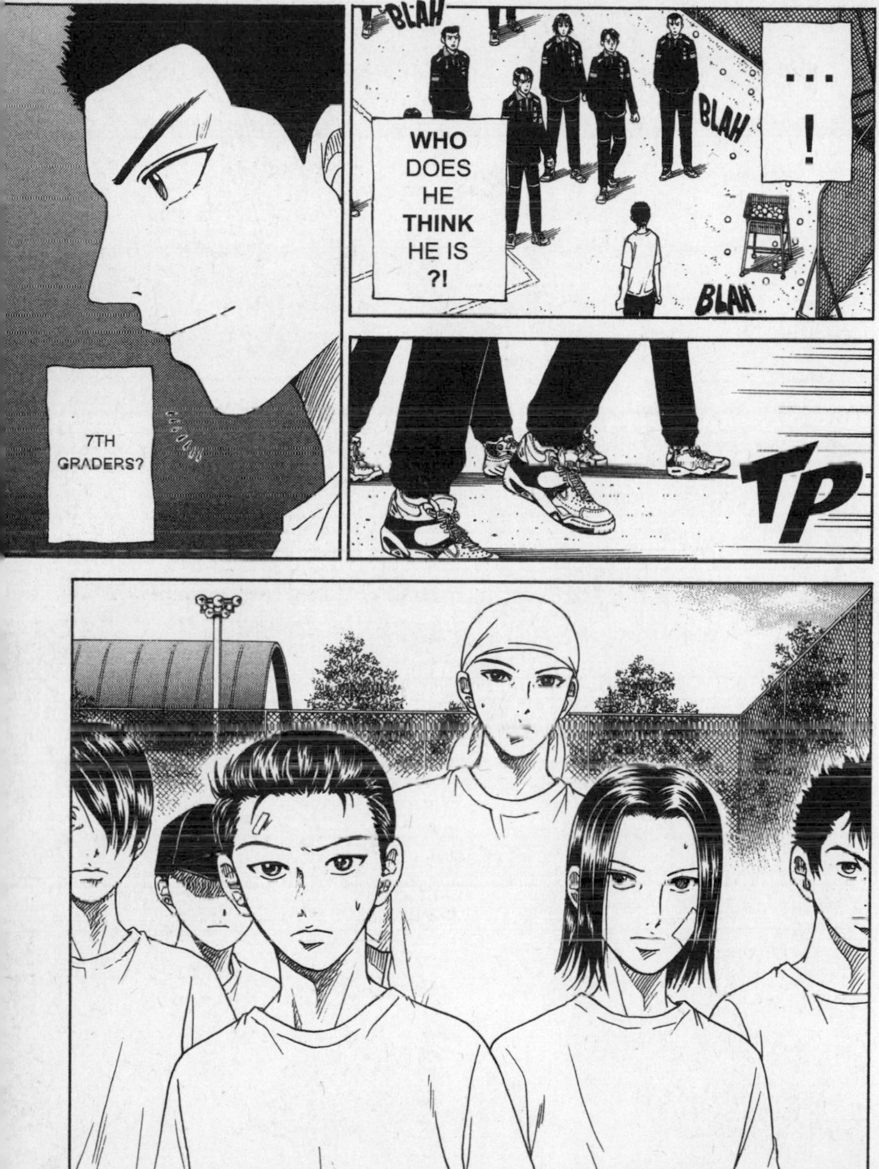

...!
BLAH
BLAH
WHO DOES HE THINK HE IS ?!
BLAH
TP
7TH GRADERS?

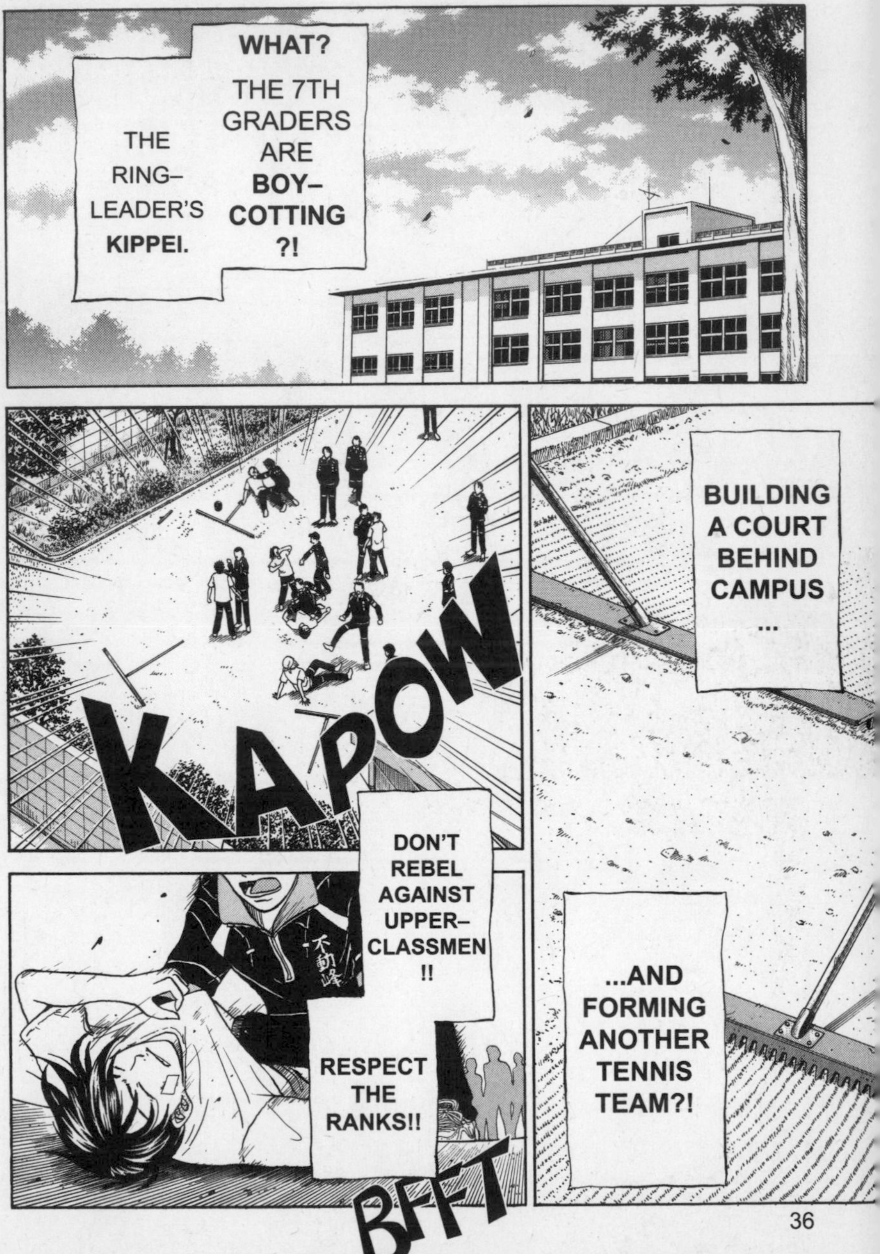
WHAT?
THE 7TH GRADERS ARE BOY–COTTING?!
THE RING–LEADER'S KIPPEI.
BUILDING A COURT BEHIND CAMPUS...
...AND FORMING ANOTHER TENNIS TEAM?!
KAPOW
DON'T REBEL AGAINST UPPER–CLASSMEN!!
RESPECT THE RANKS!!
BFFT

READ THIS WAY

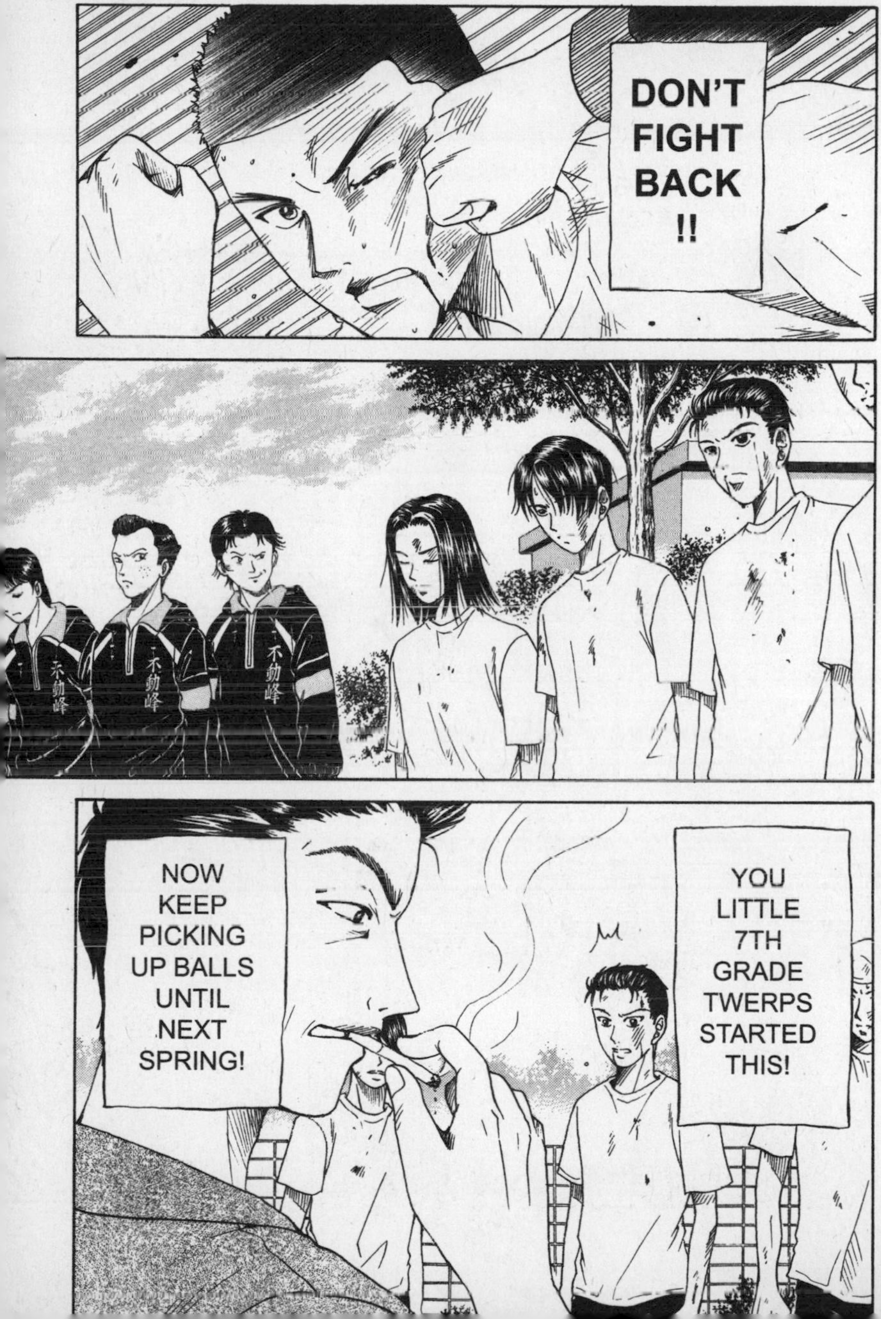
DON'T FIGHT BACK !!
不動峰
不動峰
不動峰
YOU LITTLE 7TH GRADE TWERPS STARTED THIS!
NOW KEEP PICKING UP BALLS UNTIL NEXT SPRING!

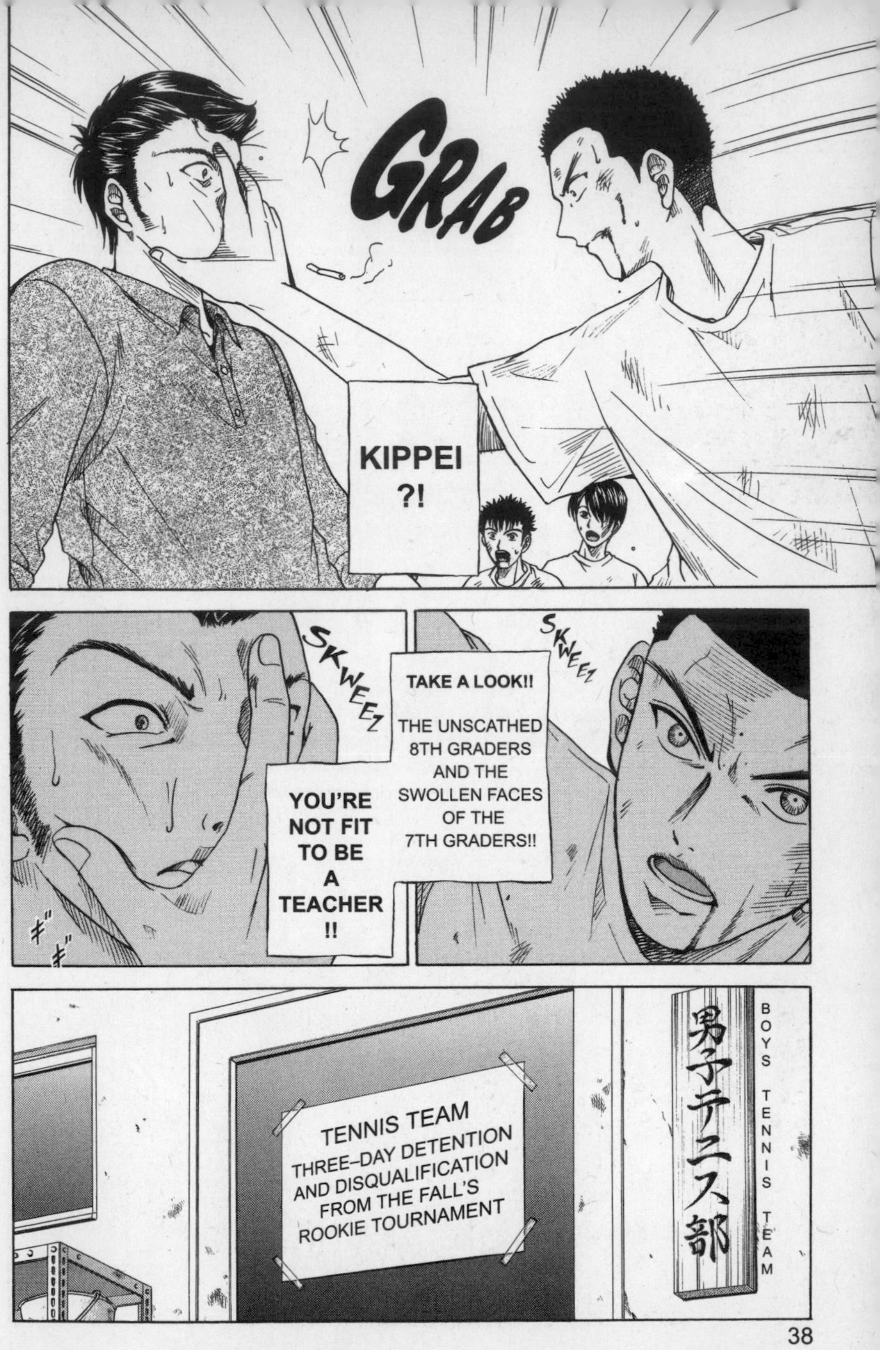
GRAB
KIPPEI ?!
SKWEEZ
TAKE A LOOK!!
THE UNSCATHED 8TH GRADERS AND THE SWOLLEN FACES OF THE 7TH GRADERS!!
SKWEEZ
YOU'RE NOT FIT TO BE A TEACHER !!
ギギ
男子テニス部
BOYS TENNIS TEAM
TENNIS TEAM
THREE-DAY DETENTION AND DISQUALIFICATION FROM THE FALL'S ROOKIE TOURNAMENT

READ THIS WAY

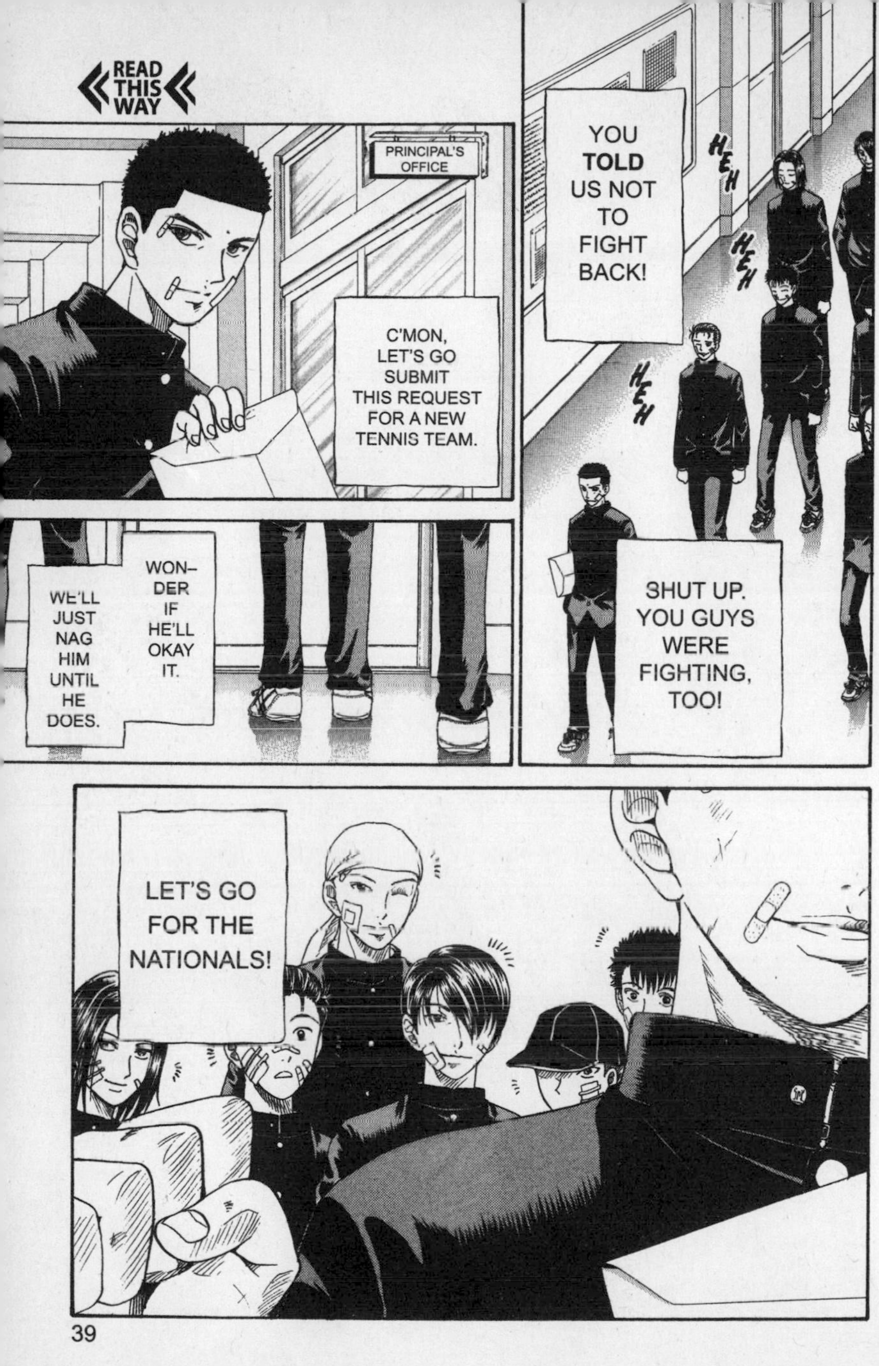

YOU TOLD US NOT TO FIGHT BACK!
HEH
HEH
HEH
SHUT UP. YOU GUYS WERE FIGHTING, TOO!
PRINCIPAL'S OFFICE
C'MON, LET'S GO SUBMIT THIS REQUEST FOR A NEW TENNIS TEAM.
WON-DER IF HE'LL OKAY IT.
WE'LL JUST NAG HIM UNTIL HE DOES.
LET'S GO FOR THE NATIONALS!

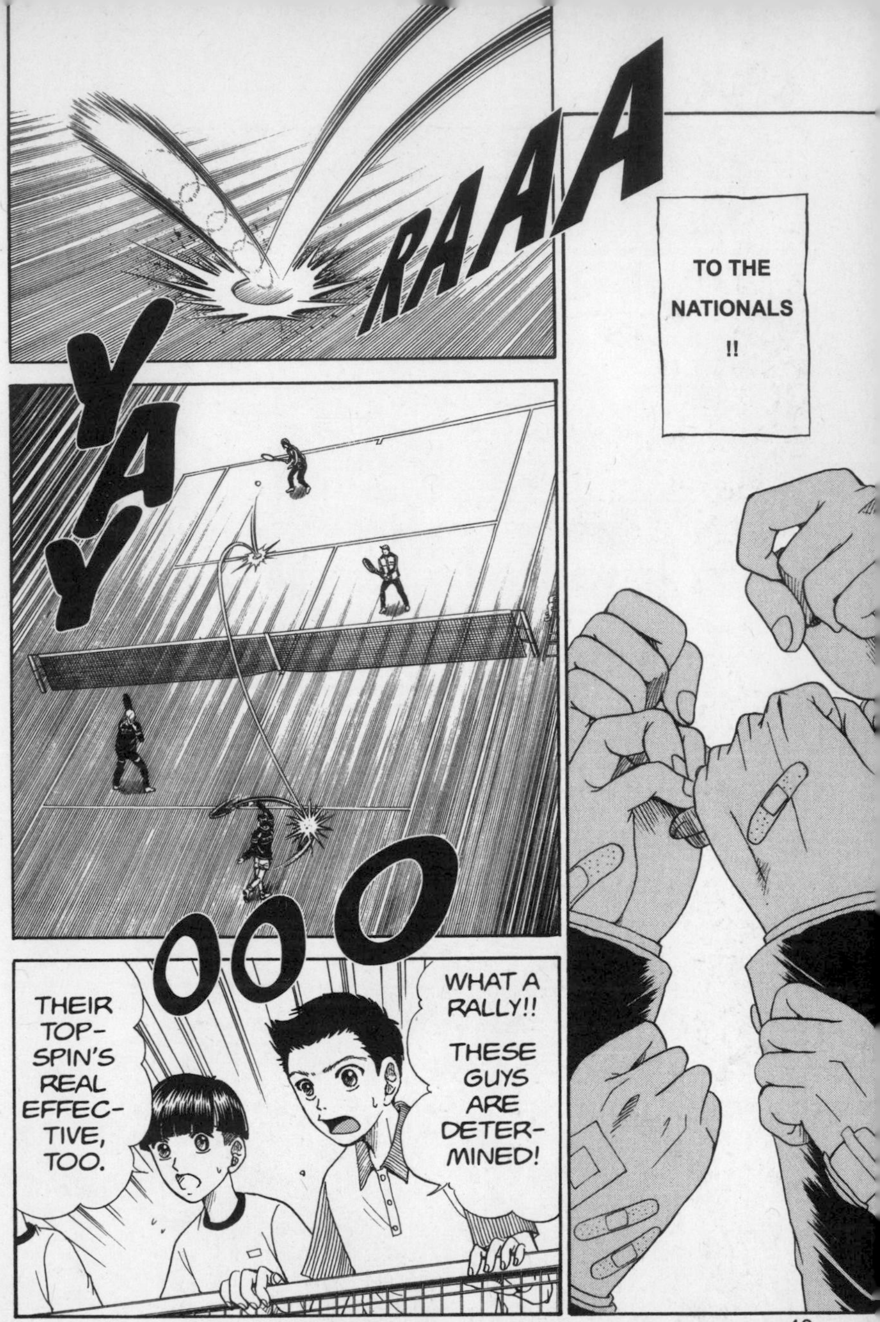
TO THE NATIONALS !!
RAAAA
YAY
OOOO
WHAT A RALLY!!
THESE GUYS ARE DETER-MINED!
THEIR TOP-SPIN'S REAL EFFEC-TIVE, TOO.

READ THIS WAY

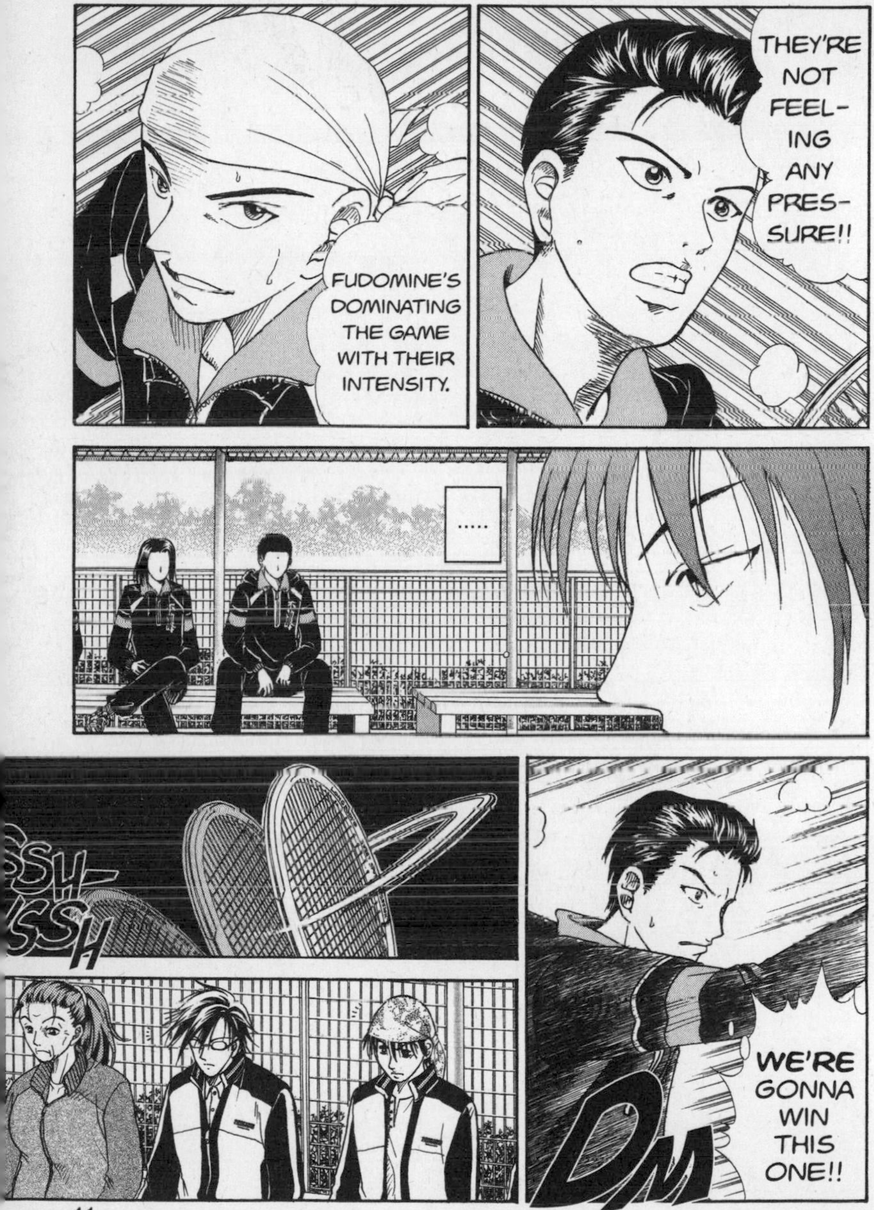
THEY'RE NOT FEEL- ING ANY PRES- SURE!!
FUDOMINE'S DOMINATING THE GAME WITH THEIR INTENSITY.
.....
WE'RE GONNA WIN THIS ONE!!
DM

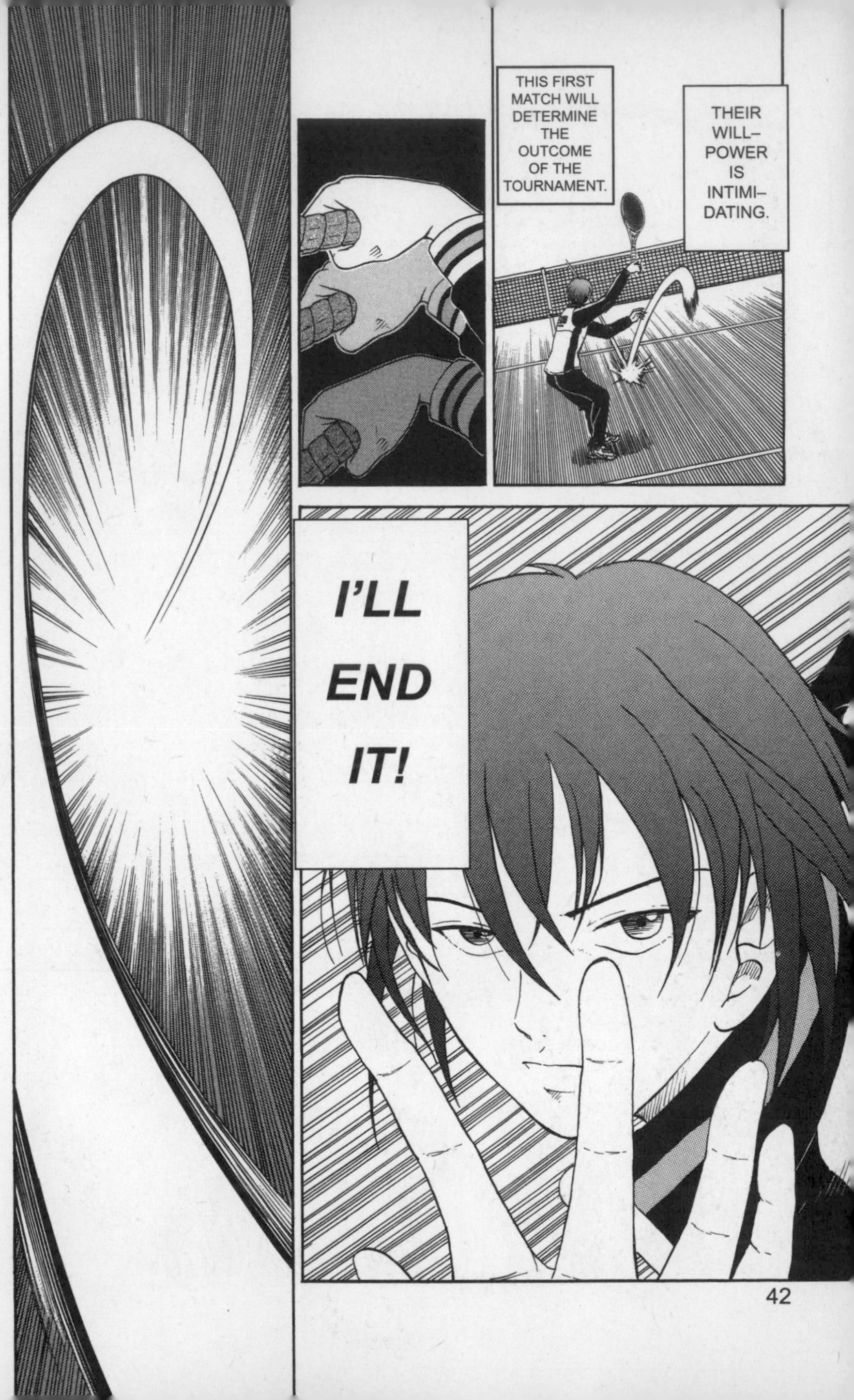
THEIR WILL–POWER IS INTIMI–DATING.
THIS FIRST MATCH WILL DETERMINE THE OUTCOME OF THE TOURNAMENT.
I'LL END IT!

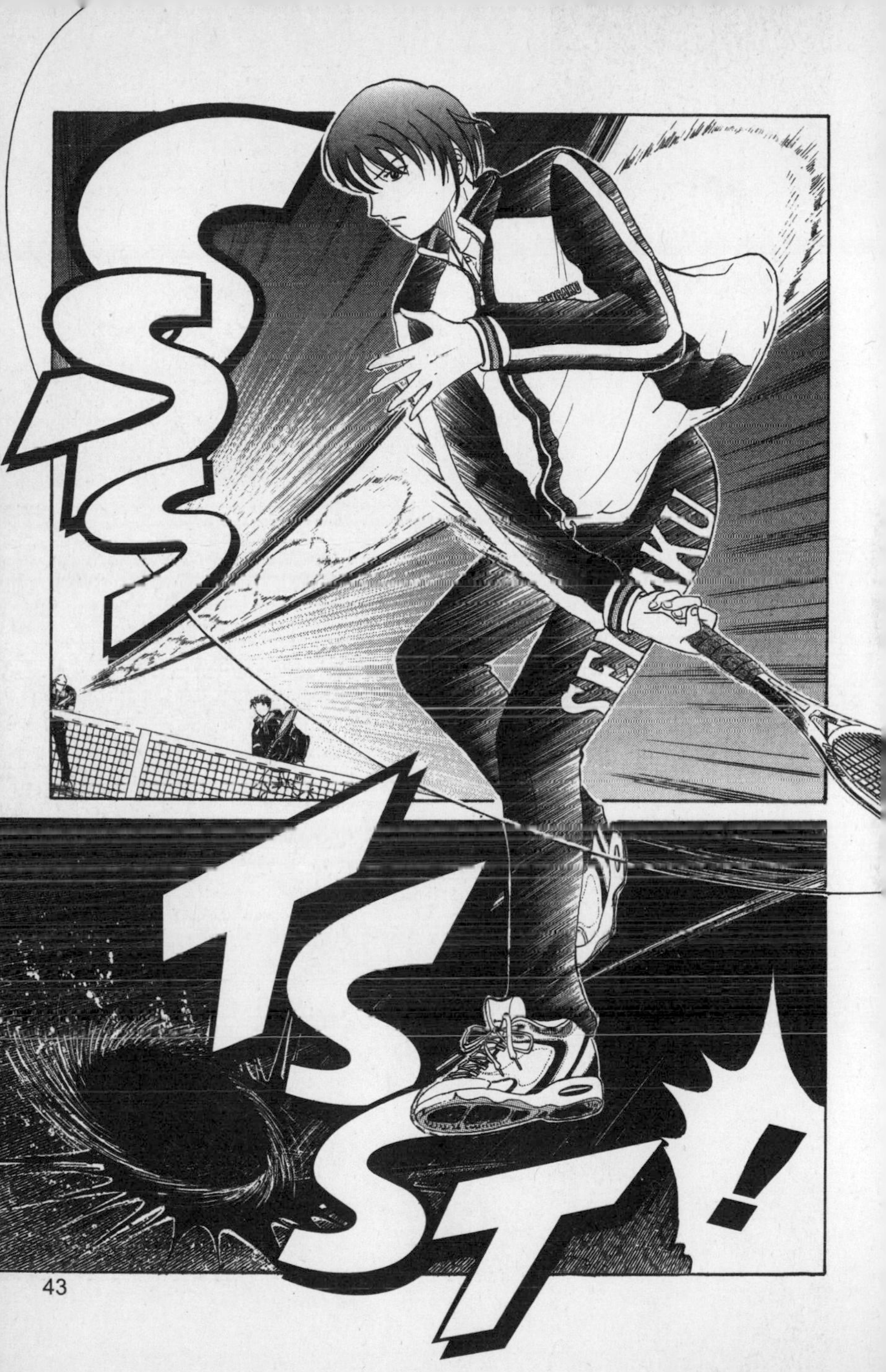
SSS
TSST!

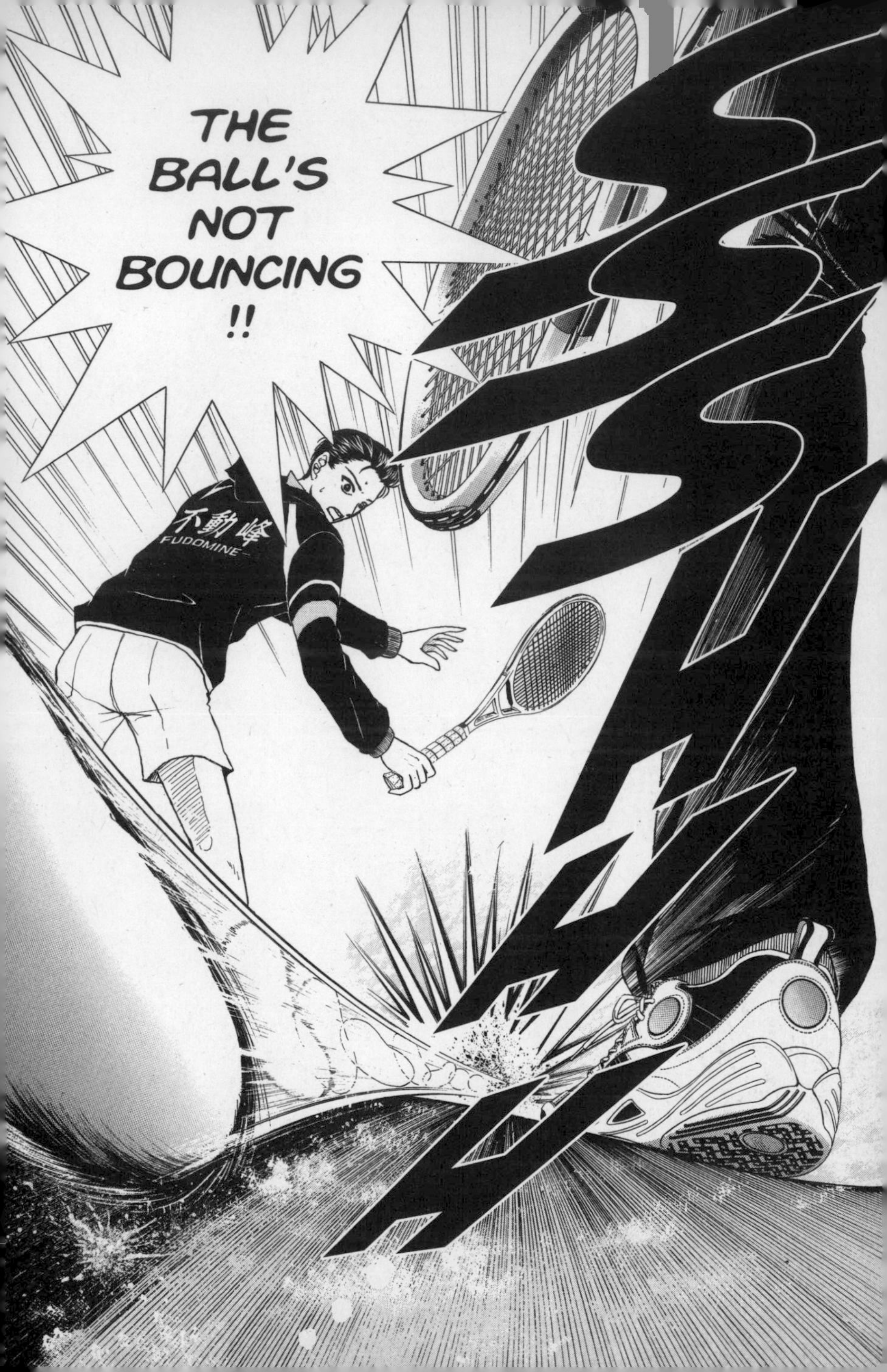
THE BALL'S NOT BOUNCING !!
不動峰
FUDOMINE

READ THIS WAY

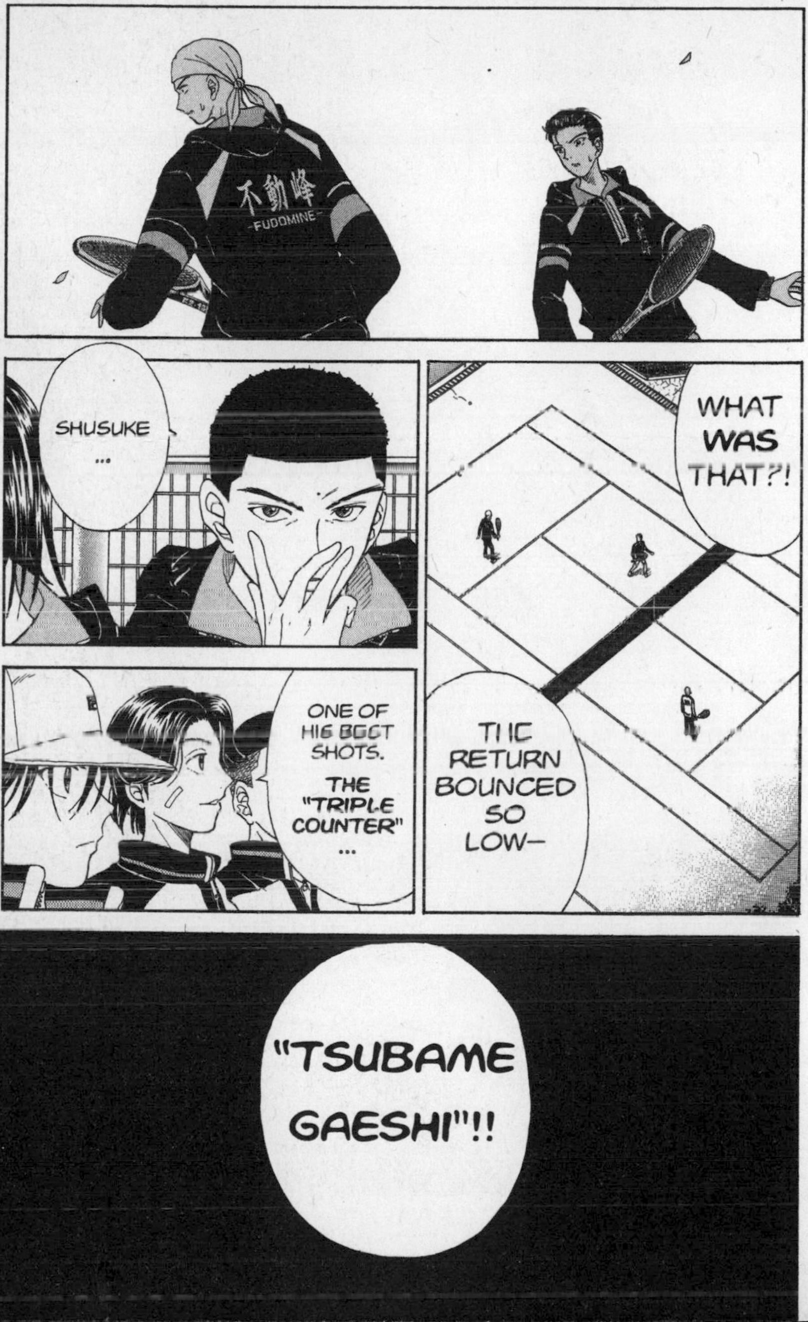

不動峰
-FUDOMINE-
WHAT WAS THAT?!
THE RETURN BOUNCED SO LOW–
SHUSUKE ...
ONE OF HIS BEST SHOTS.
THE "TRIPLE COUNTER" ...
"TSUBAME GAESHI"!!

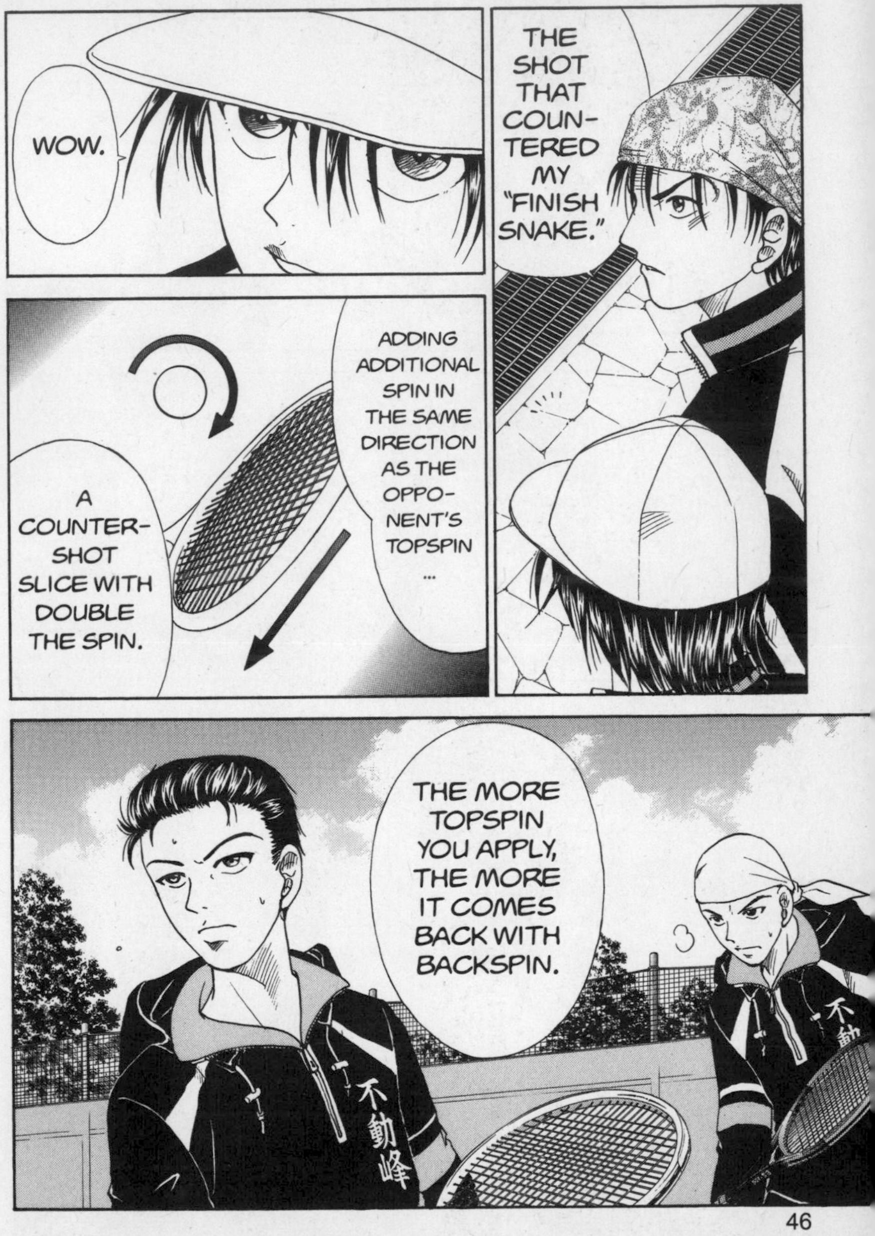
THE SHOT THAT COUNTERED MY "FINISH SNAKE."
WOW.
ADDING ADDITIONAL SPIN IN THE SAME DIRECTION AS THE OPPONENT'S TOPSPIN ...
A COUNTER-SHOT SLICE WITH DOUBLE THE SPIN.
THE MORE TOPSPIN YOU APPLY, THE MORE IT COMES BACK WITH BACKSPIN.
不動峰

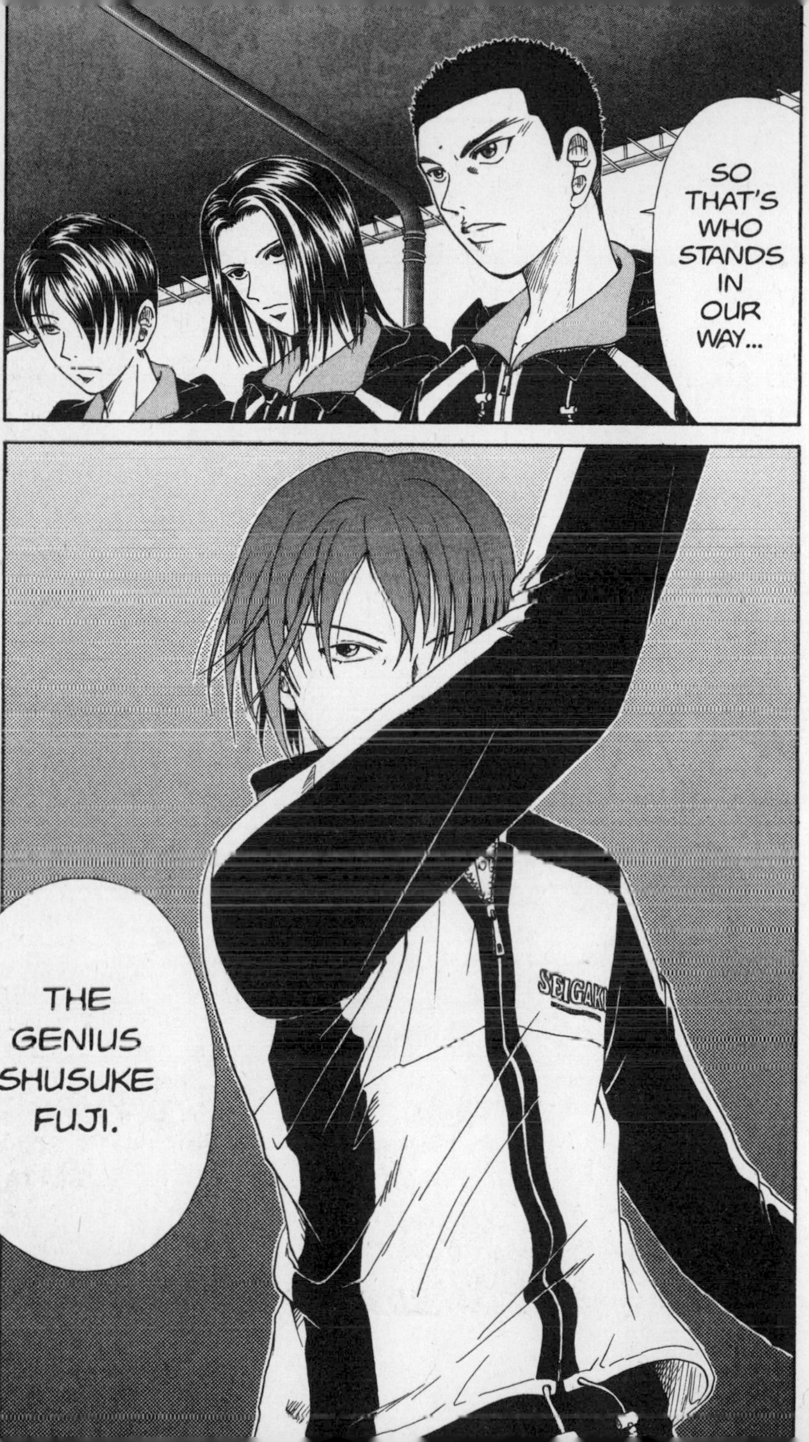
SO THAT'S WHO STANDS IN OUR WAY...
SEIGAKU
THE GENIUS SHUSUKE FUJI.

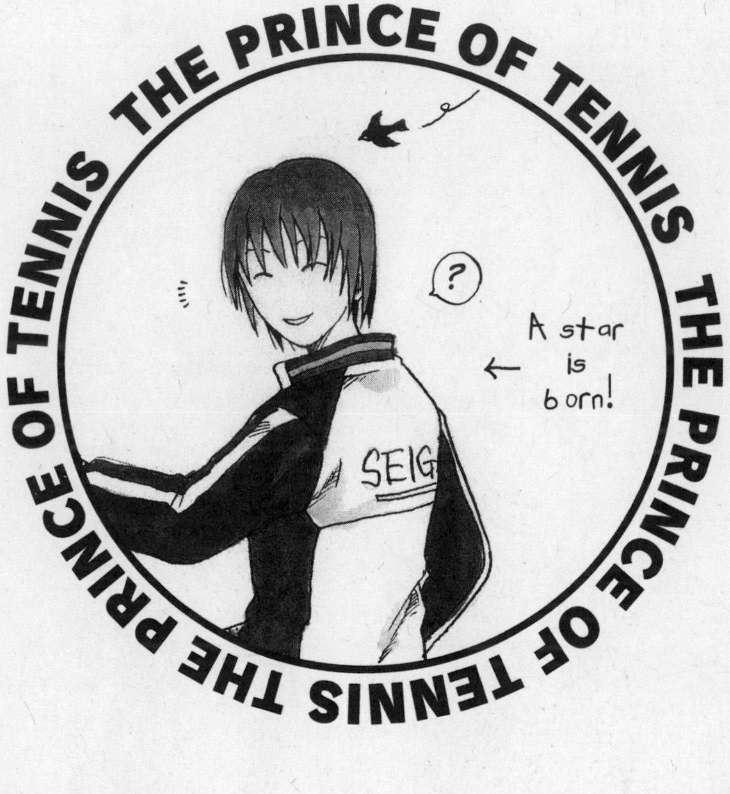
THE PRINCE OF TENNIS THE PRINCE OF TENNIS THE PRINCE OF TENNIS
?
A star is born!
SEIG

Genius 28:

GENIUS VS. POWER

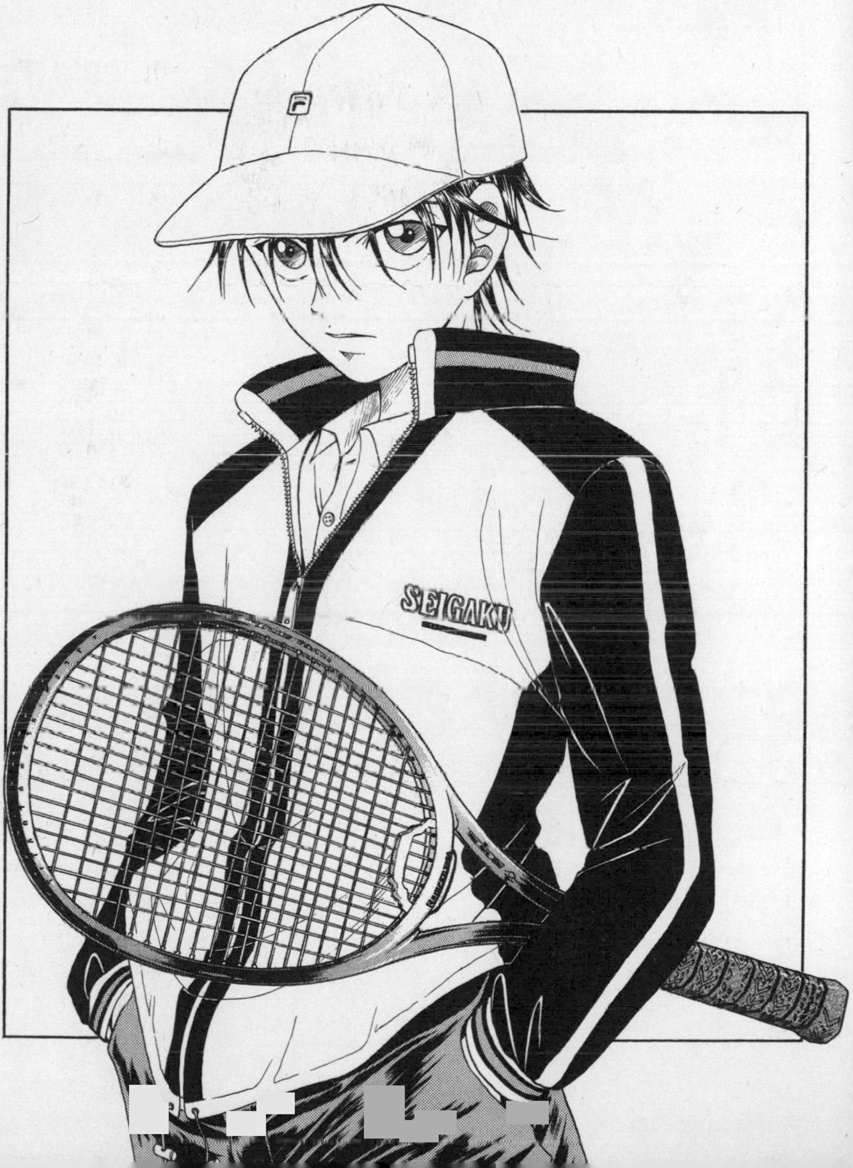
SEIGAKU

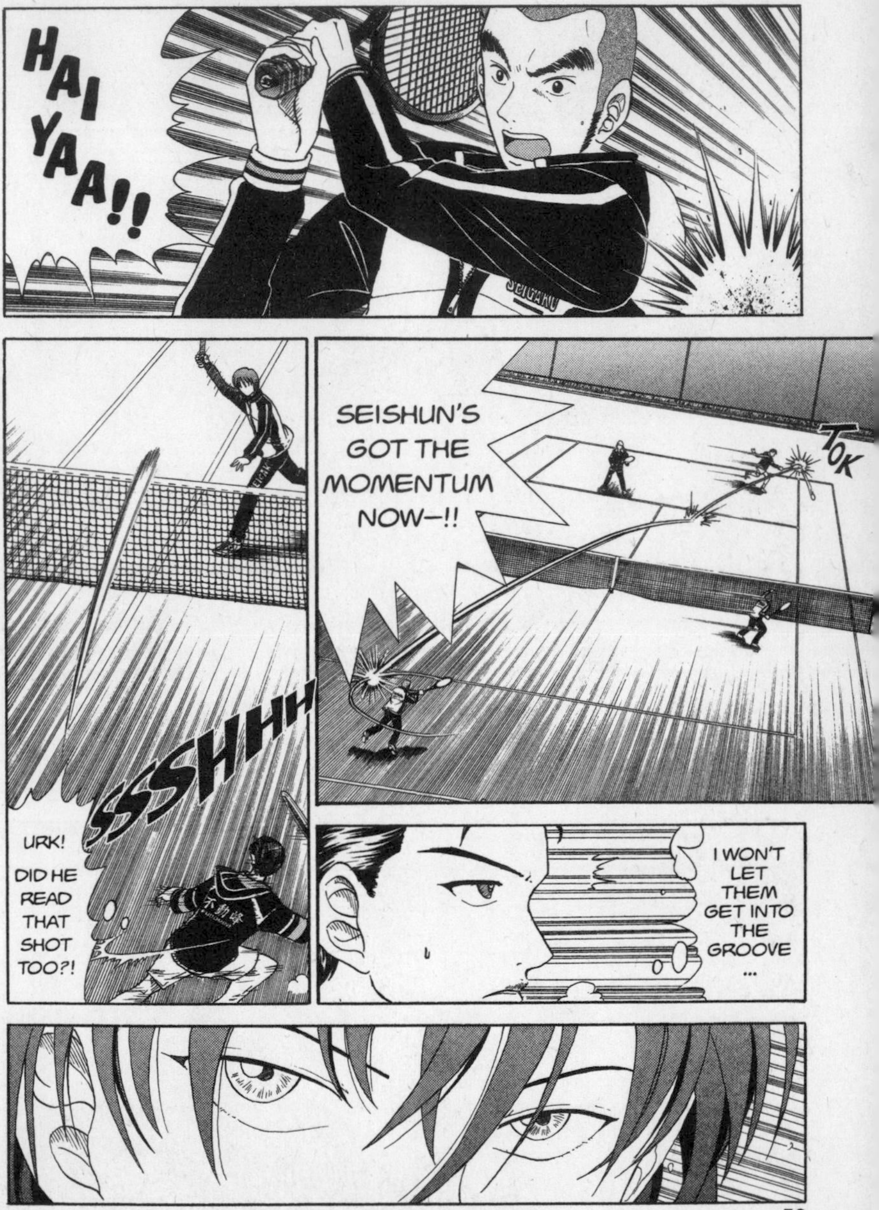
HAI YAA!!
SEISHUN'S GOT THE MOMENTUM NOW-!!
TOK
I WON'T LET THEM GET INTO THE GROOVE ...
SSSHHH
URK!
DID HE READ THAT SHOT TOO?!

READ THIS WAY

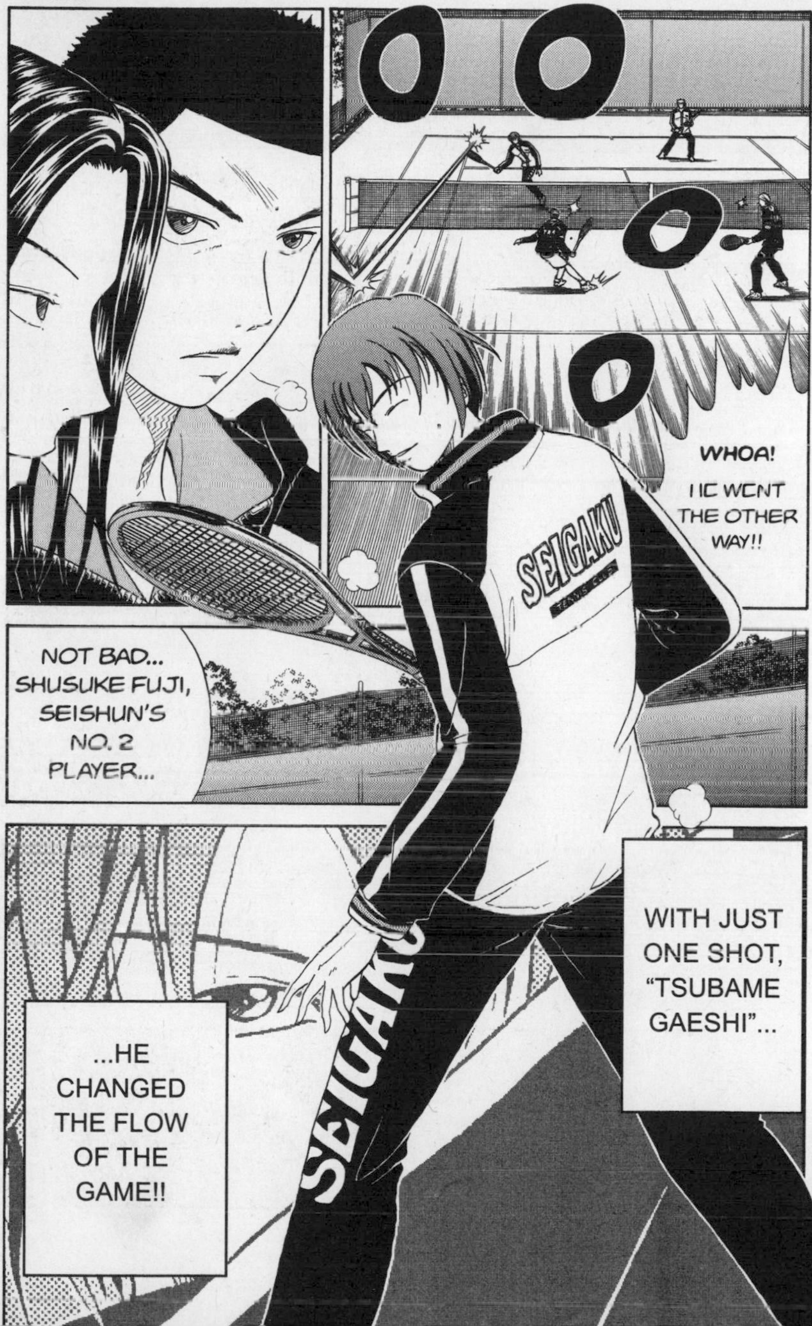
OOOO
WHOA!
HE WENT THE OTHER WAY!!
SEIGAKU
NOT BAD... SHUSUKE FUJI, SEISHUN'S NO. 2 PLAYER...
WITH JUST ONE SHOT, "TSUBAME GAESHI"...
...HE CHANGED THE FLOW OF THE GAME!!
SEIGAKU

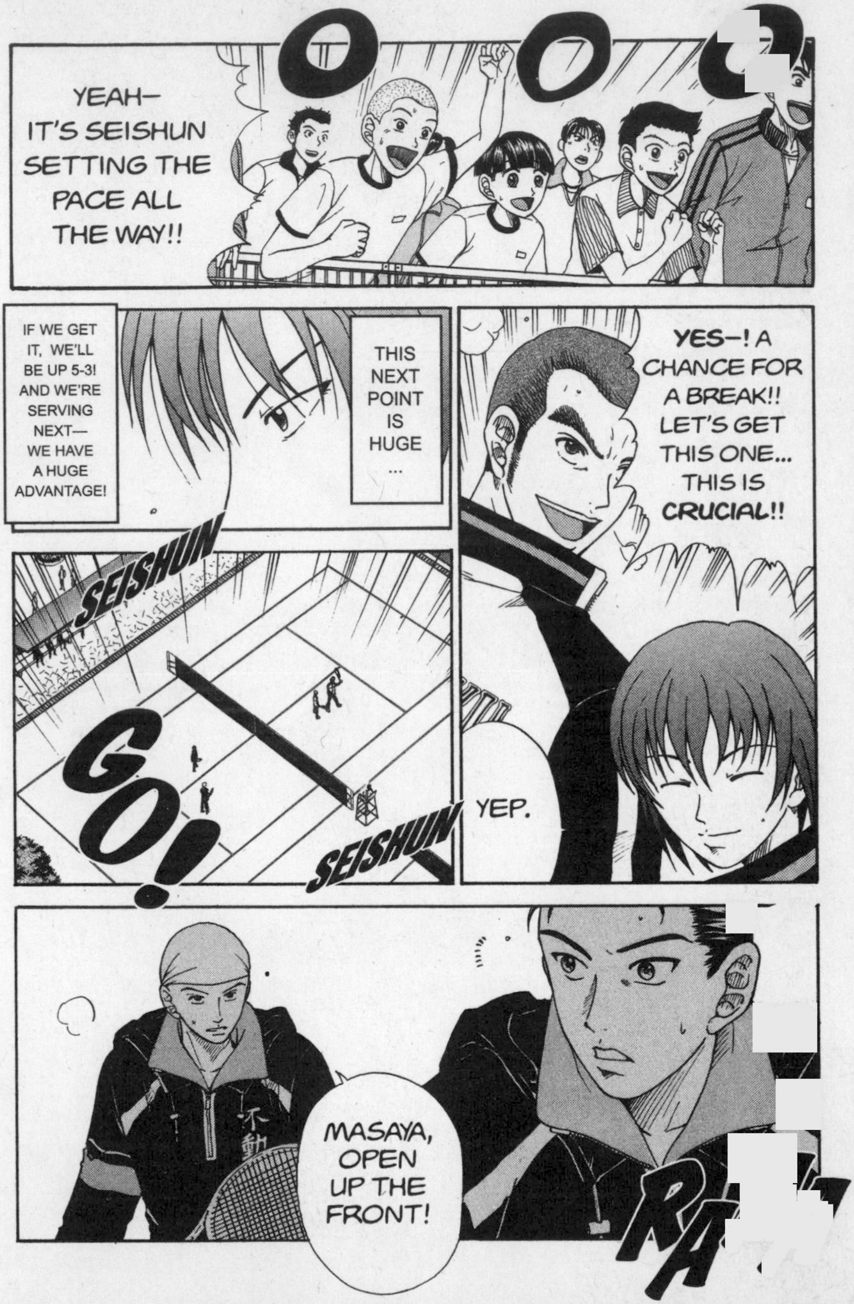
OO
YEAH— IT'S SEISHUN SETTING THE PACE ALL THE WAY!!
YES—! A CHANCE FOR A BREAK!! LET'S GET THIS ONE... THIS IS CRUCIAL!!
YEP.
THIS NEXT POINT IS HUGE ...
IF WE GET IT, WE'LL BE UP 5-3! AND WE'RE SERVING NEXT— WE HAVE A HUGE ADVANTAGE!
SEISHUN
GO!
SEISHUN
MASAYA, OPEN UP THE FRONT!

READ THIS WAY

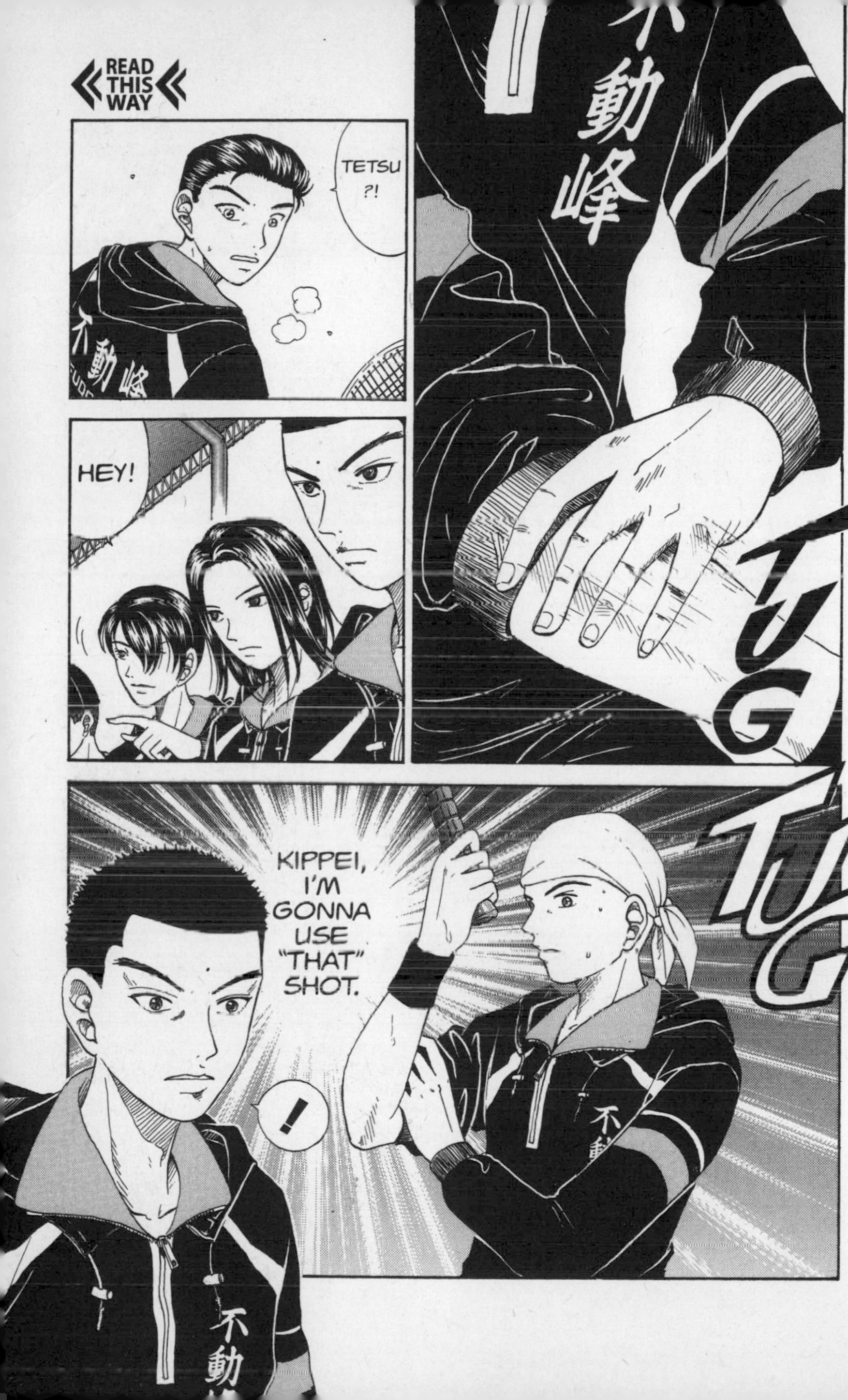
TUG
TETSU ?!
HEY!
TUG
KIPPEI, I'M GONNA USE "THAT" SHOT.
!

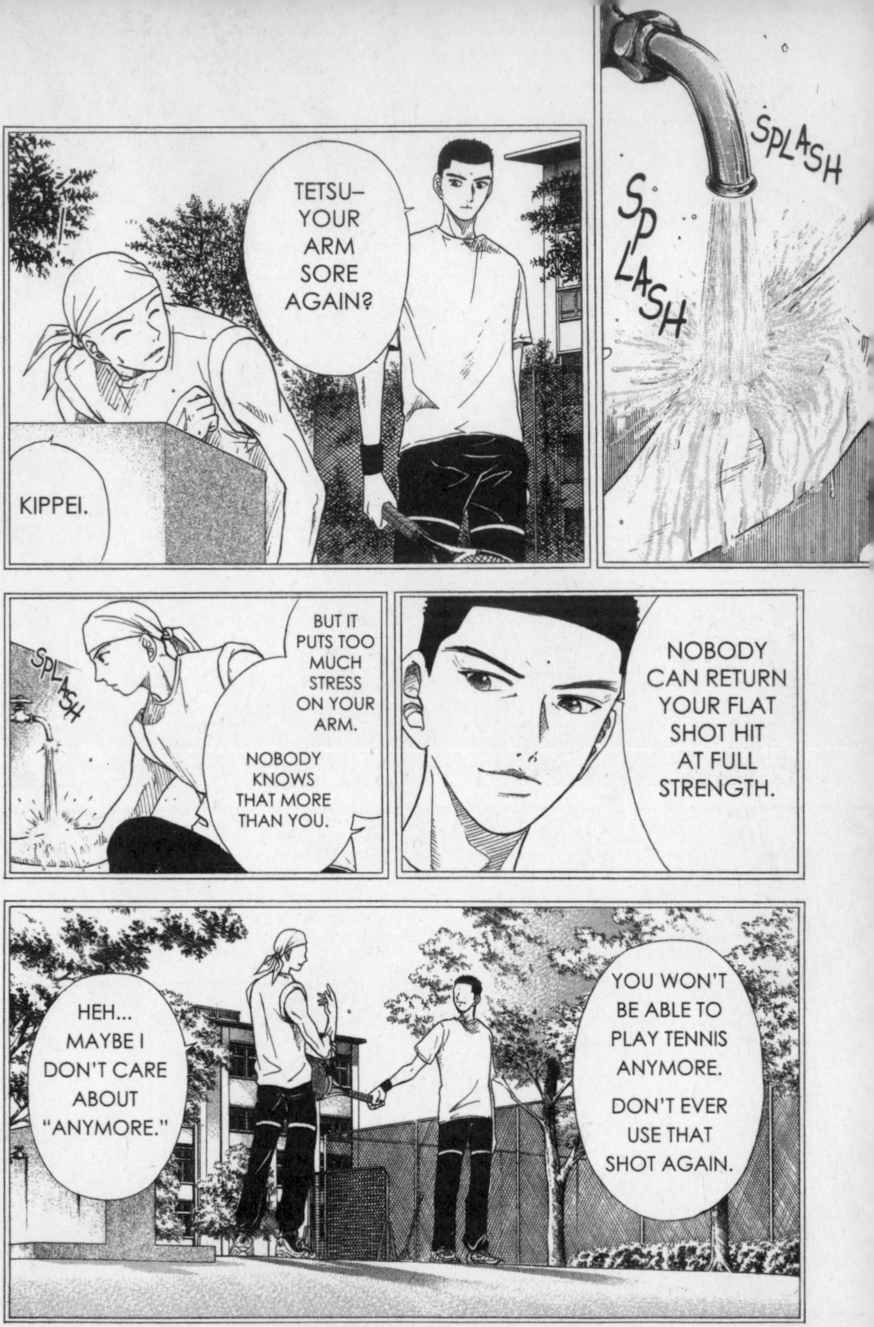
SPLASH
SPLASH
TETSU— YOUR ARM SORE AGAIN?
KIPPEI.
NOBODY CAN RETURN YOUR FLAT SHOT HIT AT FULL STRENGTH.
BUT IT PUTS TOO MUCH STRESS ON YOUR ARM.
NOBODY KNOWS THAT MORE THAN YOU.
SPLASH
YOU WON'T BE ABLE TO PLAY TENNIS ANYMORE.
DON'T EVER USE THAT SHOT AGAIN.
HEH... MAYBE I DON'T CARE ABOUT "ANYMORE."

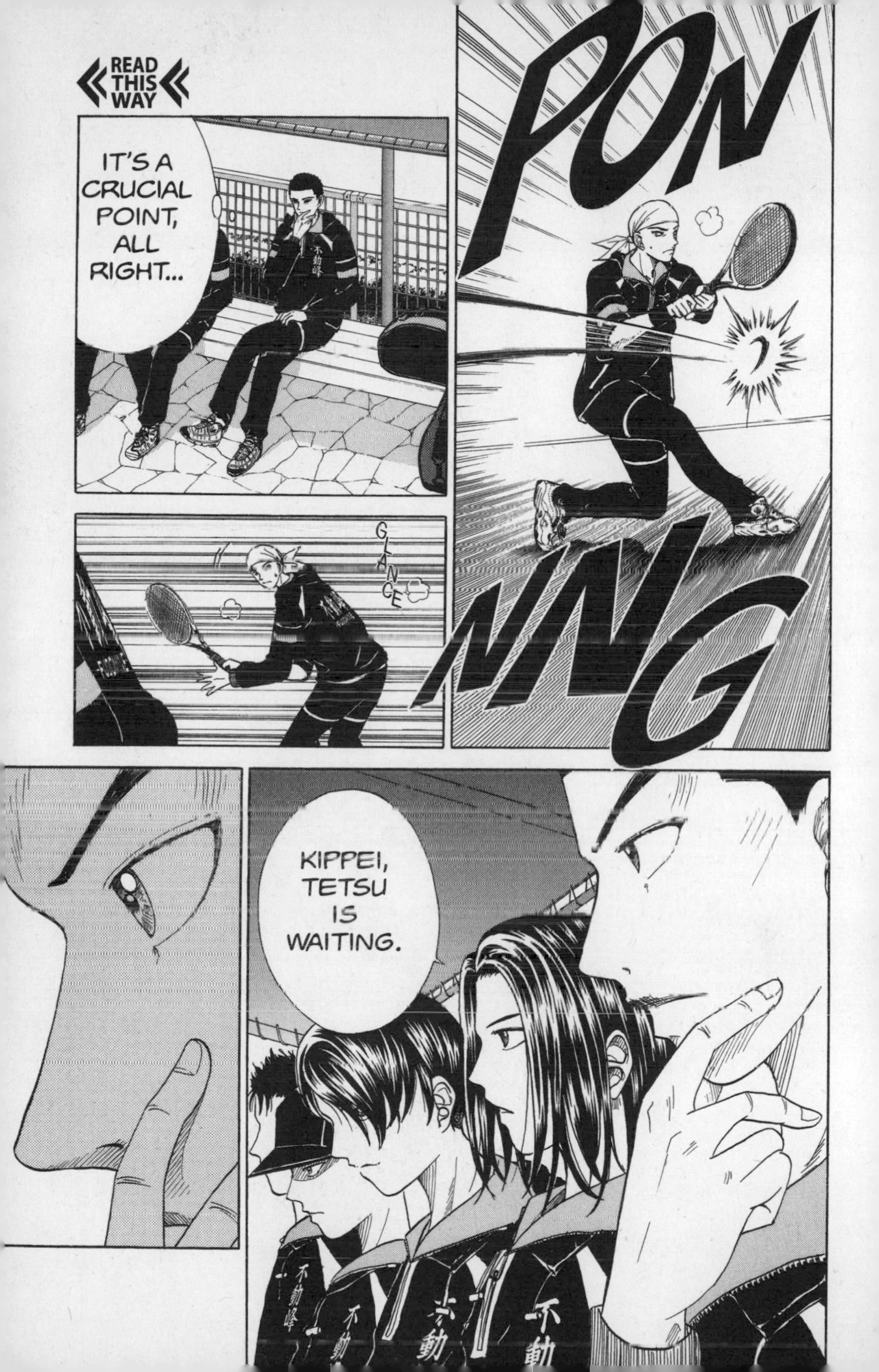
READ THIS WAY
PONNNG
IT'S A CRUCIAL POINT, ALL RIGHT...
GLANCE
KIPPEI, TETSU IS WAITING.

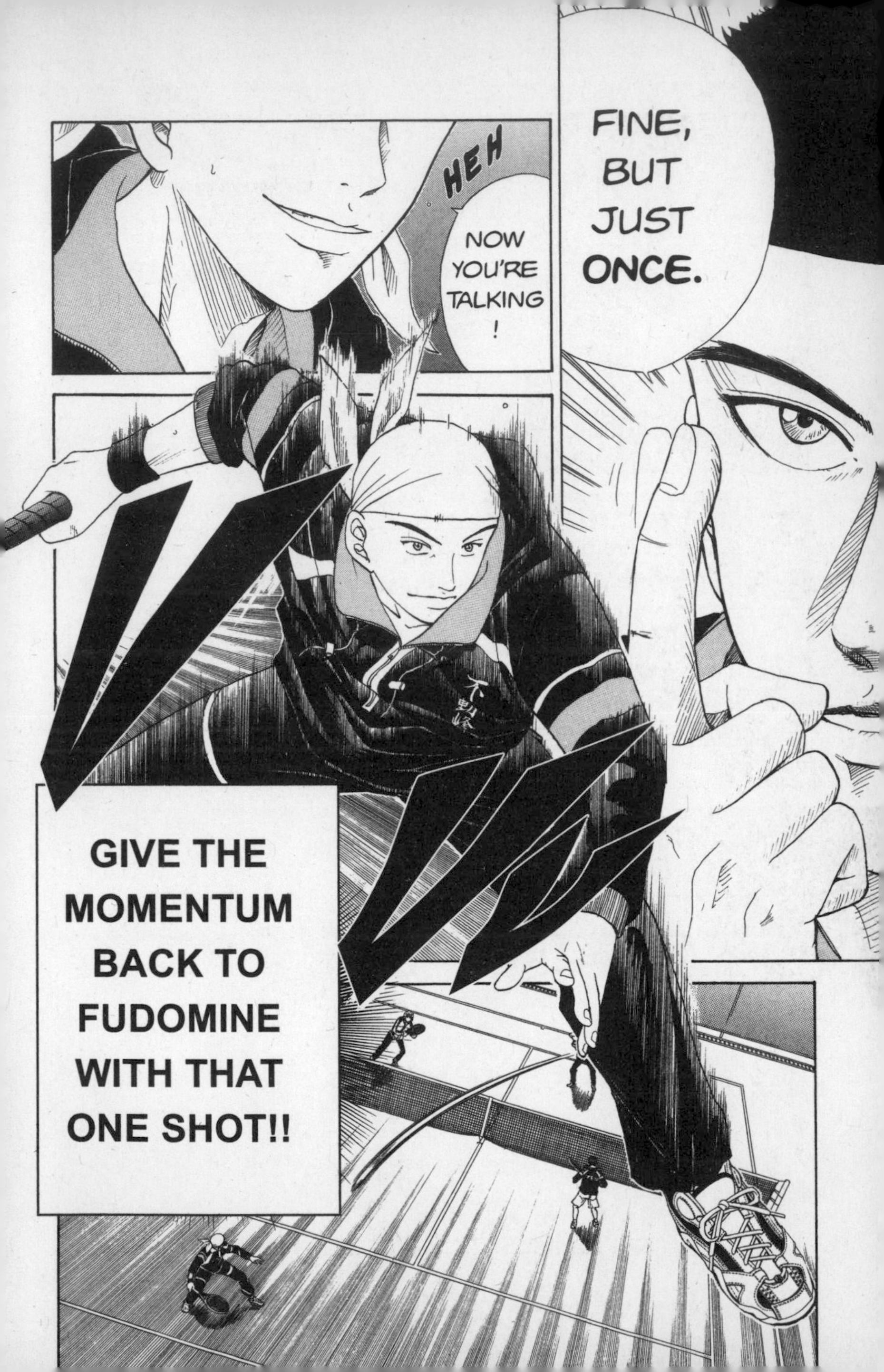
FINE, BUT JUST ONCE.
HEH
NOW YOU'RE TALKING!
GIVE THE MOMENTUM BACK TO FUDOMINE WITH THAT ONE SHOT!!

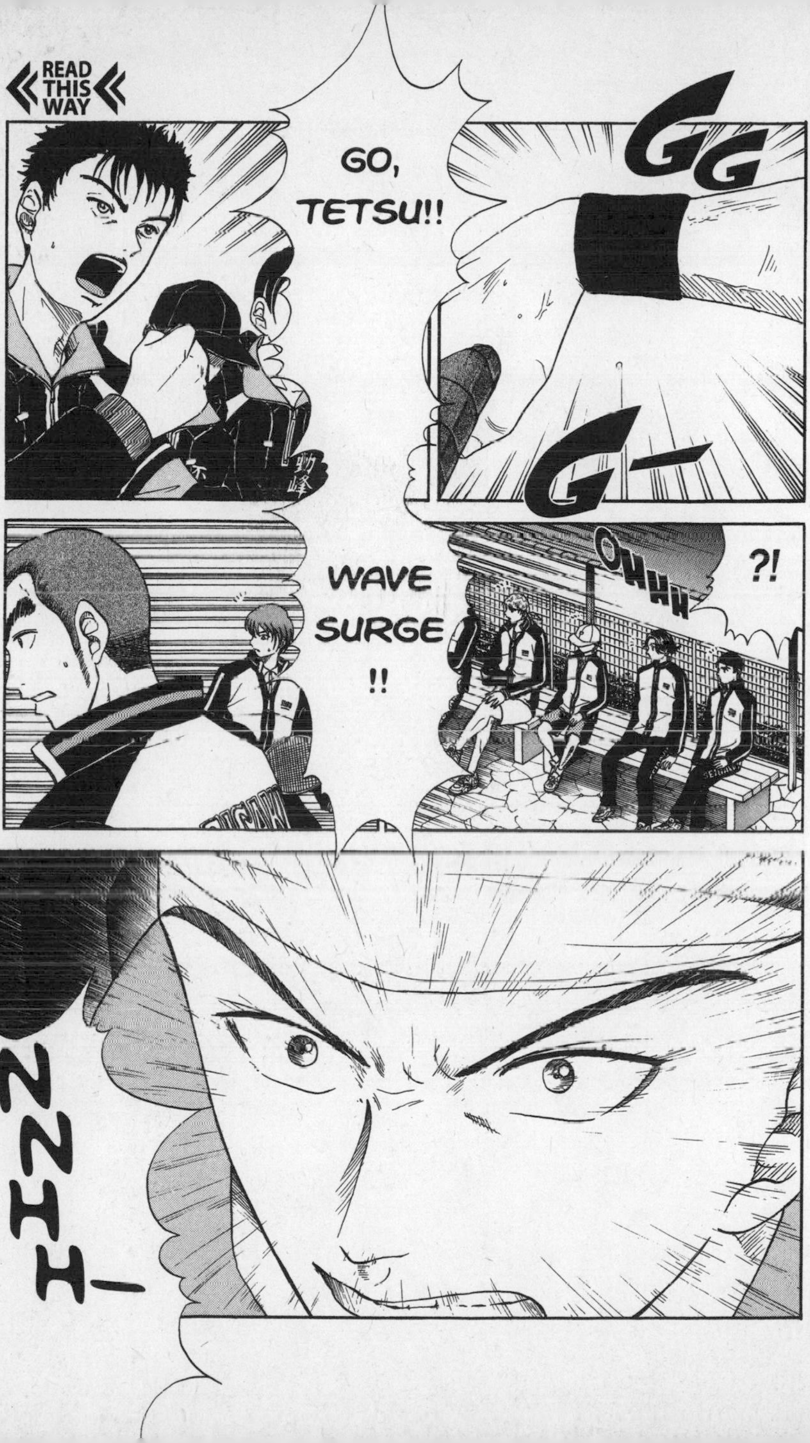
READ THIS WAY
GG
G-
GO, TETSU!!
OHHH
?!
WAVE SURGE !!
ZZII–

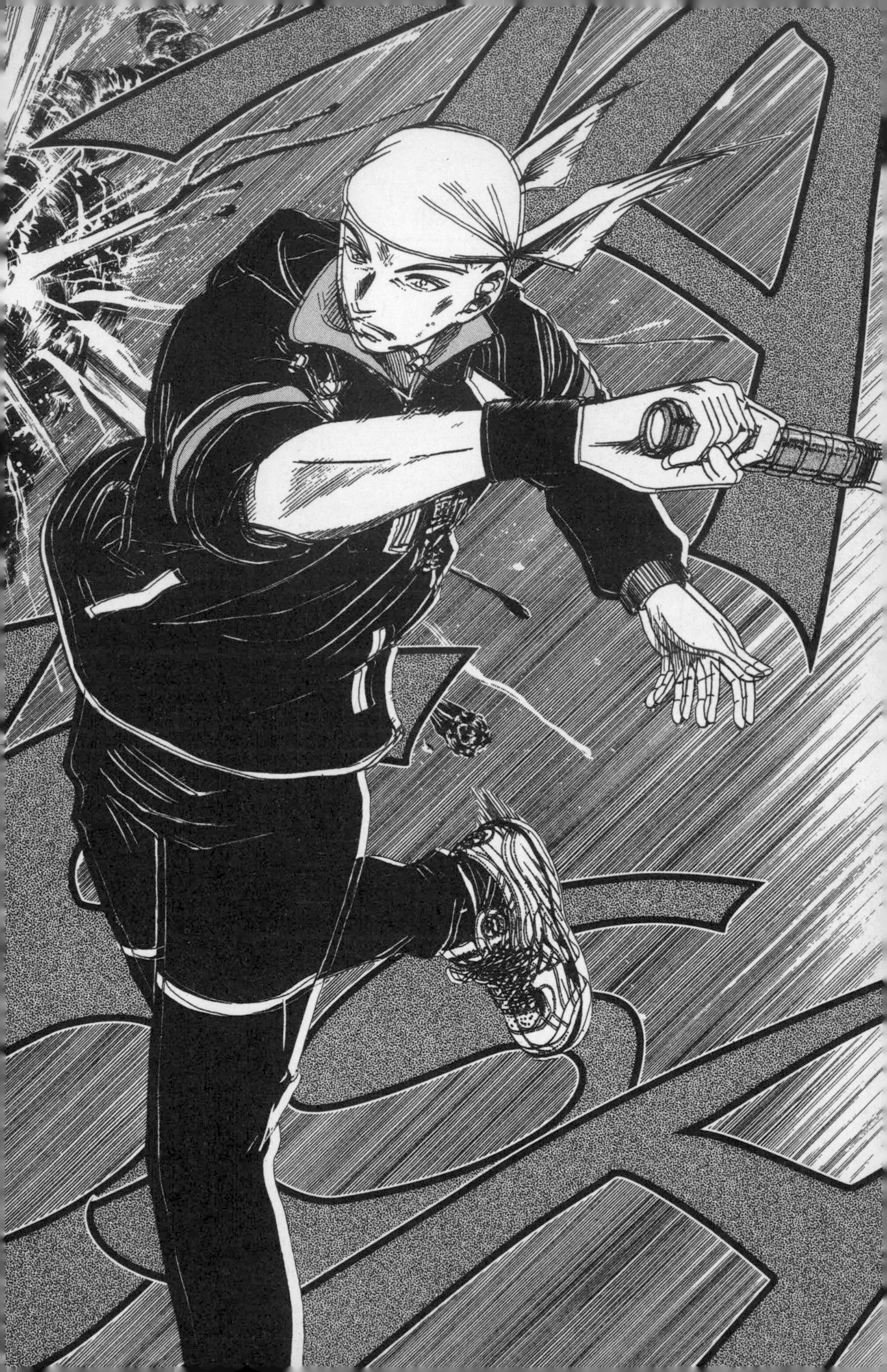

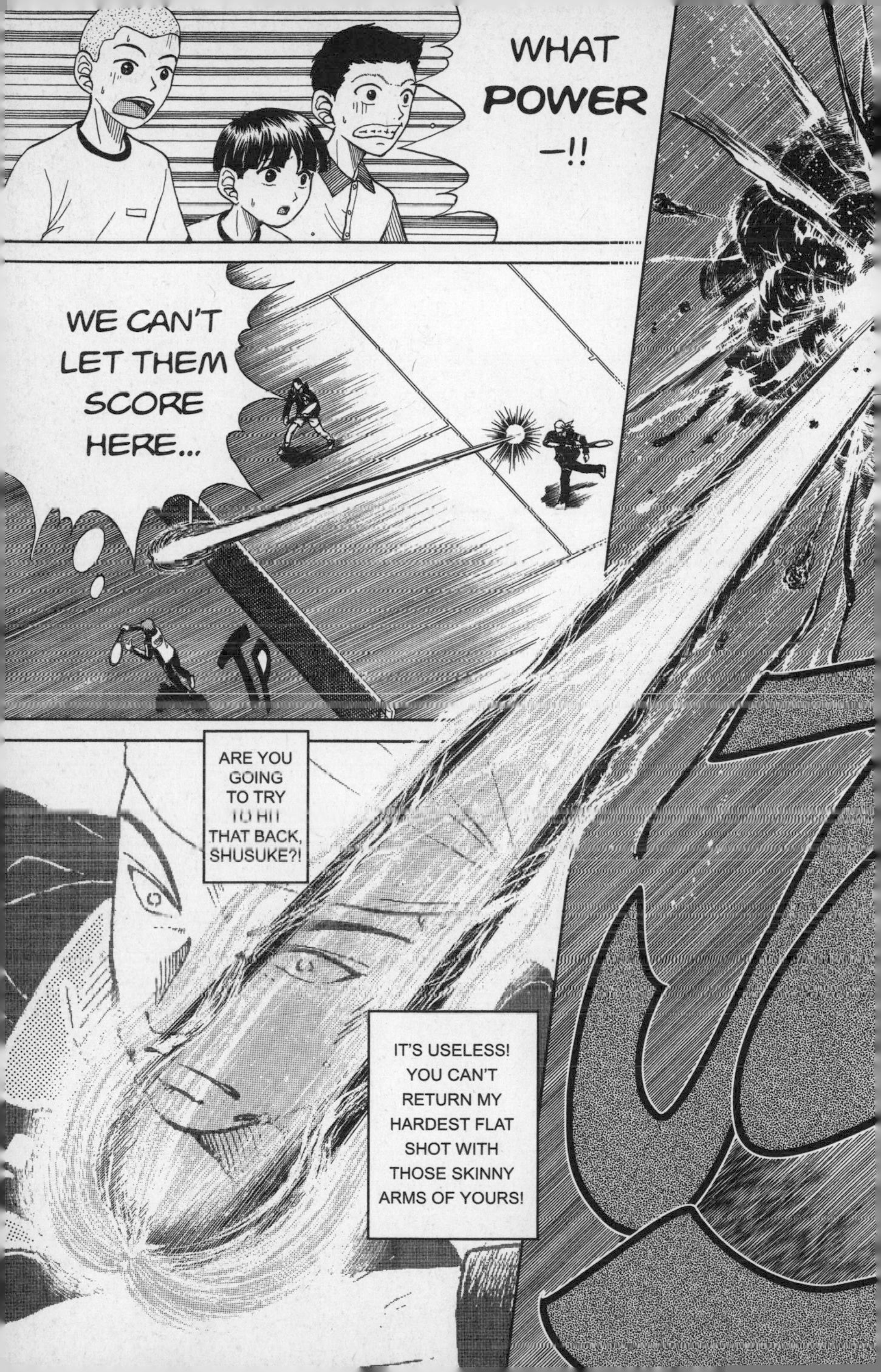
WHAT POWER—!!
WE CAN'T LET THEM SCORE HERE...
ARE YOU GOING TO TRY TO HIT THAT BACK, SHUSUKE?!
IT'S USELESS! YOU CAN'T RETURN MY HARDEST FLAT SHOT WITH THOSE SKINNY ARMS OF YOURS!

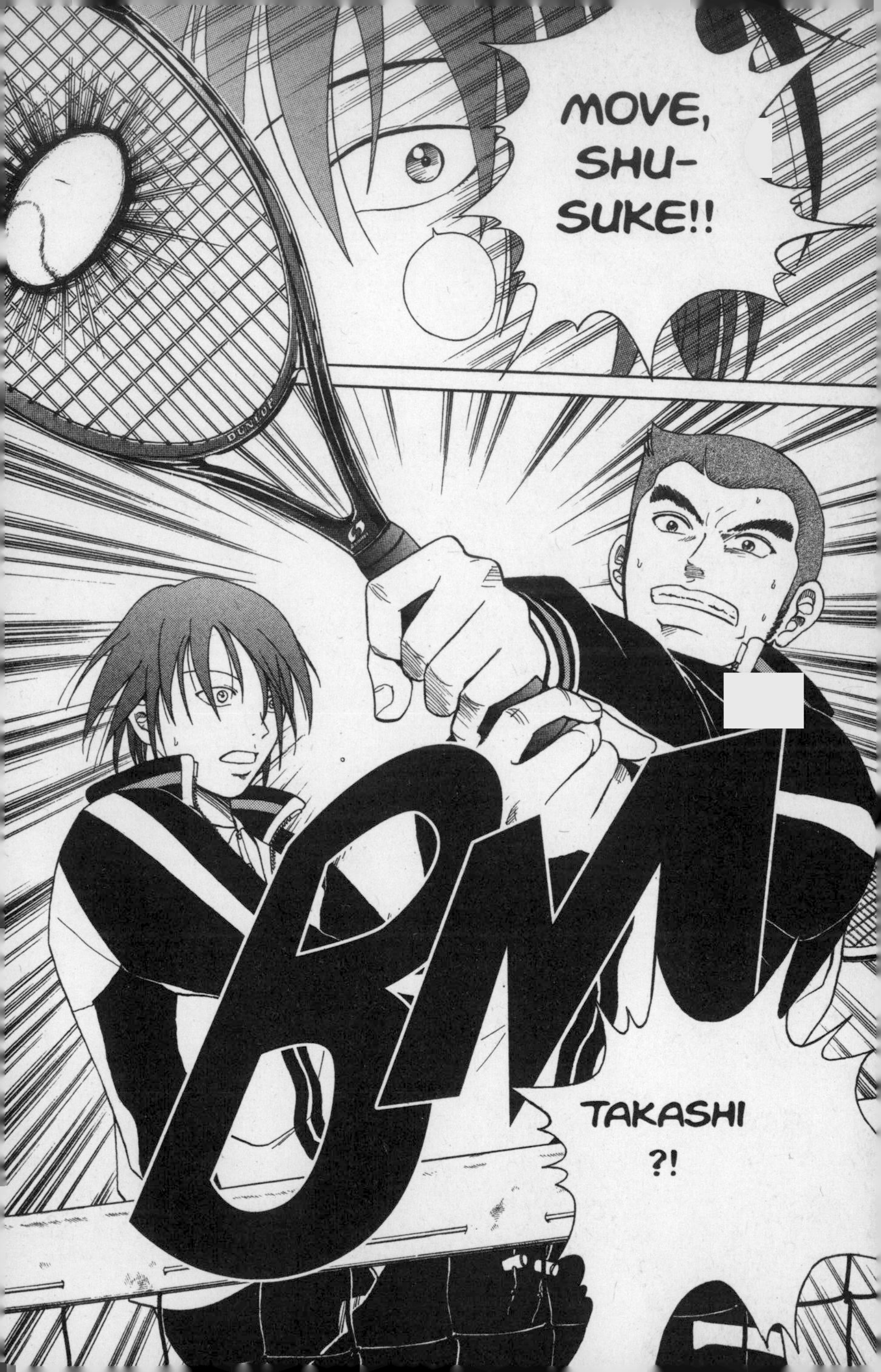
MOVE, SHU-SUKE!!
BAM
TAKASHI ?!

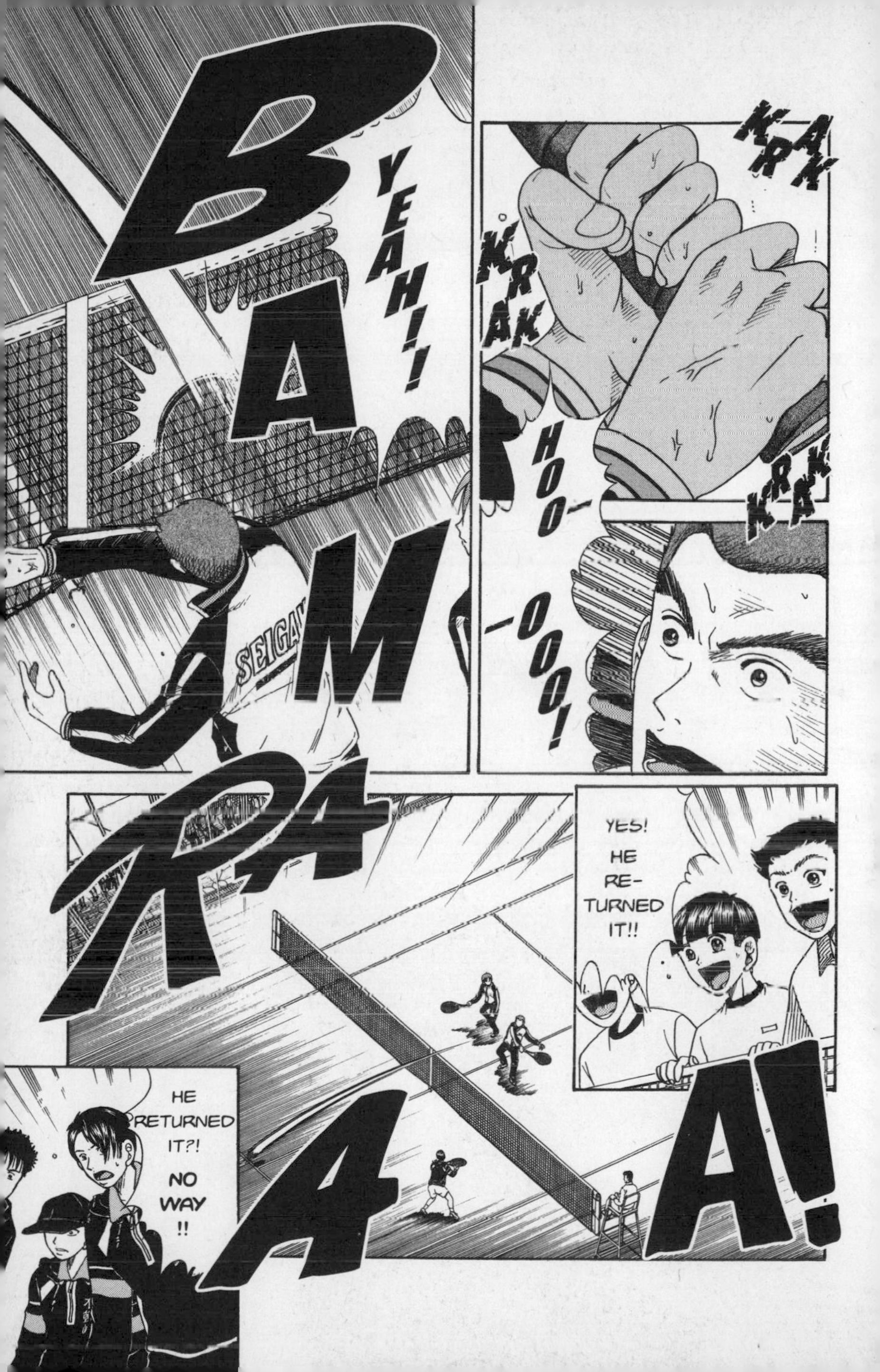
KRAK
KRAK
KRAK
HOO--OOOO!
YEAH!!
BAMRAAA!
YES! HE RE-TURNED IT!!
HE RETURNED IT?!
NO WAY!!

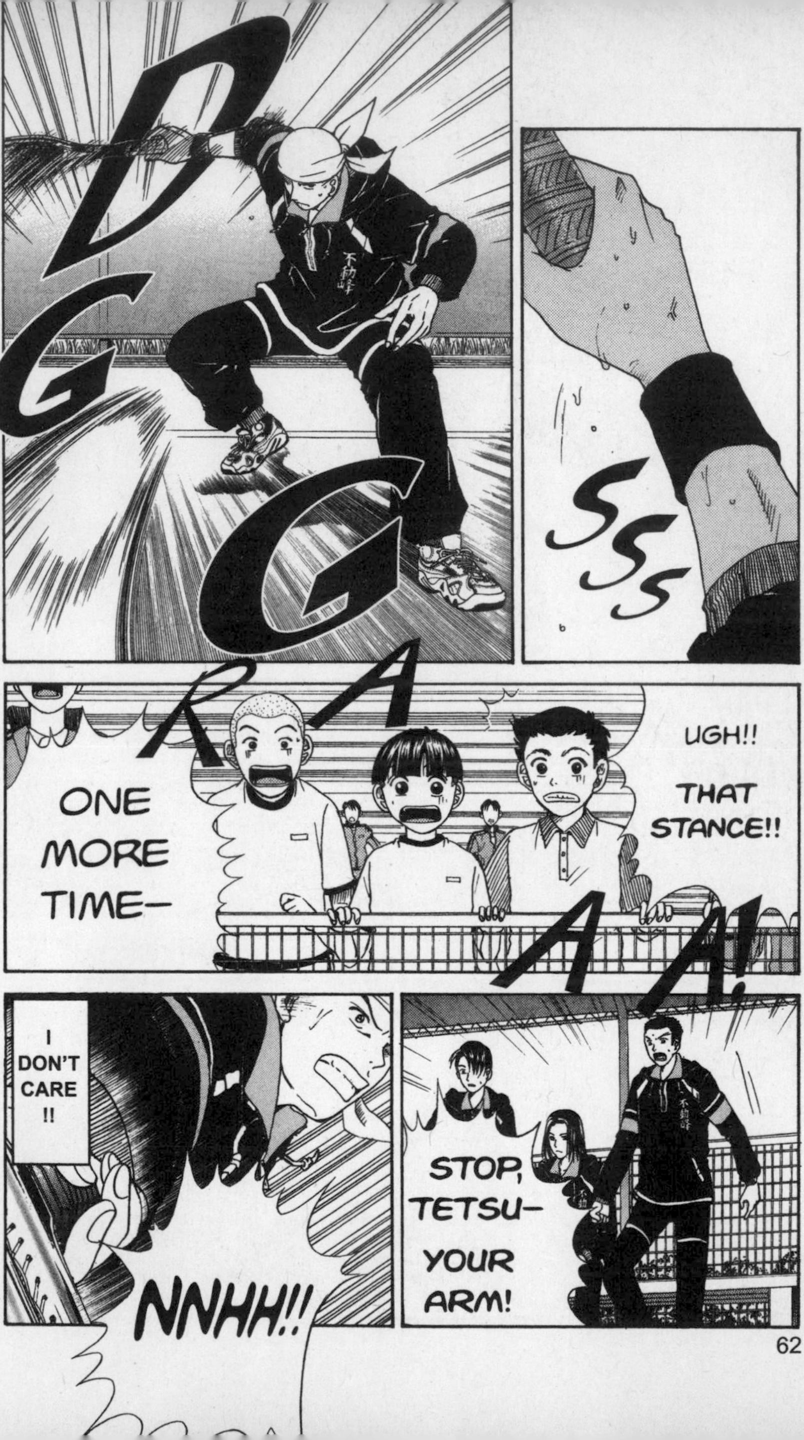
SSS
DGGRAAA!
UGH!!
THAT STANCE!!
ONE MORE TIME–
STOP, TETSU–
YOUR ARM!
I DON'T CARE !!
NNHH!!

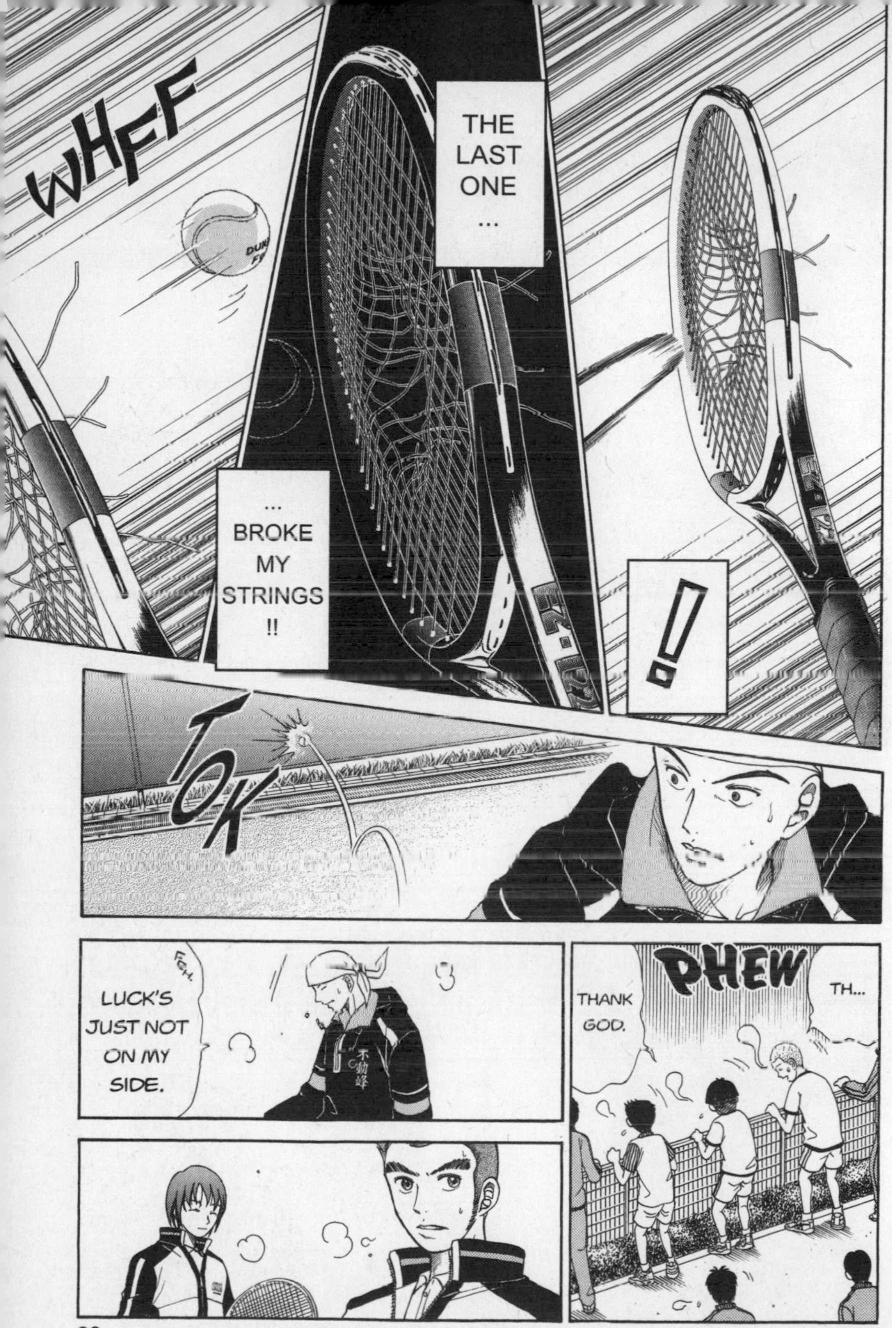
!
THE LAST ONE ...
... BROKE MY STRINGS !!
WHFF
TOK
TH...
PHEW
THANK GOD.
FCH.
LUCK'S JUST NOT ON MY SIDE.

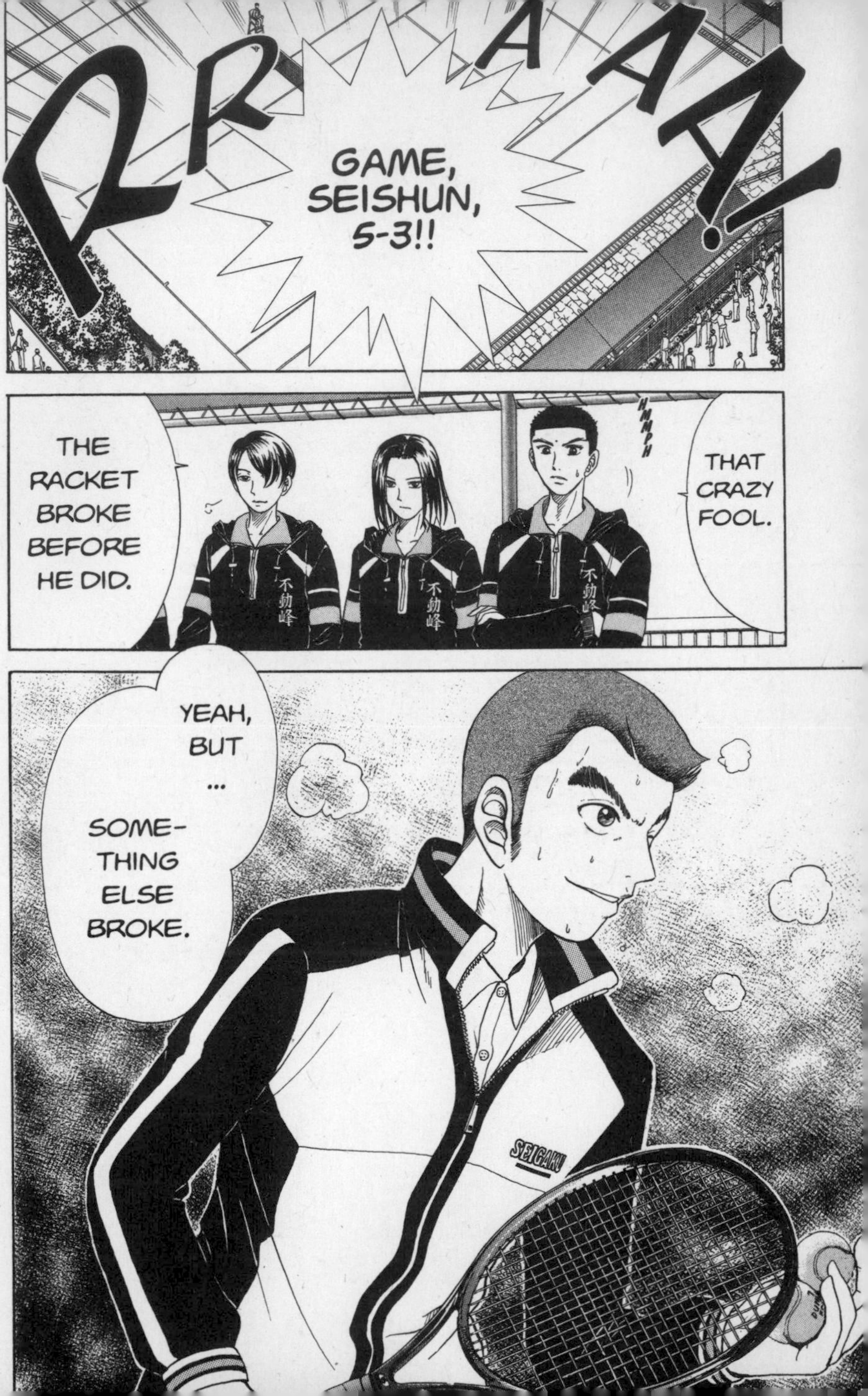
RRAAA!
GAME, SEISHUN, 5-3!!
THAT CRAZY FOOL.
HMMPH
THE RACKET BROKE BEFORE HE DID.
YEAH, BUT ... SOME-THING ELSE BROKE.
SEIGAKU

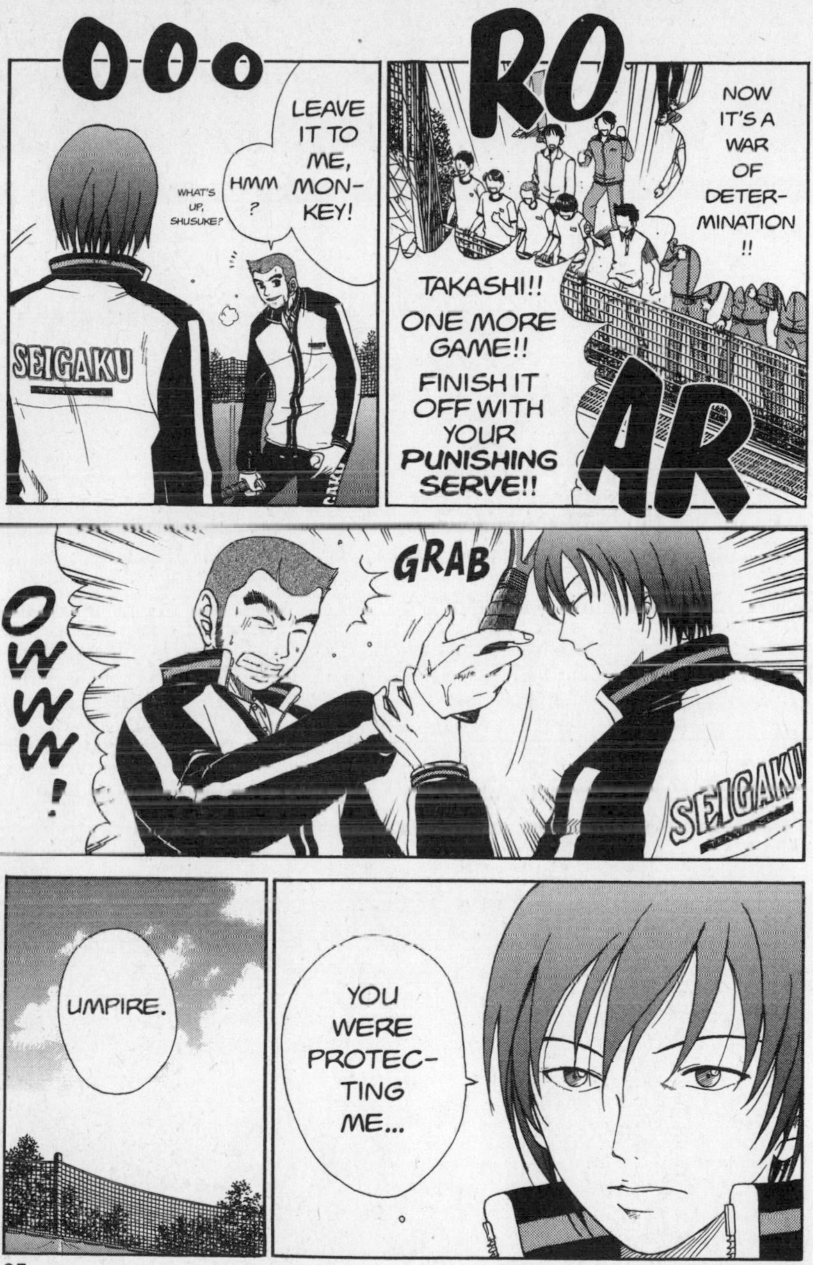
OOO
RO
AR
NOW IT'S A WAR OF DETERMINATION!!
TAKASHI!! ONE MORE GAME!! FINISH IT OFF WITH YOUR PUNISHING SERVE!!
LEAVE IT TO ME, MONKEY!
HMM?
WHAT'S UP, SHUSUKE?
GRAB
OWWW!
YOU WERE PROTECTING ME...
UMPIRE.

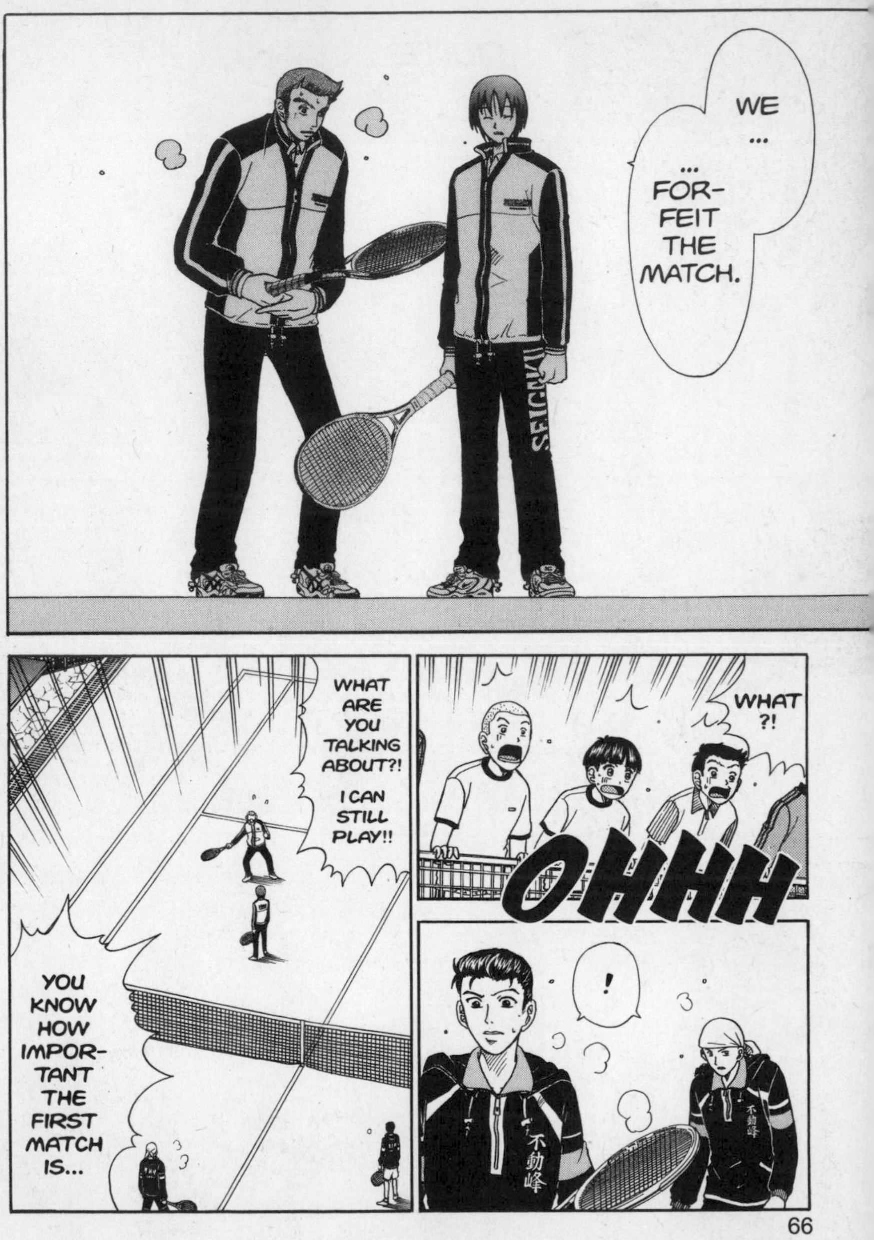
WE ...
... FORFEIT THE MATCH.
WHAT ?!
OHHH
!
WHAT ARE YOU TALKING ABOUT?!
I CAN STILL PLAY!!
YOU KNOW HOW IMPORTANT THE FIRST MATCH IS...

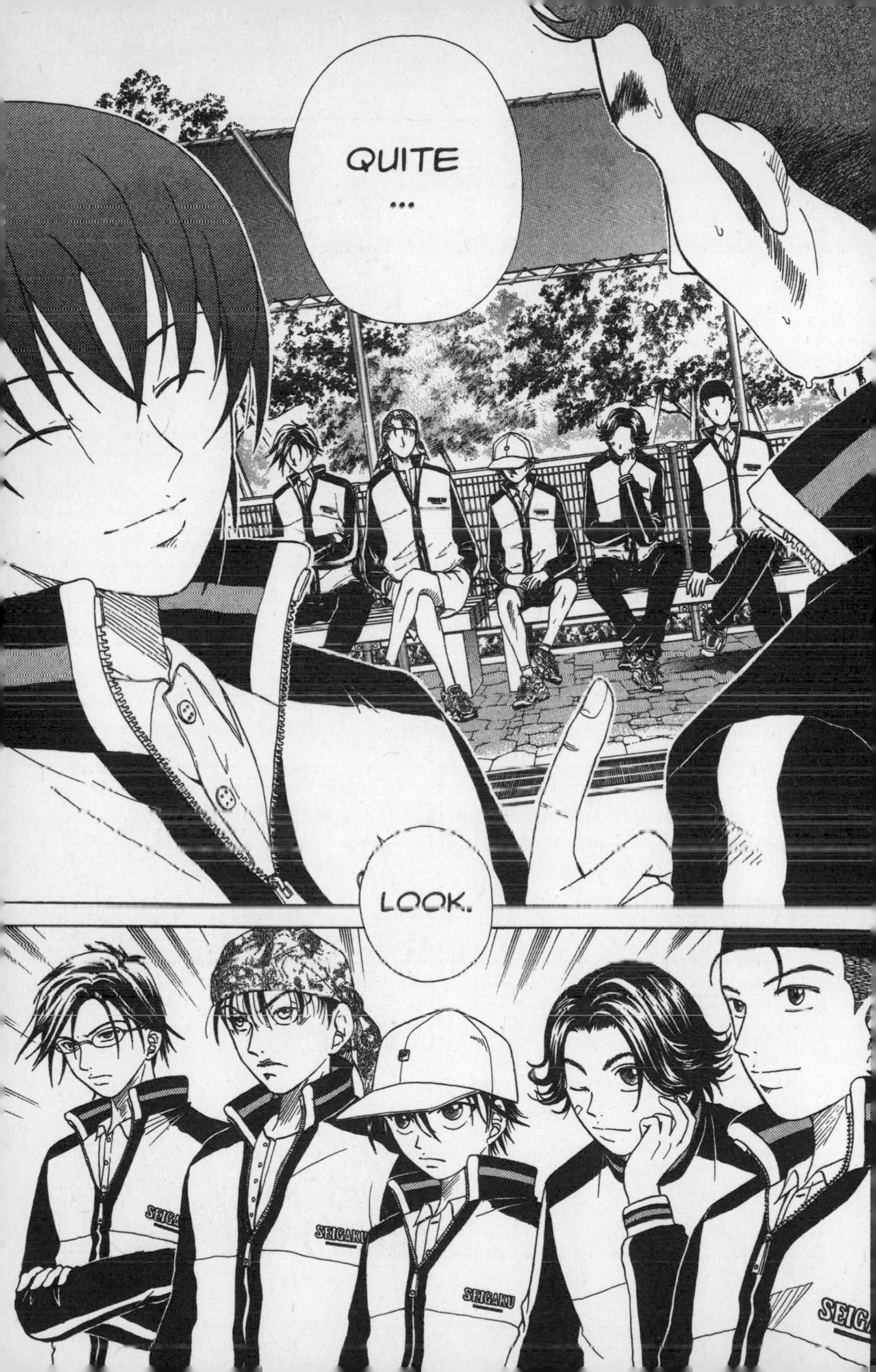
QUITE ...
LOOK.
SEIGAKU
SEIGAKU
SEIGAKU

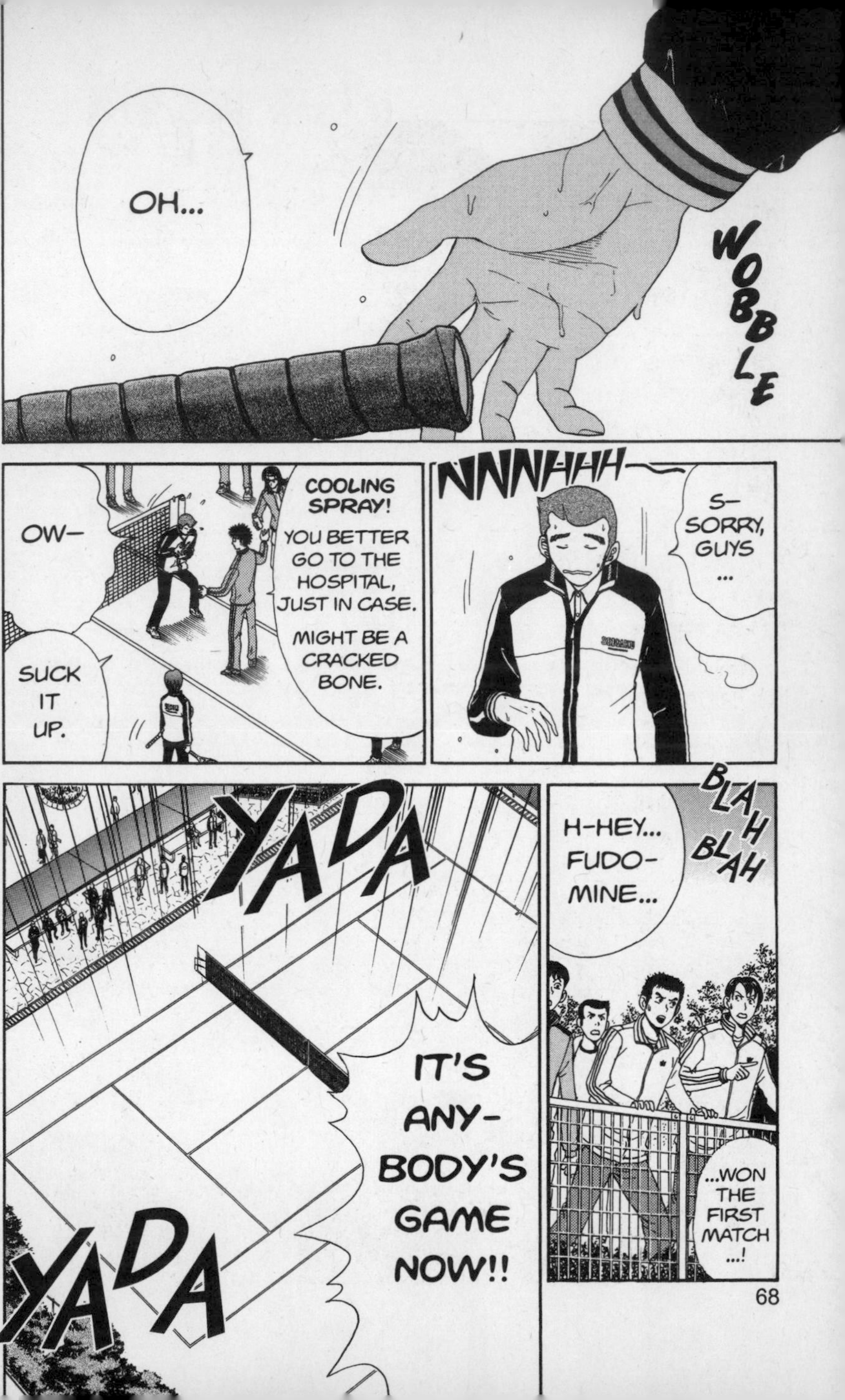
WOBBLE
OH...
NNNHHH~
S-SORRY, GUYS...
COOLING SPRAY!
YOU BETTER GO TO THE HOSPITAL, JUST IN CASE.
MIGHT BE A CRACKED BONE.
OW—
SUCK IT UP.
BLAH BLAH
H-HEY... FUDO-MINE...
...WON THE FIRST MATCH...!
YADA
IT'S ANY-BODY'S GAME NOW!!
YADA

READ THIS WAY

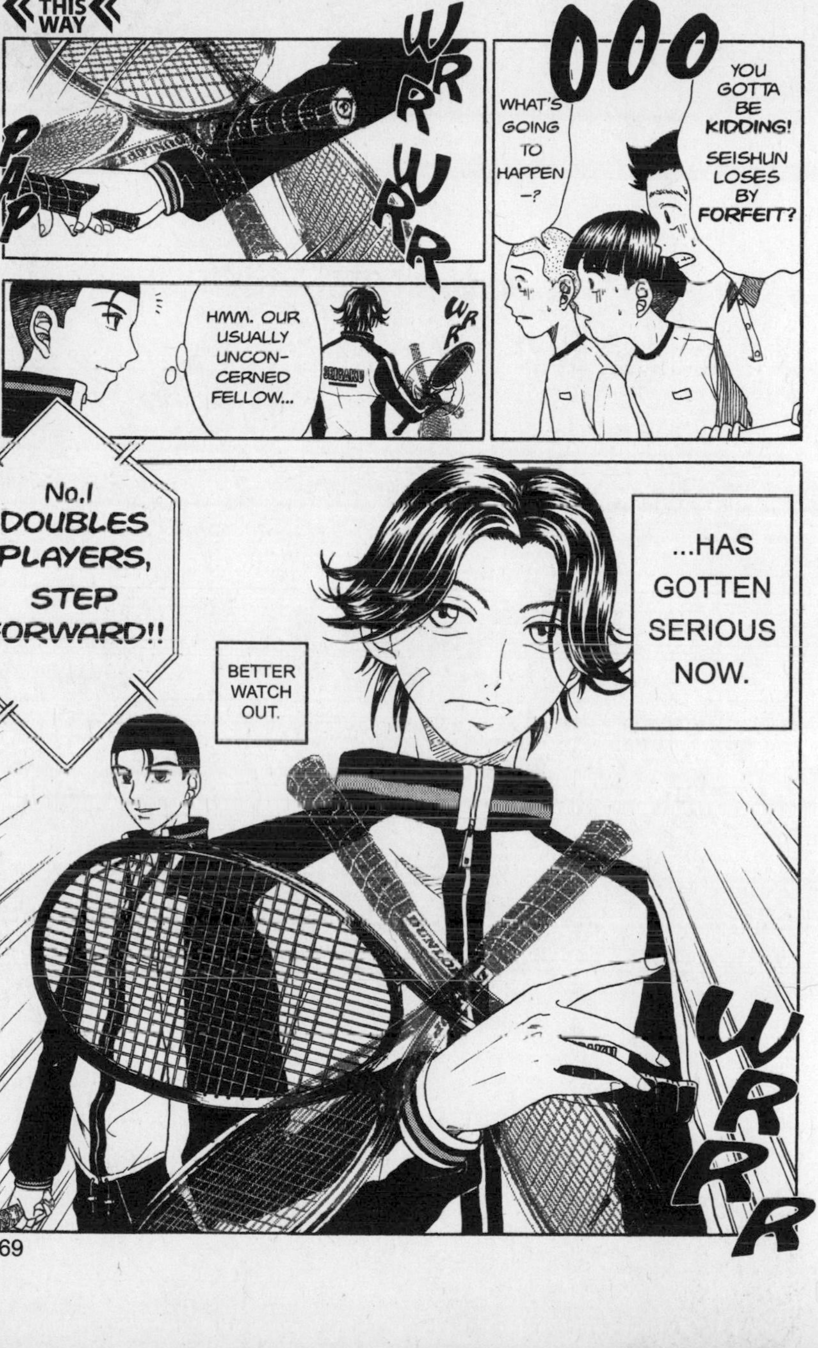
OOO
YOU GOTTA BE KIDDING! SEISHUN LOSES BY FORFEIT?
WHAT'S GOING TO HAPPEN—?
WRR WRR WRR
PAP
HMM. OUR USUALLY UNCONCERNED FELLOW...
WRR
...HAS GOTTEN SERIOUS NOW.
BETTER WATCH OUT.
No.1 DOUBLES PLAYERS, STEP FORWARD!!
WRRR

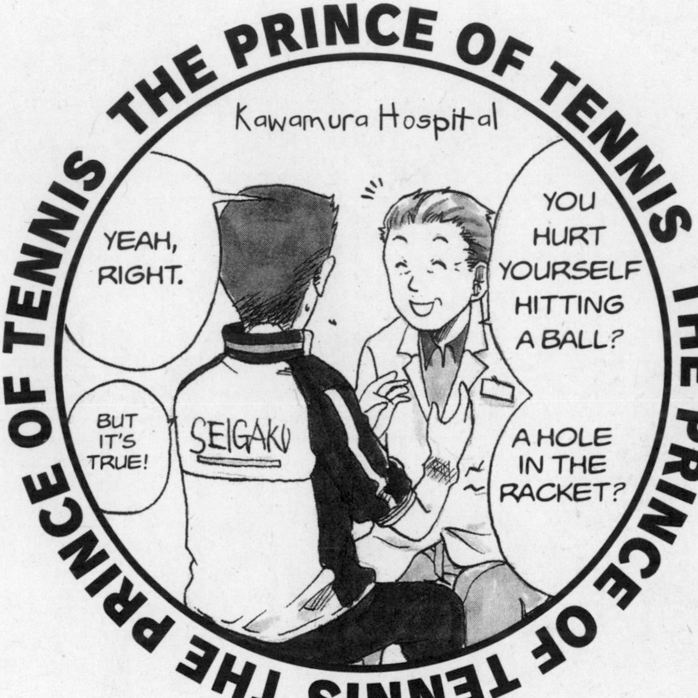
THE PRINCE OF TENNIS THE PRINCE OF TENNIS THE PRINCE OF TENNIS
Kawamura Hospital
YOU HURT YOURSELF HITTING A BALL?
YEAH, RIGHT.
A HOLE IN THE RACKET?
BUT IT'S TRUE!
SEIGAKU

Genius 29: EVERYONE'S OPPONENT

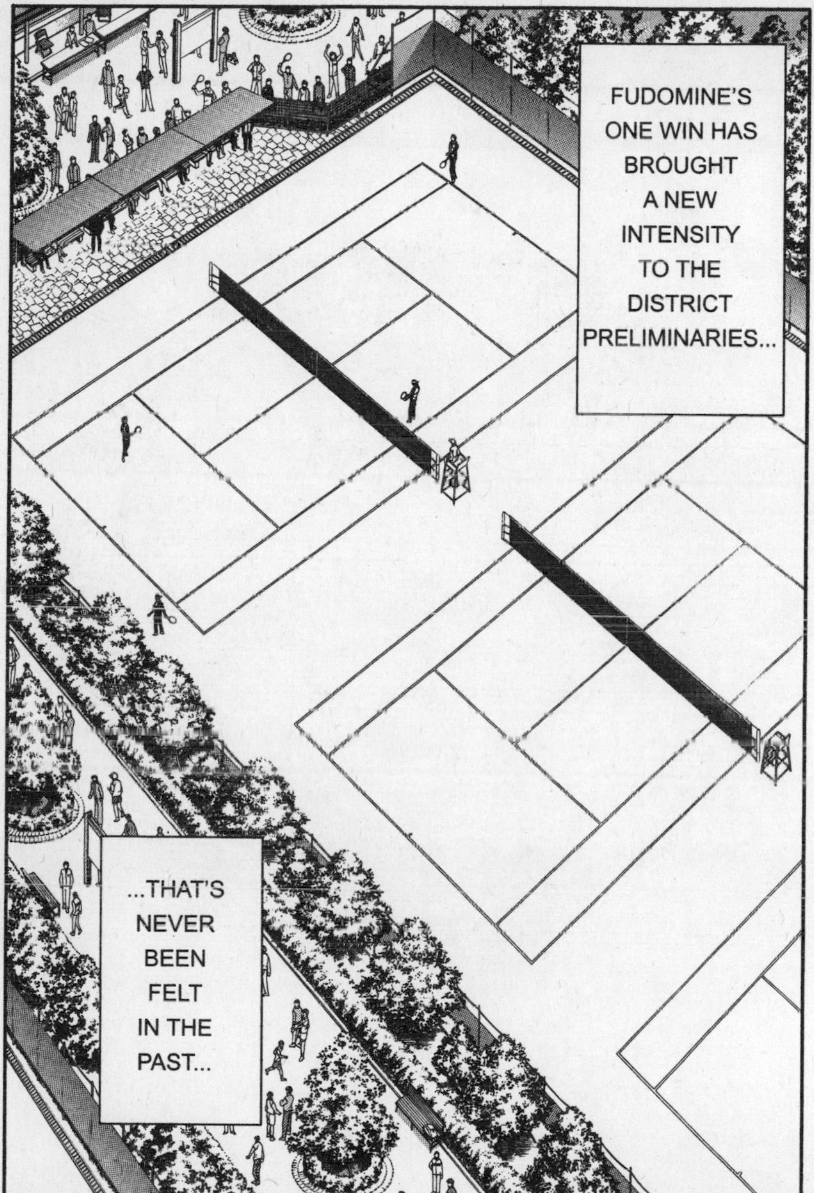
FUDOMINE'S ONE WIN HAS BROUGHT A NEW INTENSITY TO THE DISTRICT PRELIMINARIES...
...THAT'S NEVER BEEN FELT IN THE PAST...

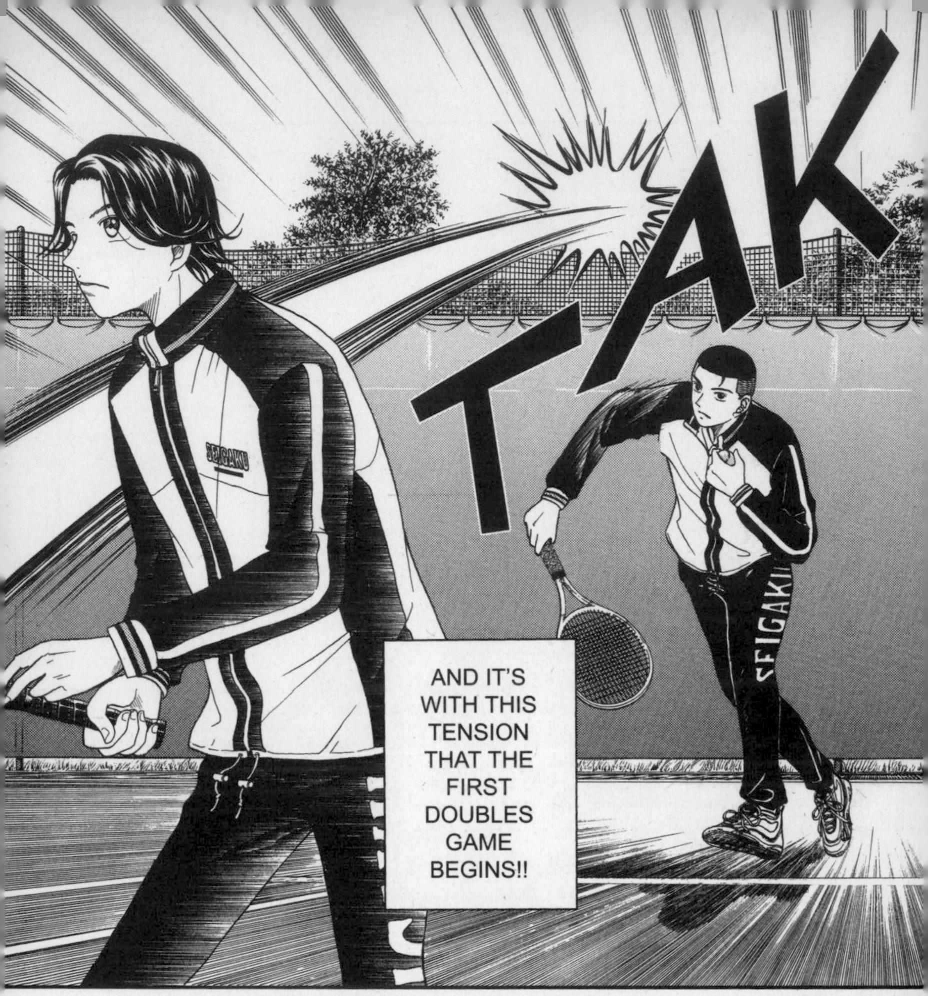
TAK
AND IT'S WITH THIS TENSION THAT THE FIRST DOUBLES GAME BEGINS!!

Genius 29:

EVERYONE'S OPPONENT

READ THIS WAY

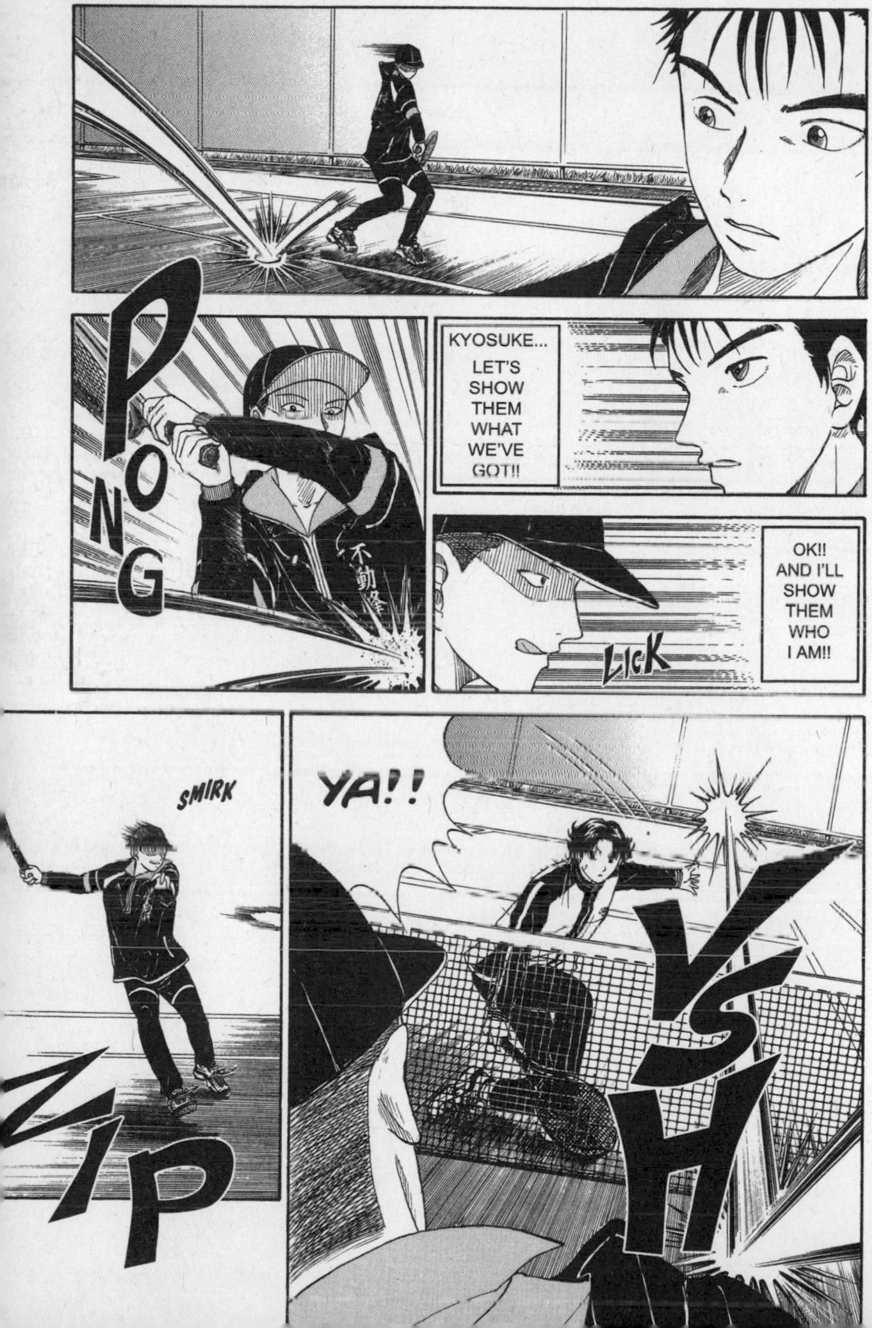

KYOSUKE... LET'S SHOW THEM WHAT WE'VE GOT!!
OK!! AND I'LL SHOW THEM WHO I AM!!
LICK
PONG
不動峰
YA!!
YSH!!
SMIRK
ZIP

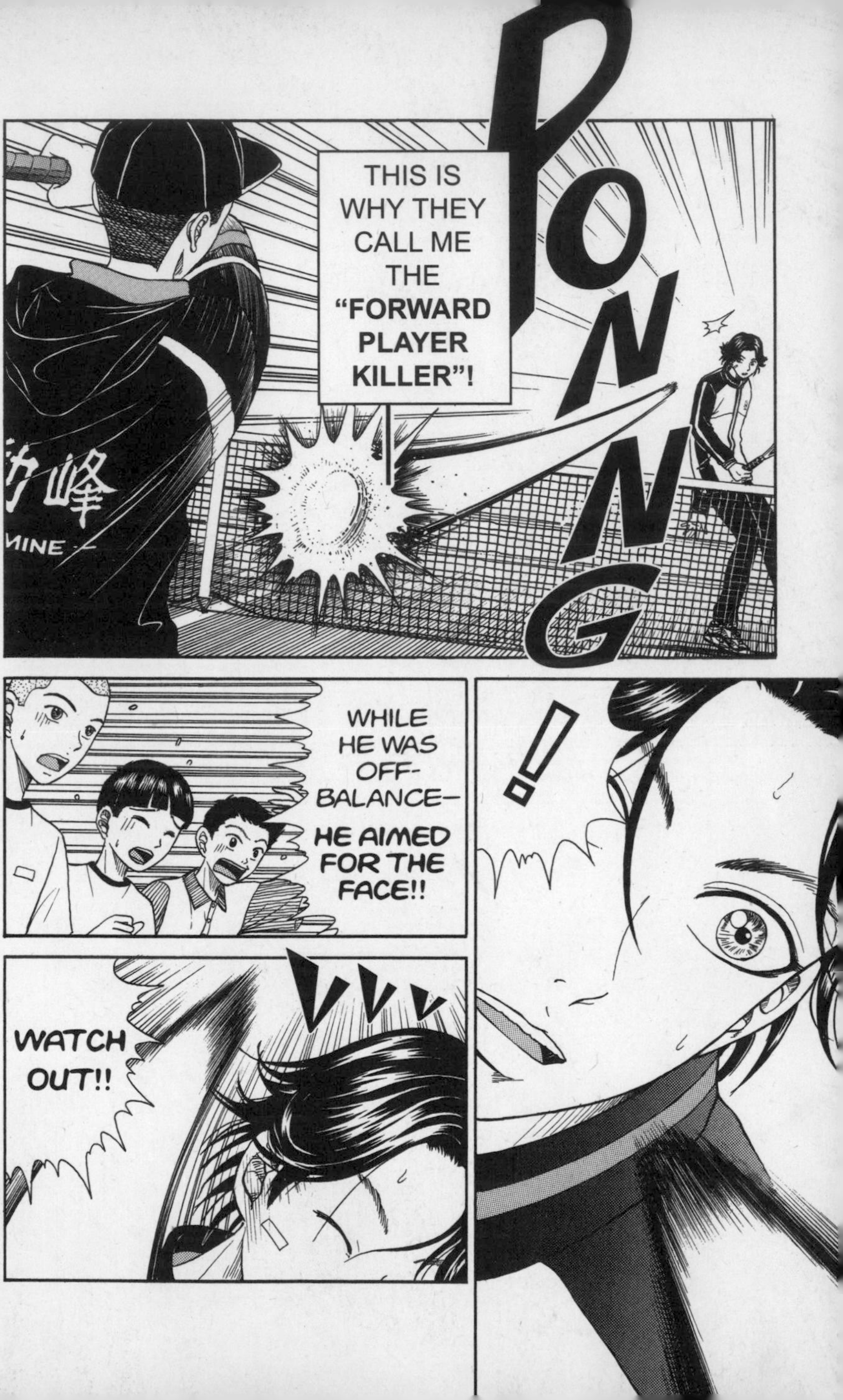
PONNG
THIS IS WHY THEY CALL ME THE "FORWARD PLAYER KILLER"!
!
WHILE HE WAS OFF-BALANCE—
HE AIMED FOR THE FACE!!
WATCH OUT!!

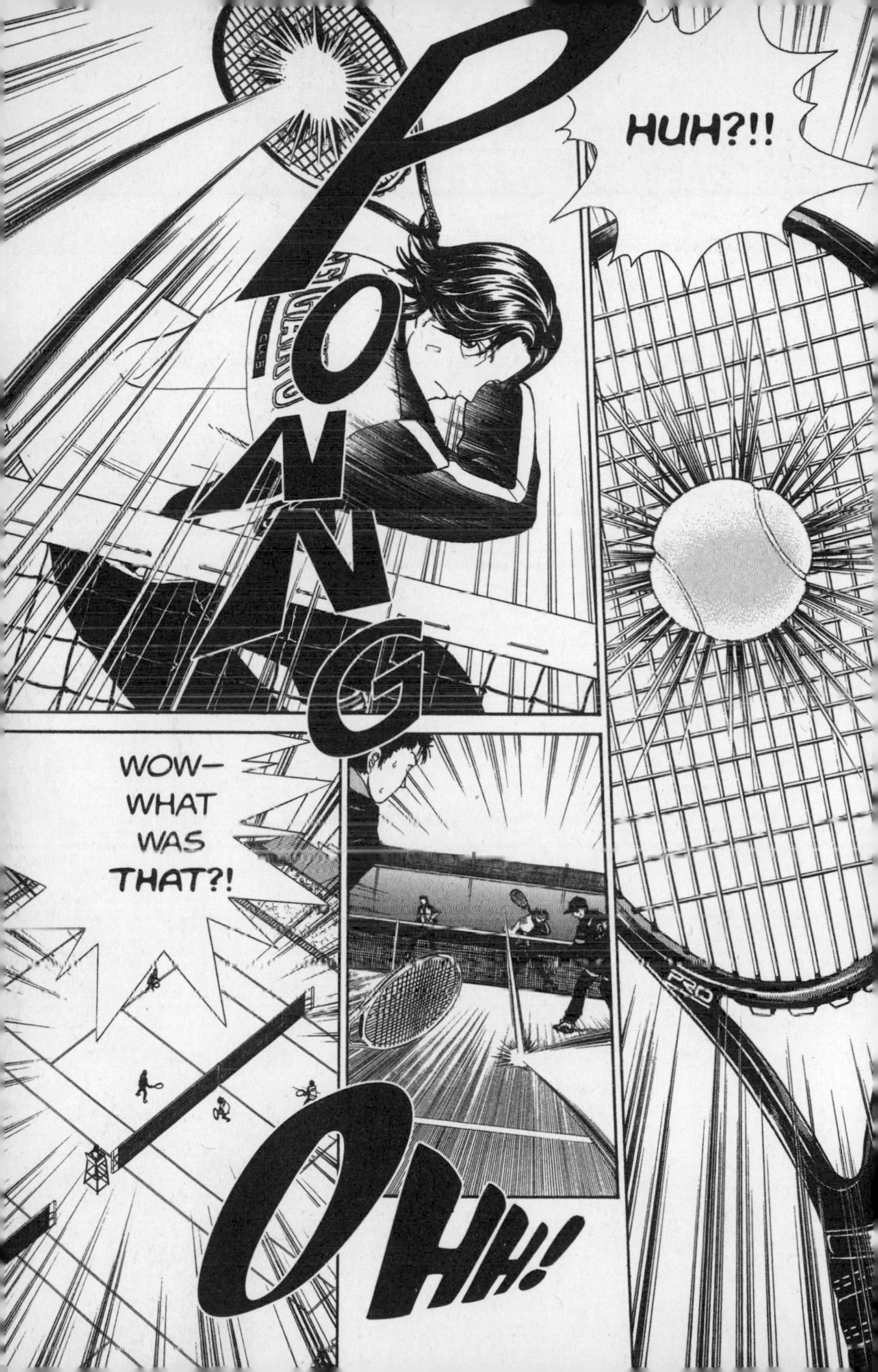
HUH?!!
PONNG
WOW—WHAT WAS THAT?!
OHH!

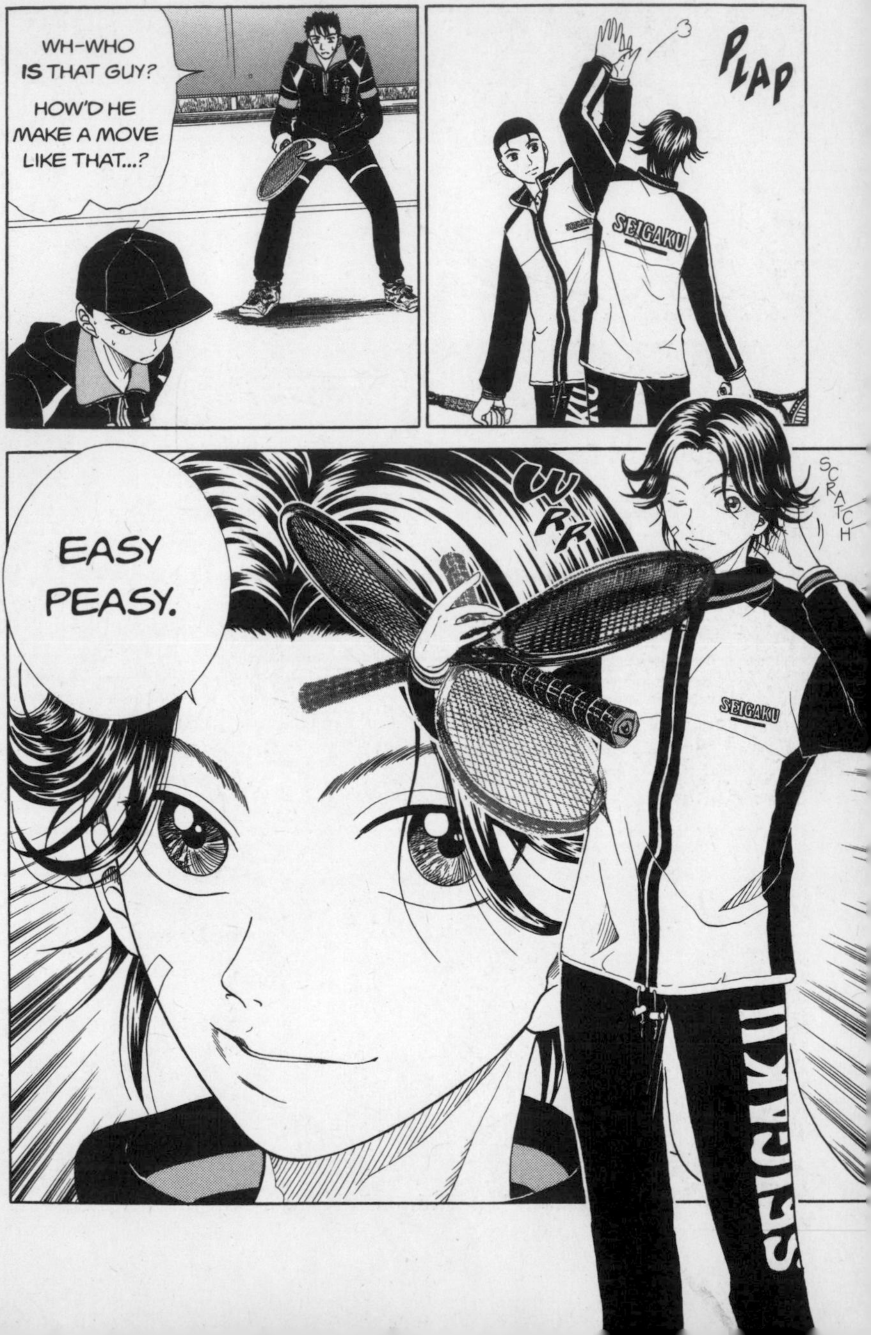
PLAP
WH-WHO IS THAT GUY?
HOW'D HE MAKE A MOVE LIKE THAT...?
SCRATCH
WRR
EASY PEASY.

READ THIS WAY

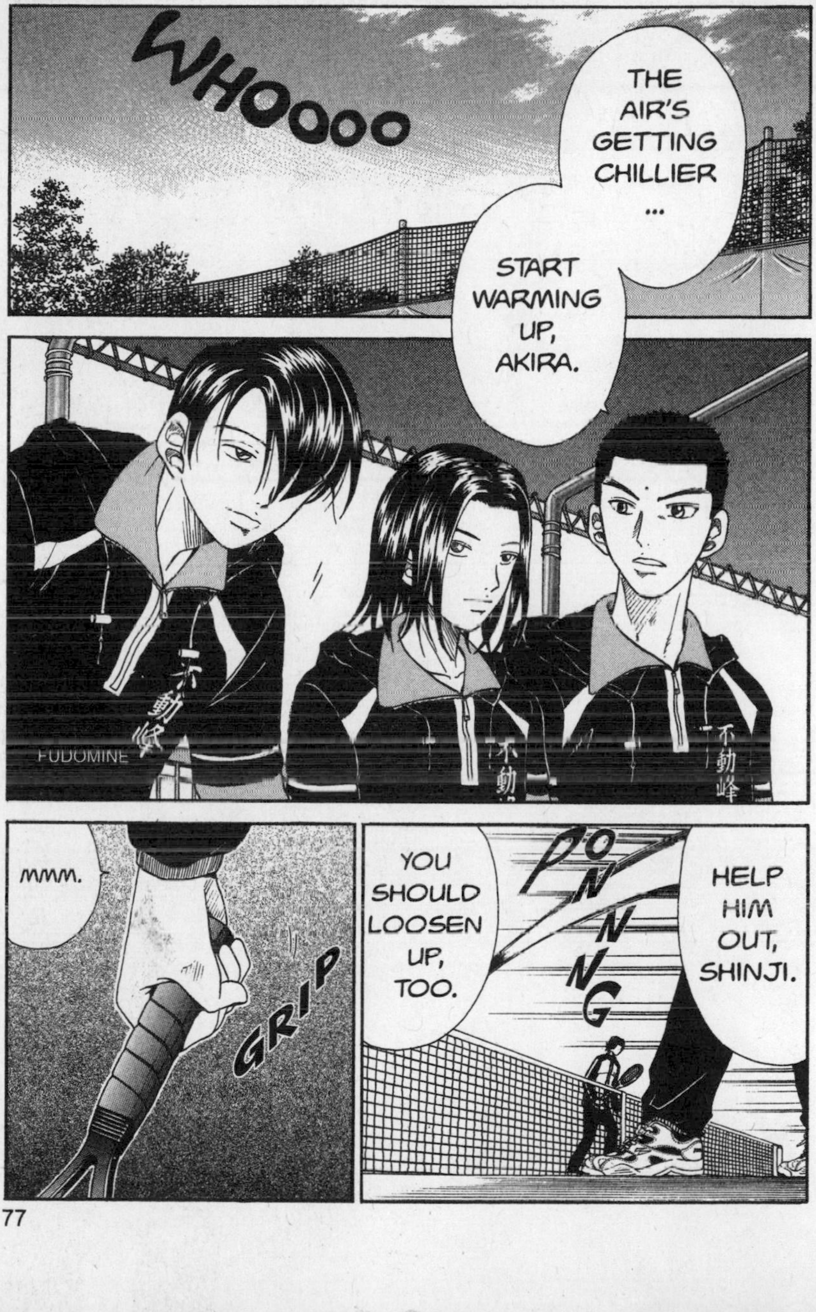
WHOOOO
THE AIR'S GETTING CHILLIER ...
START WARMING UP, AKIRA.
不動峰
FUDOMINE
HELP HIM OUT, SHINJI.
PONNNG
YOU SHOULD LOOSEN UP, TOO.
MMM.
GRIP

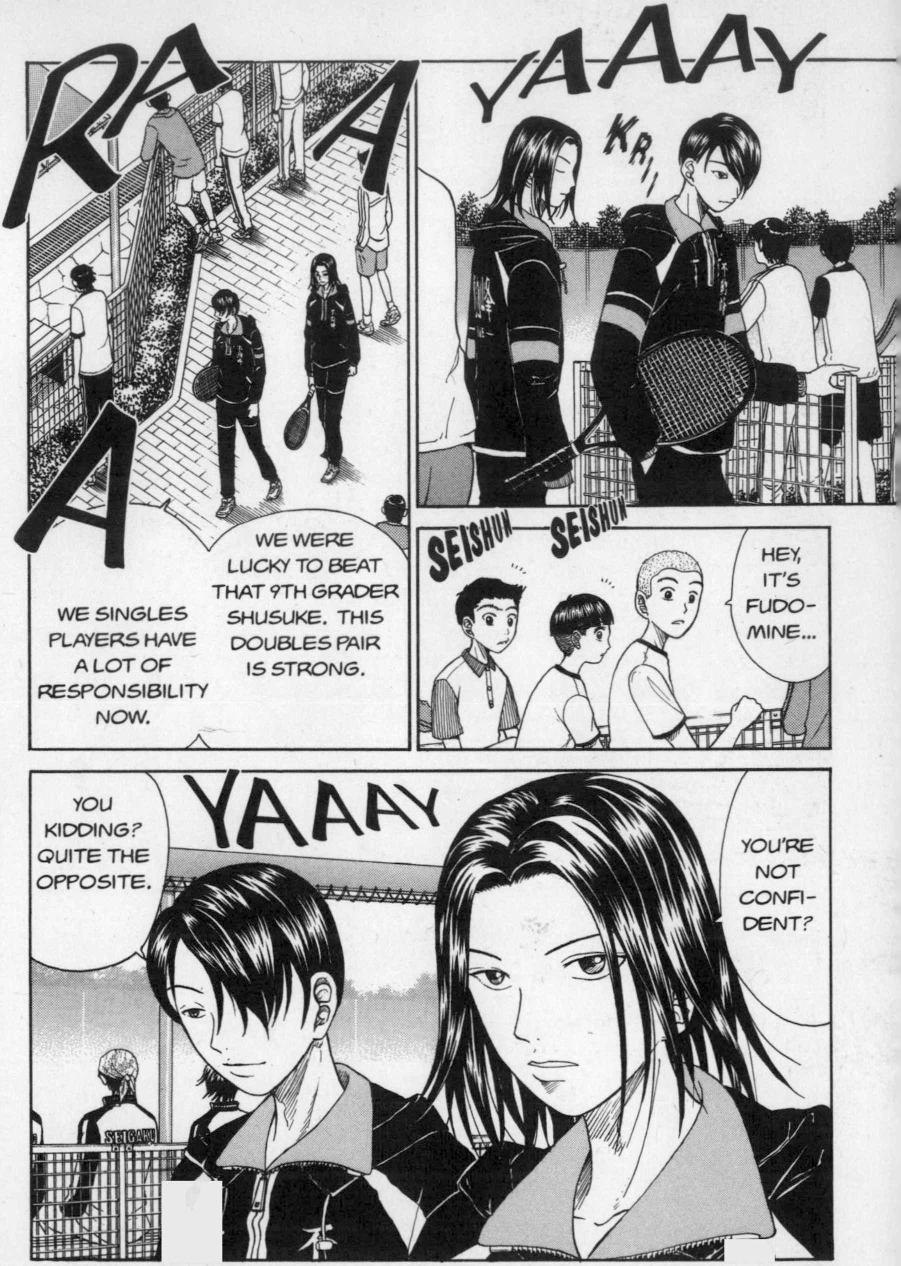
YAAAAY
KRI
SEISHUN SEISHUN
HEY, IT'S FUDO-MINE...
RAAAA
WE WERE LUCKY TO BEAT THAT 9TH GRADER SHUSUKE. THIS DOUBLES PAIR IS STRONG.
WE SINGLES PLAYERS HAVE A LOT OF RESPONSIBILITY NOW.
YOU'RE NOT CONFI-DENT?
YAAAY
YOU KIDDING? QUITE THE OPPOSITE.
SEIGAKU

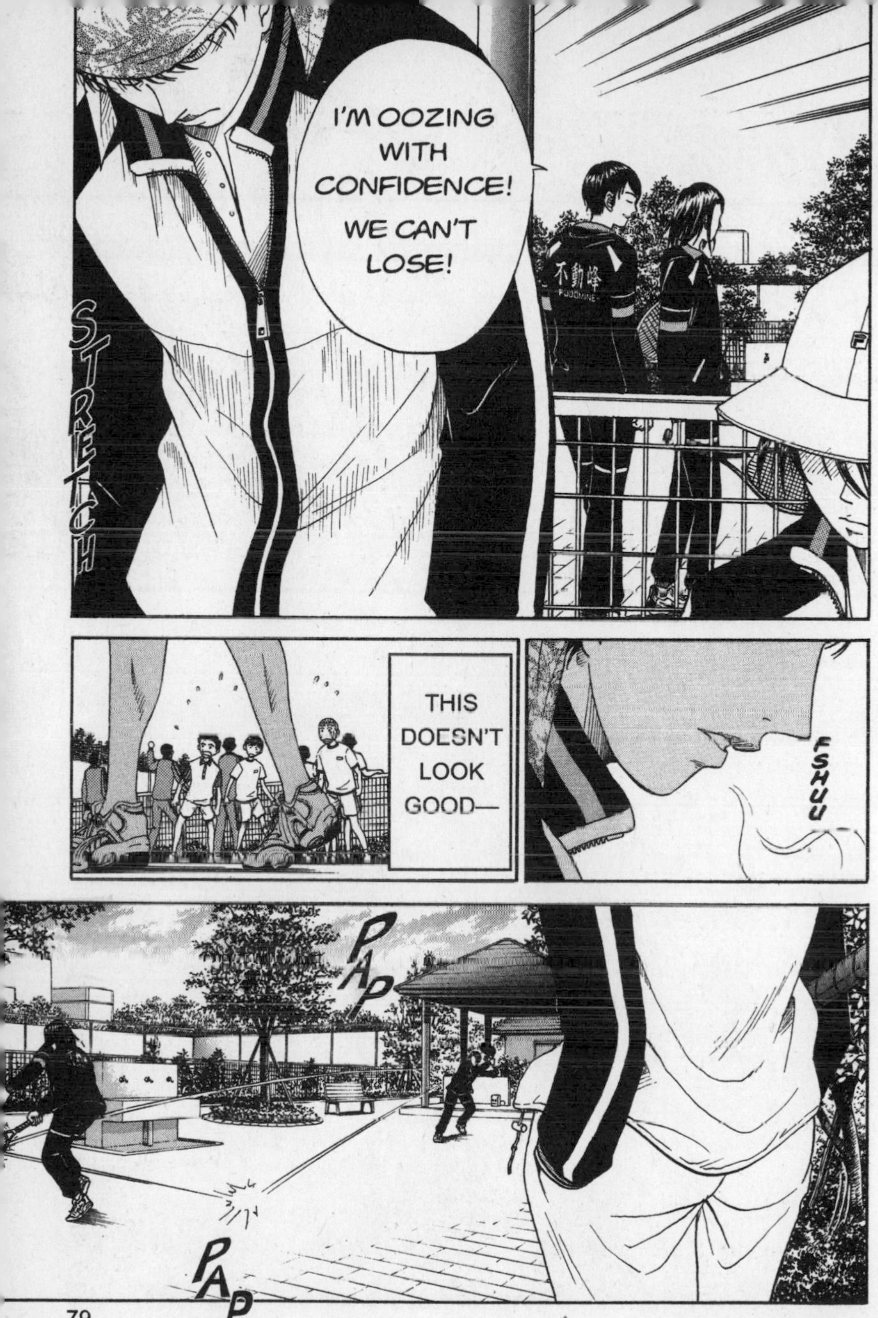

I'M OOZING WITH CONFIDENCE!
WE CAN'T LOSE!
不動峰
STRETCH
FSHUU
THIS DOESN'T LOOK GOOD—
PAP
PAP

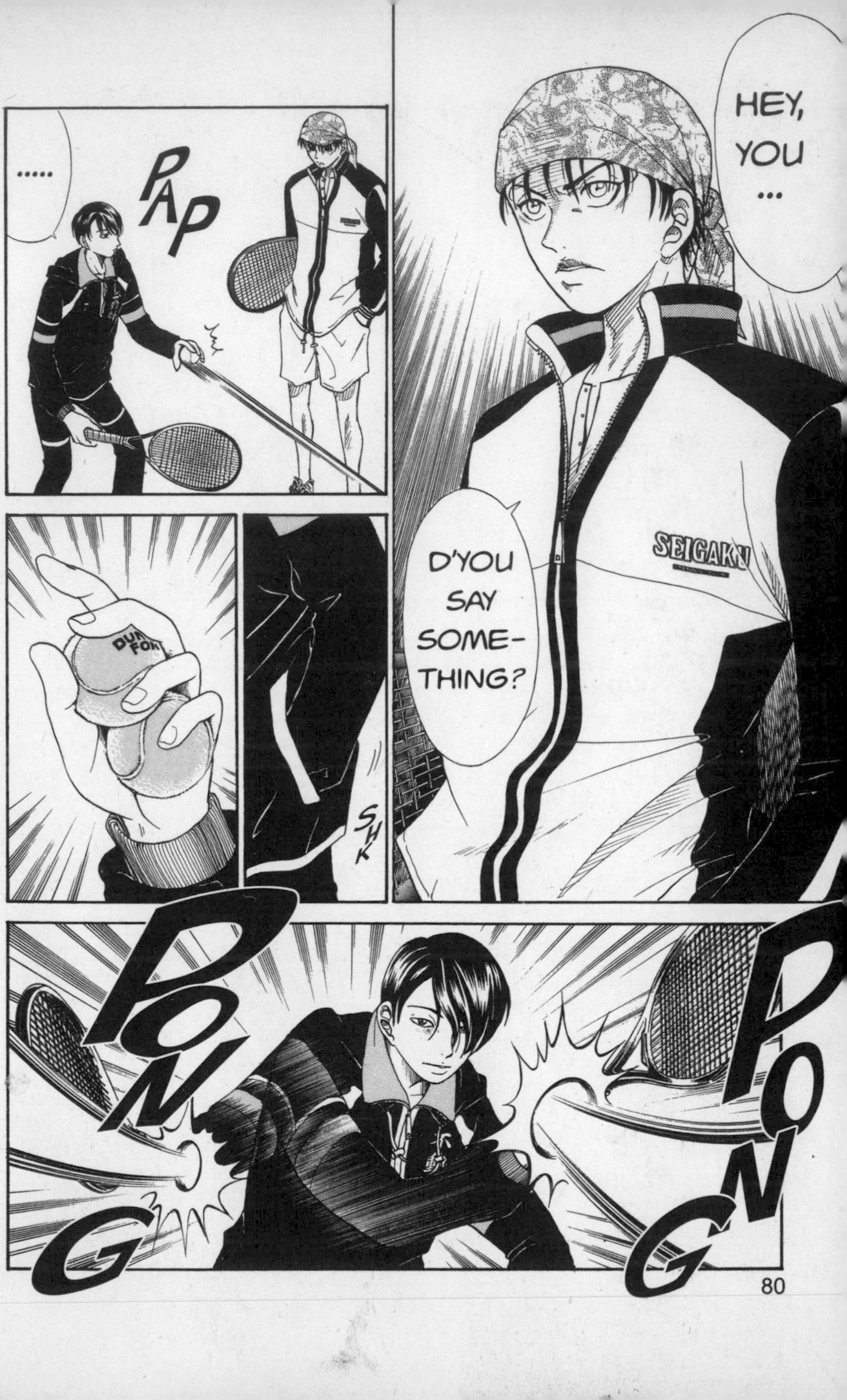
HEY, YOU ...
SEIGAKU
D'YOU SAY SOME- THING?
.....
PAP
SHK
PONG
PONG

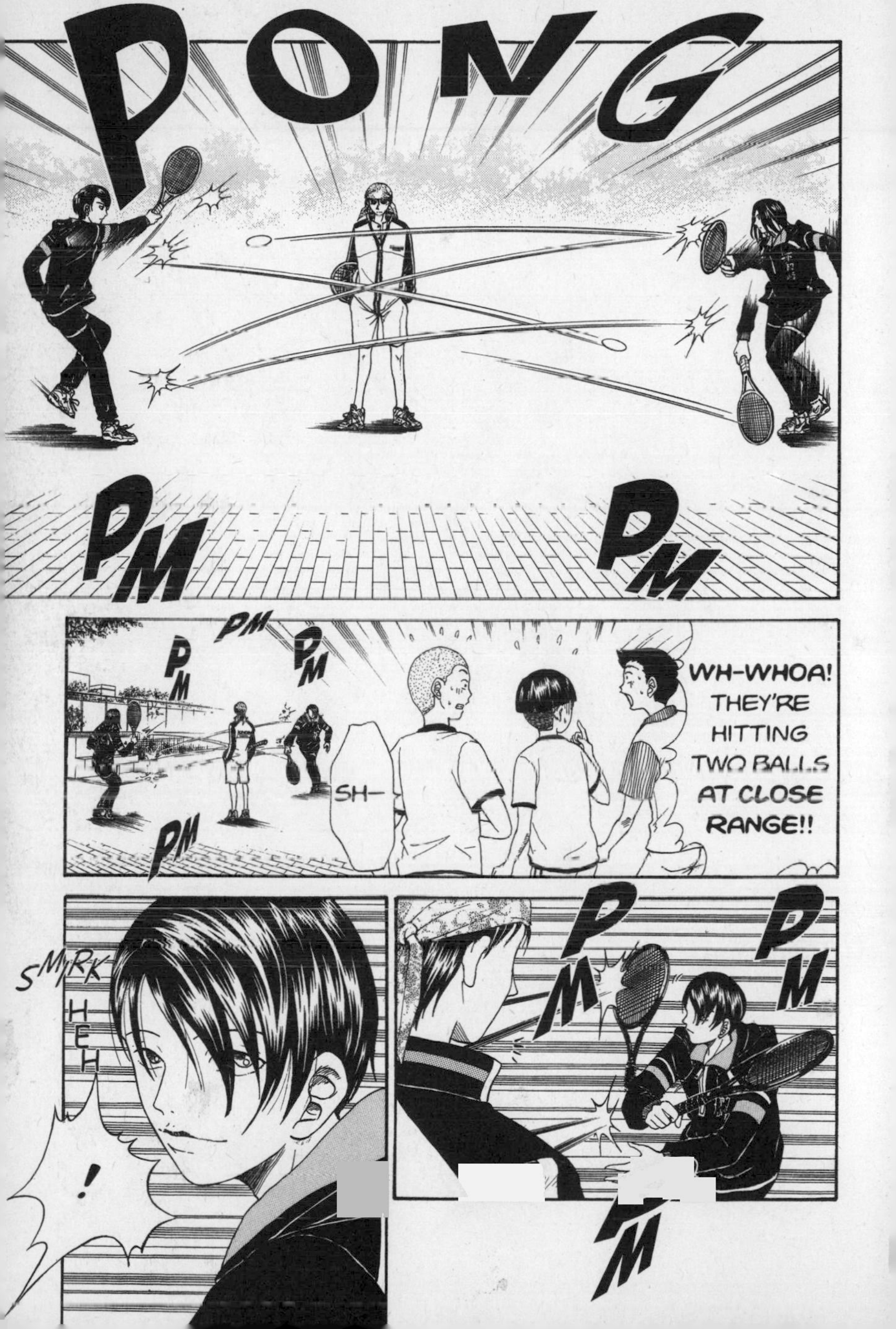
PONG
PM
PM
WH-WHOA! THEY'RE HITTING TWO BALLS AT CLOSE RANGE!!
SH-
PM
PM
PM
PM
PM
PM
PM
SMIRK
HEH
!

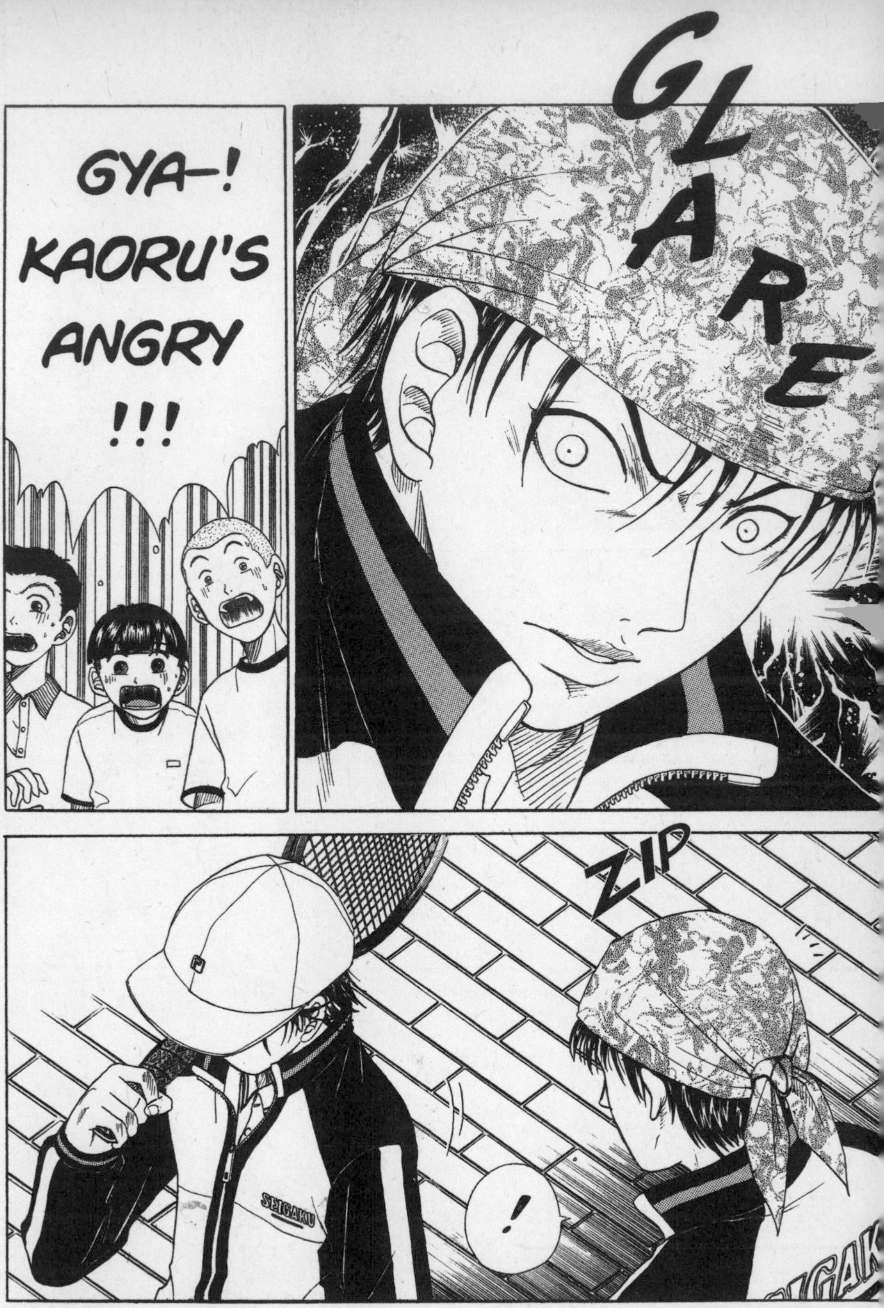
GLARE
GYA—! KAORU'S ANGRY !!!
ZIP
!
SEIGAKU

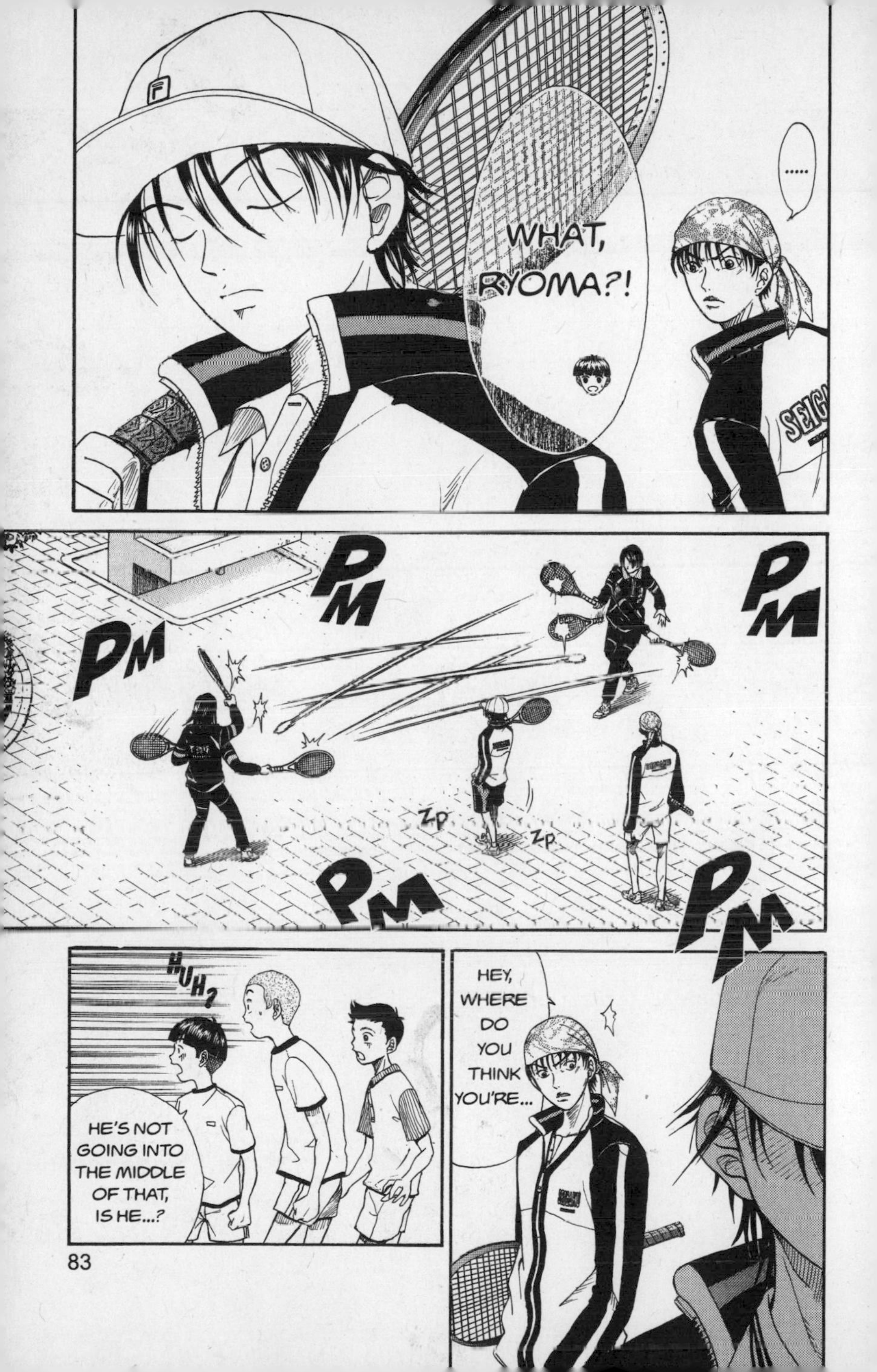
......
WHAT, RYOMA?!
PM
PM
PM
PM
PM
ZP
ZP
HEY, WHERE DO YOU THINK YOU'RE...
HUH?
HE'S NOT GOING INTO THE MIDDLE OF THAT, IS HE...?

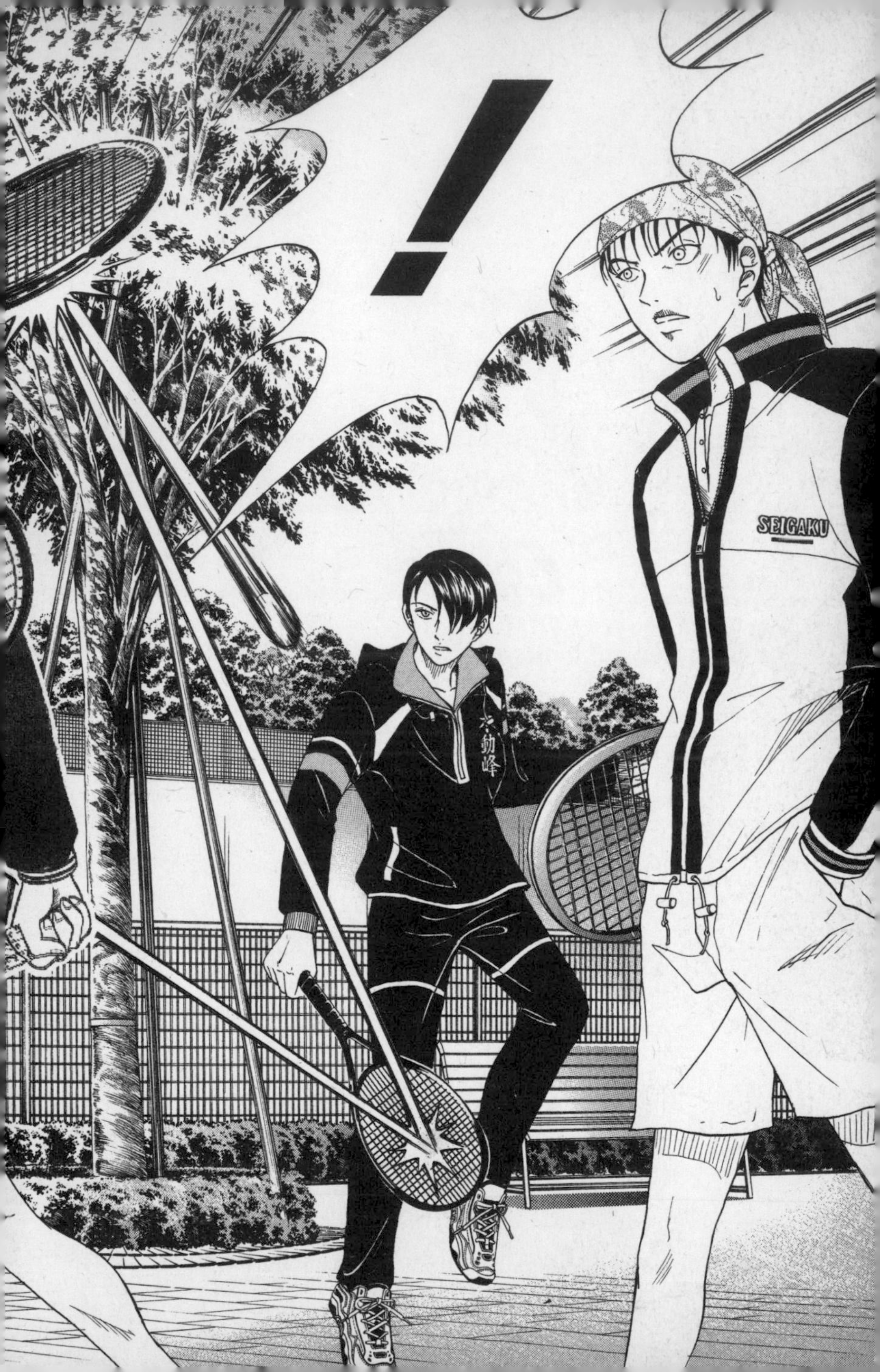
!
SEIGAKU

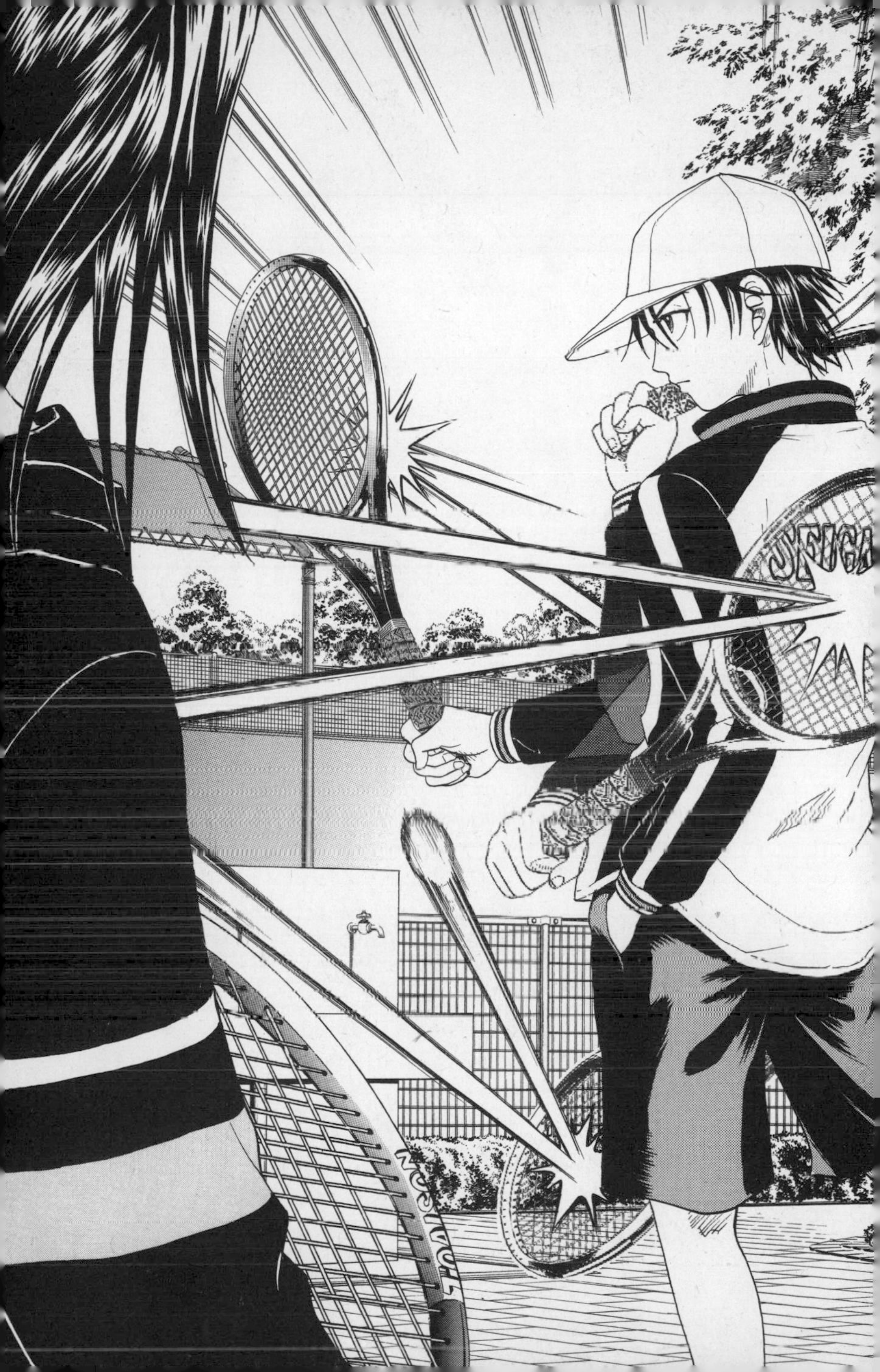

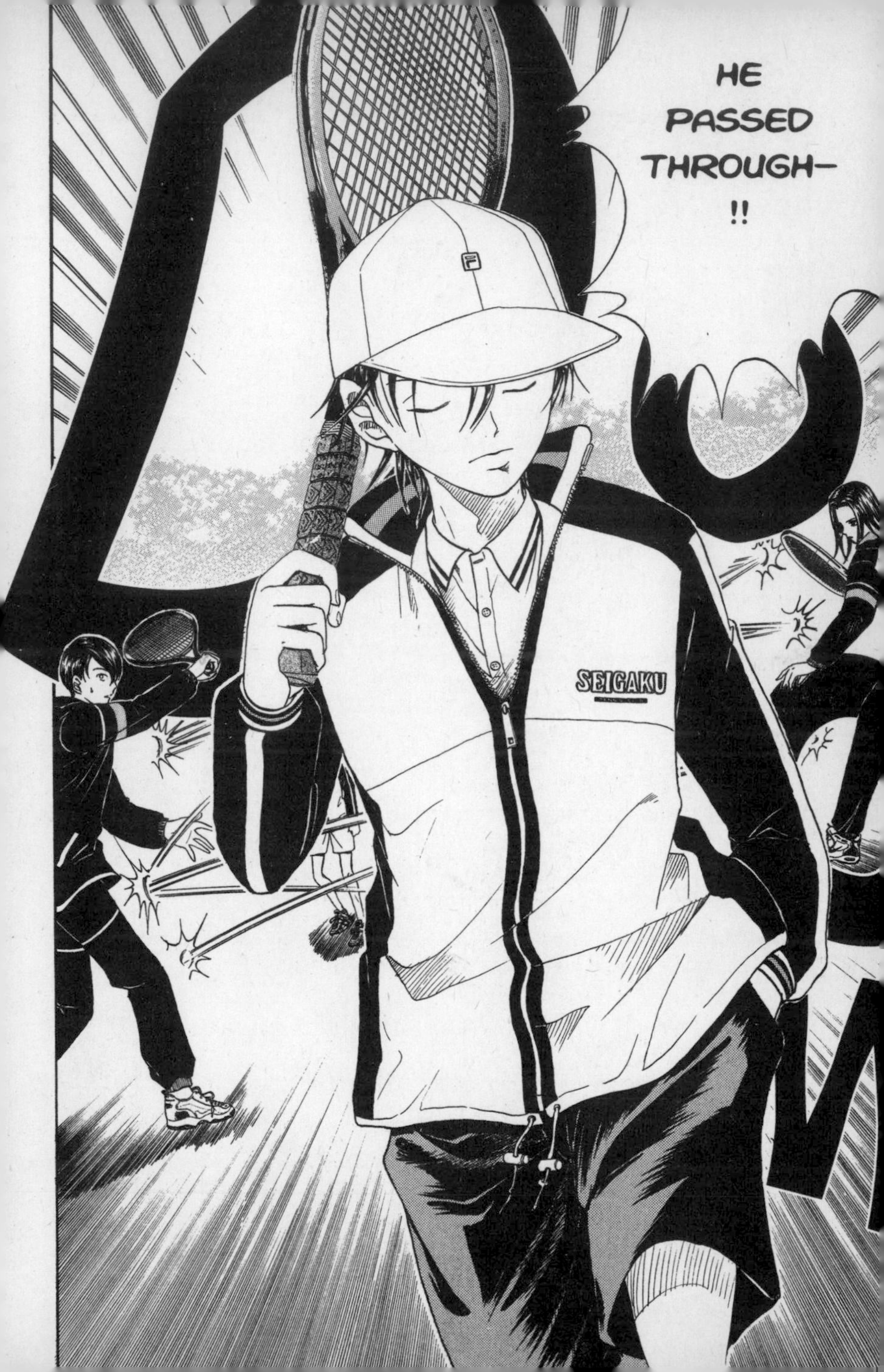
HE PASSED THROUGH—!!
SEIGAKU

READ THIS WAY

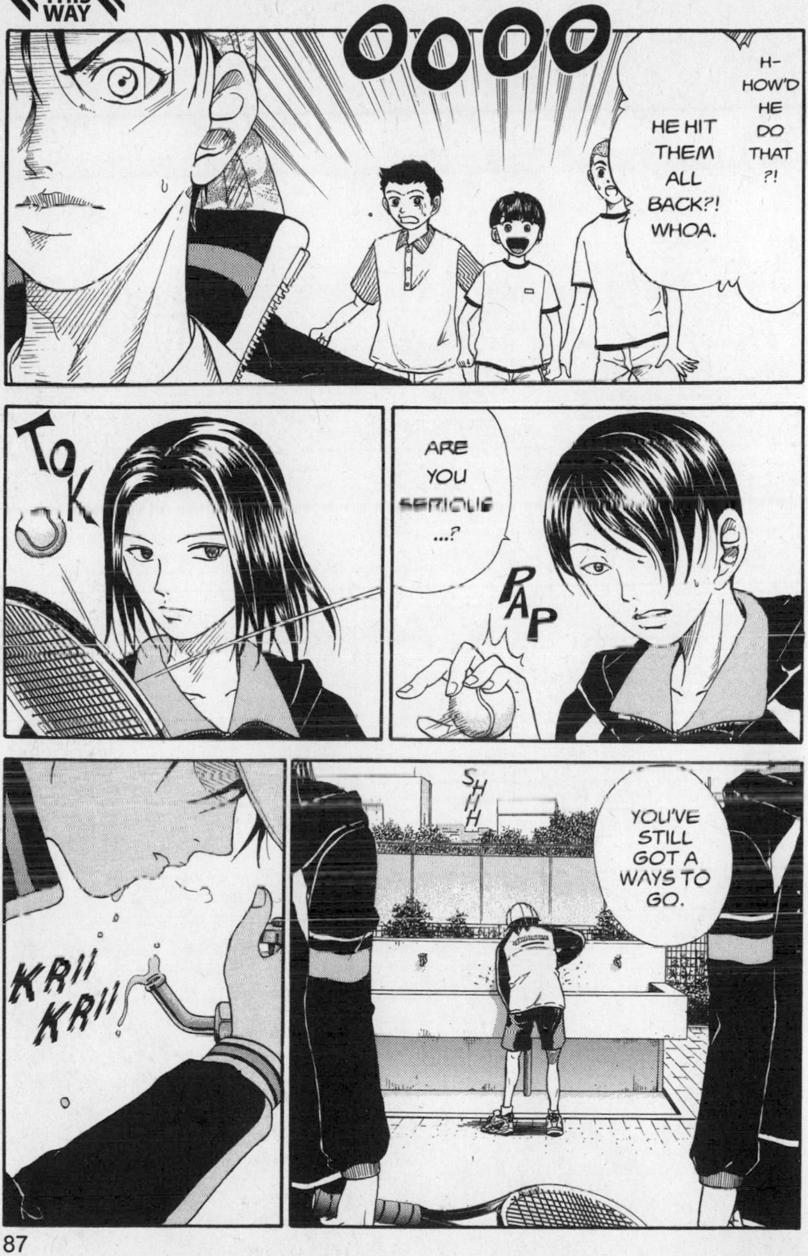
OOOO
H- HOW'D HE DO THAT?!
HE HIT THEM ALL BACK?! WHOA.
ARE YOU SERIOUS ...?
PAP
TOK
SHHH
YOU'VE STILL GOT A WAYS TO GO.
KRII KRII

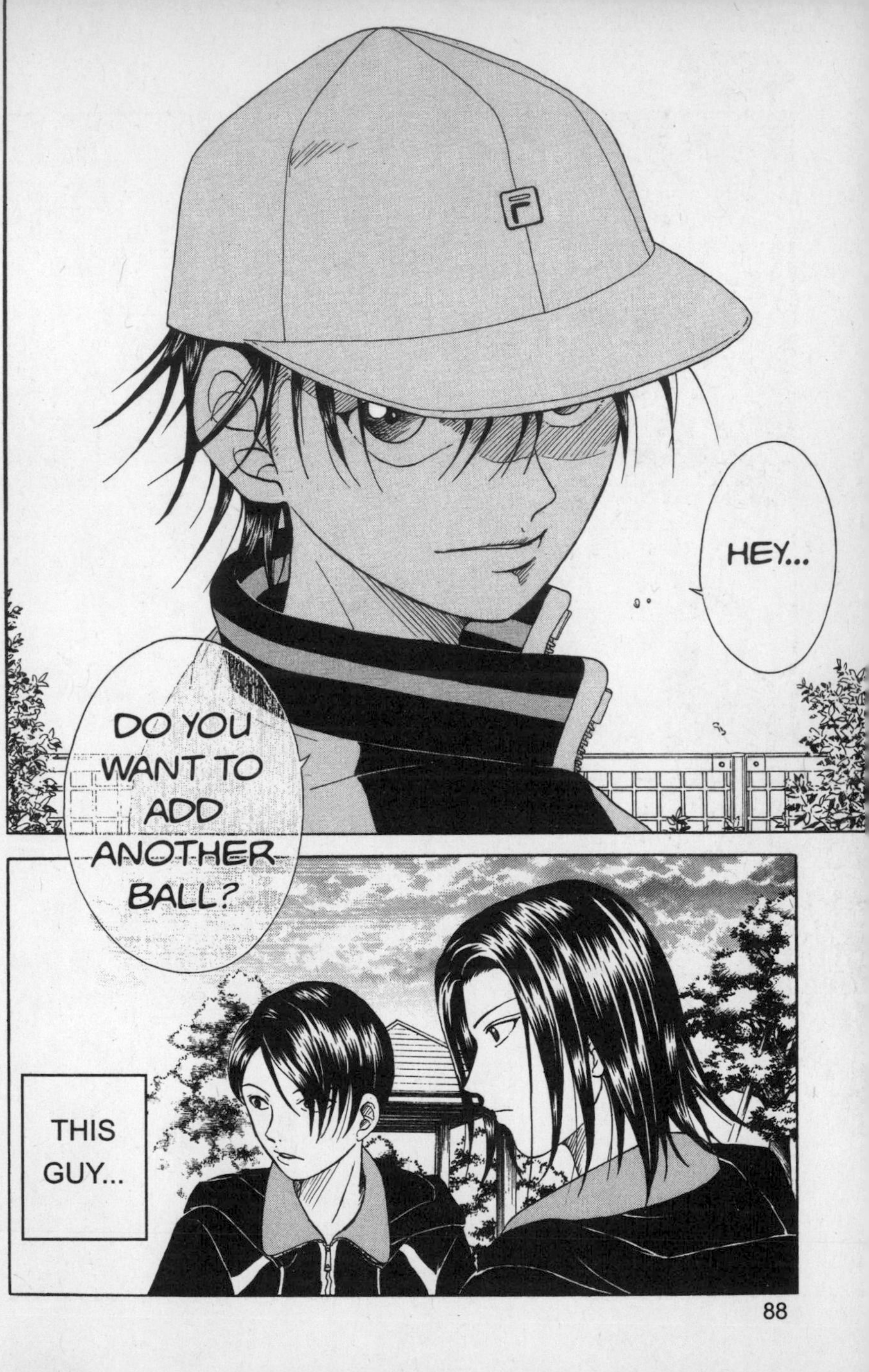
HEY...
DO YOU WANT TO ADD ANOTHER BALL?
THIS GUY...

READ THIS WAY

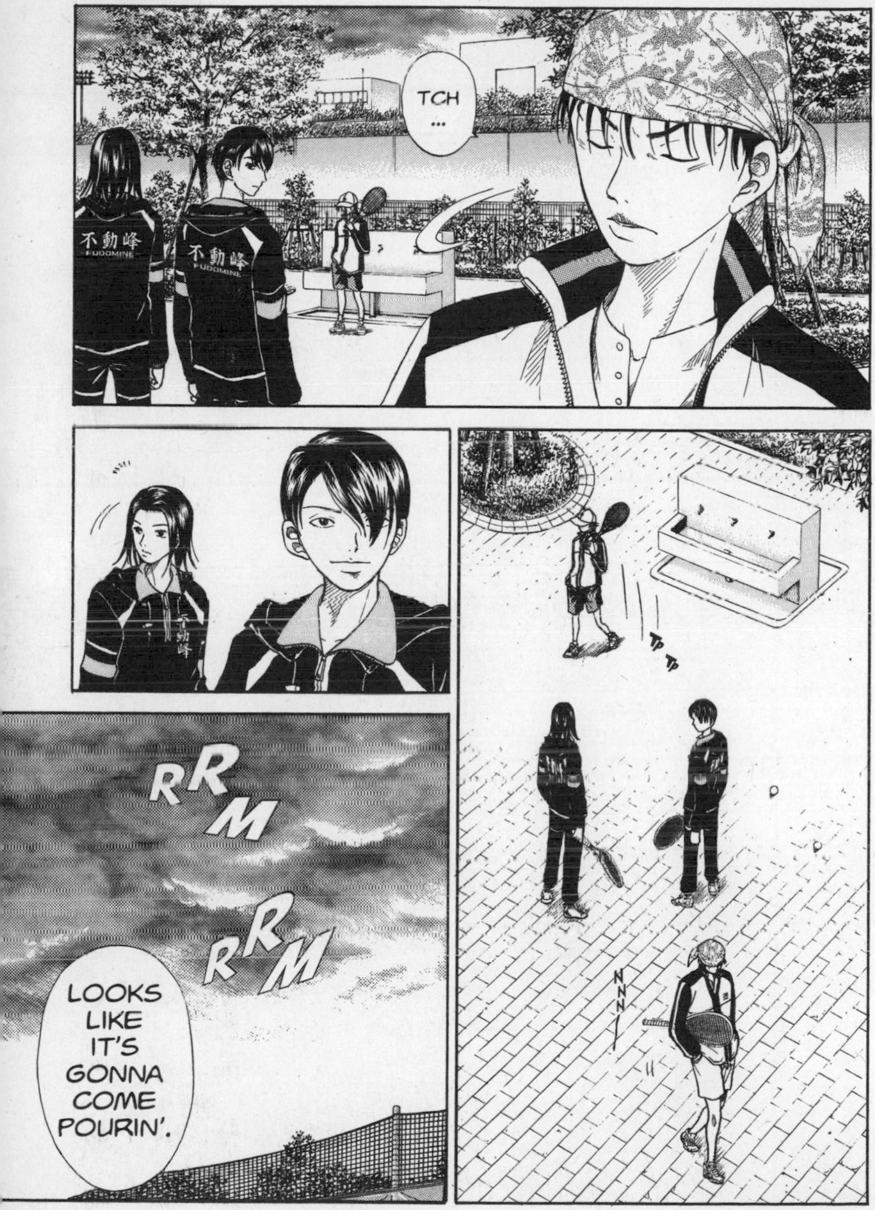
TCH ...
Tp Tp
NNN
RRRM
RRRM
LOOKS LIKE IT'S GONNA COME POURIN'.

Thanks for reading *The Prince of Tennis* Volume 4! And thanks for all of your letters. Some of them say, "I've started to play tennis," which is especially pleasing. Speaking of tennis, I've received a few letters saying, "I learned how to hit a shot like that at soft-tennis"—meaning, Shusuke's best move, "Tsubame Gaeshi," from this volume. Wow!! The "twist" and "snake" still seem difficult, though... Anyway, I'm happy people are becoming interested in tennis because of my comic!! And now, I have two announcements to make...

Fan Project Part 1

I'm thinking of letting the fans who have sent letters choose the topic for the cover of volume 5.

1. Genius 35: "Shock Them!" *Jump* Issue 17
2. Genius 43: "Sign of Strength" *Jump* Issue 26

Just write 1 or 2 in green ink on the "outside" of the postcard or envelope! The number with the most votes will be chosen as the cover. The deadline is 8/11/2000.

Fan Project Part 2

In response to the overwhelming requests by fans for "Ryoma's Classmate," here's a preview—!! We're planning on announcing the project in *Shukan Shonen Jump* Issue 38, which will be on sale in the middle of August 2000. For those who were "too late"—please join!! The application procedures will be slightly different from the last time. Check out *Jump* for more details!! (There will be other surprising projects, too.)

Anyway, keep supporting Prince of Tennis and Ryoma!! See you in the next volume!

テニスの王子様☆
T. KONOMI
2000. 7. 3

Note from the Editor: Projects and contests were held only in Japan. Entries are no longer being accepted.

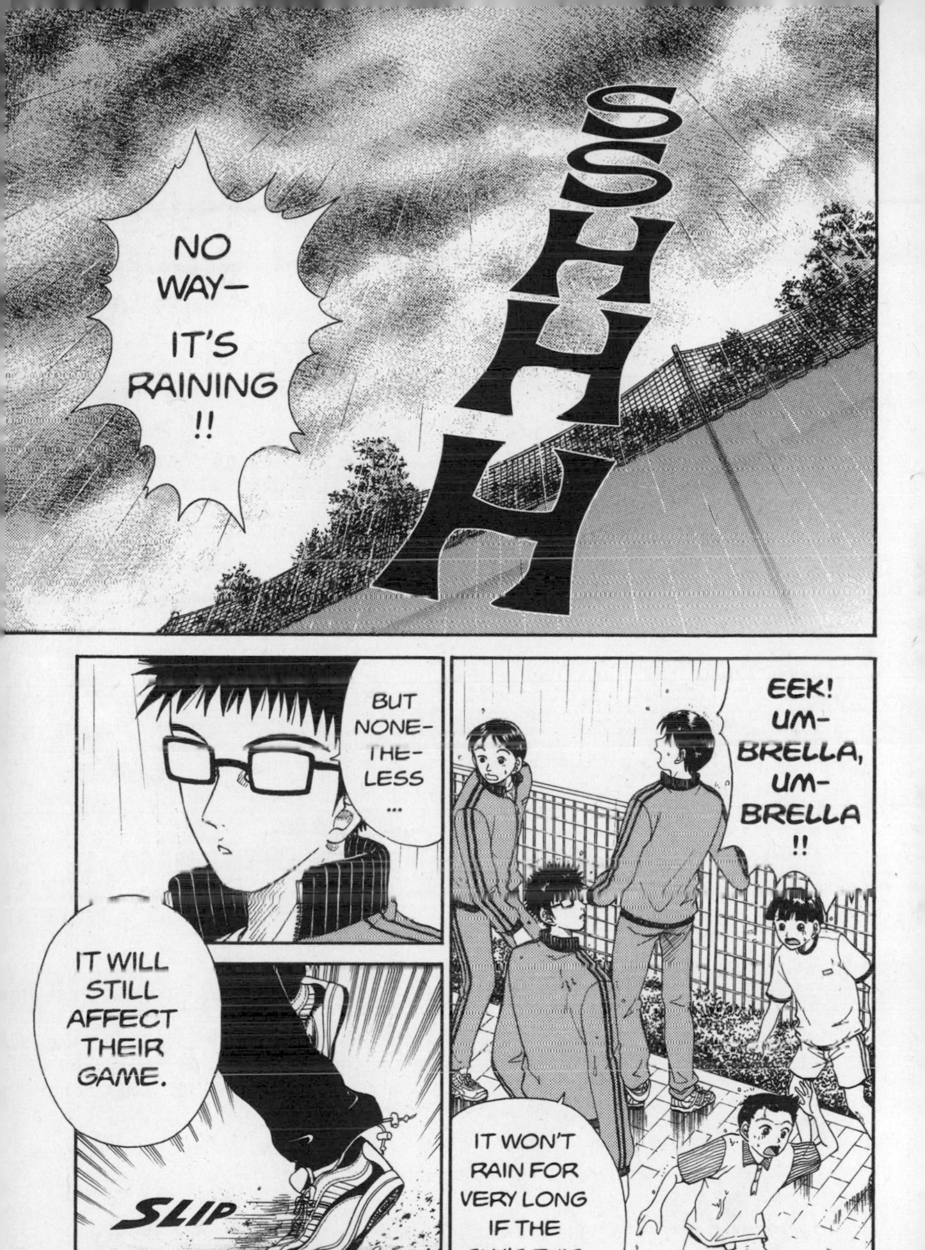
SSHHH
NO WAY— IT'S RAINING !!
EEK! UM-BRELLA, UM-BRELLA !!
IT WON'T RAIN FOR VERY LONG IF THE SKY'S THIS BRIGHT.
BUT NONE-THE-LESS ...
IT WILL STILL AFFECT THEIR GAME.
SLIP

Genius 30: ACE OF SPEED

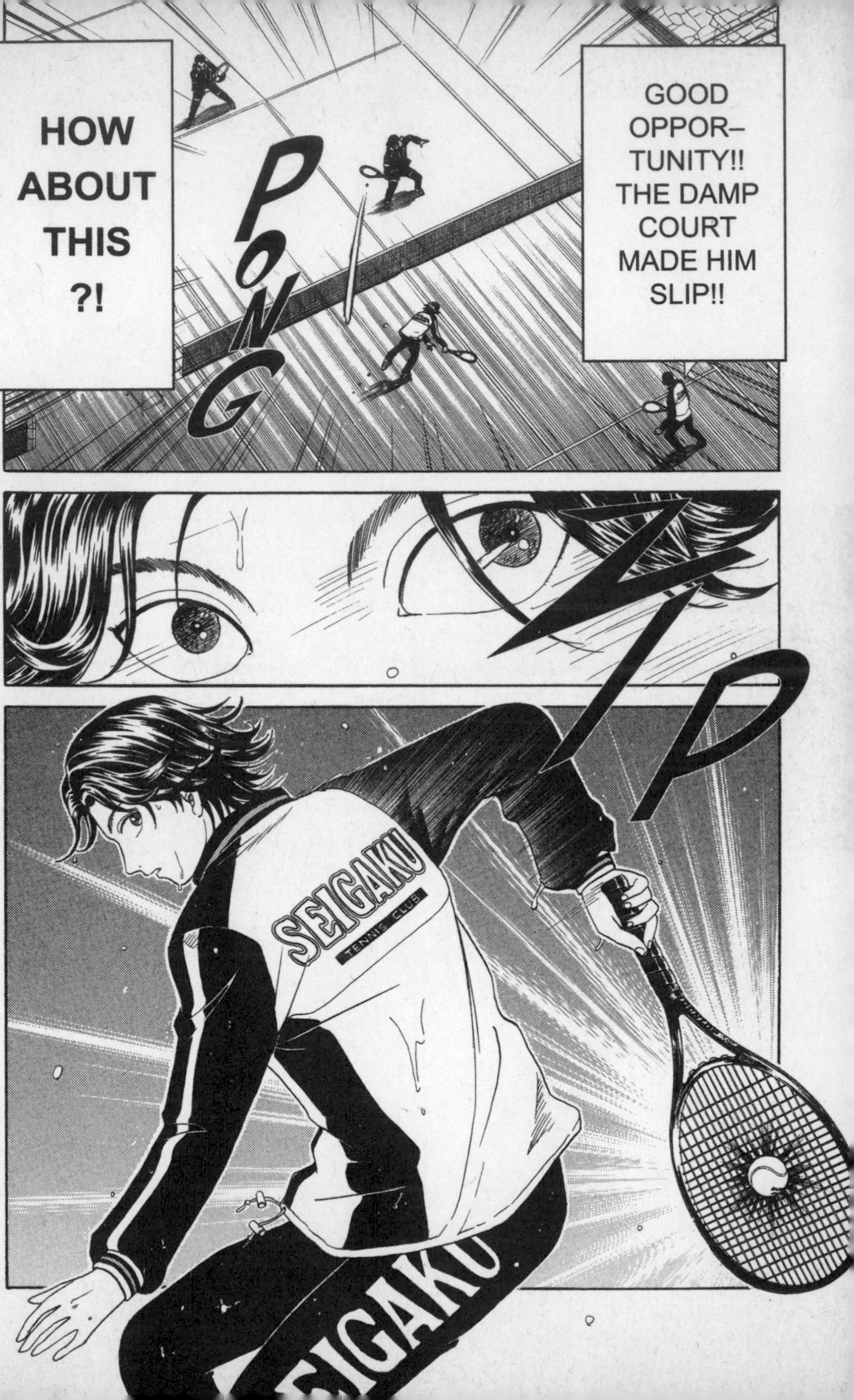
GOOD OPPOR–TUNITY!! THE DAMP COURT MADE HIM SLIP!!
PONG
HOW ABOUT THIS ?!
ZIP
SEIGAKU
TENNIS CLUB
SEIGAKU

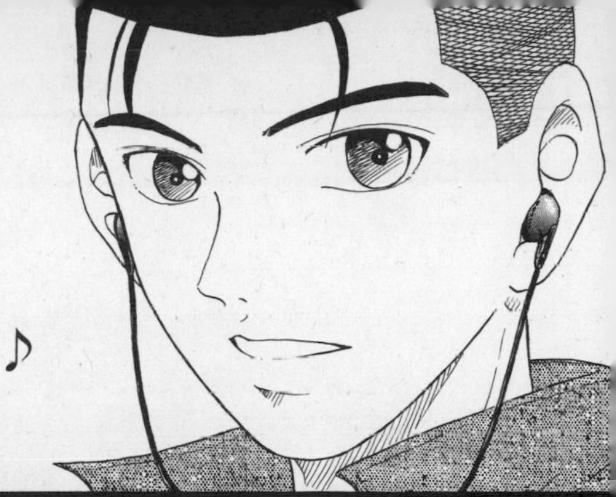

Genius 30: ACE OF SPEED

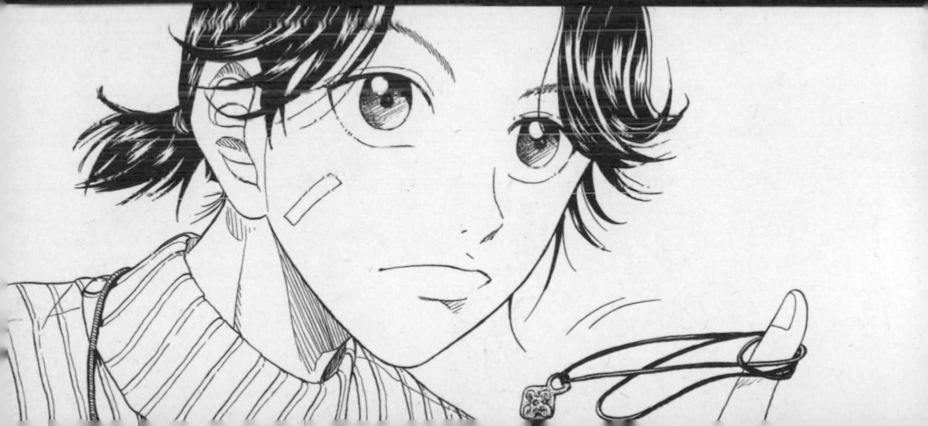

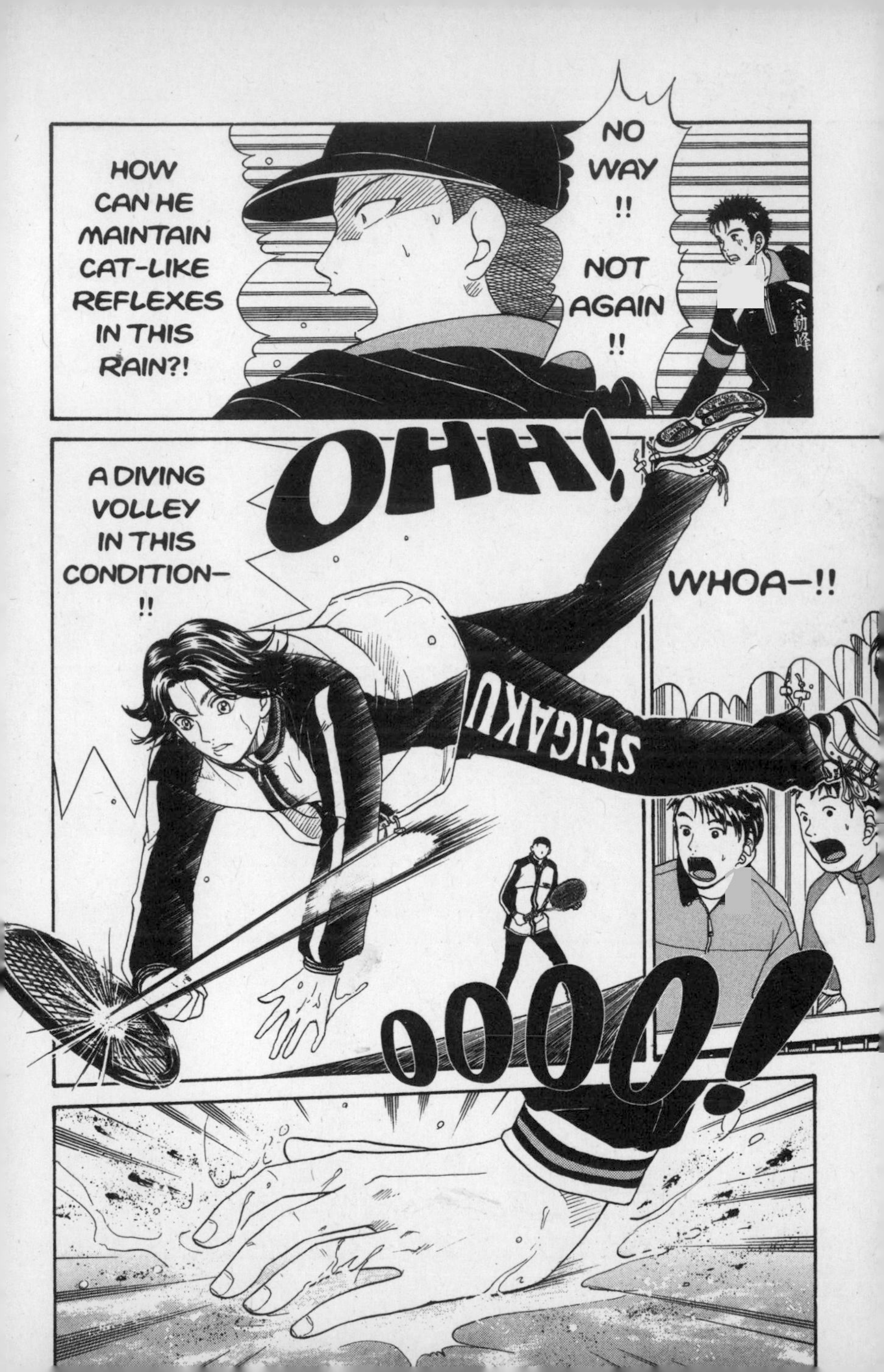
NO WAY !! NOT AGAIN !!
HOW CAN HE MAINTAIN CAT-LIKE REFLEXES IN THIS RAIN?!
OHH!
WHOA-!!
A DIVING VOLLEY IN THIS CONDITION-!!
SEIGAKU
OOOO!

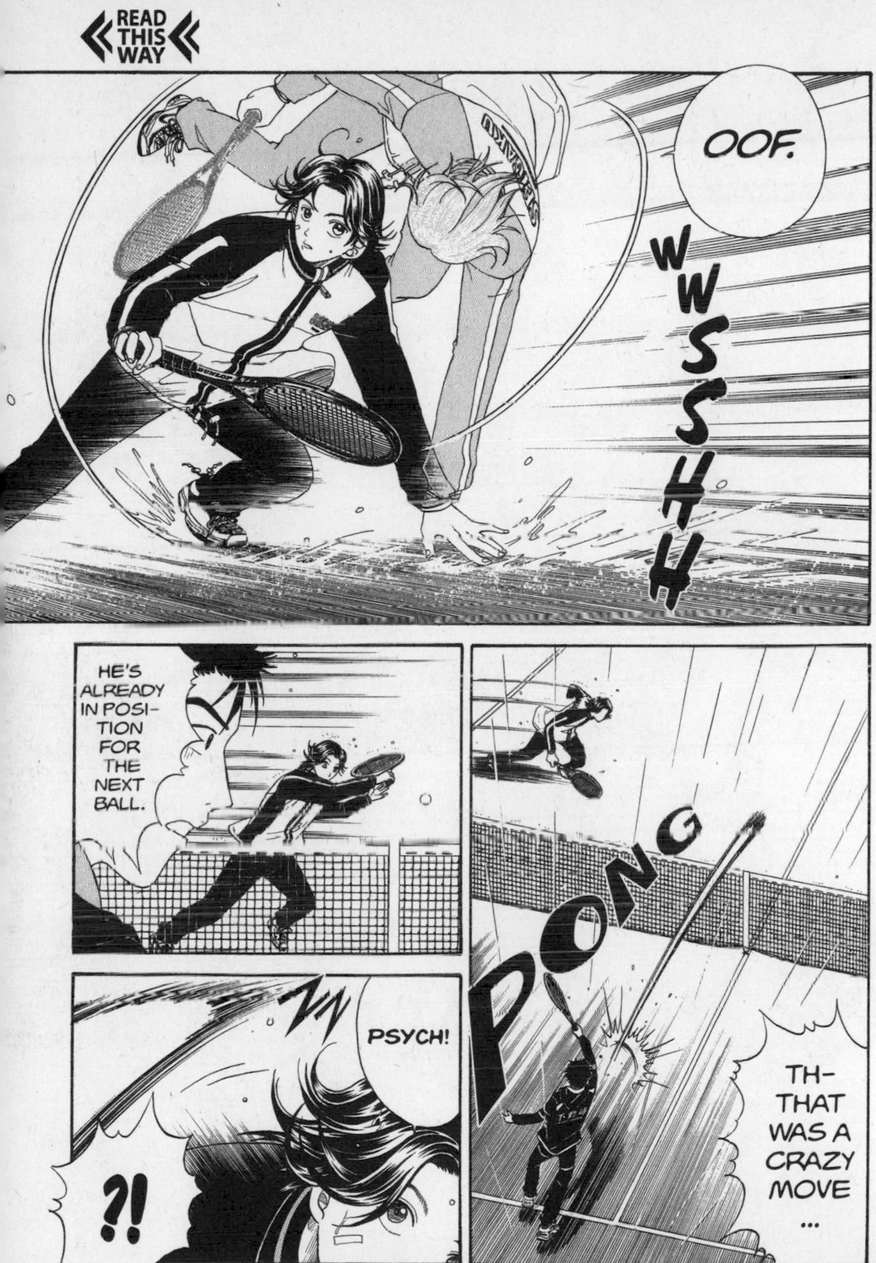
READ THIS WAY
OOF.
WWSSHH
PONG
TH-THAT WAS A CRAZY MOVE ...
HE'S ALREADY IN POSITION FOR THE NEXT BALL.
PSYCH!
?!

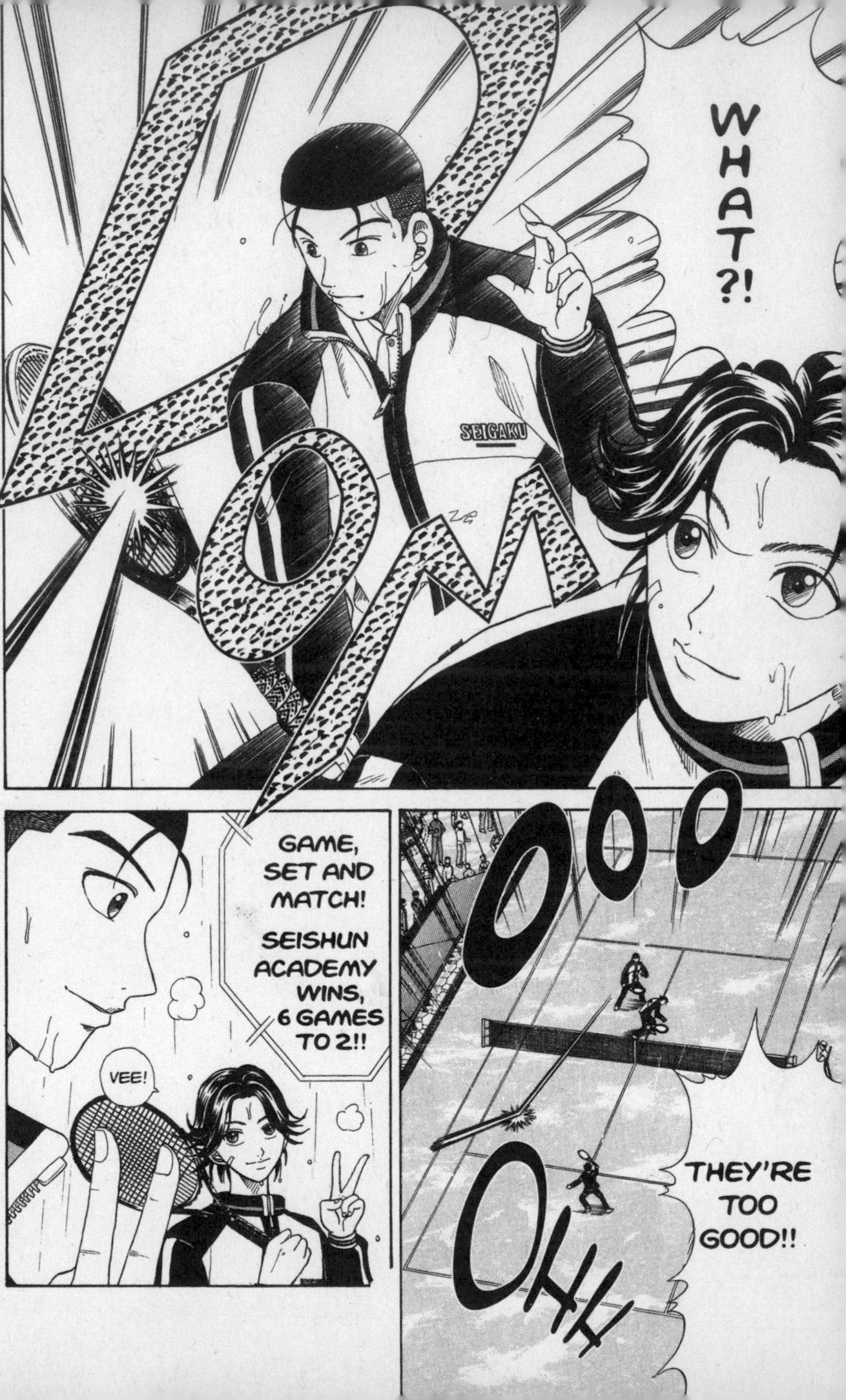
WHAT?!
OOOOOHH
THEY'RE TOO GOOD!!
GAME, SET AND MATCH!
SEISHUN ACADEMY WINS, 6 GAMES TO 2!!
VEE!

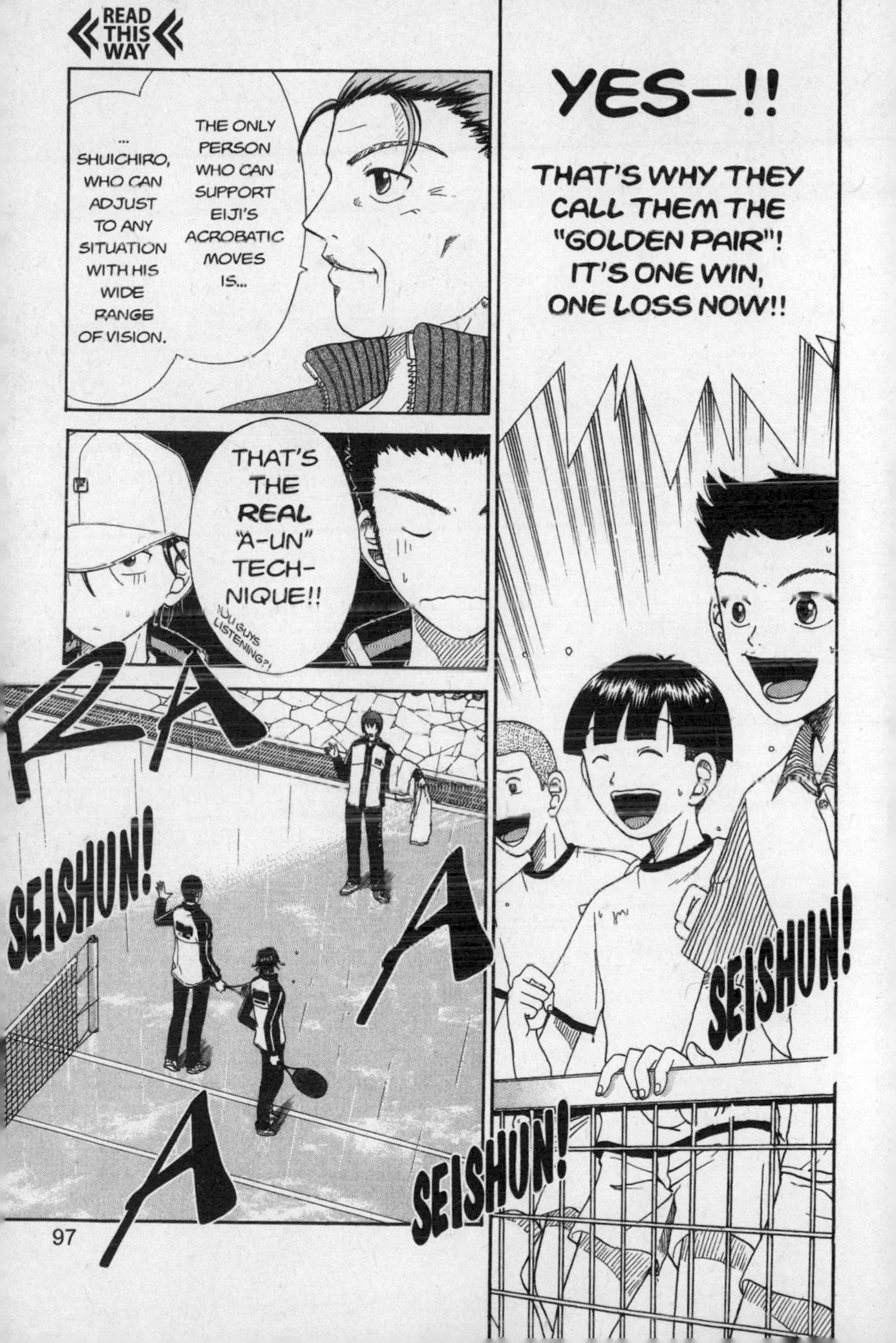
READ THIS WAY
YES—!!
THAT'S WHY THEY CALL THEM THE "GOLDEN PAIR"! IT'S ONE WIN, ONE LOSS NOW!!
SEISHUN!
SEISHUN!
THE ONLY PERSON WHO CAN SUPPORT EIJI'S ACROBATIC MOVES IS...
... SHUICHIRO, WHO CAN ADJUST TO ANY SITUATION WITH HIS WIDE RANGE OF VISION.
THAT'S THE REAL "A-UN" TECHNIQUE!!
YOU GUYS LISTENING?!
SEISHUN!
SEISHUN!
AAA

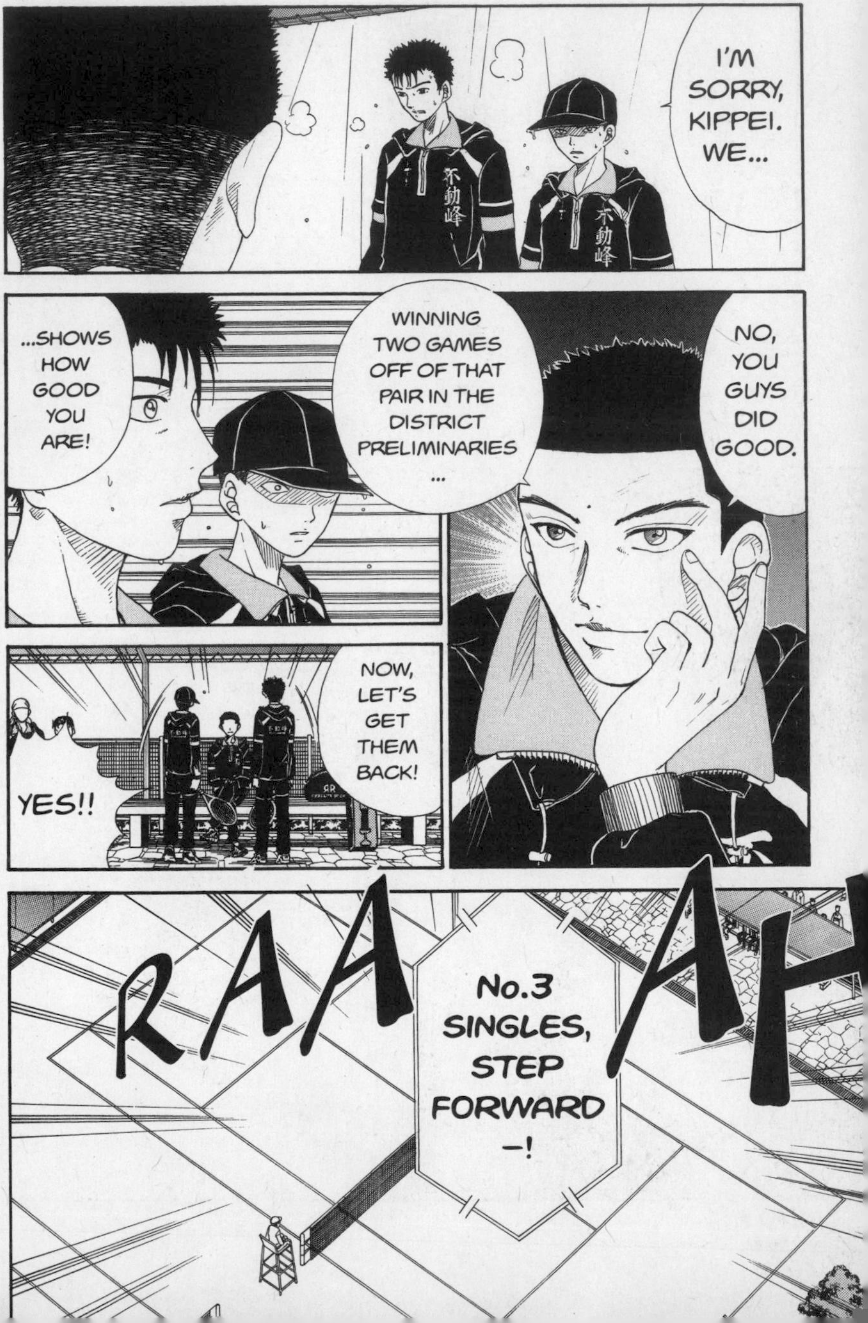
I'M SORRY, KIPPEI. WE...
NO, YOU GUYS DID GOOD.
WINNING TWO GAMES OFF OF THAT PAIR IN THE DISTRICT PRELIMINARIES...
...SHOWS HOW GOOD YOU ARE!
NOW, LET'S GET THEM BACK!
YES!!
RAAAH
No.3 SINGLES, STEP FORWARD—!

READ THIS WAY

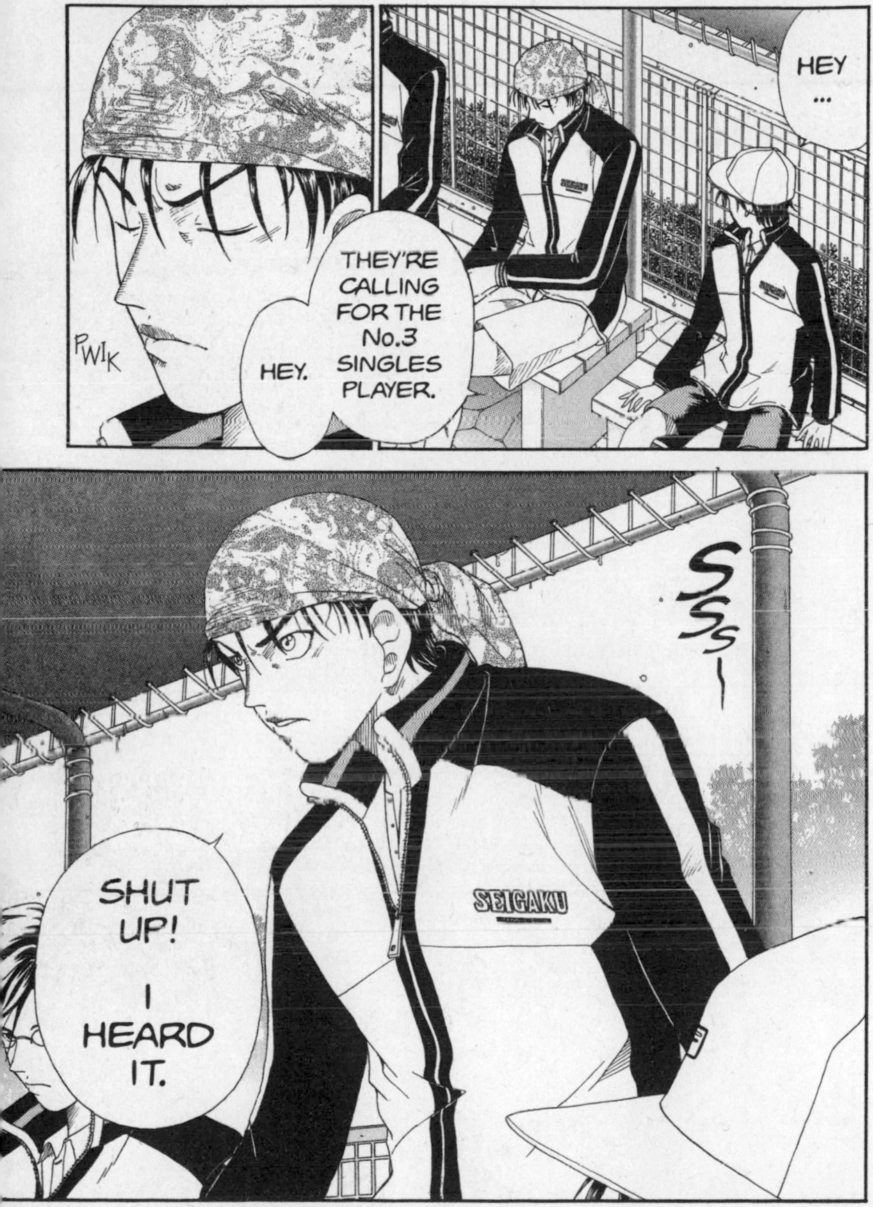

HEY ...
THEY'RE CALLING FOR THE No.3 SINGLES PLAYER.
HEY.
PWIK
SSS
SEIGAKU
SHUT UP! I HEARD IT.

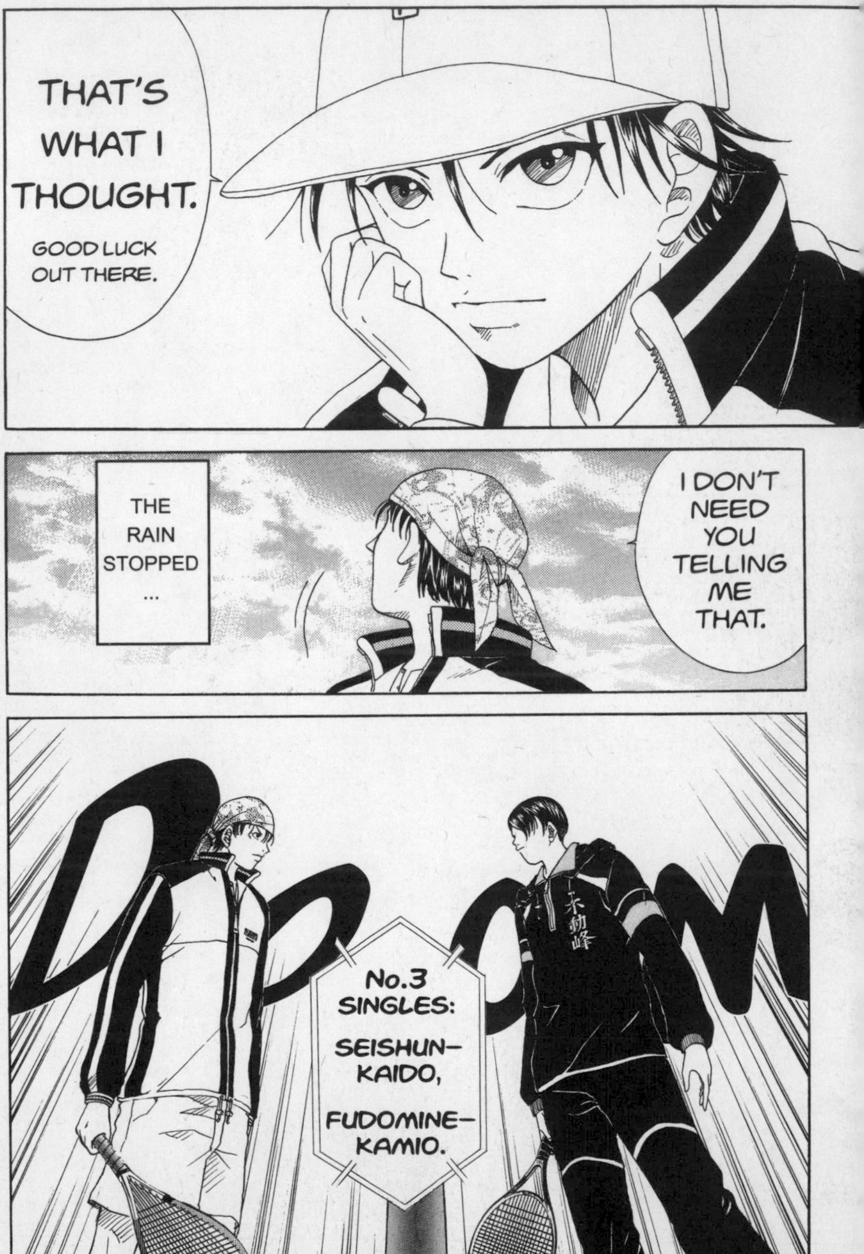
THAT'S WHAT I THOUGHT.
GOOD LUCK OUT THERE.
I DON'T NEED YOU TELLING ME THAT.
THE RAIN STOPPED ...
No.3 SINGLES: SEISHUN-KAIDO, FUDOMINE-KAMIO.
不動峰

READ THIS WAY

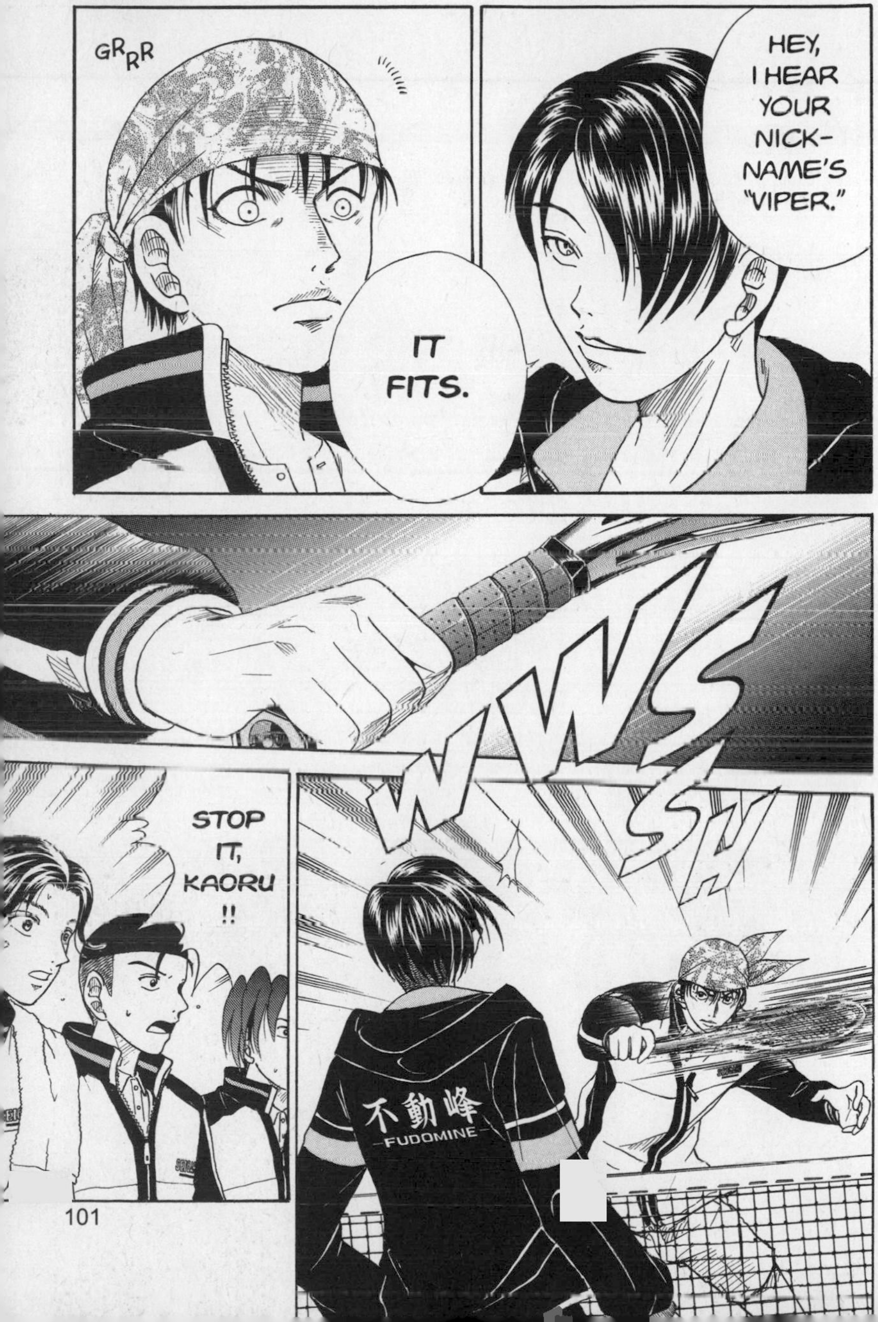

HEY, I HEAR YOUR NICK-NAME'S "VIPER."
GRRR
IT FITS.
WWSSH
不動峰
-FUDOMINE-
STOP IT, KAORU!!

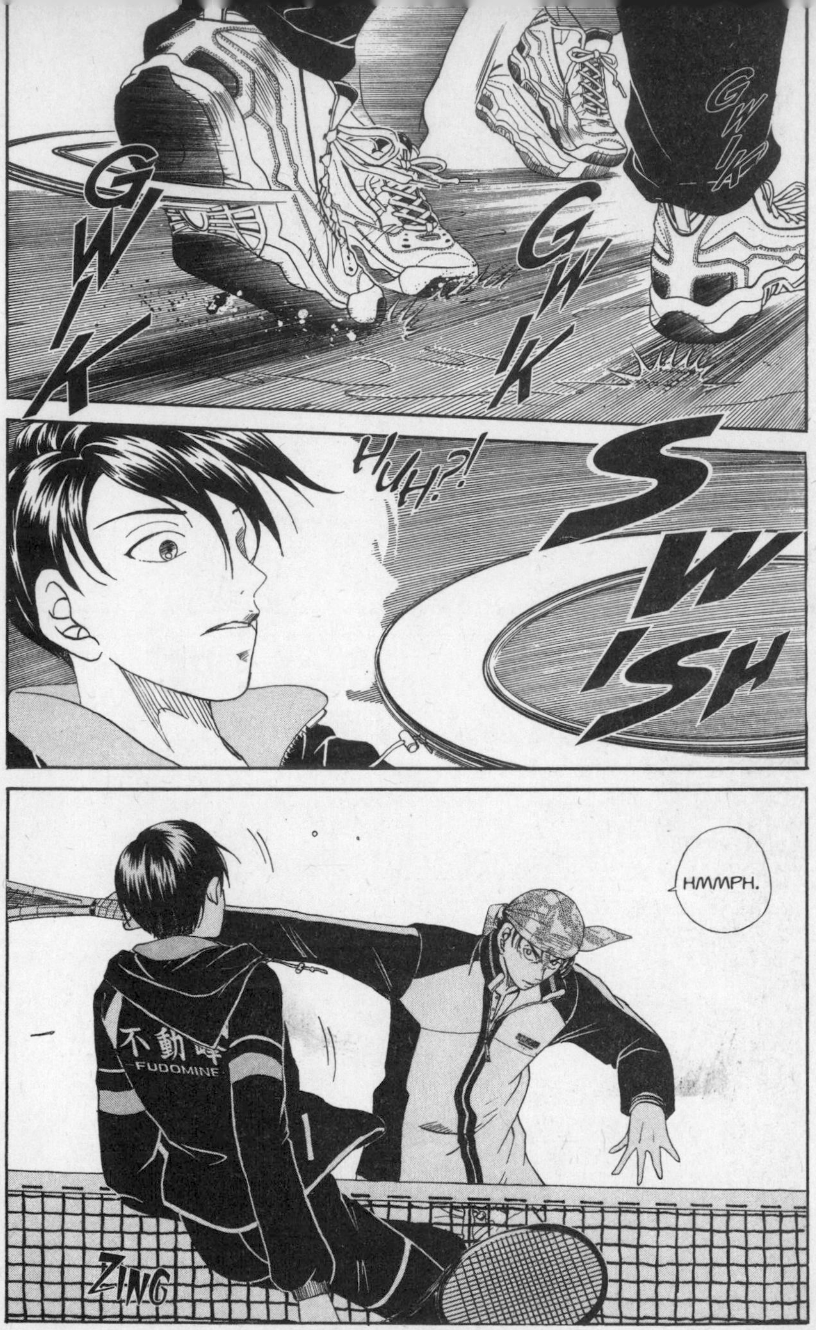
GWIK
GWIK
GWIK
SWISH
HUH?!
HMMPH.
不動峰
FUDOMINE
ZING

READ THIS WAY

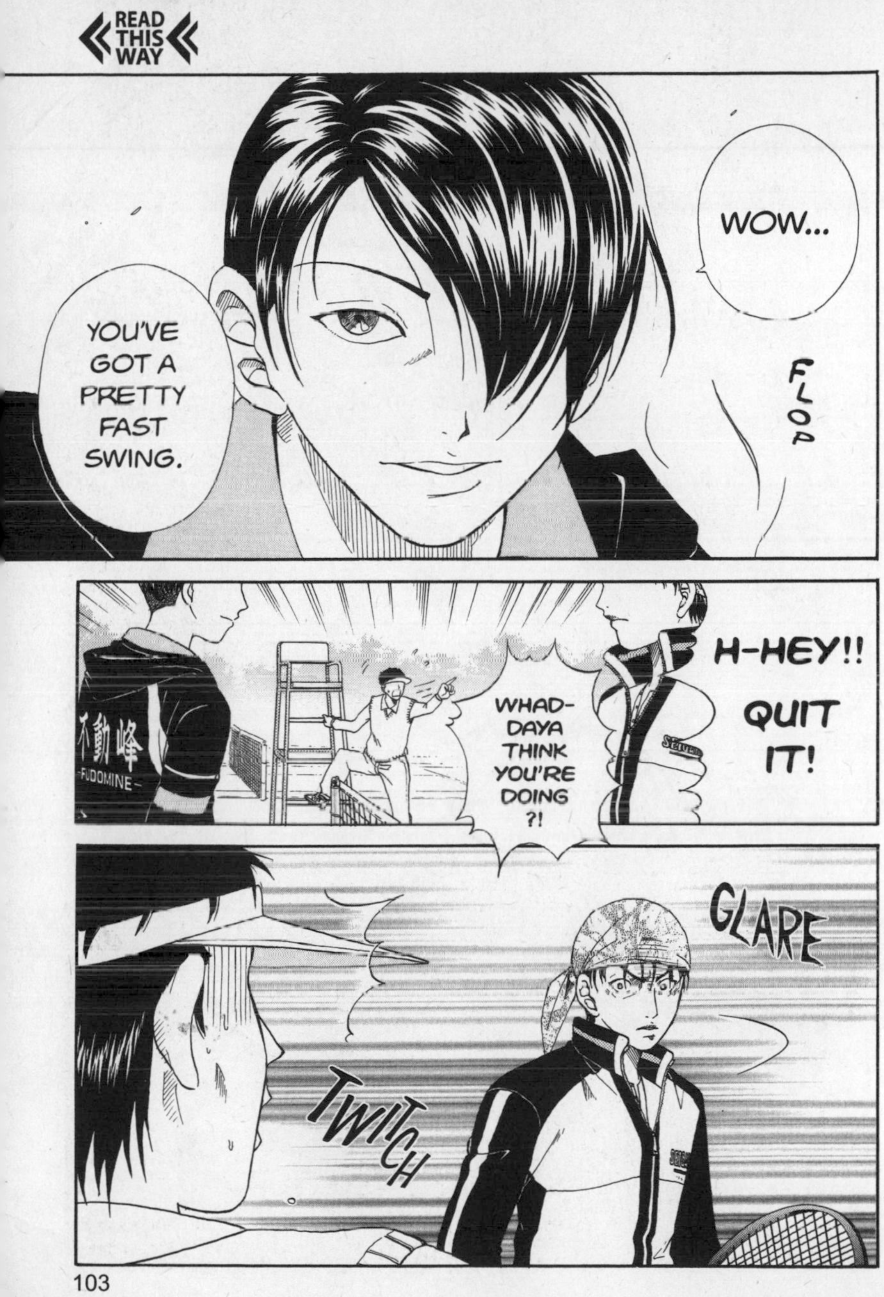

WOW...
FLOP
YOU'VE GOT A PRETTY FAST SWING.
H-HEY!! QUIT IT!
WHAD-DAYA THINK YOU'RE DOING ?!
GLARE
TWITCH

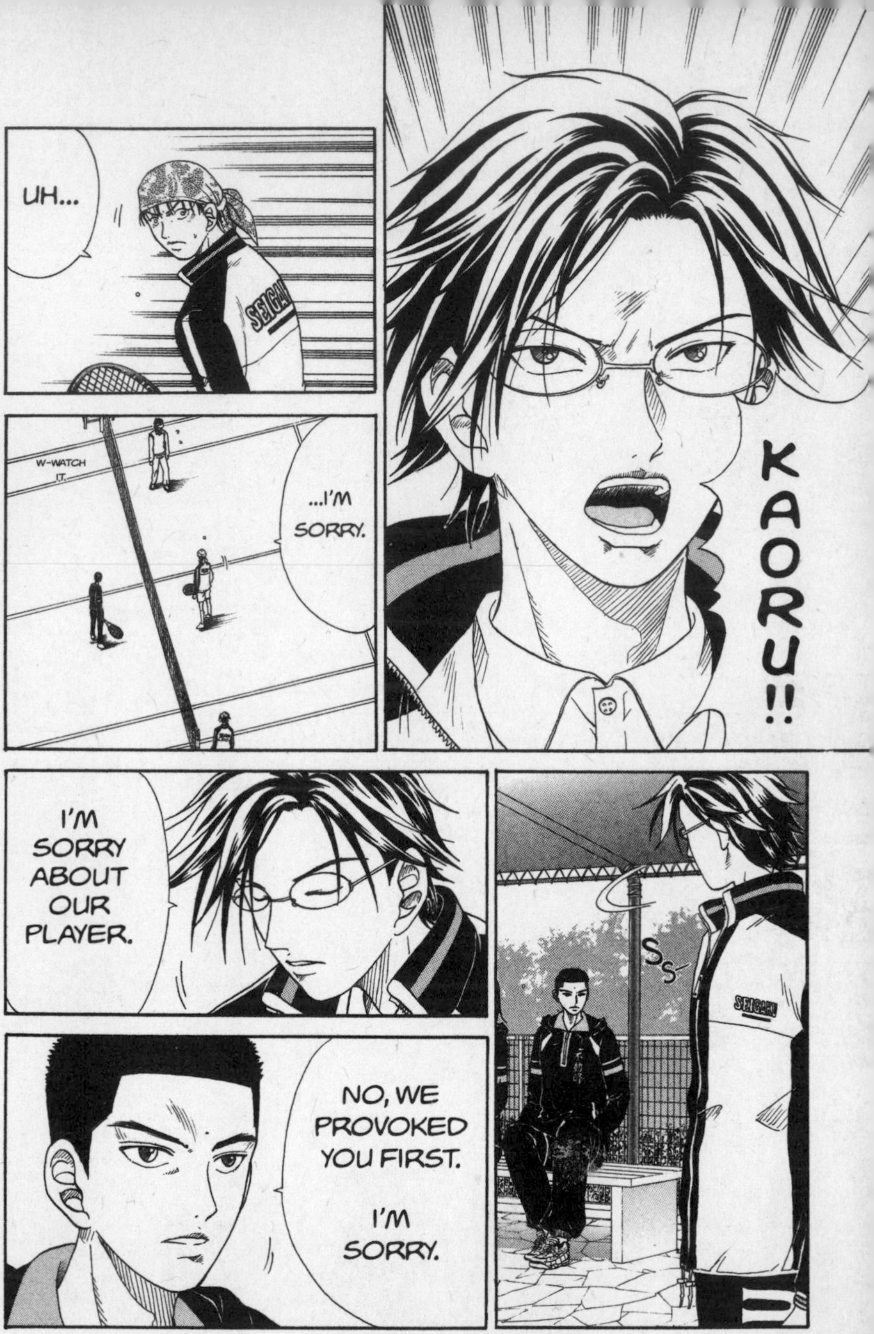

KAORU!!
UH...
...I'M SORRY.
W-WATCH IT.
SS
I'M SORRY ABOUT OUR PLAYER.
NO, WE PROVOKED YOU FIRST.
I'M SORRY.

READ THIS WAY

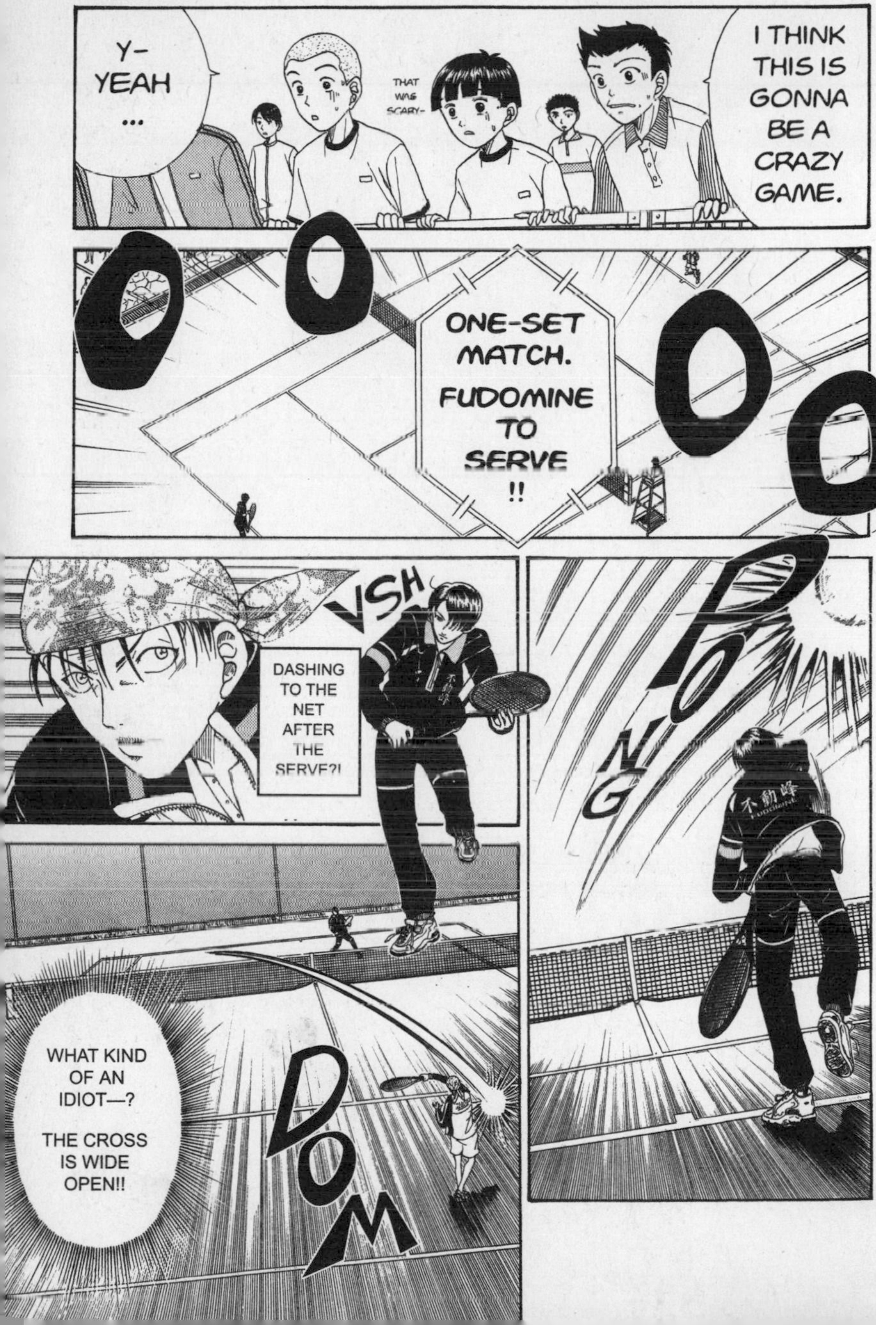
I THINK THIS IS GONNA BE A CRAZY GAME.
THAT WAS SCARY-
Y-YEAH...
OOOOO
ONE-SET MATCH. FUDOMINE TO SERVE!!
PONG
VSH
DASHING TO THE NET AFTER THE SERVE?!
WHAT KIND OF AN IDIOT—?
THE CROSS IS WIDE OPEN!!
DOM

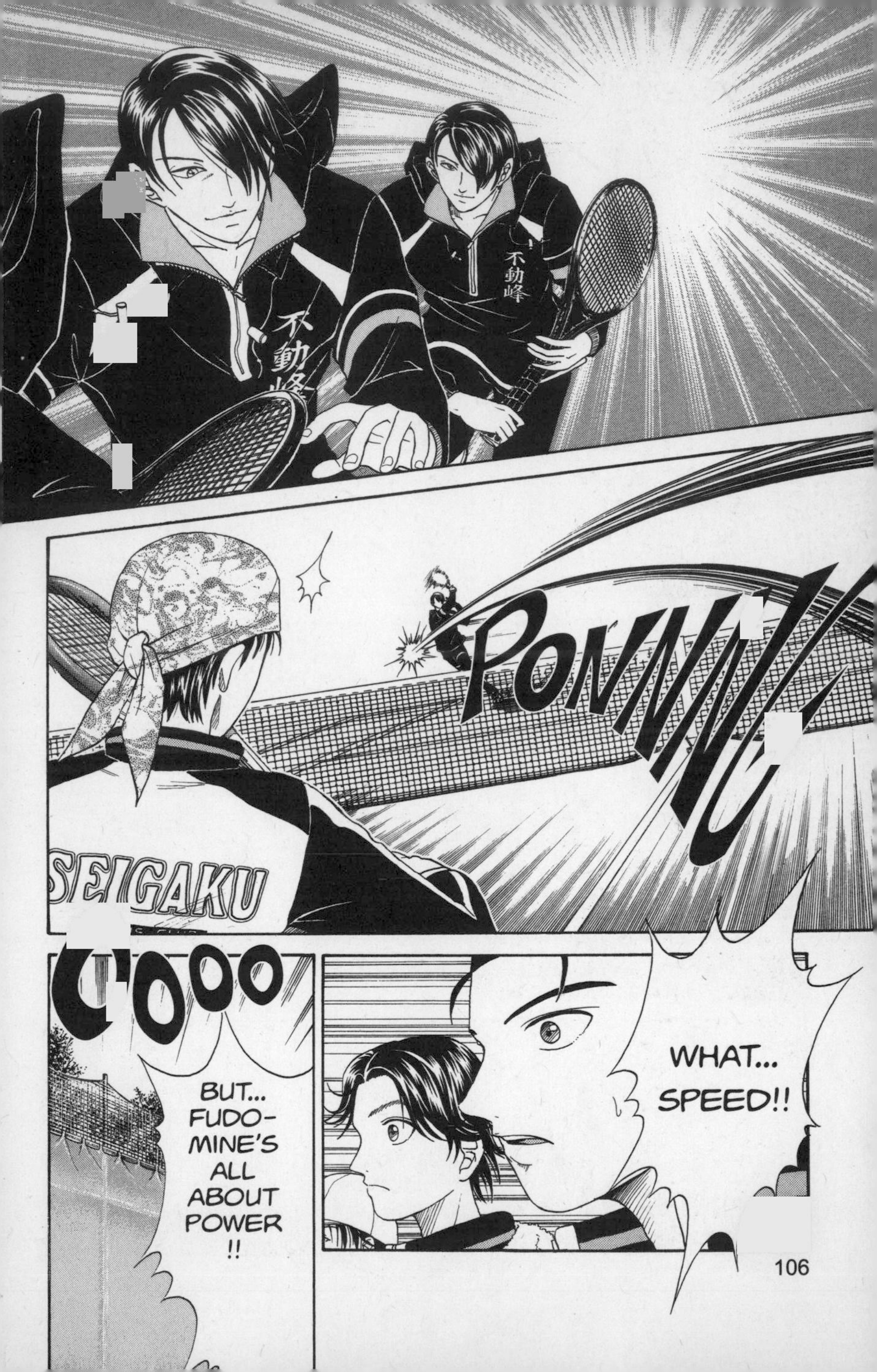
不動峰
不動峰
PONNN
WHAT... SPEED!!
GOOO
BUT... FUDO-MINE'S ALL ABOUT POWER!!
SEIGAKU

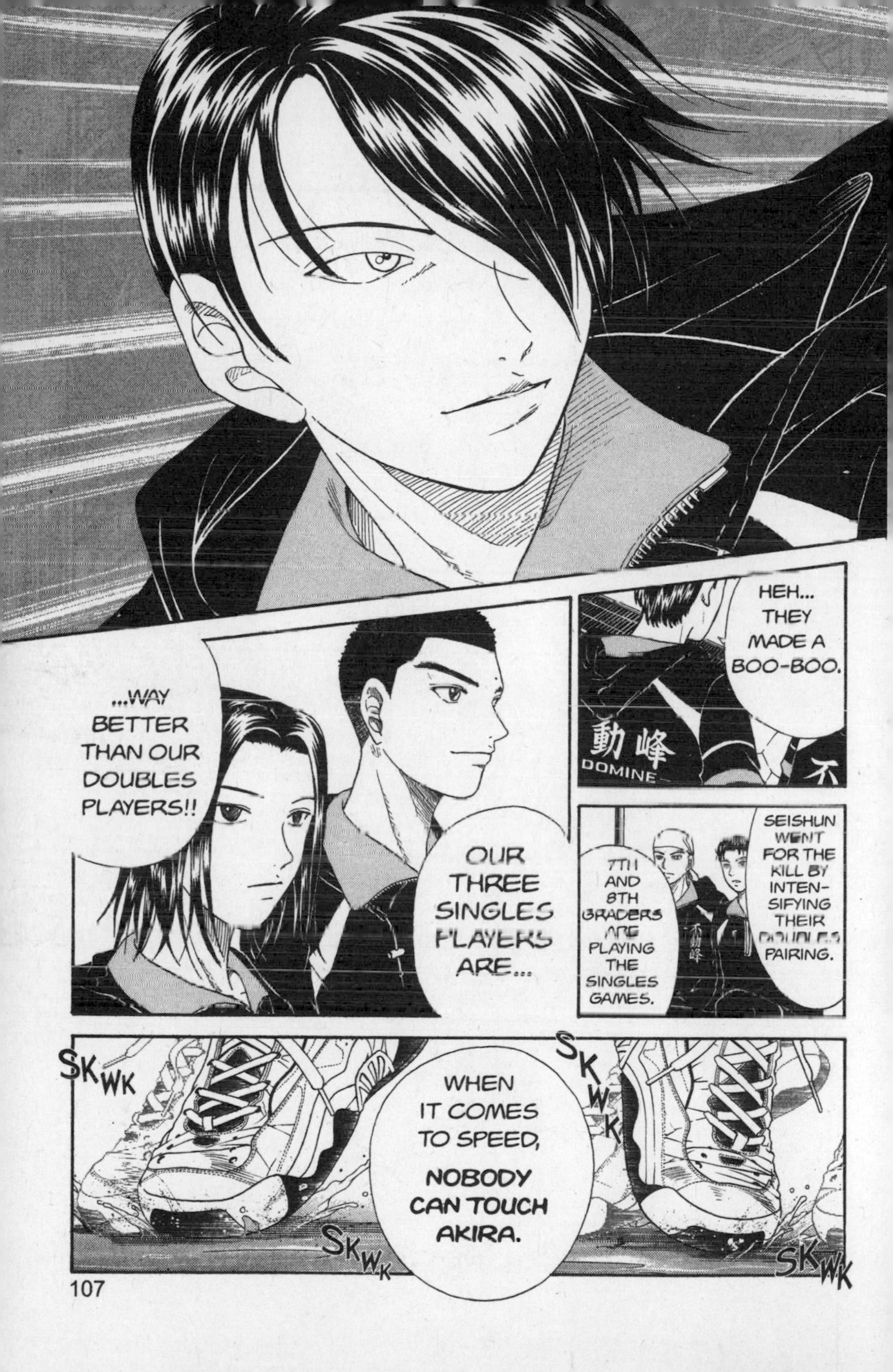
HEH... THEY MADE A BOO-BOO.
動峰
DOMINE
SEISHUN WENT FOR THE KILL BY INTENSIFYING THEIR DOUBLES PAIRING.
7TH AND 8TH GRADERS ARE PLAYING THE SINGLES GAMES.
OUR THREE SINGLES PLAYERS ARE...
...WAY BETTER THAN OUR DOUBLES PLAYERS!!
SKWK
SKWK
WHEN IT COMES TO SPEED,
NOBODY CAN TOUCH AKIRA.
SKWK
SKWK

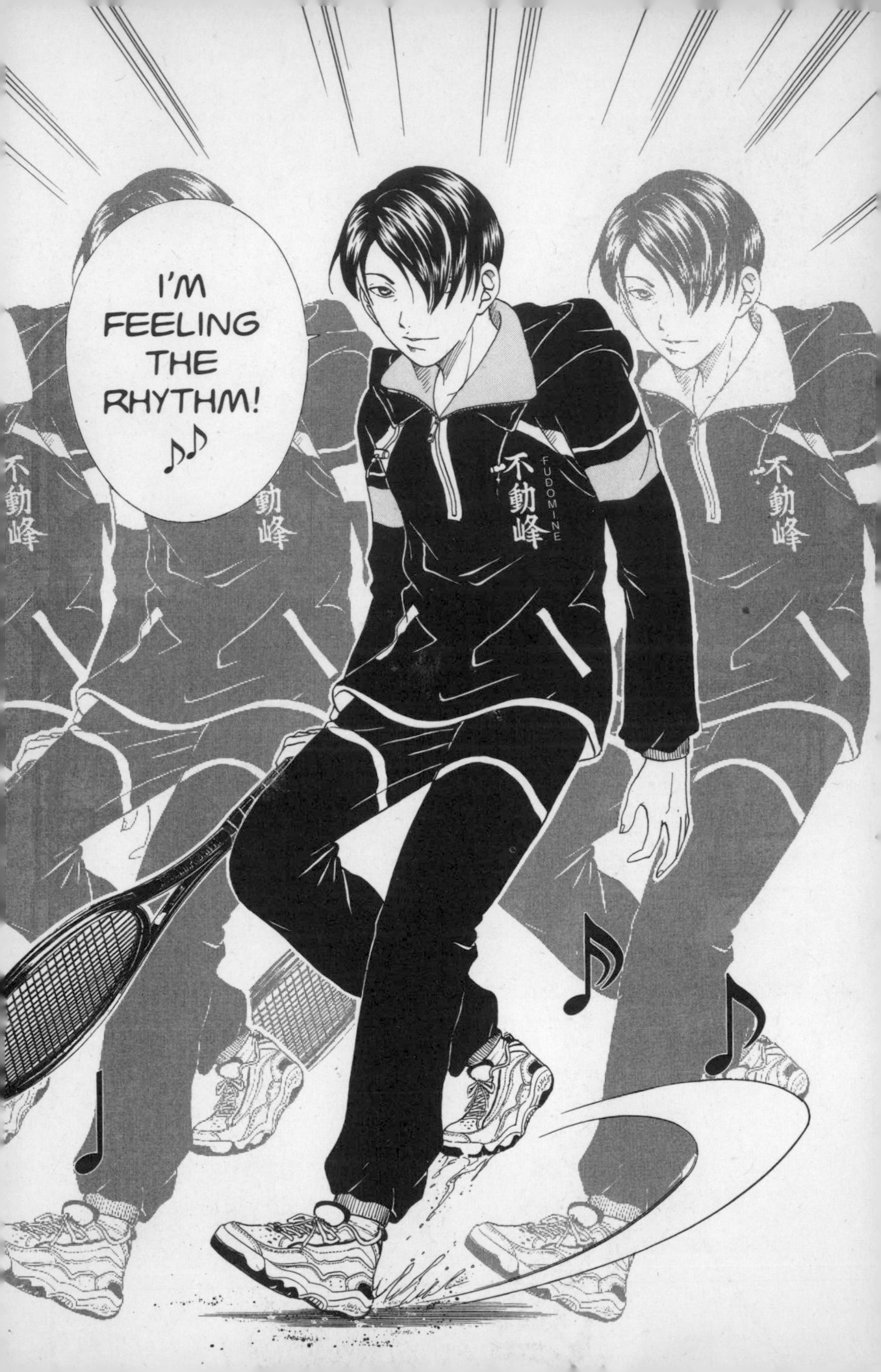
I'M FEELING THE RHYTHM! ♪♪
不動峰 FUDOMINE

READ THIS WAY

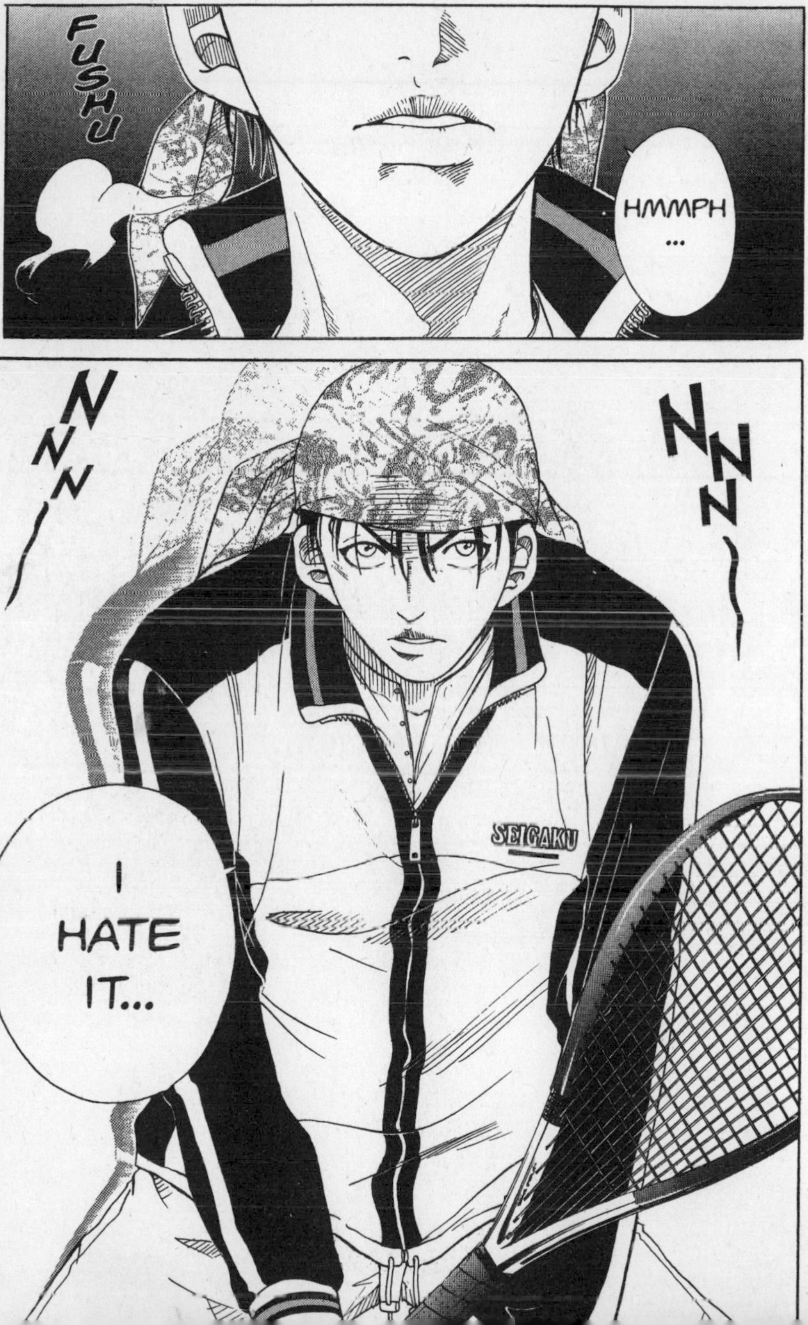
HMMPH ...
FUSHU
NNN~
NNN~
SEIGAKU
I HATE IT...

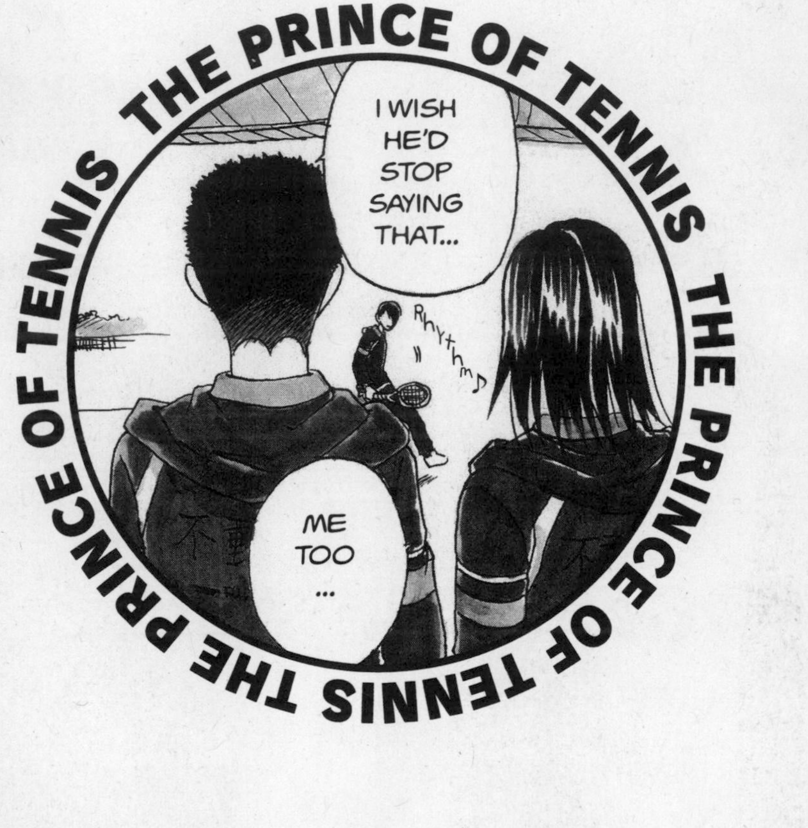
THE PRINCE OF TENNIS THE PRINCE OF TENNIS THE PRINCE OF TENNIS
I WISH HE'D STOP SAYING THAT...
Rhythm♪
ME TOO ...

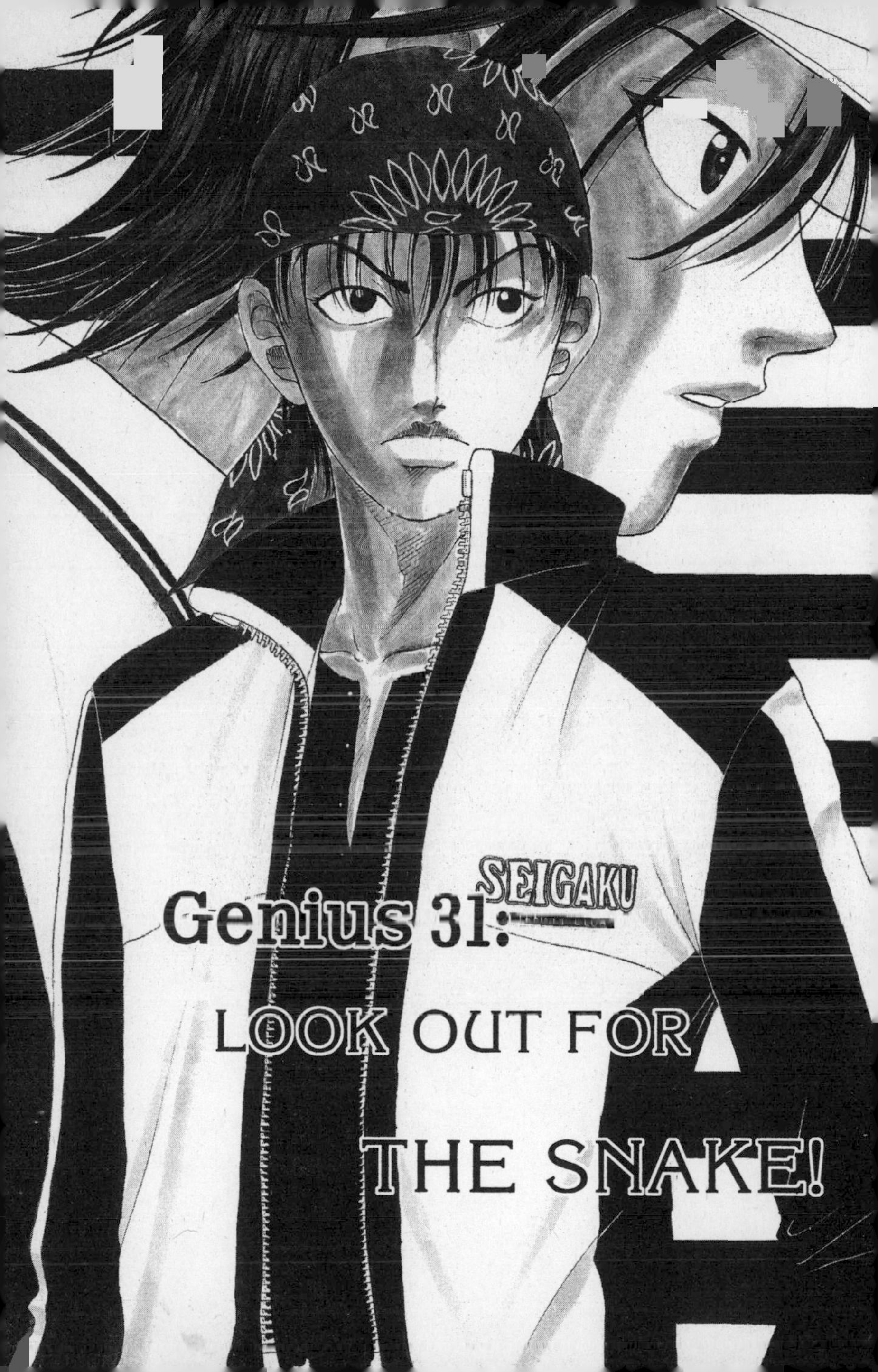
SEIGAKU
Genius 31:
LOOK OUT FOR THE SNAKE!

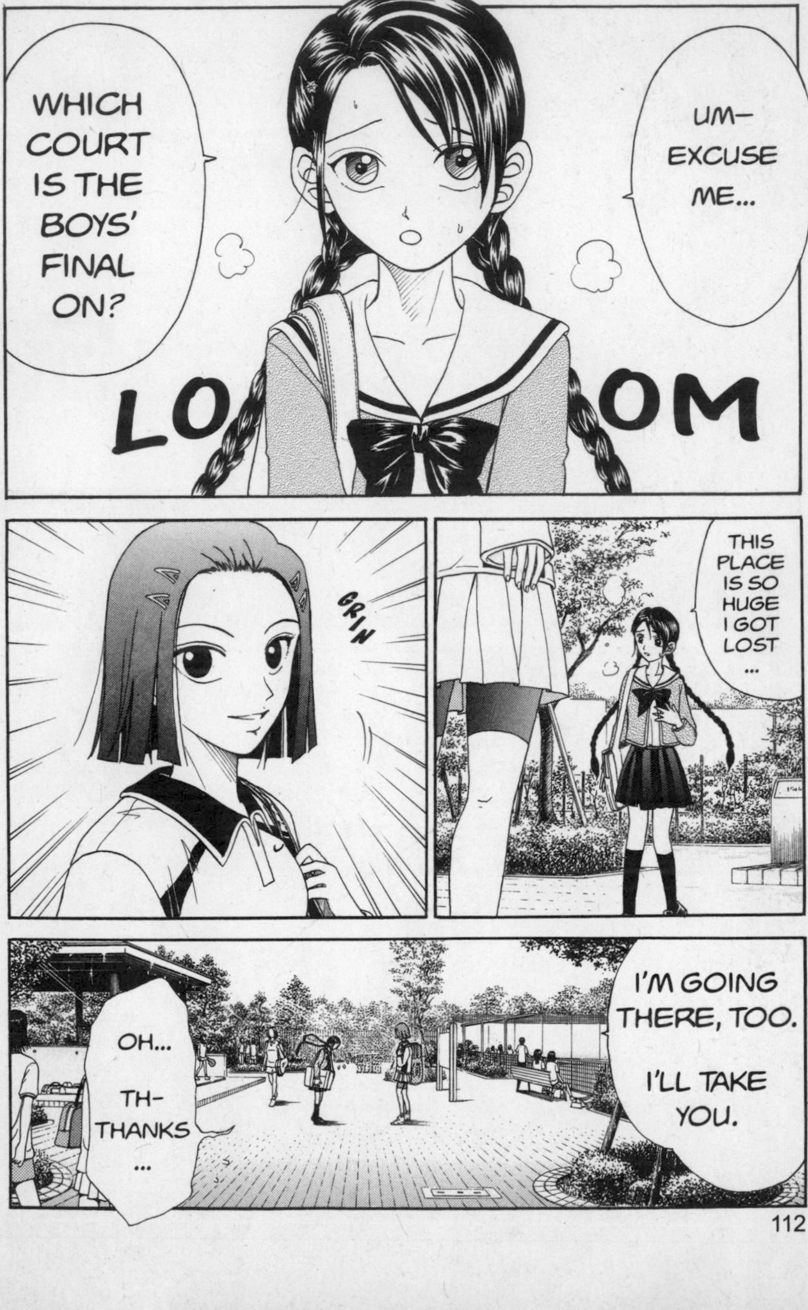
UM— EXCUSE ME...
WHICH COURT IS THE BOYS' FINAL ON?
LO OM
THIS PLACE IS SO HUGE I GOT LOST ...
GRIN
I'M GOING THERE, TOO.
I'LL TAKE YOU.
OH...
TH-THANKS ...

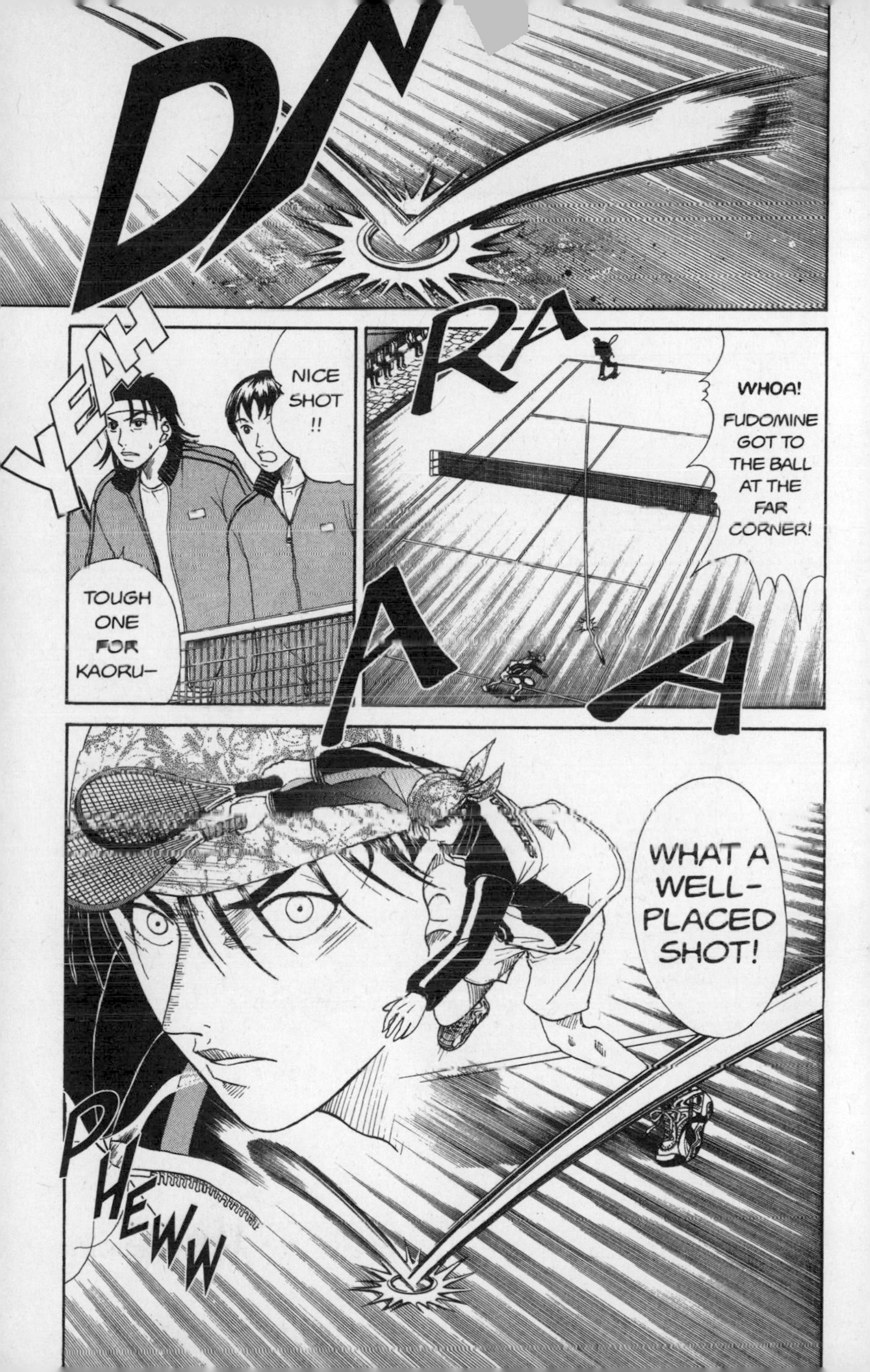
DN
WHOA!
FUDOMINE GOT TO THE BALL AT THE FAR CORNER!
RA A A
NICE SHOT !!
YEAH
TOUGH ONE FOR KAORU–
WHAT A WELL-PLACED SHOT!
PHEWW

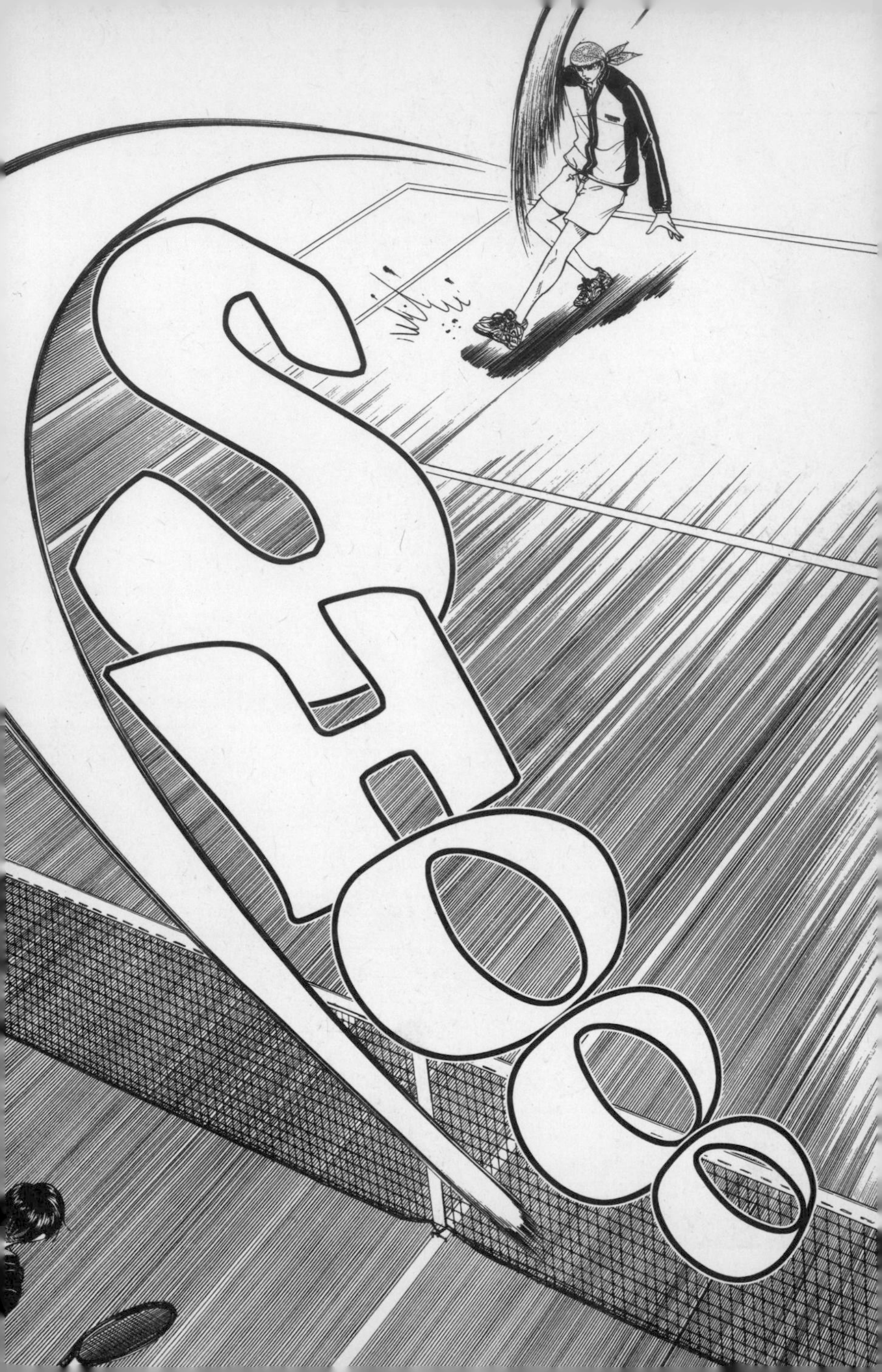
SHOOO

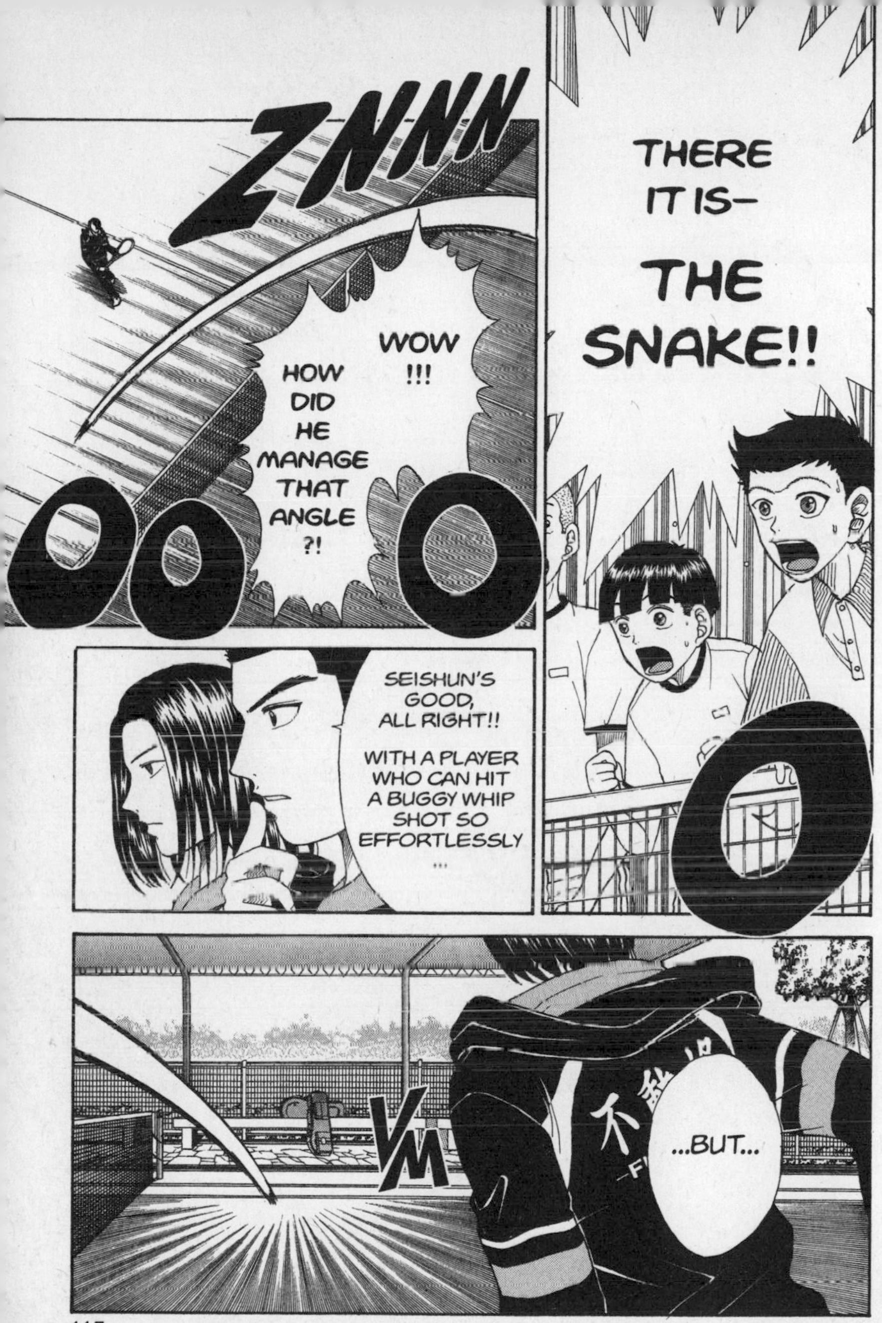
THERE IT IS—
THE SNAKE!!
O
ZNNNN
WOW!!!
HOW DID HE MANAGE THAT ANGLE?!
OOO
SEISHUN'S GOOD, ALL RIGHT!!
WITH A PLAYER WHO CAN HIT A BUGGY WHIP SHOT SO EFFORTLESSLY...
VM
...BUT...

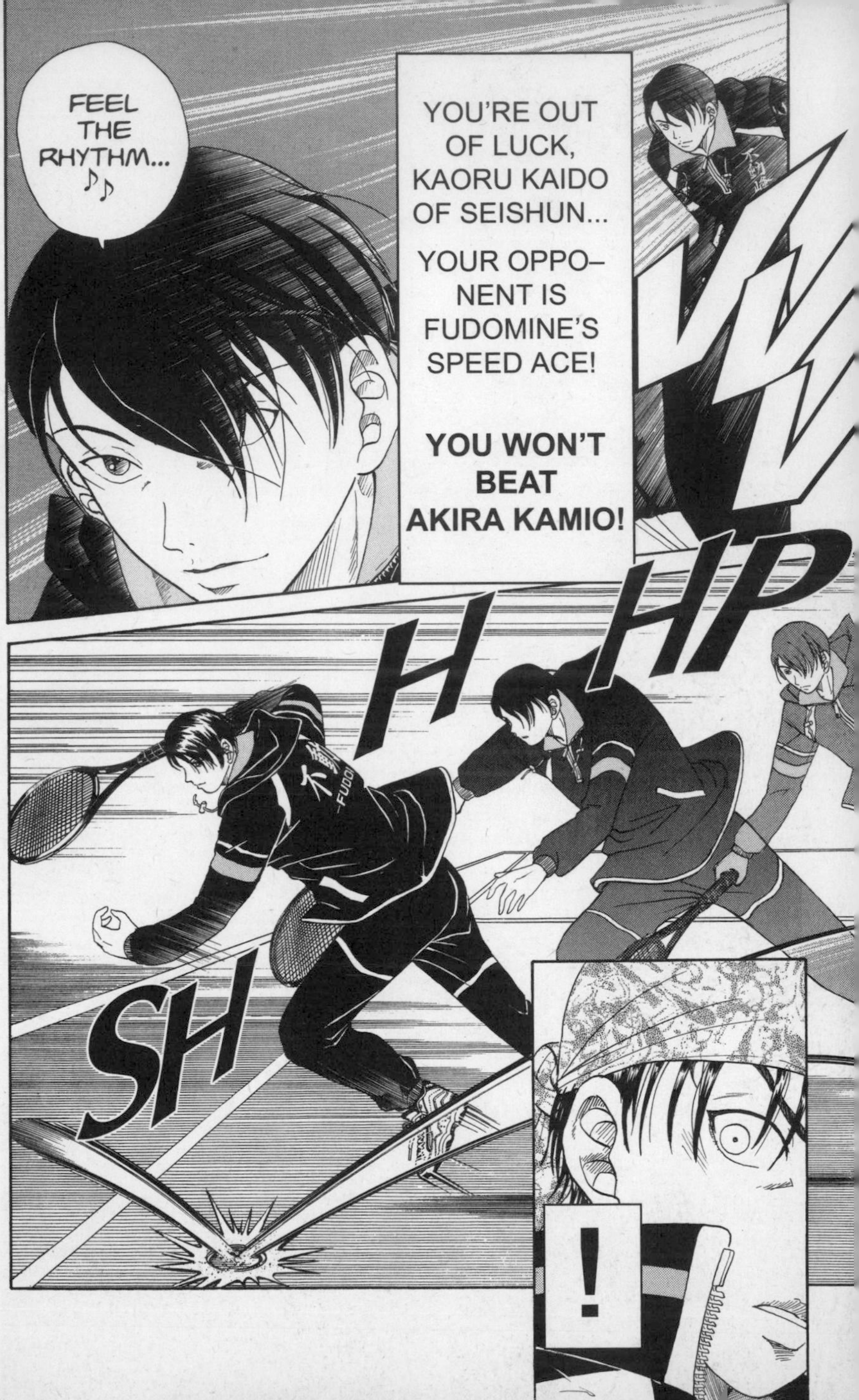
YOU'RE OUT OF LUCK, KAORU KAIDO OF SEISHUN...
YOUR OPPO–NENT IS FUDOMINE'S SPEED ACE!
YOU WON'T BEAT AKIRA KAMIO!
WHIP
FEEL THE RHYTHM... ♪♪
H
SH
!

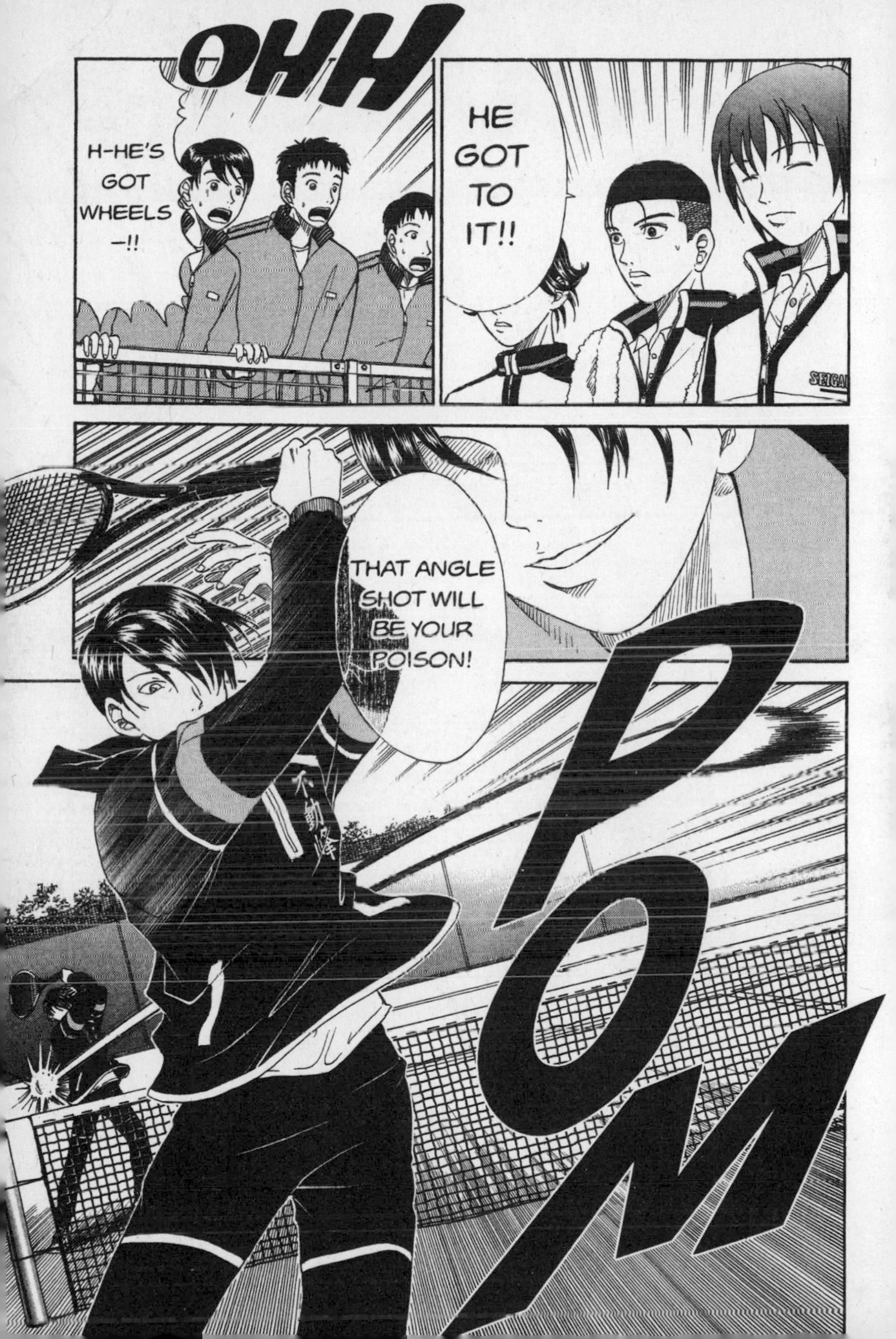
HE GOT TO IT!!
OHH
H-HE'S GOT WHEELS—!!
THAT ANGLE SHOT WILL BE YOUR POISON!
SEIGAKU
DOM

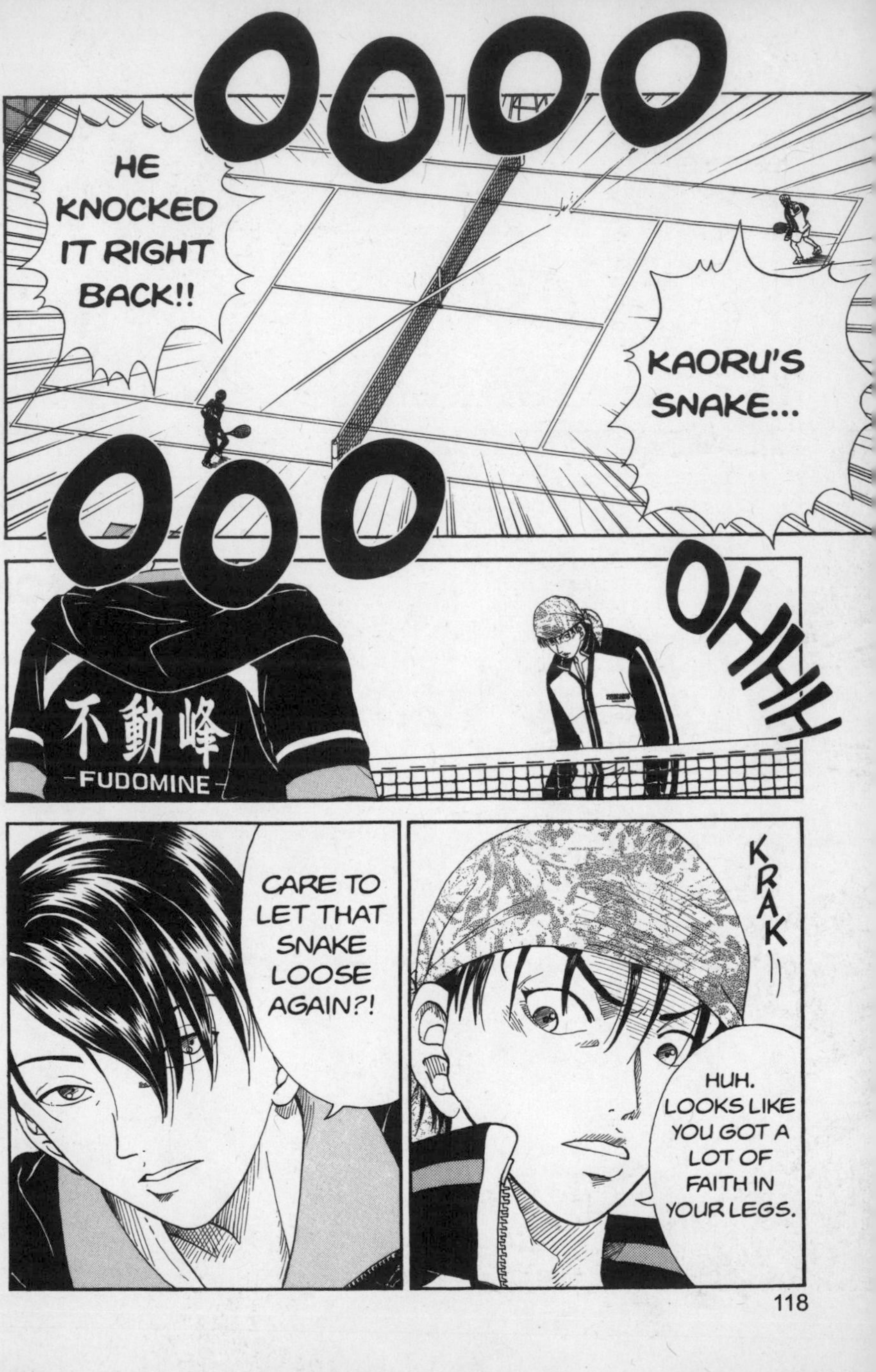
KAORU'S SNAKE...
HE KNOCKED IT RIGHT BACK!!
OOOO
OOO
OHHHH
不動峰
-FUDOMINE-
KRAK
HUH. LOOKS LIKE YOU GOT A LOT OF FAITH IN YOUR LEGS.
CARE TO LET THAT SNAKE LOOSE AGAIN?!

READ THIS WAY

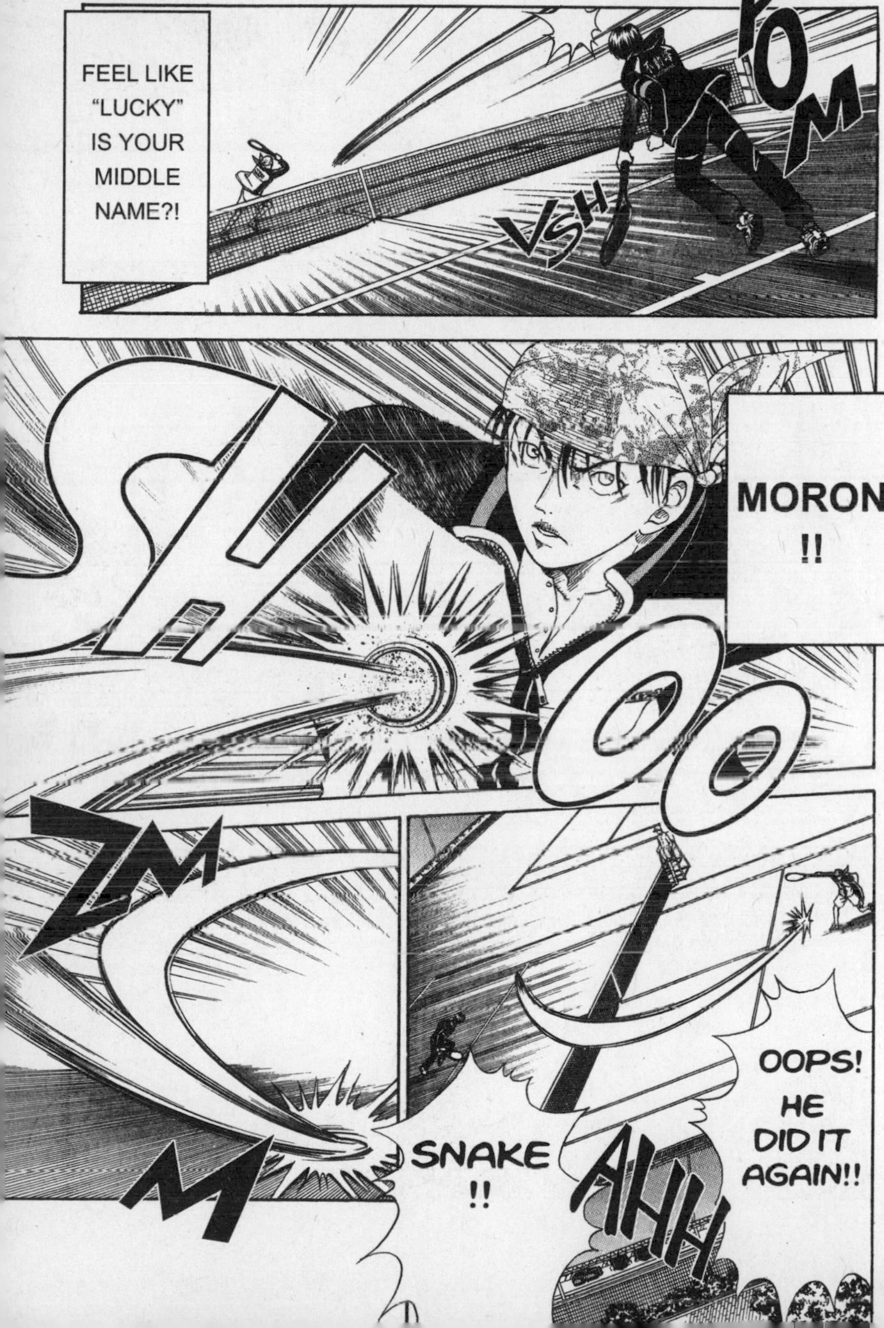
POM
VSH
FEEL LIKE "LUCKY" IS YOUR MIDDLE NAME?!
MORON !!
SHOO
OOPS! HE DID IT AGAIN!!
AHH
SNAKE !!
ZM
M

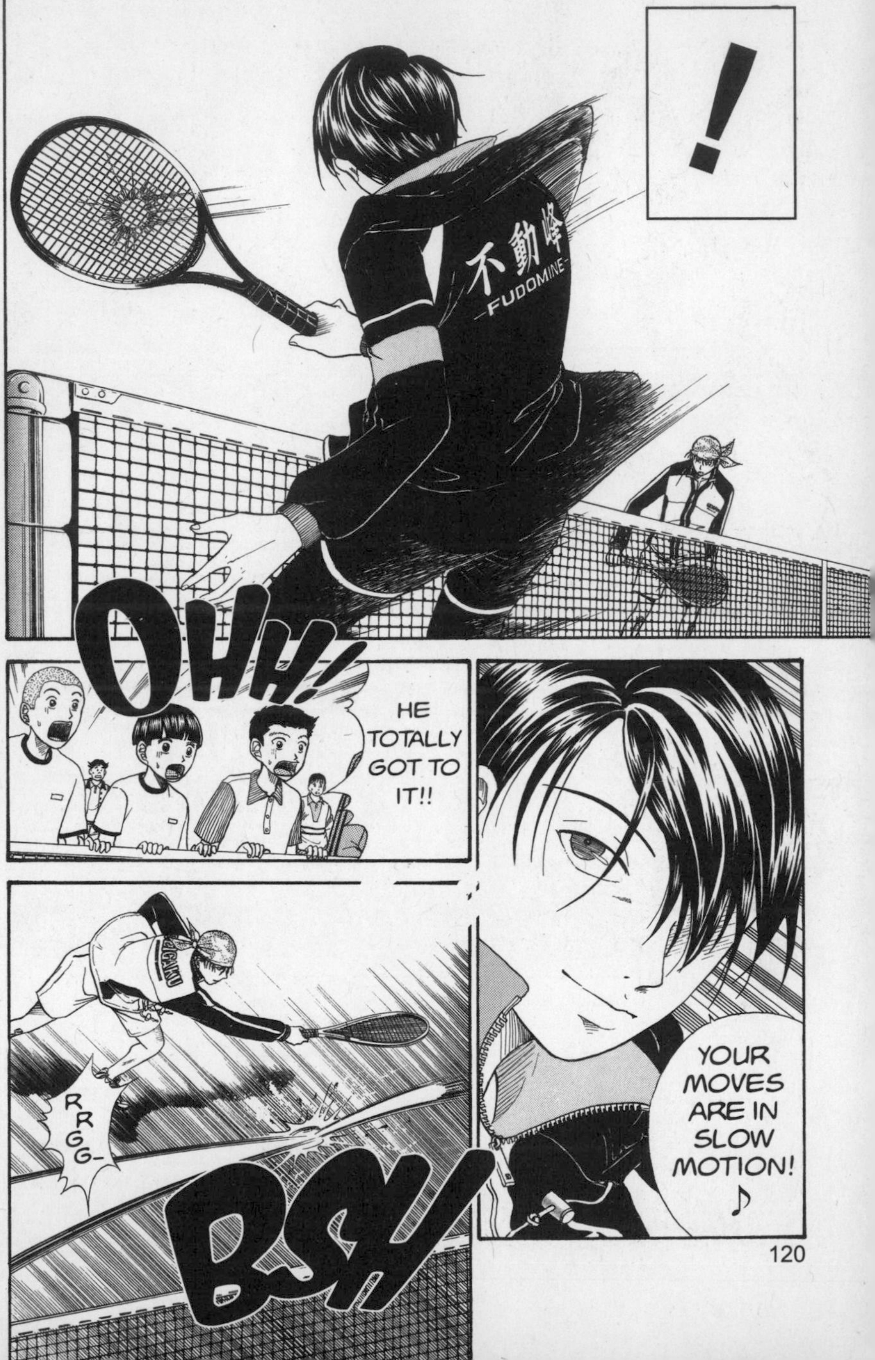
!
不動峰
-FUDOMINE-
OHH!!
YOUR MOVES ARE IN SLOW MOTION! ♪
HE TOTALLY GOT TO IT!!
RRGG-
BASH!

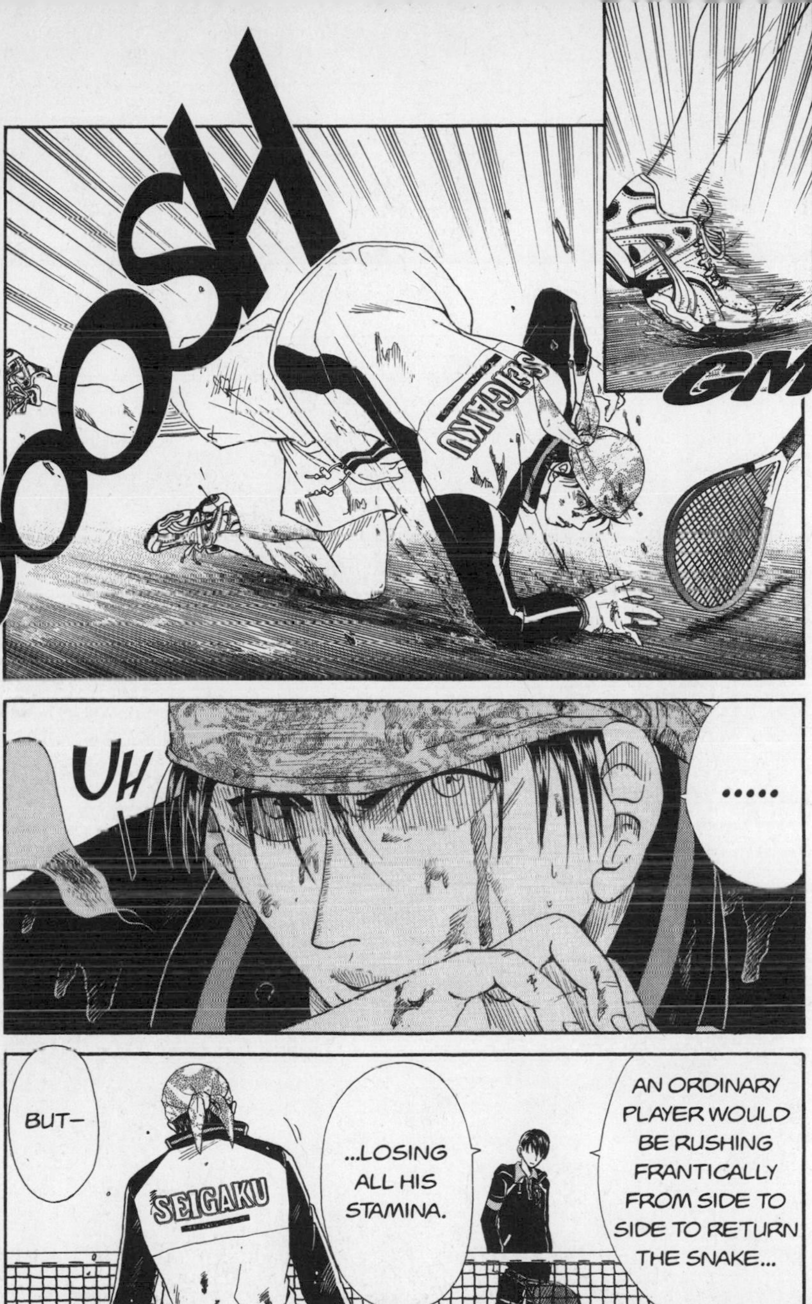
GM
DOOOSH
.....
UH
AN ORDINARY PLAYER WOULD BE RUSHING FRANTICALLY FROM SIDE TO SIDE TO RETURN THE SNAKE...
...LOSING ALL HIS STAMINA.
BUT—

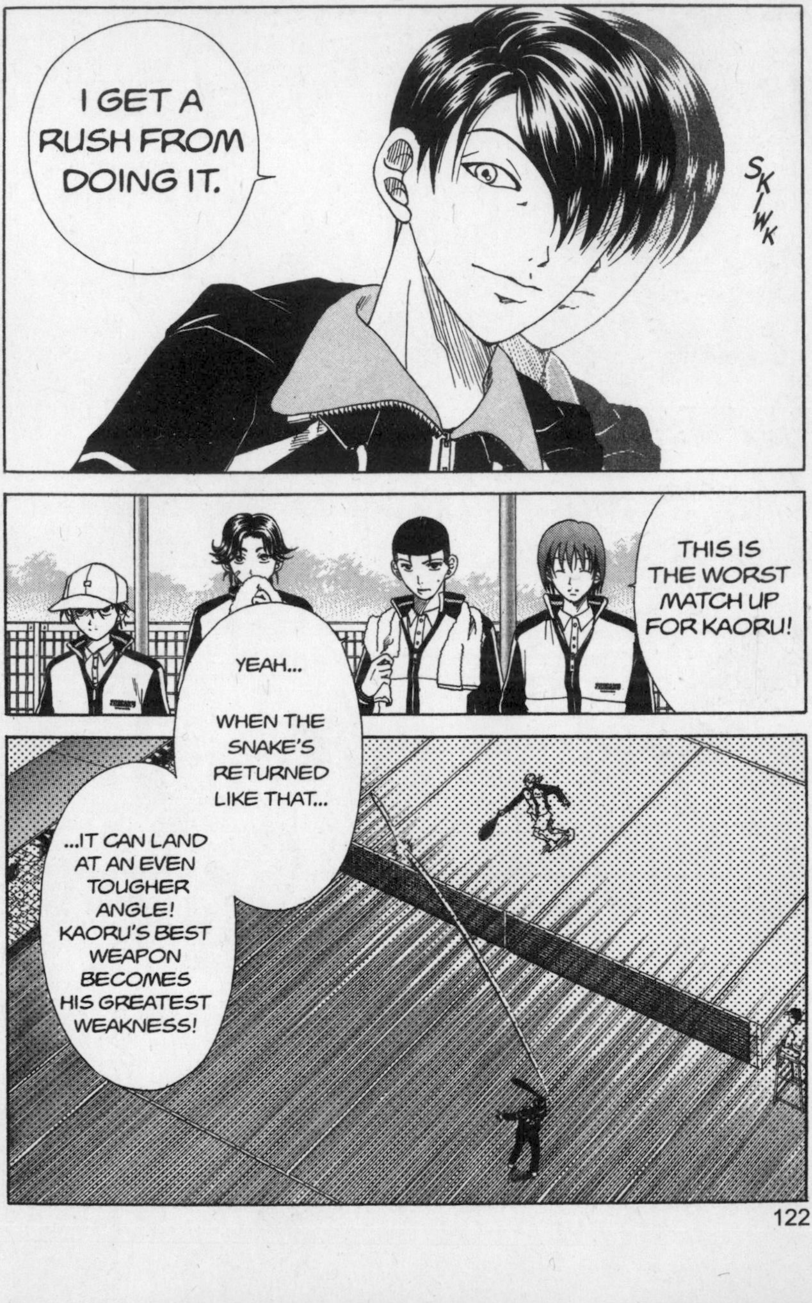
I GET A RUSH FROM DOING IT.
SKIWK
THIS IS THE WORST MATCH UP FOR KAORU!
YEAH...
WHEN THE SNAKE'S RETURNED LIKE THAT...
...IT CAN LAND AT AN EVEN TOUGHER ANGLE! KAORU'S BEST WEAPON BECOMES HIS GREATEST WEAKNESS!

READ THIS WAY

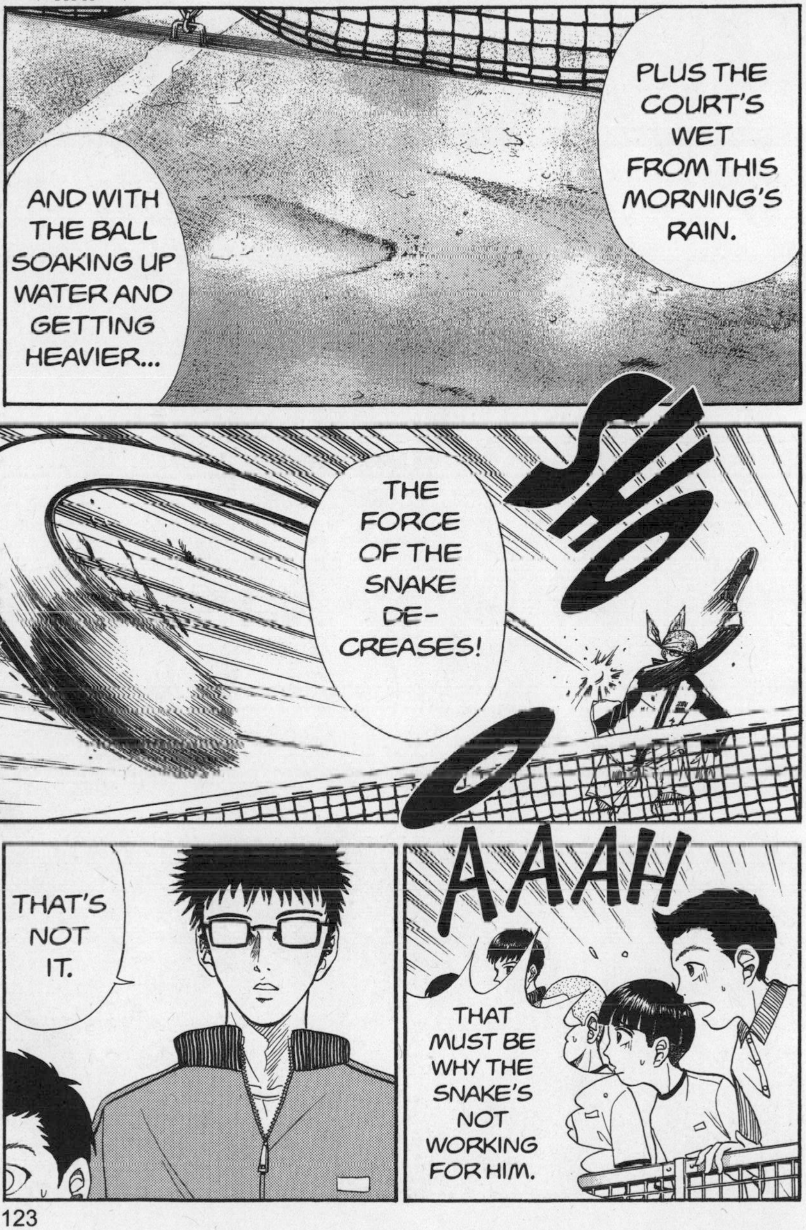

PLUS THE COURT'S WET FROM THIS MORNING'S RAIN.
AND WITH THE BALL SOAKING UP WATER AND GETTING HEAVIER...
SHOO
THE FORCE OF THE SNAKE DE-CREASES!
AAAH
THAT MUST BE WHY THE SNAKE'S NOT WORKING FOR HIM.
THAT'S NOT IT.

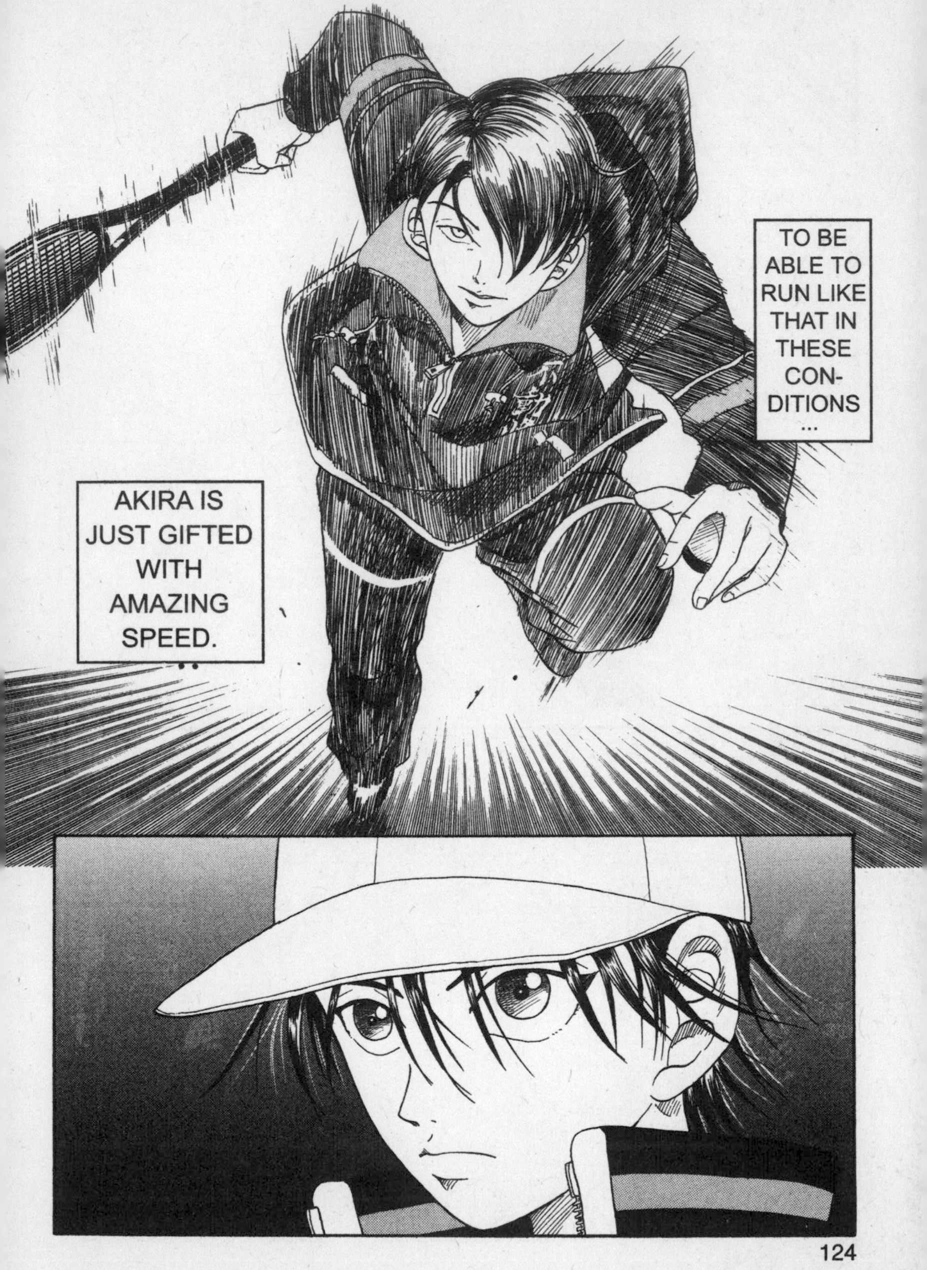
TO BE ABLE TO RUN LIKE THAT IN THESE CON-DITIONS ...
AKIRA IS JUST GIFTED WITH AMAZING SPEED.

READ THIS WAY

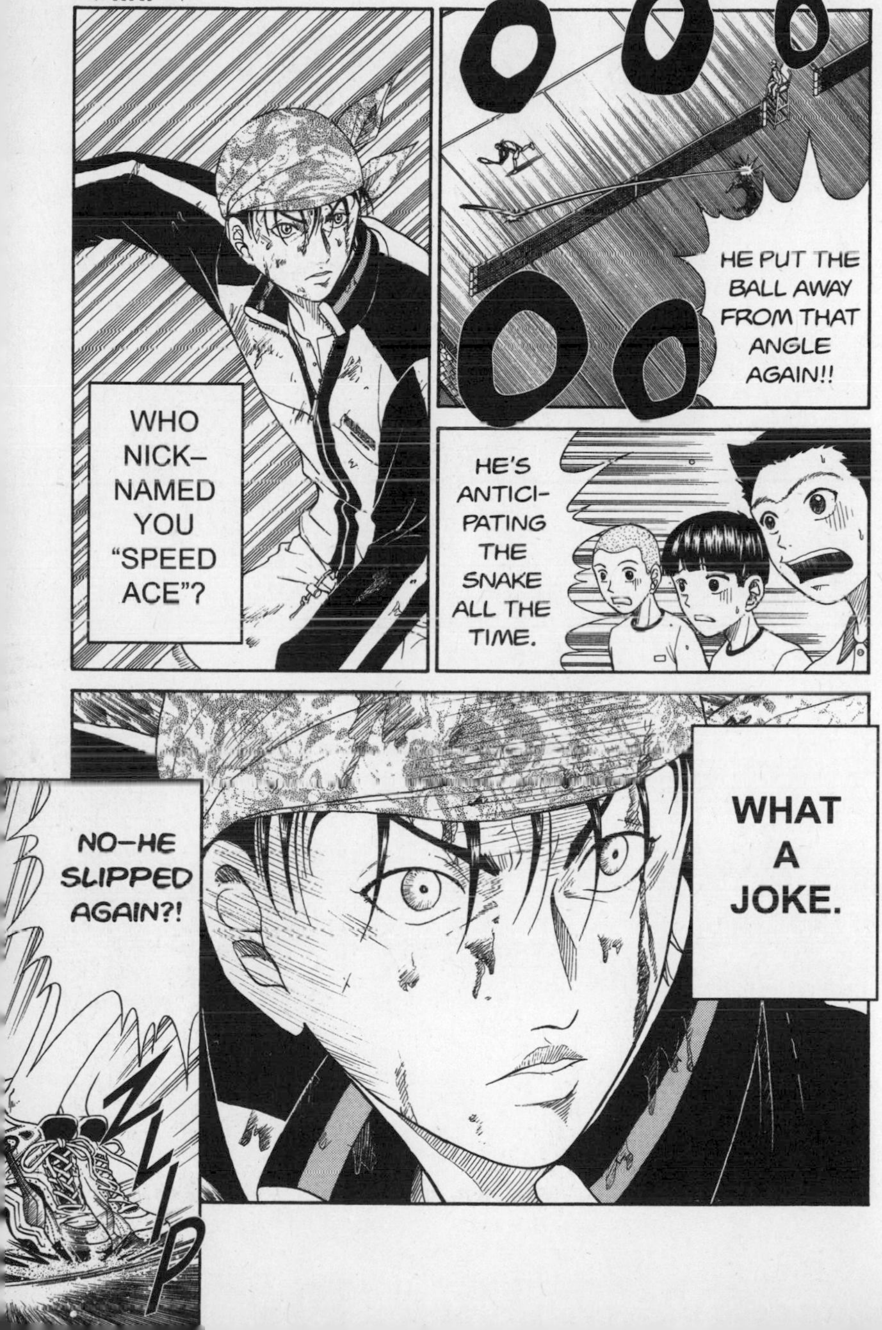
HE PUT THE BALL AWAY FROM THAT ANGLE AGAIN!!
HE'S ANTICIPATING THE SNAKE ALL THE TIME.
WHO NICKNAMED YOU "SPEED ACE"?
WHAT A JOKE.
NO—HE SLIPPED AGAIN?!
ZLIP

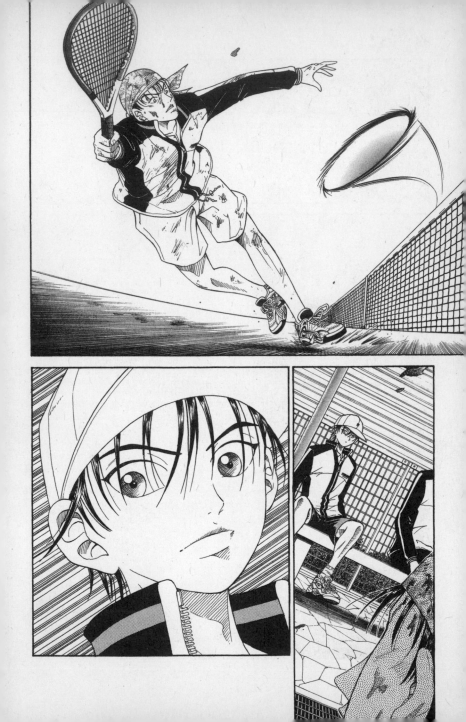

READ THIS WAY

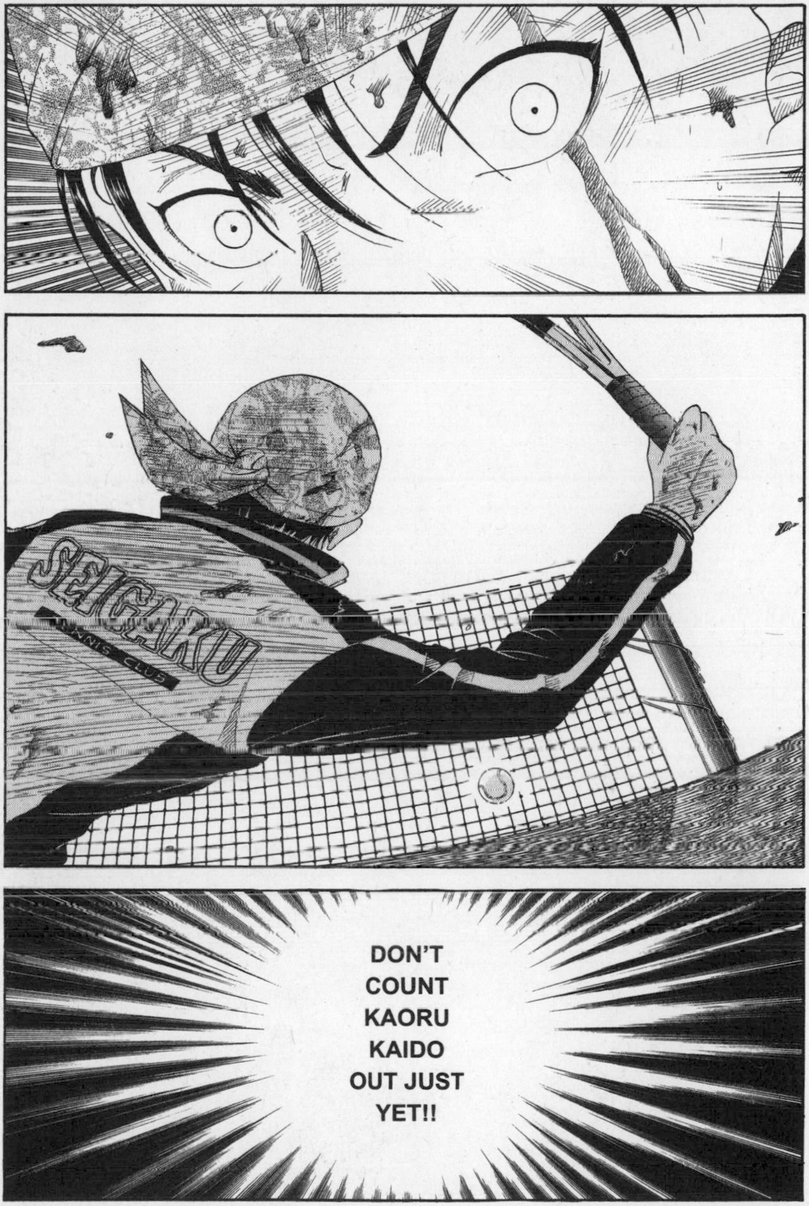
SEIGAKU
DON'T COUNT KAORU KAIDO OUT JUST YET!!

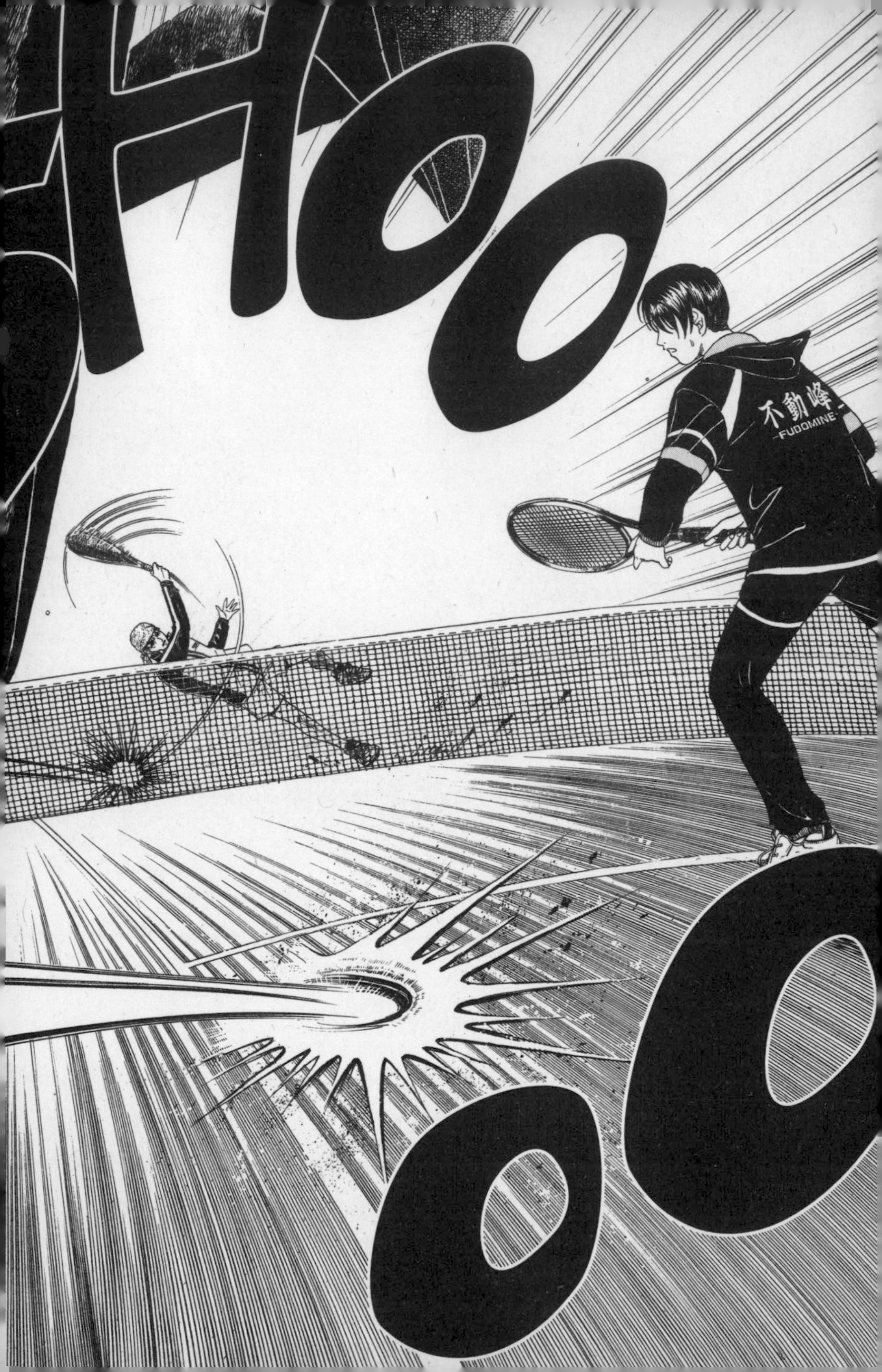

不動峰
FUDOMINE

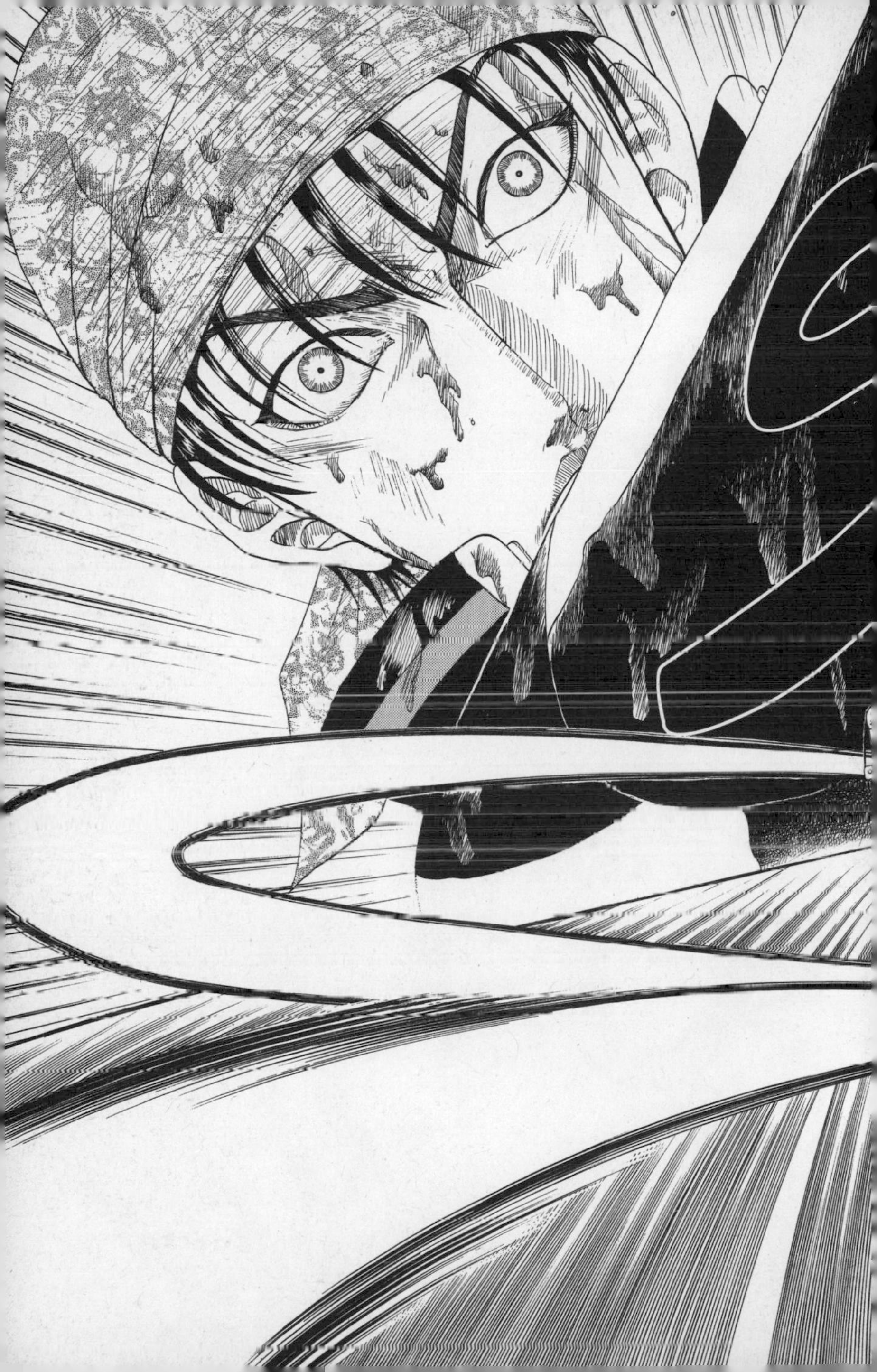

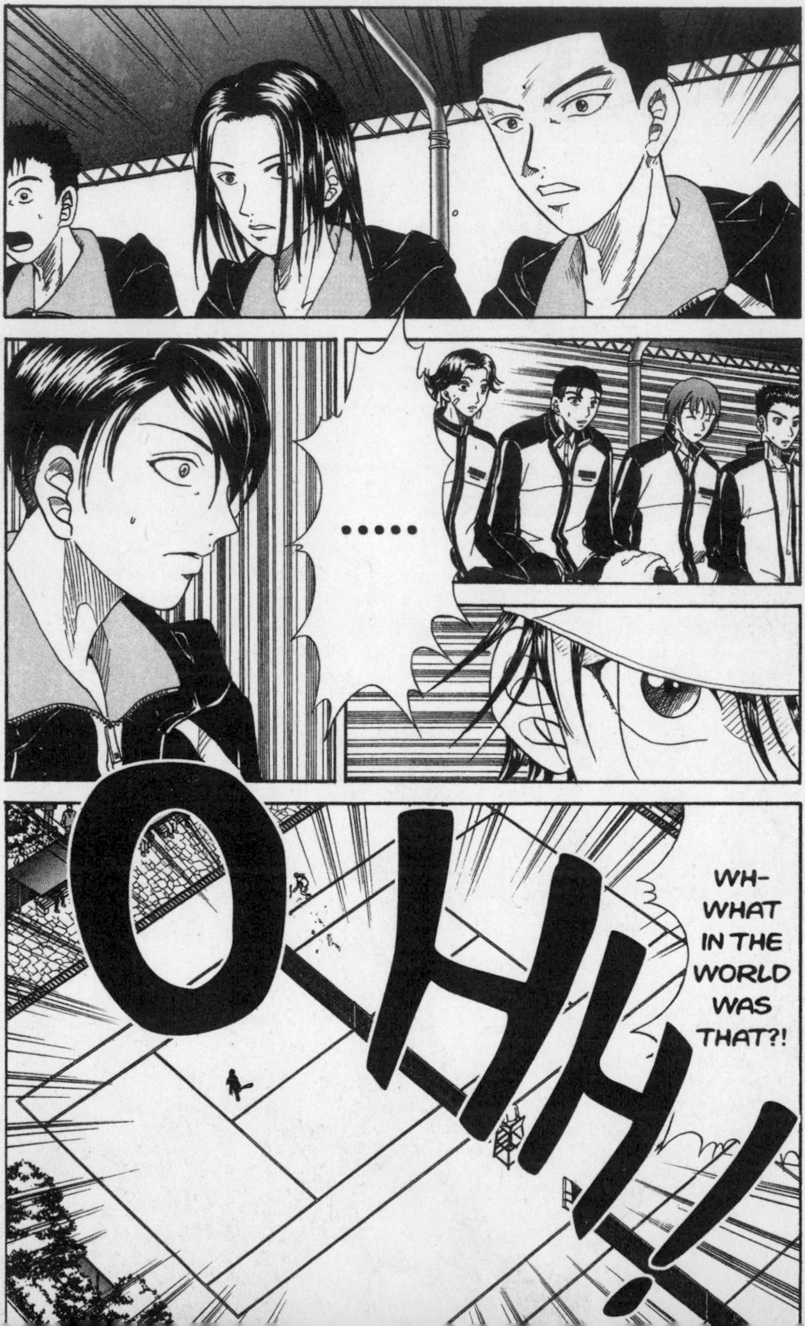
.....
WH-WHAT IN THE WORLD WAS THAT?!
O-HH!

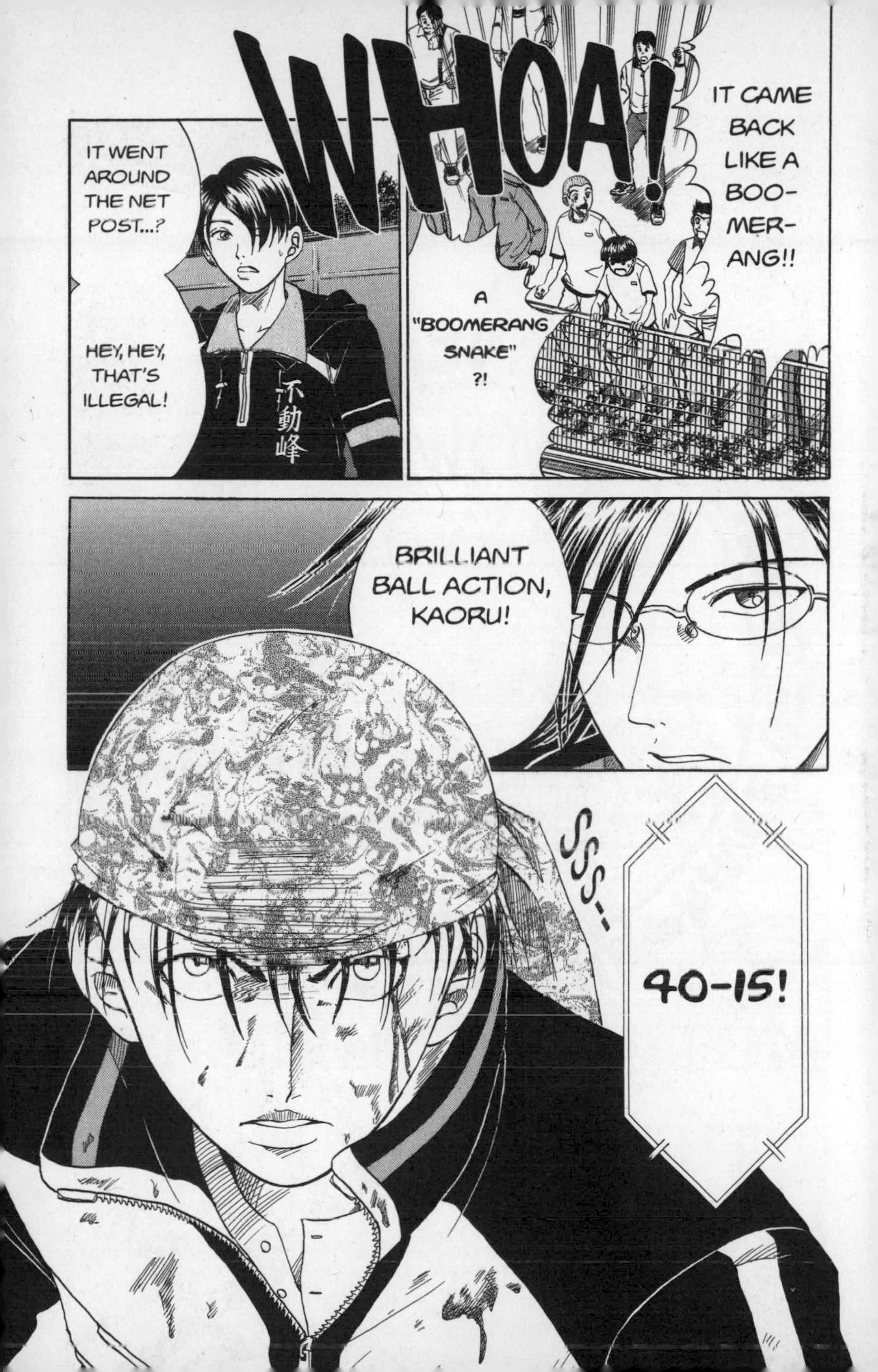
WHOA!
IT CAME BACK LIKE A BOO-MER-ANG!!
A "BOOMERANG SNAKE" ?!
IT WENT AROUND THE NET POST...?
HEY, HEY, THAT'S ILLEGAL!
不動峰
BRILLIANT BALL ACTION, KAORU!
SSS--
40-15!

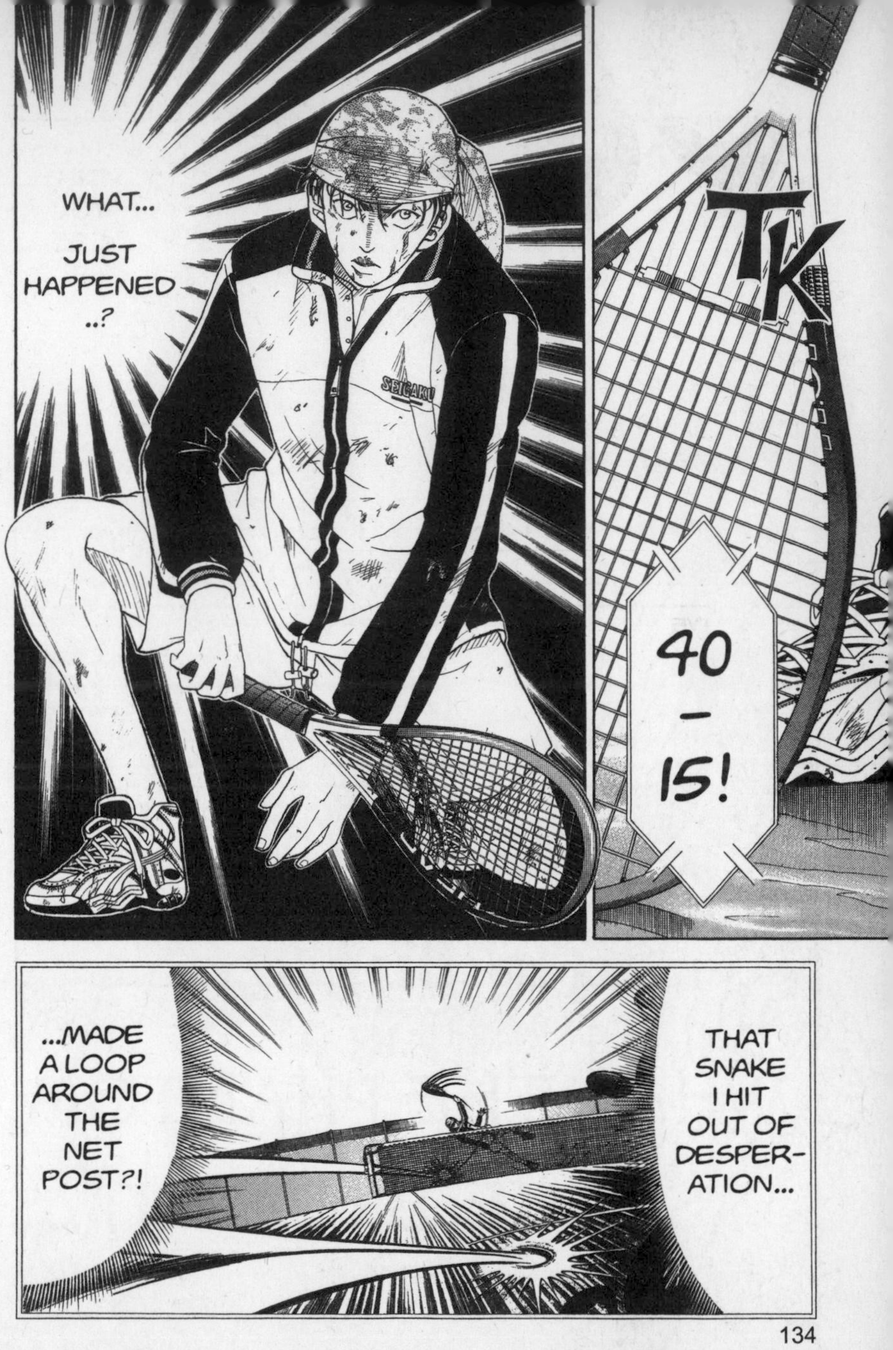
TK
40 – 15!
WHAT... JUST HAPPENED ..?
THAT SNAKE I HIT OUT OF DESPER-ATION...
...MADE A LOOP AROUND THE NET POST?!

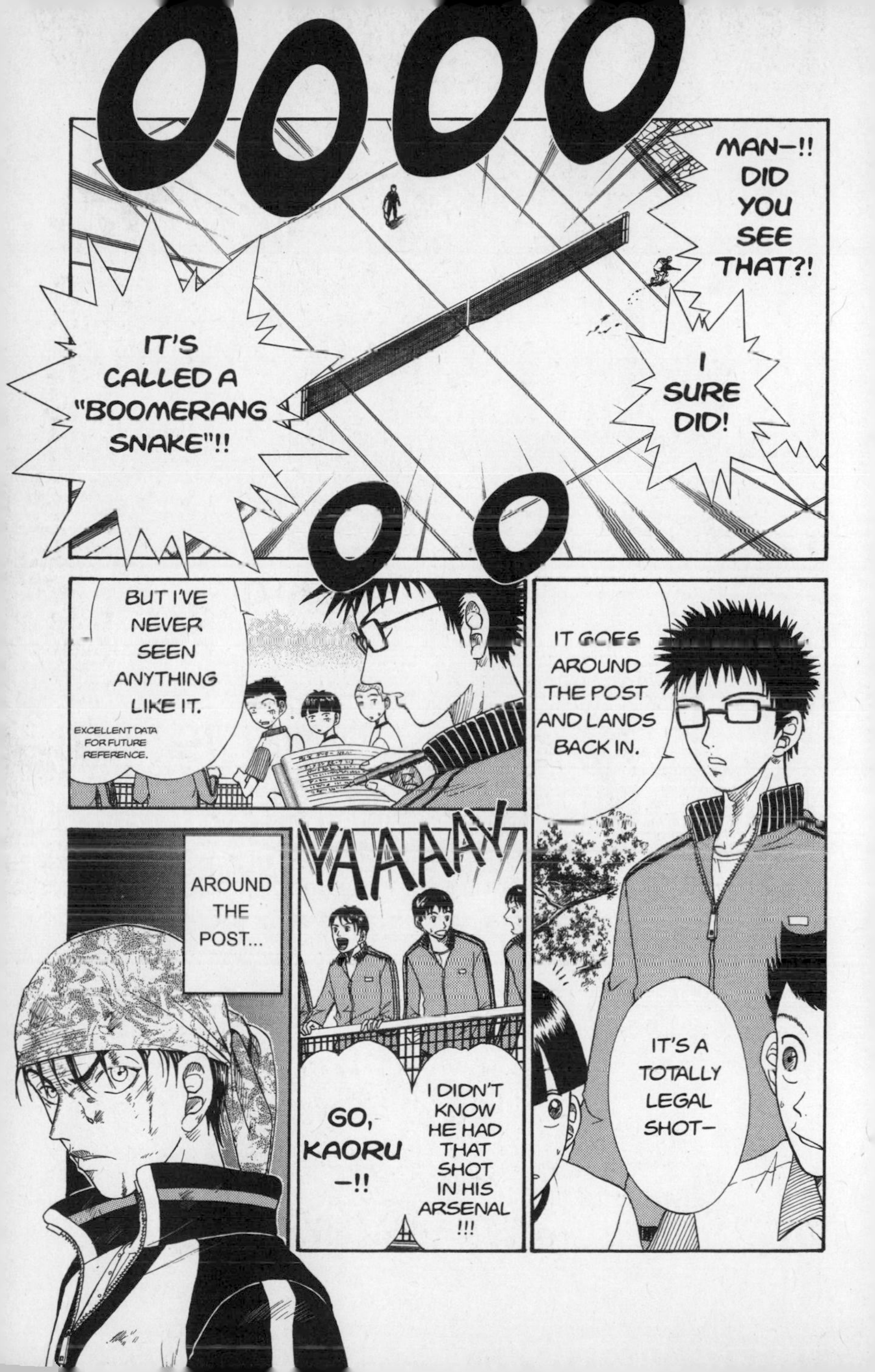
OOOO
MAN—!! DID YOU SEE THAT?!
I SURE DID!
IT'S CALLED A "BOOMERANG SNAKE"!!
OO
IT GOES AROUND THE POST AND LANDS BACK IN.
IT'S A TOTALLY LEGAL SHOT—
BUT I'VE NEVER SEEN ANYTHING LIKE IT.
EXCELLENT DATA FOR FUTURE REFERENCE.
YAAAAY
I DIDN'T KNOW HE HAD THAT SHOT IN HIS ARSENAL!!!
GO, KAORU—!!
AROUND THE POST...

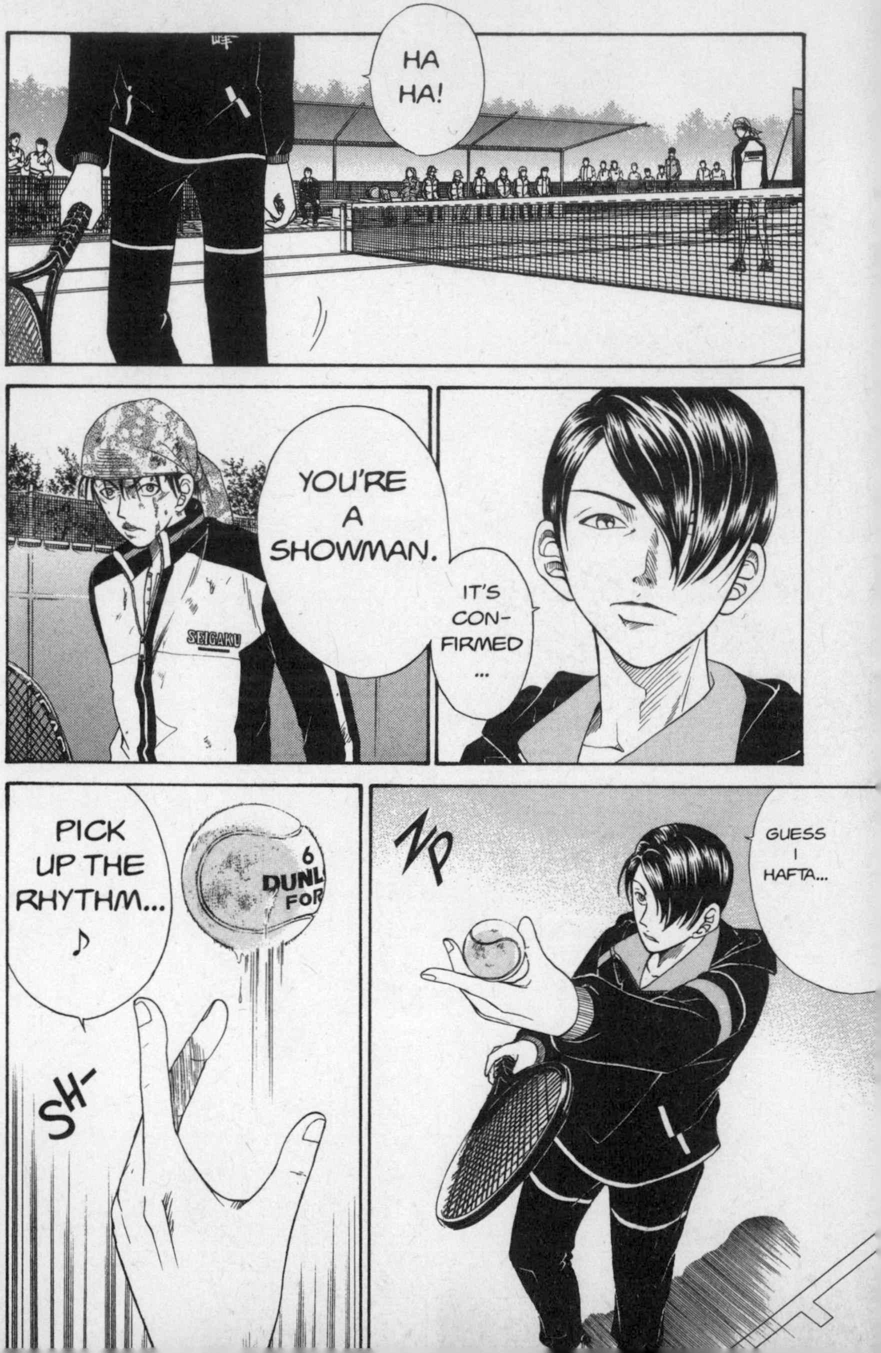
HA HA!
IT'S CONFIRMED...
YOU'RE A SHOWMAN.
GUESS I HAFTA...
PICK UP THE RHYTHM... ♪
SH-

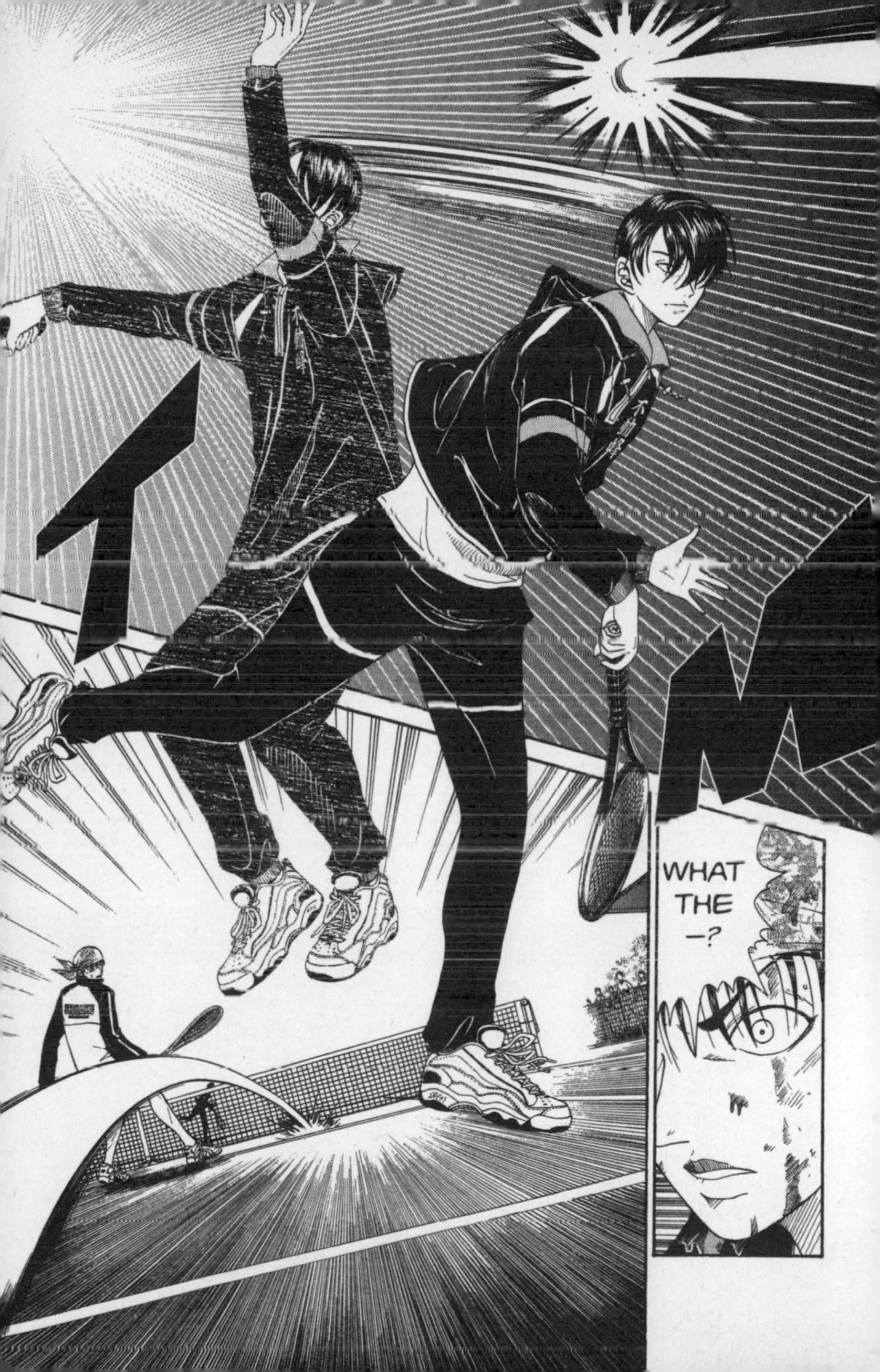
WHAT THE —?

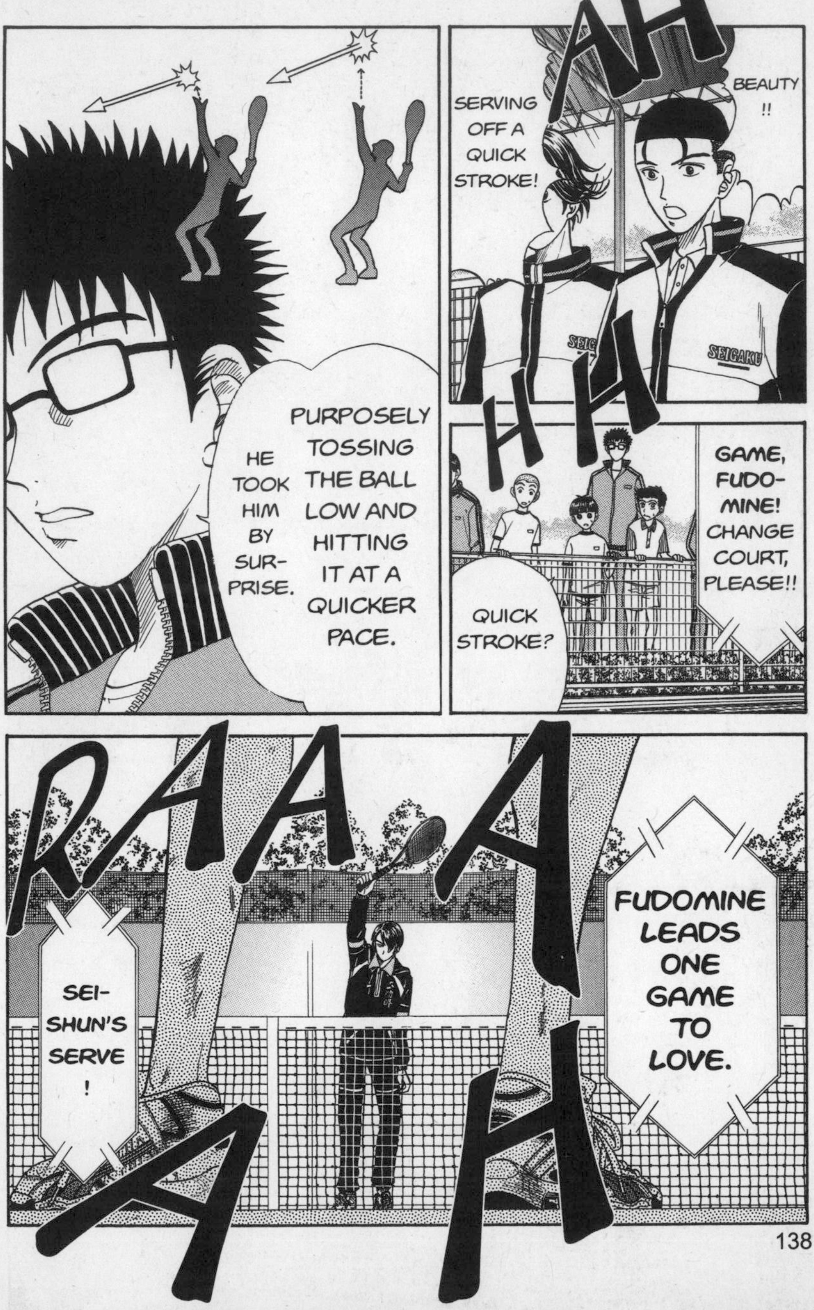
AHHHH
BEAUTY !!
SERVING OFF A QUICK STROKE!
GAME, FUDOMINE! CHANGE COURT, PLEASE!!
QUICK STROKE?
PURPOSELY TOSSING THE BALL LOW AND HITTING IT AT A QUICKER PACE.
HE TOOK HIM BY SURPRISE.
FUDOMINE LEADS ONE GAME TO LOVE.
RAAAAH
SEISHUN'S SERVE !

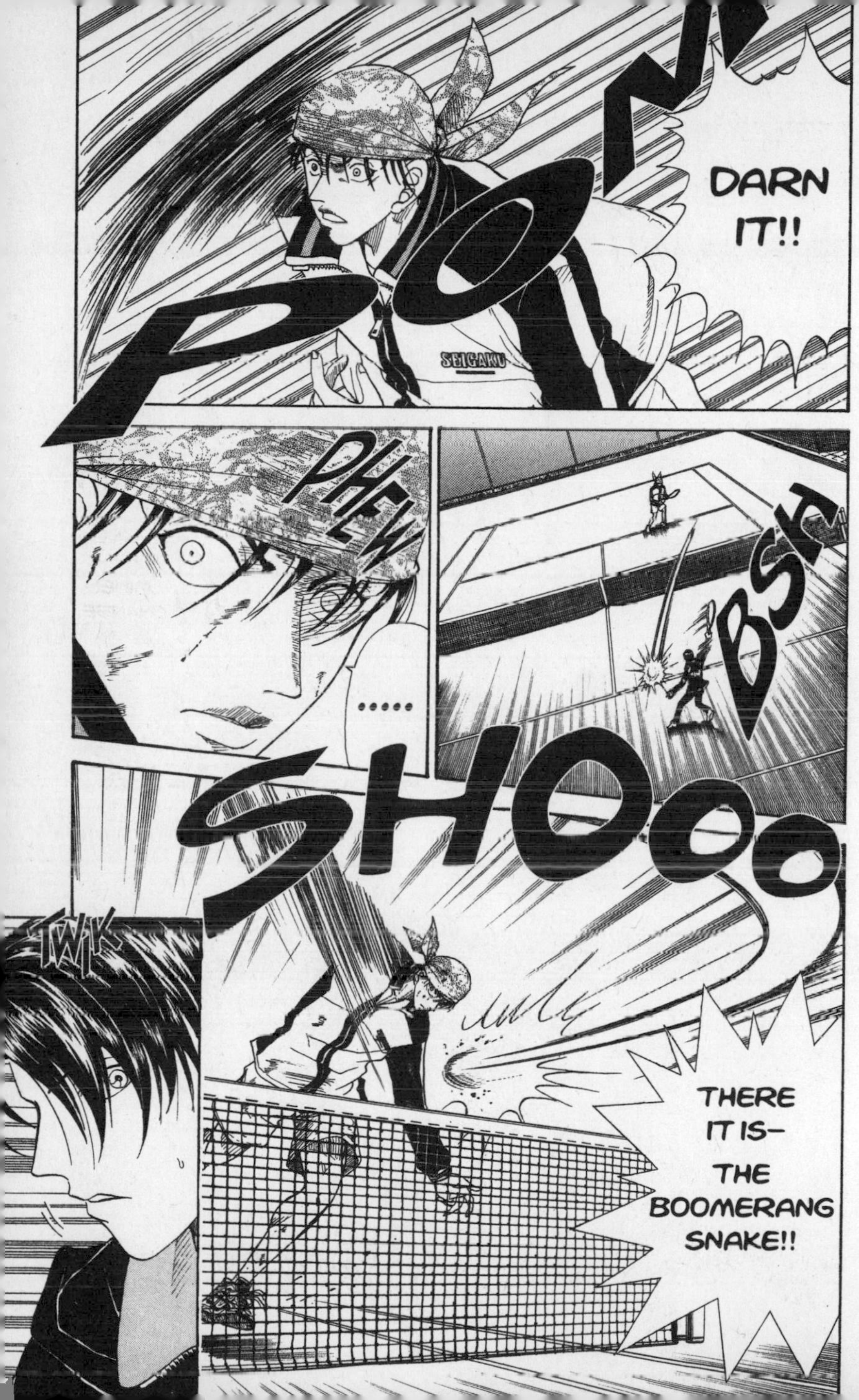
DARN IT!!
BSH
PHEW
......
SHOOO
TWIK
THERE IT IS— THE BOOMERANG SNAKE!!

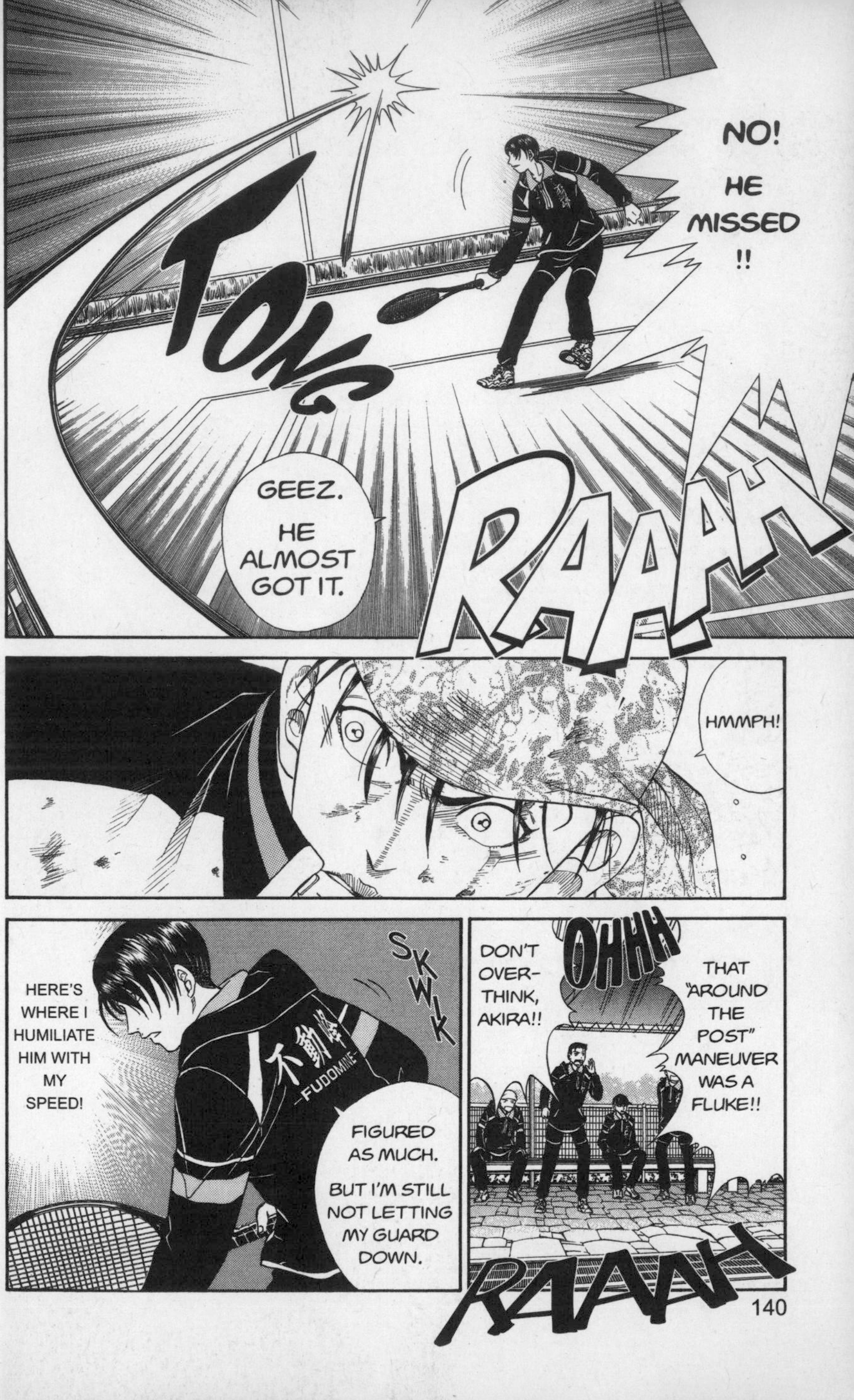
NO! HE MISSED !!
TONG
GEEZ. HE ALMOST GOT IT.
RAAAH
HMMPH!
THAT "AROUND THE POST" MANEUVER WAS A FLUKE!!
OHHH
DON'T OVER-THINK, AKIRA!!
RAAAH
SKWIK
HERE'S WHERE I HUMILIATE HIM WITH MY SPEED!
FIGURED AS MUCH.
BUT I'M STILL NOT LETTING MY GUARD DOWN.

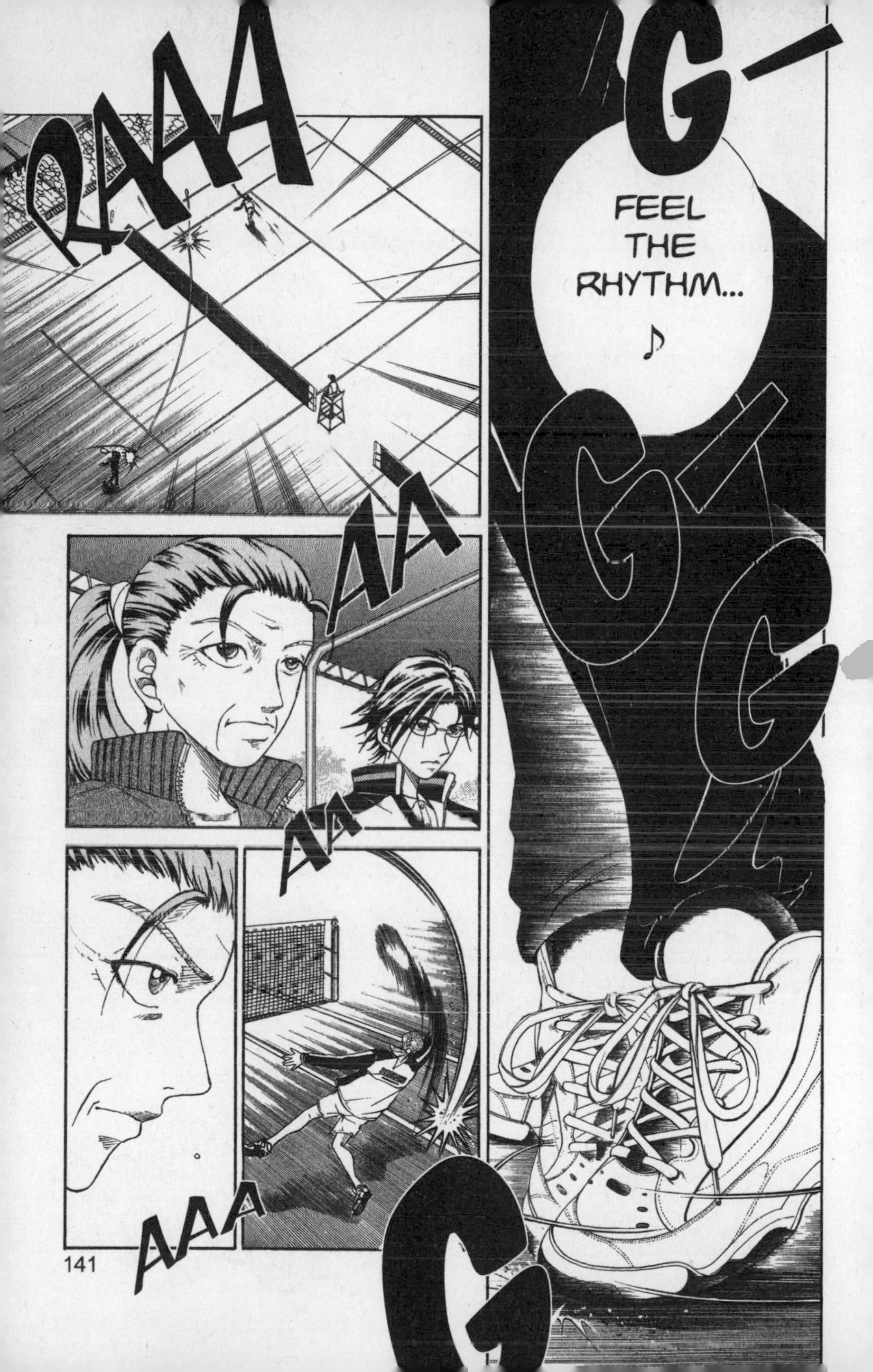
G-
FEEL THE RHYTHM... ♪
GGG
G
RAAA
AA
AA
AAA

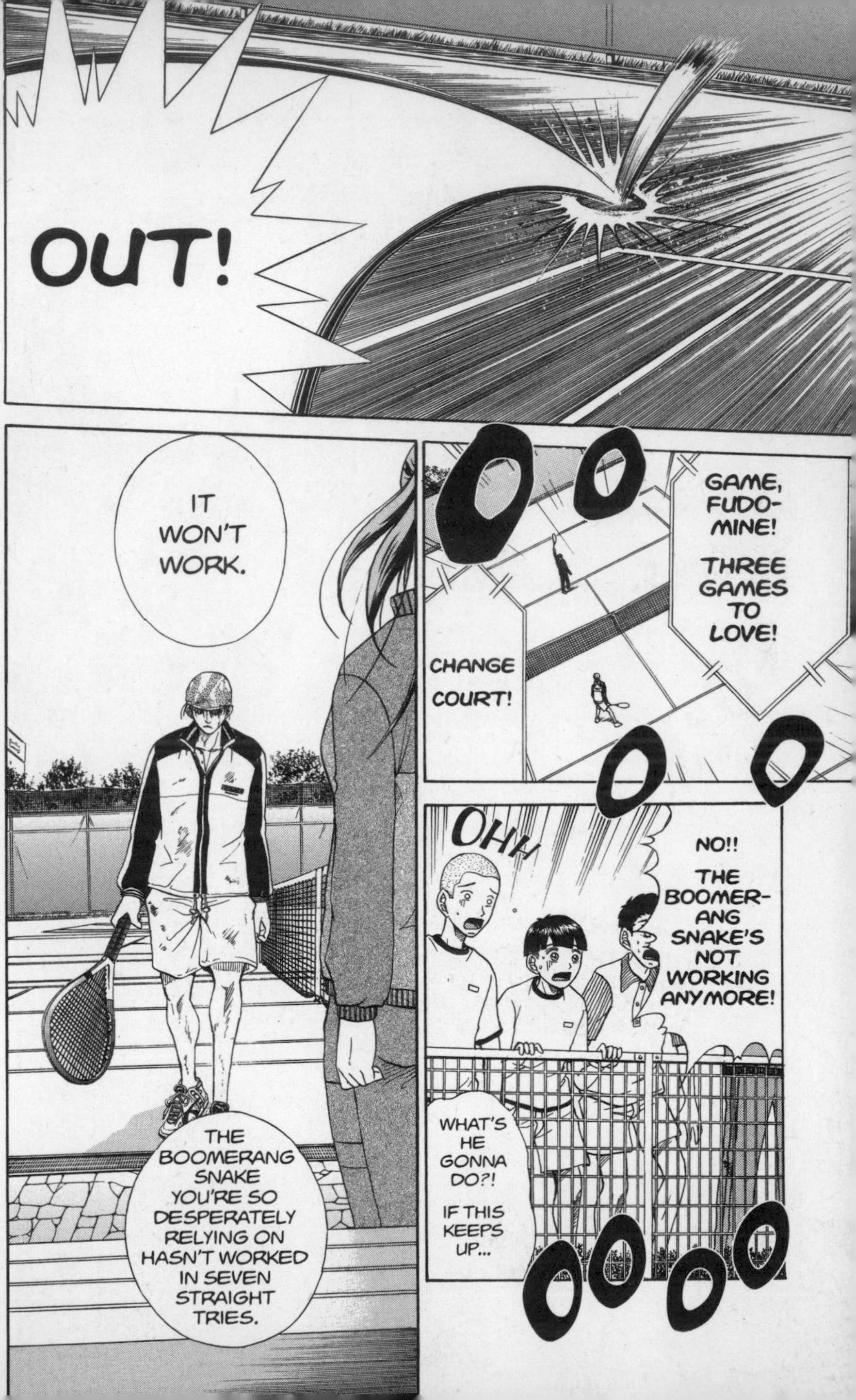
OUT!
GAME, FUDO-MINE!
THREE GAMES TO LOVE!
CHANGE COURT!
OHH
NO!!
THE BOOMER-ANG SNAKE'S NOT WORKING ANYMORE!
WHAT'S HE GONNA DO?!
IF THIS KEEPS UP...
IT WON'T WORK.
THE BOOMERANG SNAKE YOU'RE SO DESPERATELY RELYING ON HASN'T WORKED IN SEVEN STRAIGHT TRIES.

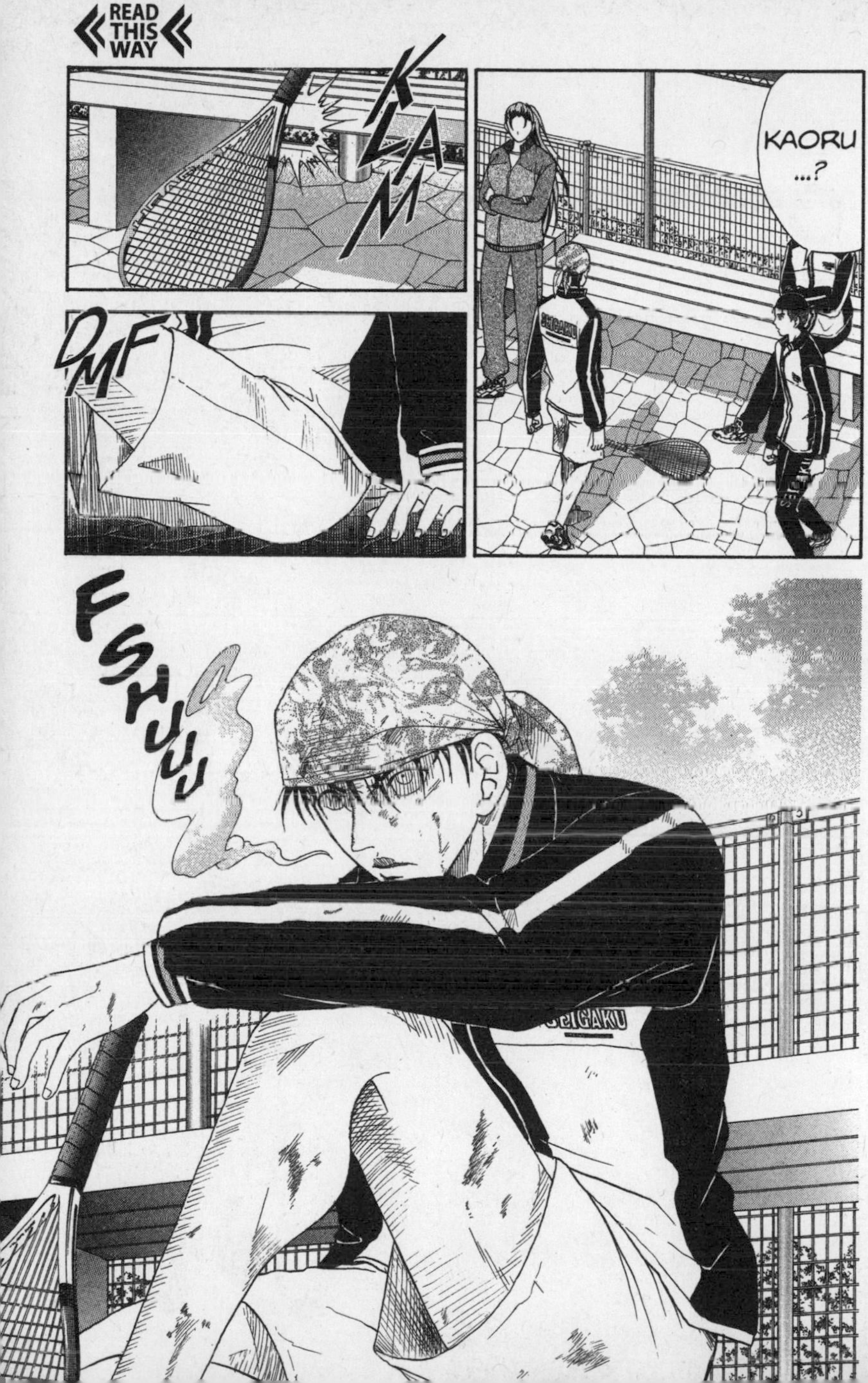
READ THIS WAY
KAORU ...?
KLAM
DMF
FSHUUU

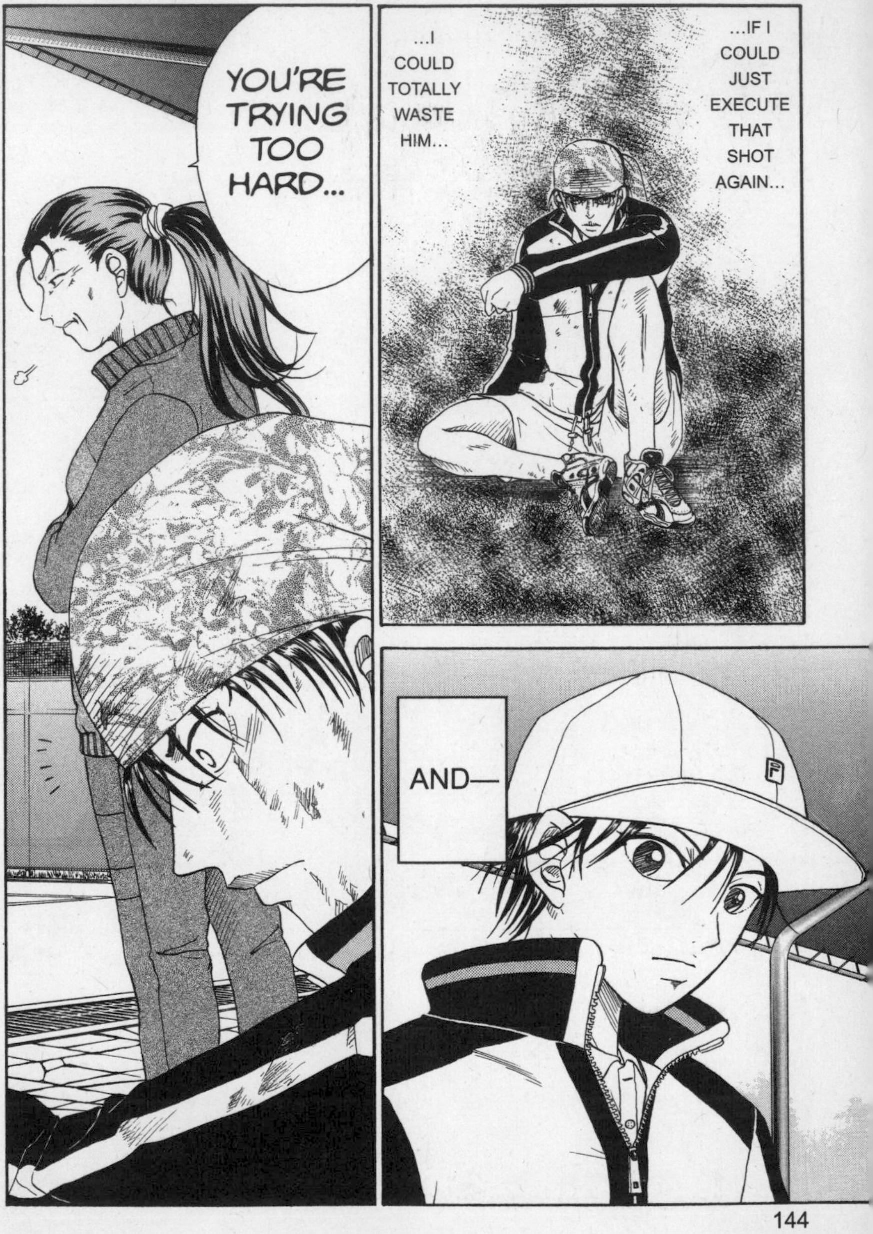
...IF I COULD JUST EXECUTE THAT SHOT AGAIN...
...I COULD TOTALLY WASTE HIM...
AND—
YOU'RE TRYING TOO HARD...

READ THIS WAY

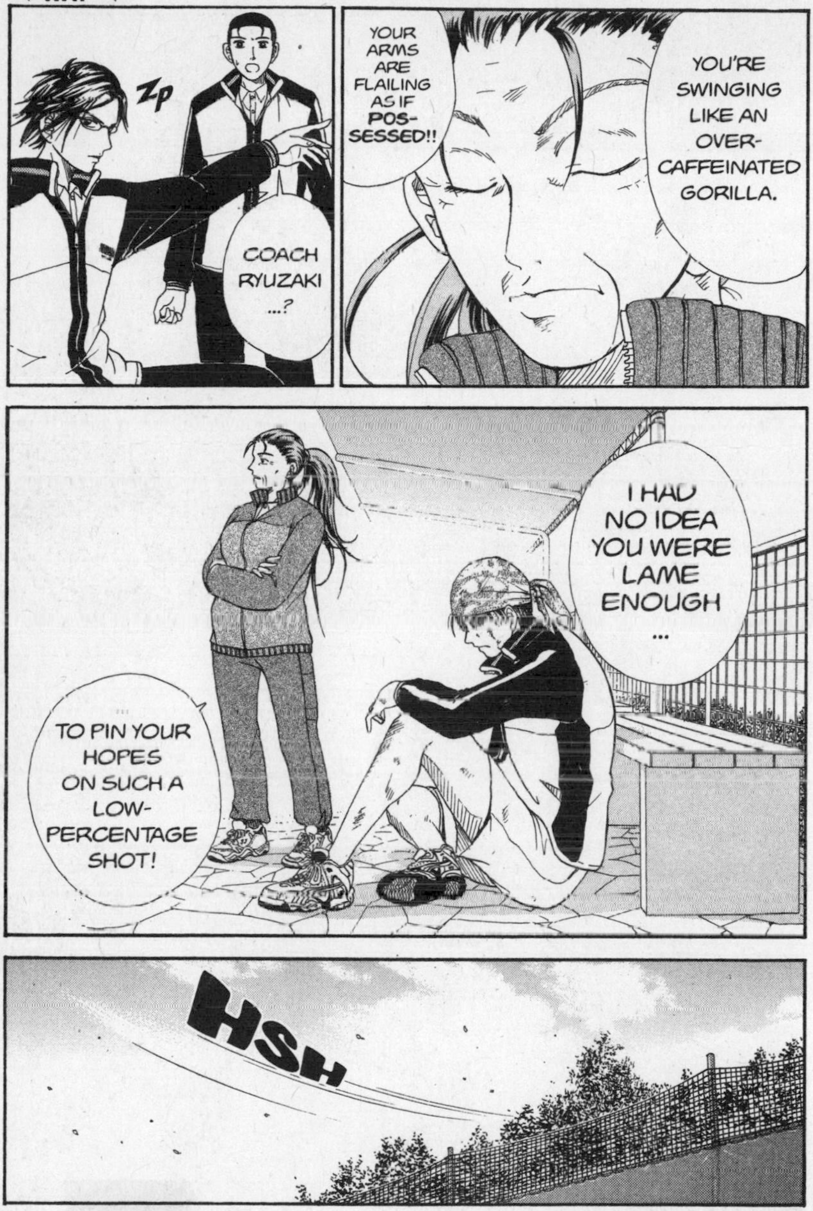

YOU'RE SWINGING LIKE AN OVER-CAFFEINATED GORILLA.
YOUR ARMS ARE FLAILING AS IF POS-SESSED!!
Zp
COACH RYUZAKI ...?
I HAD NO IDEA YOU WERE LAME ENOUGH ...
... TO PIN YOUR HOPES ON SUCH A LOW-PERCENTAGE SHOT!
HSH

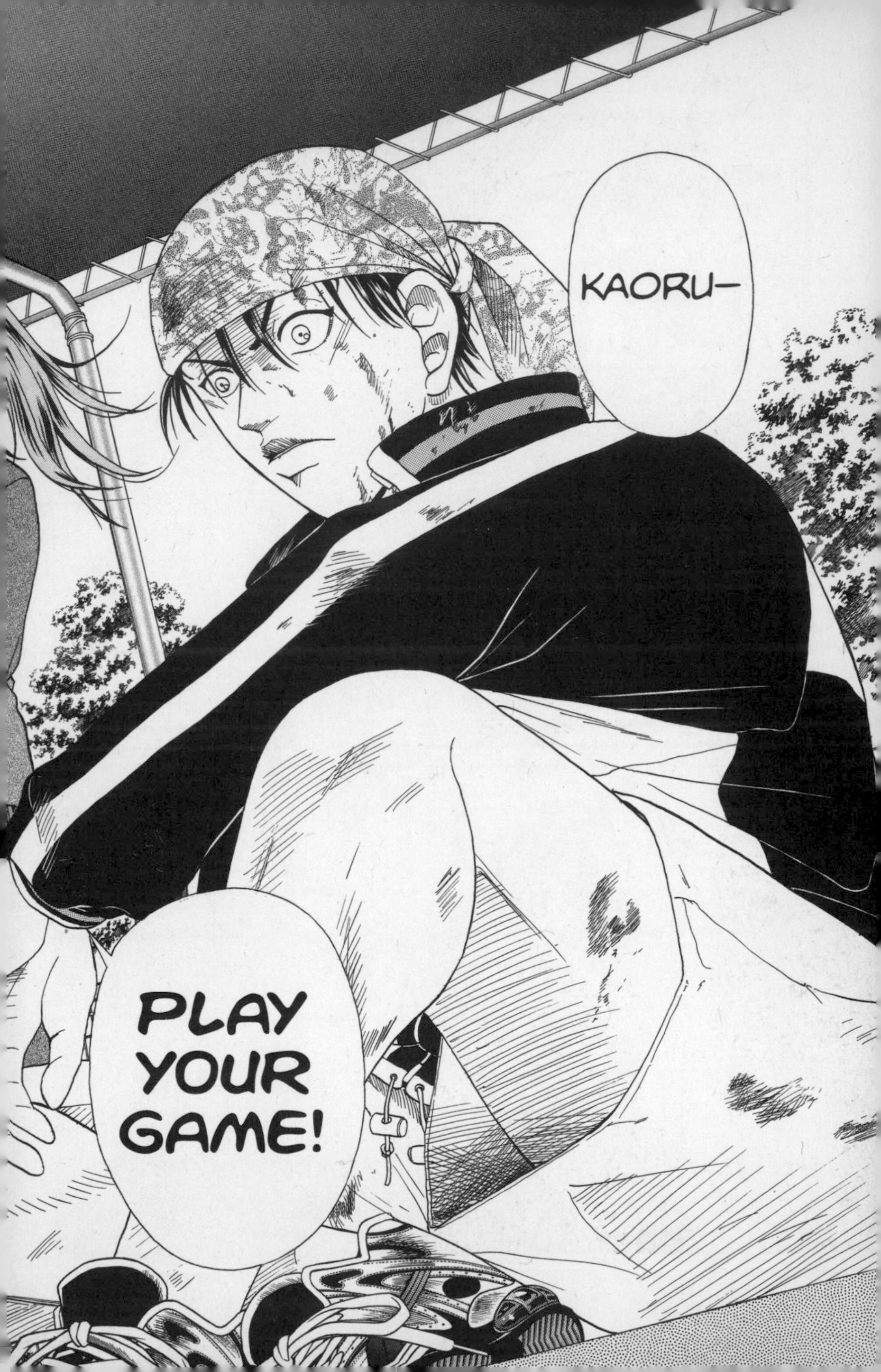
KAORU–
PLAY YOUR GAME!

READ THIS WAY

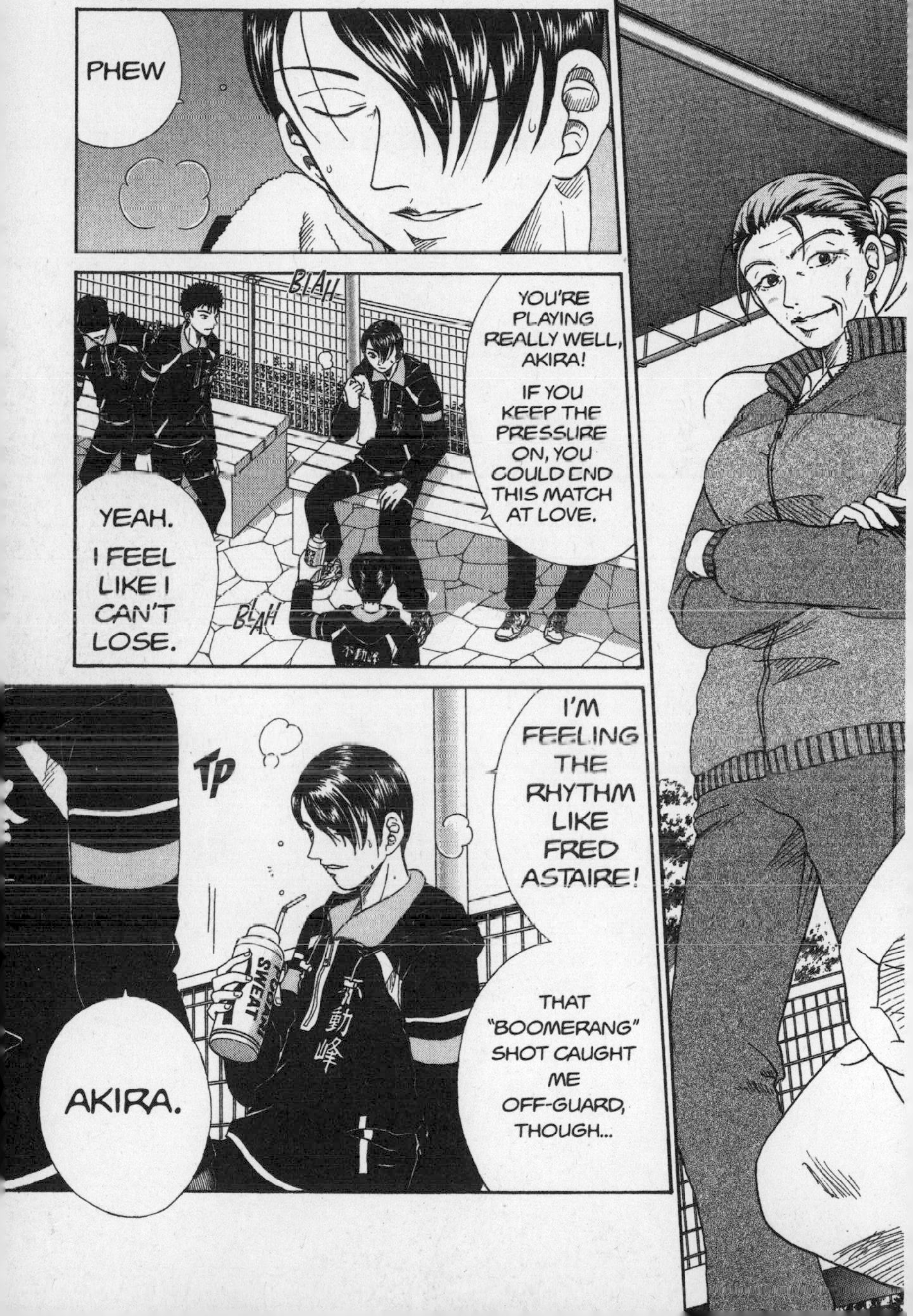
PHEW
YOU'RE PLAYING REALLY WELL, AKIRA!
IF YOU KEEP THE PRESSURE ON, YOU COULD END THIS MATCH AT LOVE.
BLAH
BLAH
YEAH.
I FEEL LIKE I CAN'T LOSE.
I'M FEELING THE RHYTHM LIKE FRED ASTAIRE!
TP
THAT "BOOMERANG" SHOT CAUGHT ME OFF-GUARD, THOUGH...
AKIRA.

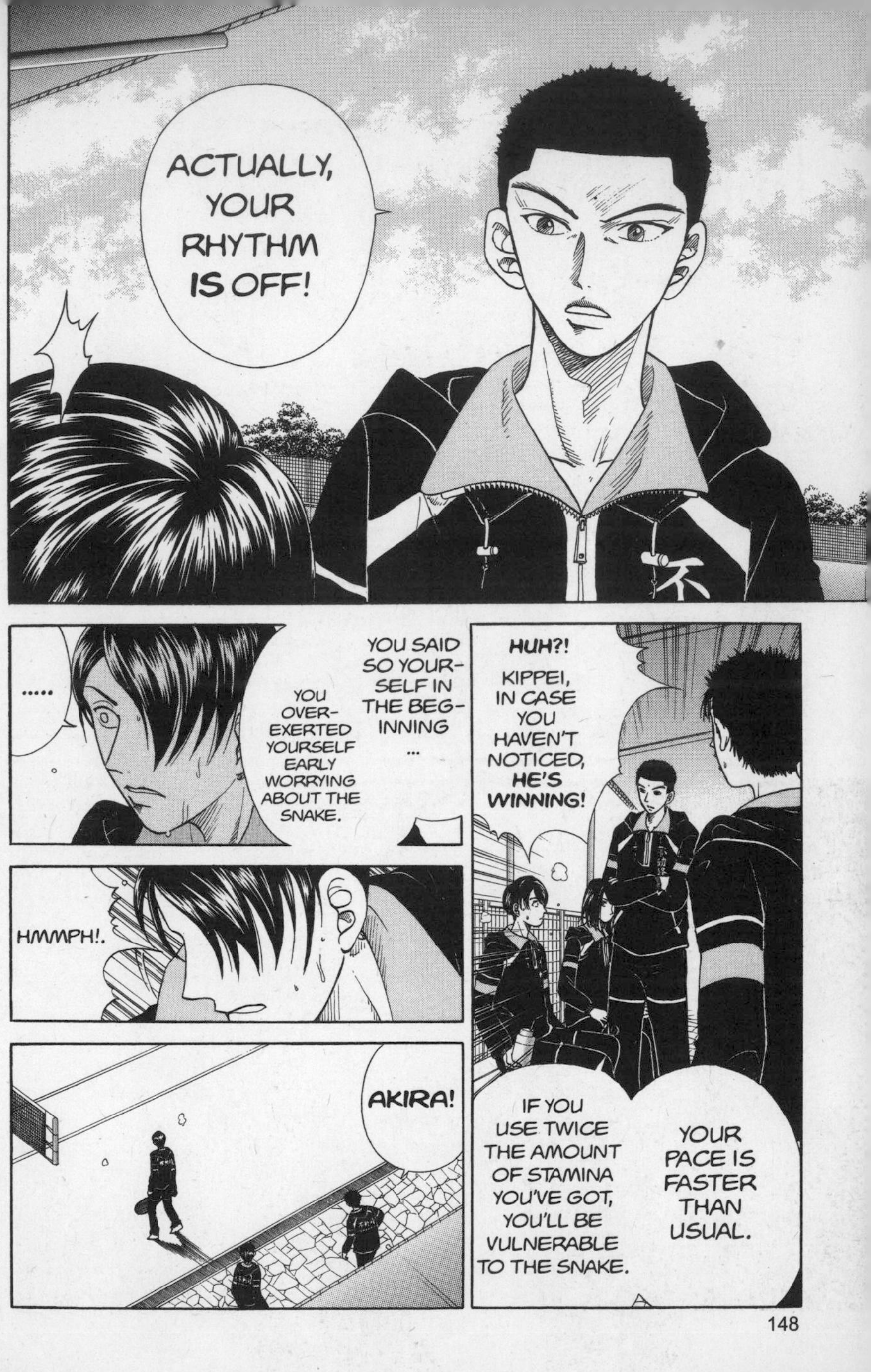

ACTUALLY, YOUR RHYTHM IS OFF!
HUH?!
KIPPEI, IN CASE YOU HAVEN'T NOTICED, HE'S WINNING!
YOUR PACE IS FASTER THAN USUAL.
IF YOU USE TWICE THE AMOUNT OF STAMINA YOU'VE GOT, YOU'LL BE VULNERABLE TO THE SNAKE.
YOU SAID SO YOURSELF IN THE BEGINNING ...
YOU OVEREXERTED YOURSELF EARLY WORRYING ABOUT THE SNAKE.
......
HMMPH!.
AKIRA!

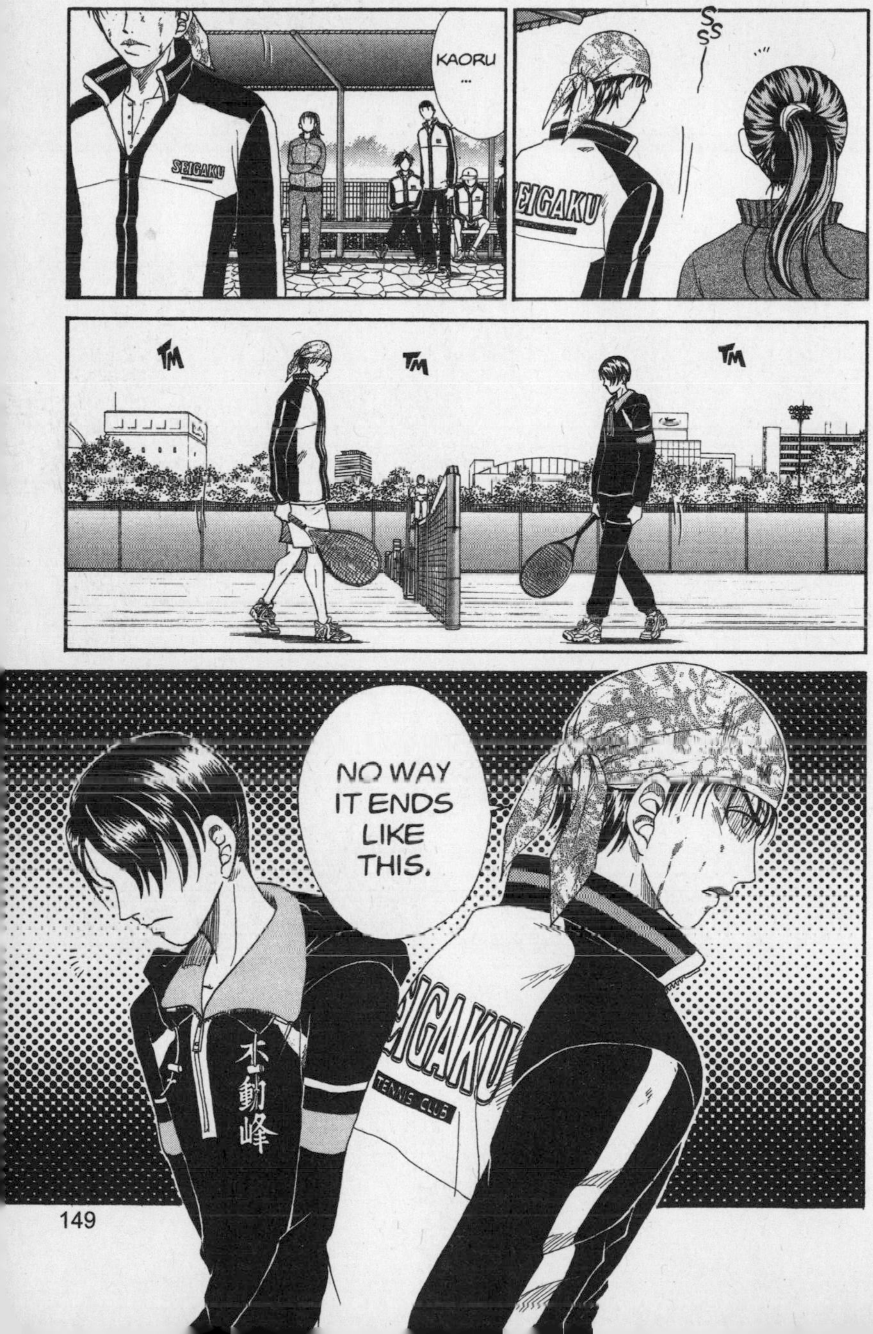
SSS
KAORU ...
TM
TM
TM
NO WAY IT ENDS LIKE THIS.

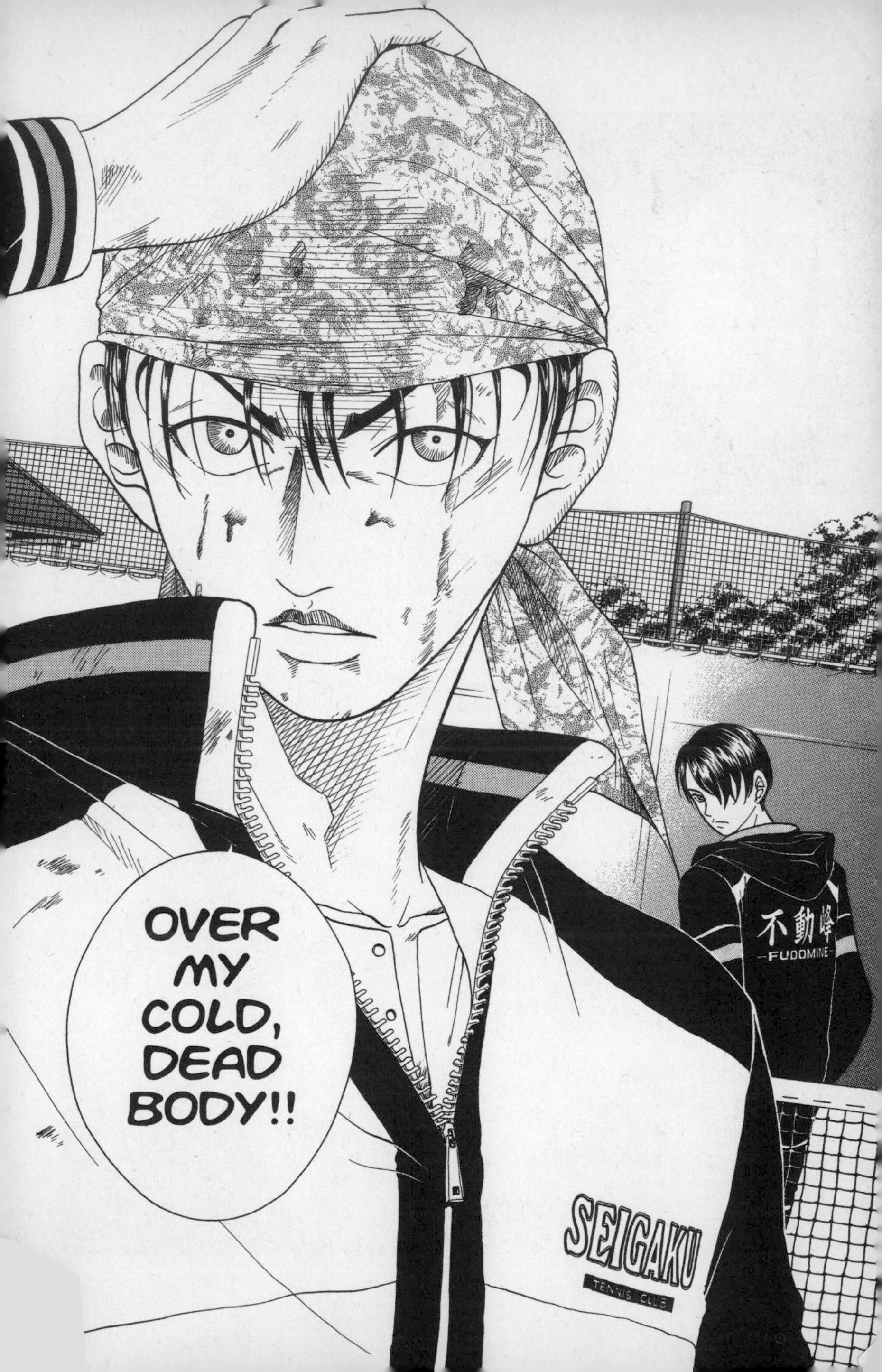
OVER MY COLD, DEAD BODY!!
不動峰
-FUDOMINE-
SEIGAKU
TENNIS CLUB

READ THIS WAY

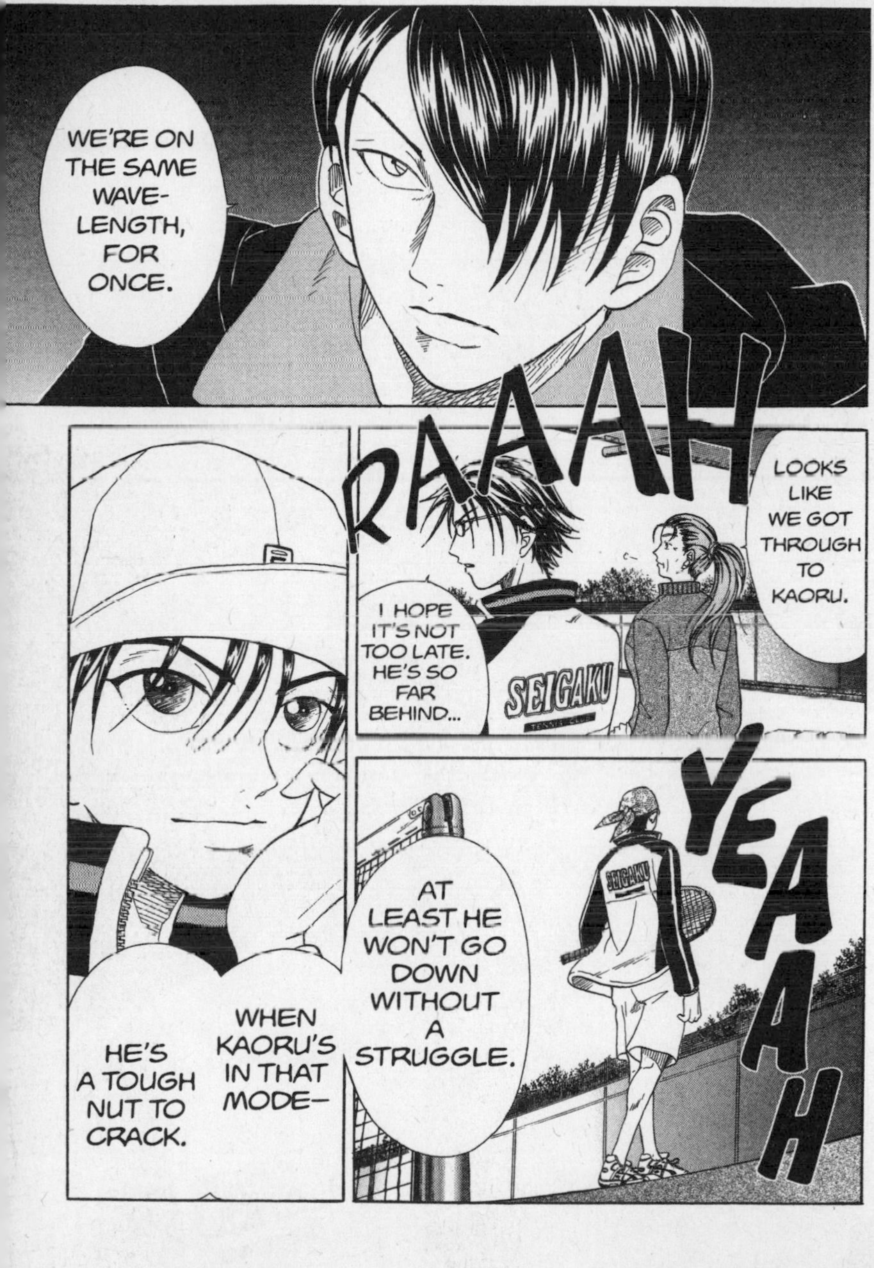
WE'RE ON THE SAME WAVE-LENGTH, FOR ONCE.
RAAAH
LOOKS LIKE WE GOT THROUGH TO KAORU.
I HOPE IT'S NOT TOO LATE. HE'S SO FAR BEHIND...
SEIGAKU
YEAAAH
AT LEAST HE WON'T GO DOWN WITHOUT A STRUGGLE.
SEIGAKU
WHEN KAORU'S IN THAT MODE—
HE'S A TOUGH NUT TO CRACK.

Date · · No. 51

Kaoru Kaido/ Right-Handed

Seishun Academy 8th Grade Class 7
Height: 173 cm/ Blood Type: B/ Born: 5/11
Favorite Brand Shoes: Puma
(Cell Factor PT0634 0067)
Racket: Head
(Ti. S7)
Best Shot: Snake
Favorite Food: Yam Soba – on a bamboo plate
Yogurt
100% fruit juice
Hobbies: Marathon, collecting bandanas

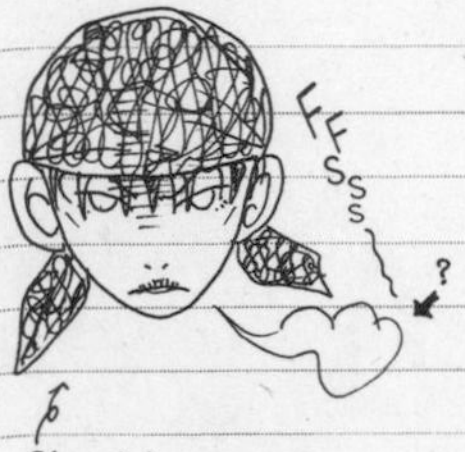
FFSSS
?

Short temper
(maybe he needs more calcium)

Kunimitsu Tezuka/Left-Handed

Seishun Academy 9th Grade Class 1
Height: 179 cm/ Blood Type: O/ Born: 10/7
Favorite Brand Shoes: Mizuno
(Wave Dual Lite 6KW93009)
Racket: Mizuno
(Pro Light S90)
Best Shot: Drop Shot
Favorite Food: Broiled eel
Hobby/Recent Pastime: Mountain climbing,
camping, fishing

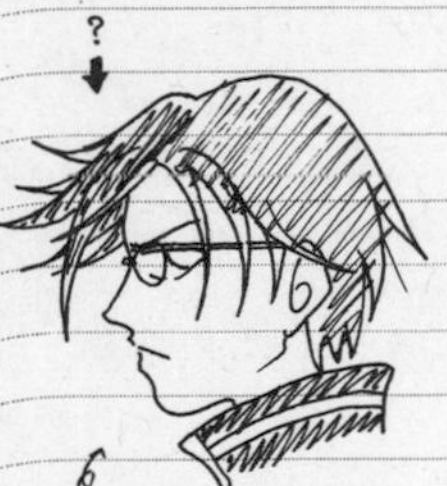
?

Captain
Hard expression

* Taken from Sadaharu Inui's Secret Data Note 51

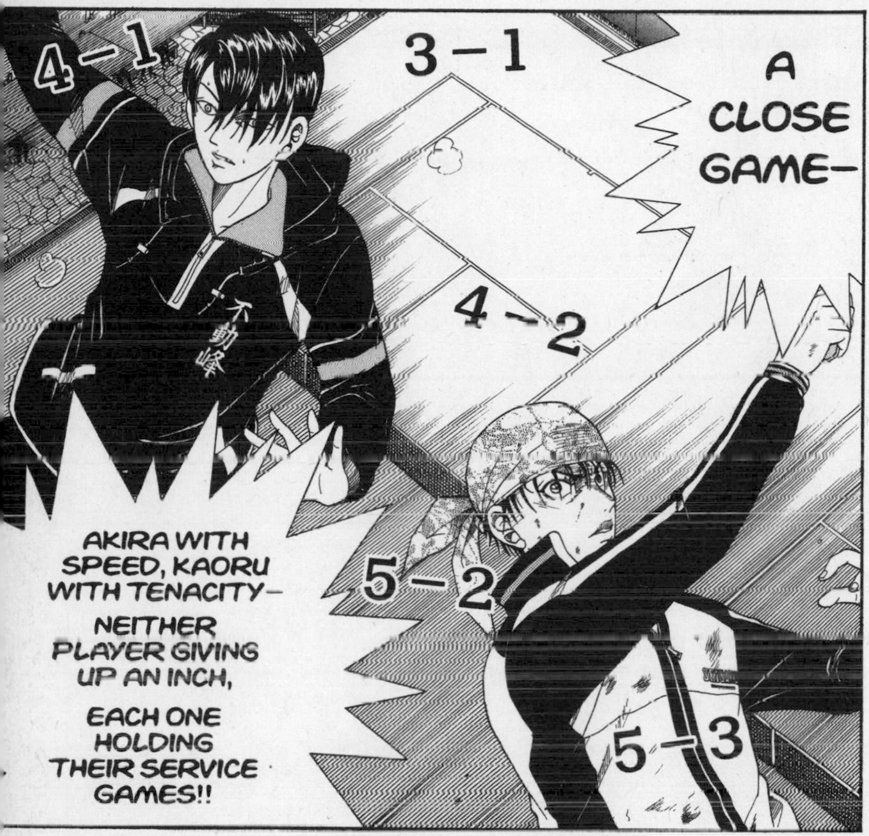
A CLOSE GAME-
3-1
4-1
不動峰
4-2
5-2
5-3
AKIRA WITH SPEED, KAORU WITH TENACITY-
NEITHER PLAYER GIVING UP AN INCH,
EACH ONE HOLDING THEIR SERVICE GAMES!!

Genius 33:

SMALL FIST PUMP

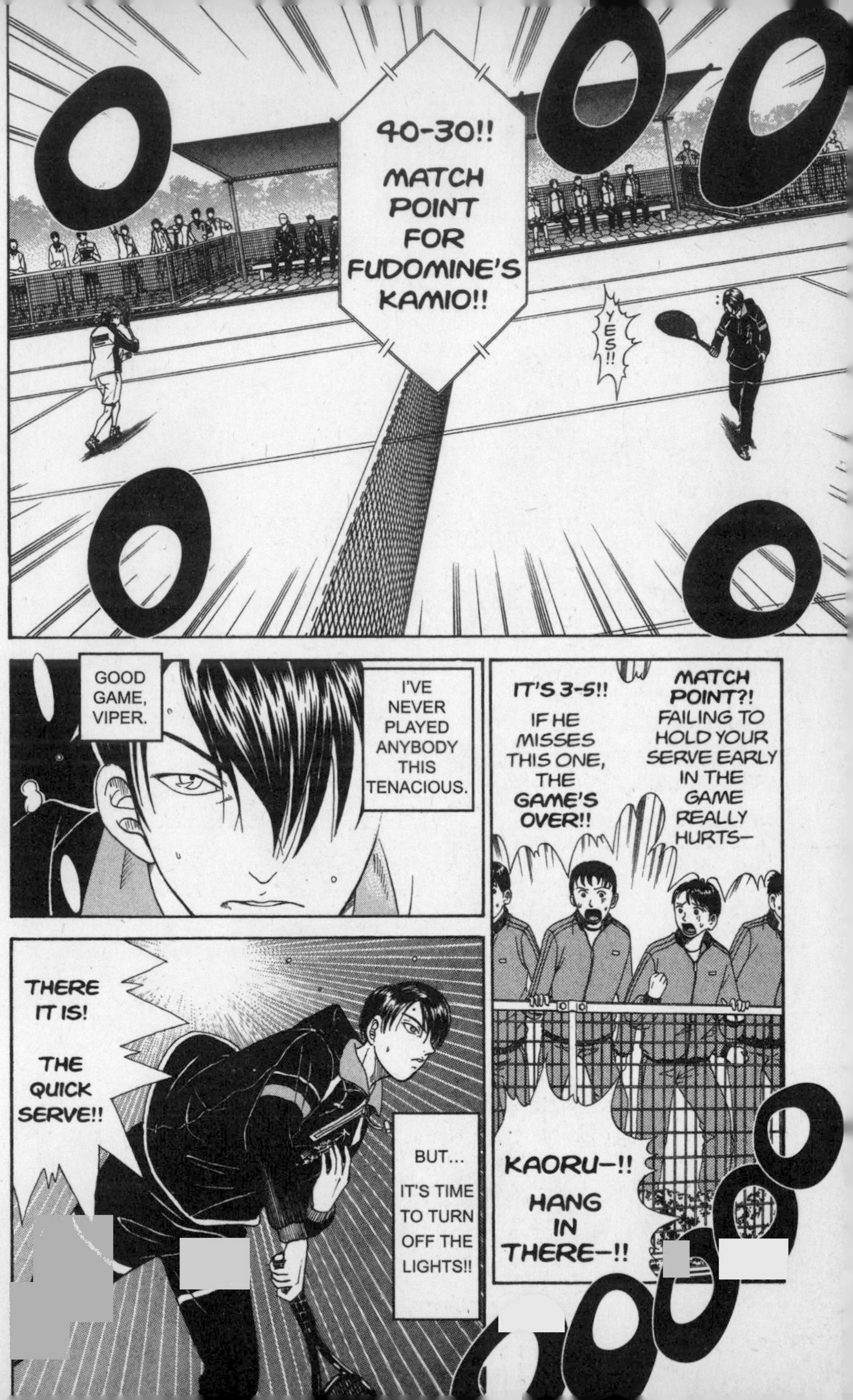
40-30!!
MATCH POINT FOR FUDOMINE'S KAMIO!!
YES!!
MATCH POINT?! FAILING TO HOLD YOUR SERVE EARLY IN THE GAME REALLY HURTS—
IT'S 3-5!!
IF HE MISSES THIS ONE, THE GAME'S OVER!!
KAORU—!!
HANG IN THERE—!!
I'VE NEVER PLAYED ANYBODY THIS TENACIOUS.
GOOD GAME, VIPER.
BUT...
IT'S TIME TO TURN OFF THE LIGHTS!!
THERE IT IS!
THE QUICK SERVE!!

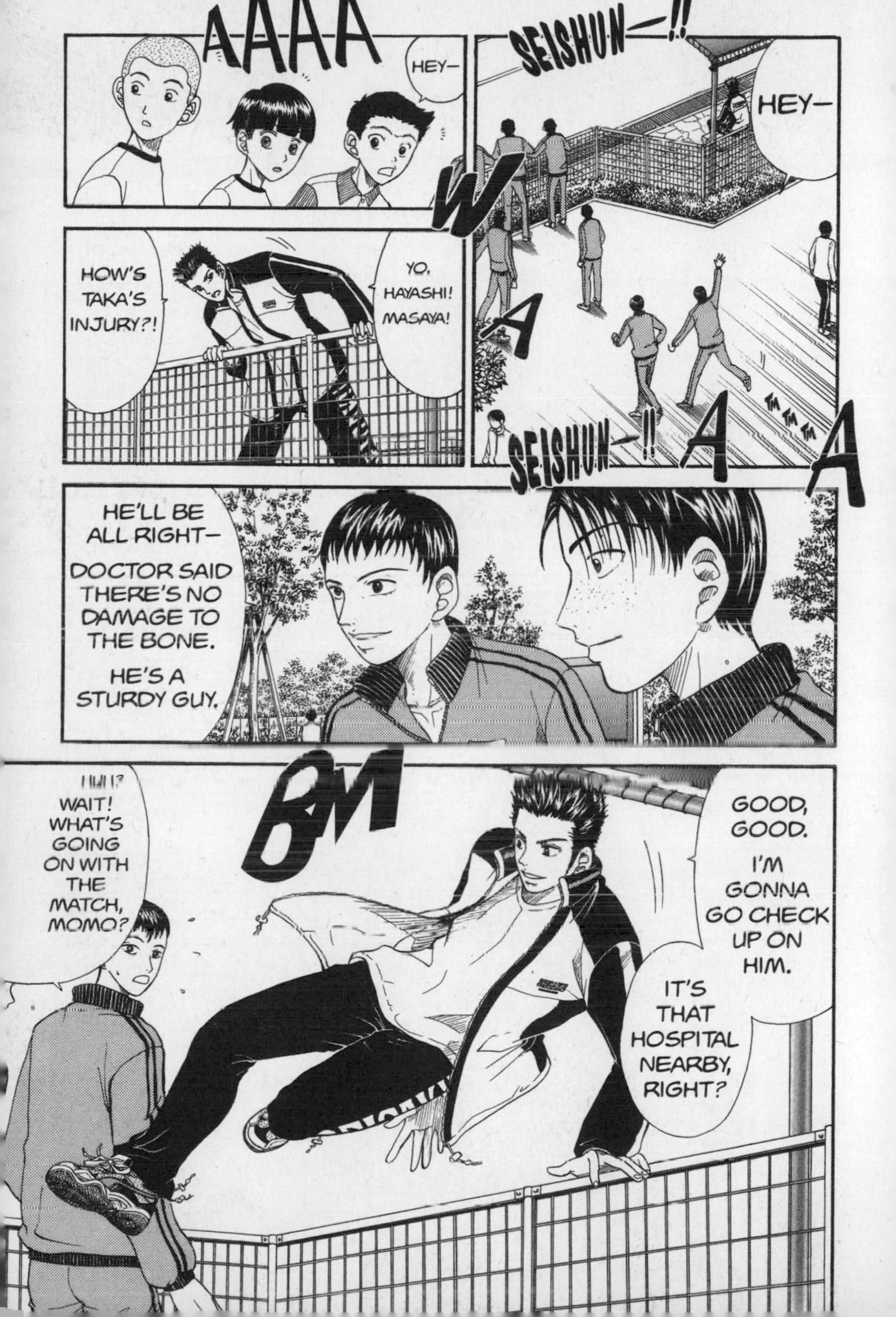
SEISHUN—!!
HEY—
W
A
SEISHUN—!!
TM TM TM
A
A
AAAA
HEY—
YO, HAYASHI! MASAYA!
HOW'S TAKA'S INJURY?!
HE'LL BE ALL RIGHT—
DOCTOR SAID THERE'S NO DAMAGE TO THE BONE.
HE'S A STURDY GUY.
BM
GOOD, GOOD.
I'M GONNA GO CHECK UP ON HIM.
IT'S THAT HOSPITAL NEARBY, RIGHT?
WAIT! WHAT'S GOING ON WITH THE MATCH, MOMO?

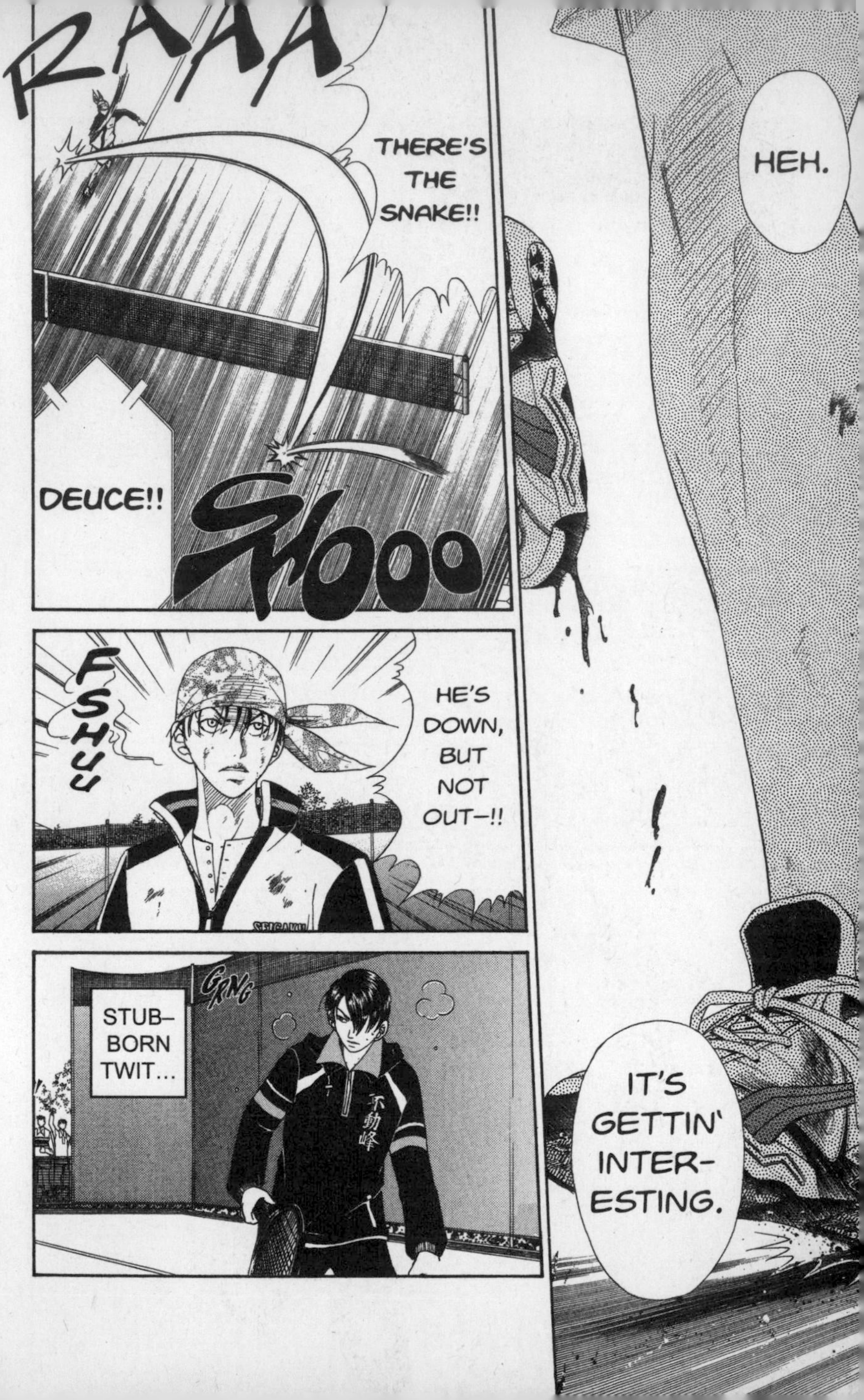
HEH.
IT'S GETTIN' INTER-ESTING.
RAAA
THERE'S THE SNAKE!!
SHOOO
DEUCE!!
HE'S DOWN, BUT NOT OUT--!!
FSHUU
GRNG
不動峰
STUB-BORN TWIT...

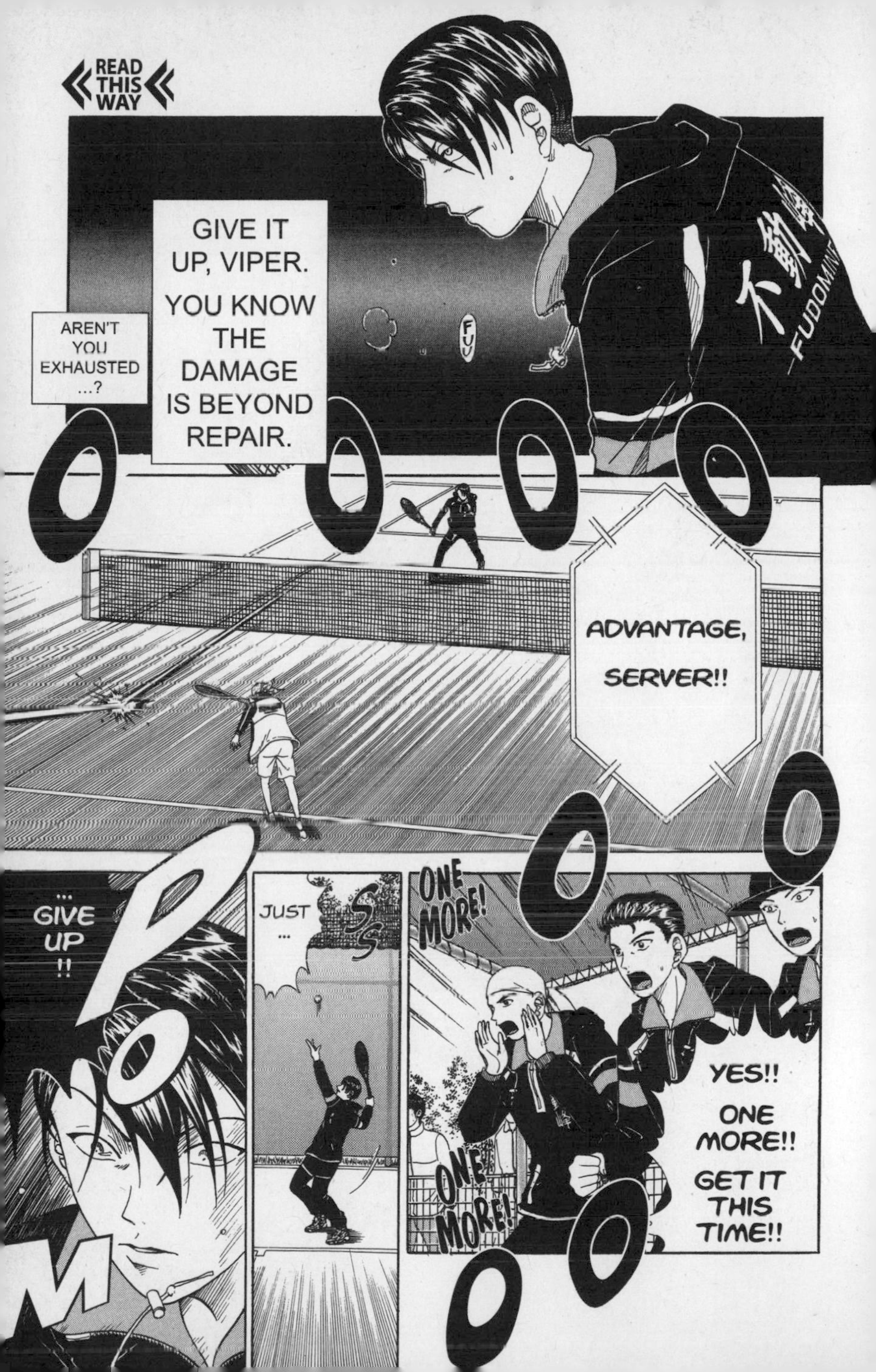
READ THIS WAY
FU
GIVE IT UP, VIPER.
YOU KNOW THE DAMAGE IS BEYOND REPAIR.
AREN'T YOU EXHAUSTED ...?
FUDOMINE
ADVANTAGE, SERVER!!
ONE MORE!
YES!!
ONE MORE!!
GET IT THIS TIME!!
ONE MORE!
SS
JUST ...
... GIVE UP !!
POM

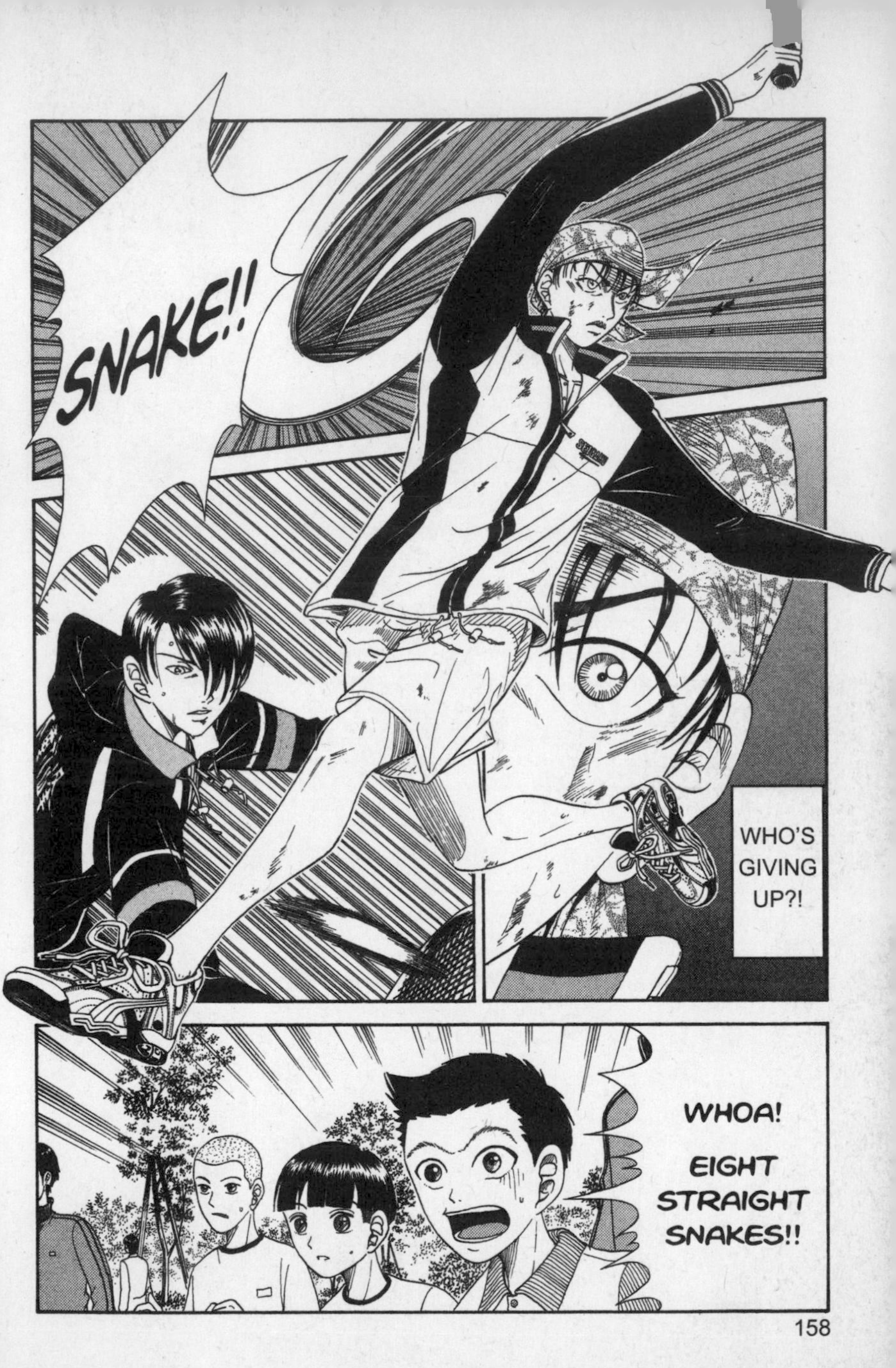
SNAKE!!
WHO'S GIVING UP?!
WHOA!
EIGHT STRAIGHT SNAKES!!

READ THIS WAY

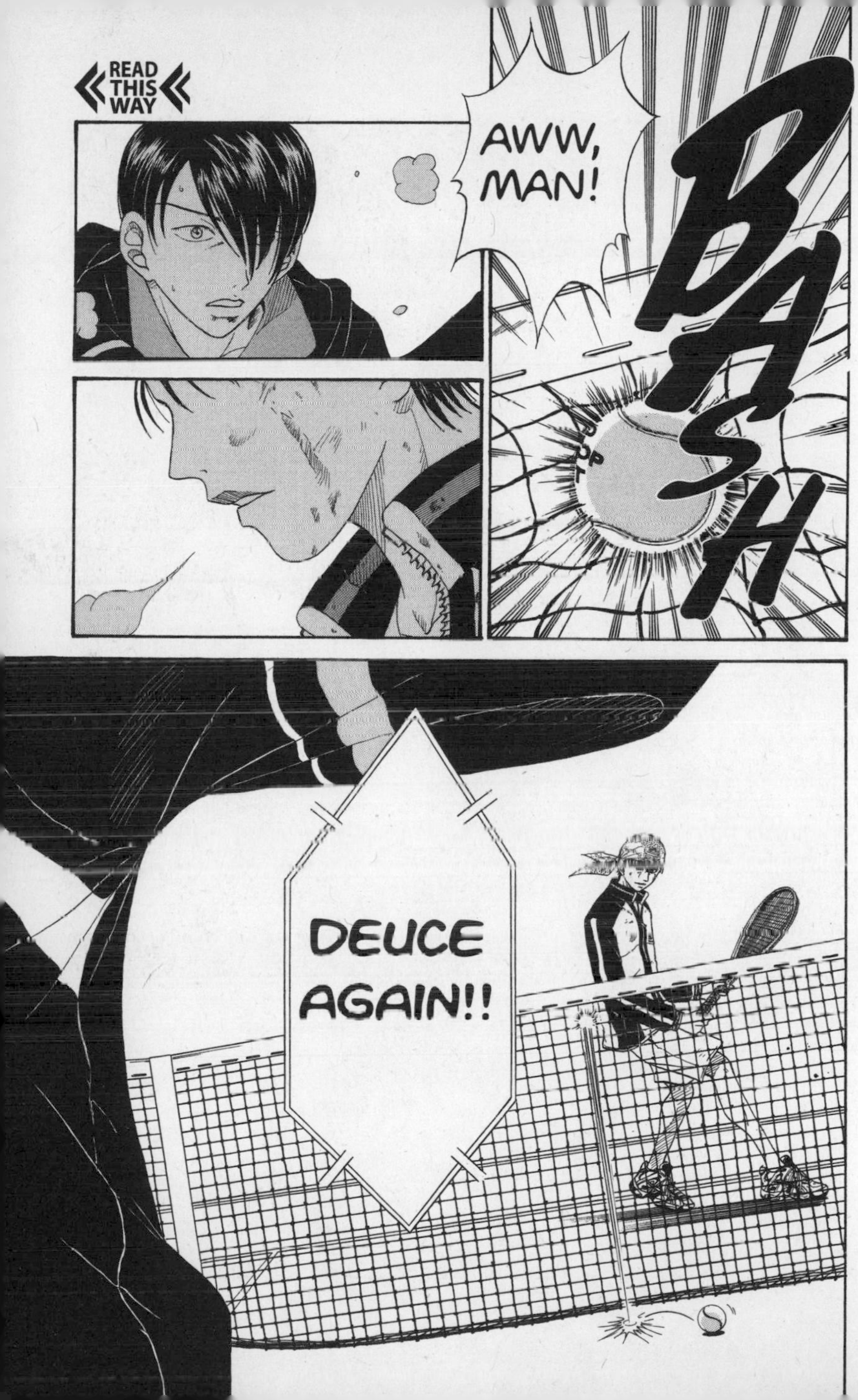
BASH
AWW, MAN!
DEUCE AGAIN!!

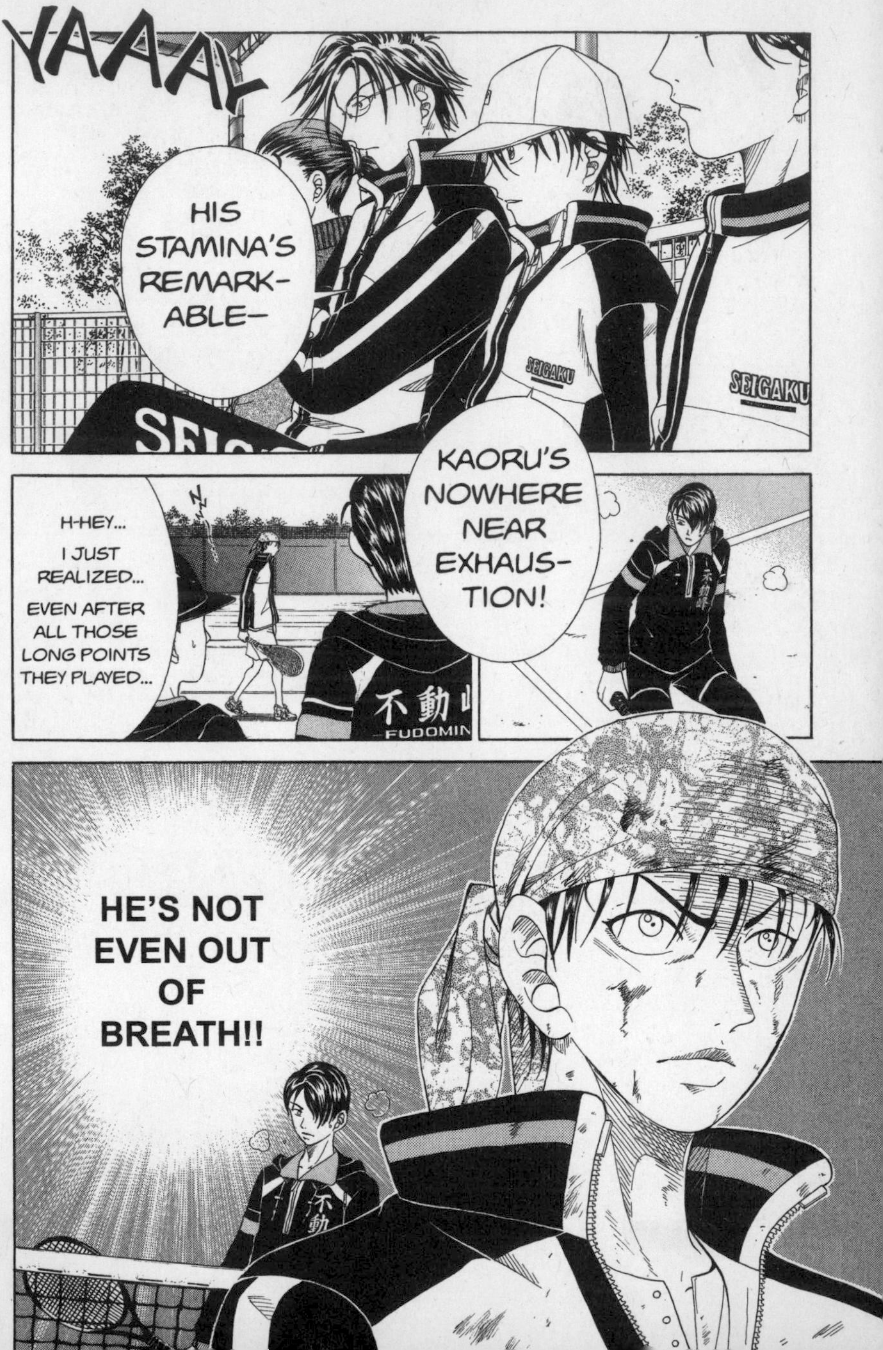
YAAAY
HIS STAMINA'S REMARK-ABLE—
KAORU'S NOWHERE NEAR EXHAUS-TION!
H-HEY... I JUST REALIZED... EVEN AFTER ALL THOSE LONG POINTS THEY PLAYED...
HE'S NOT EVEN OUT OF BREATH!!

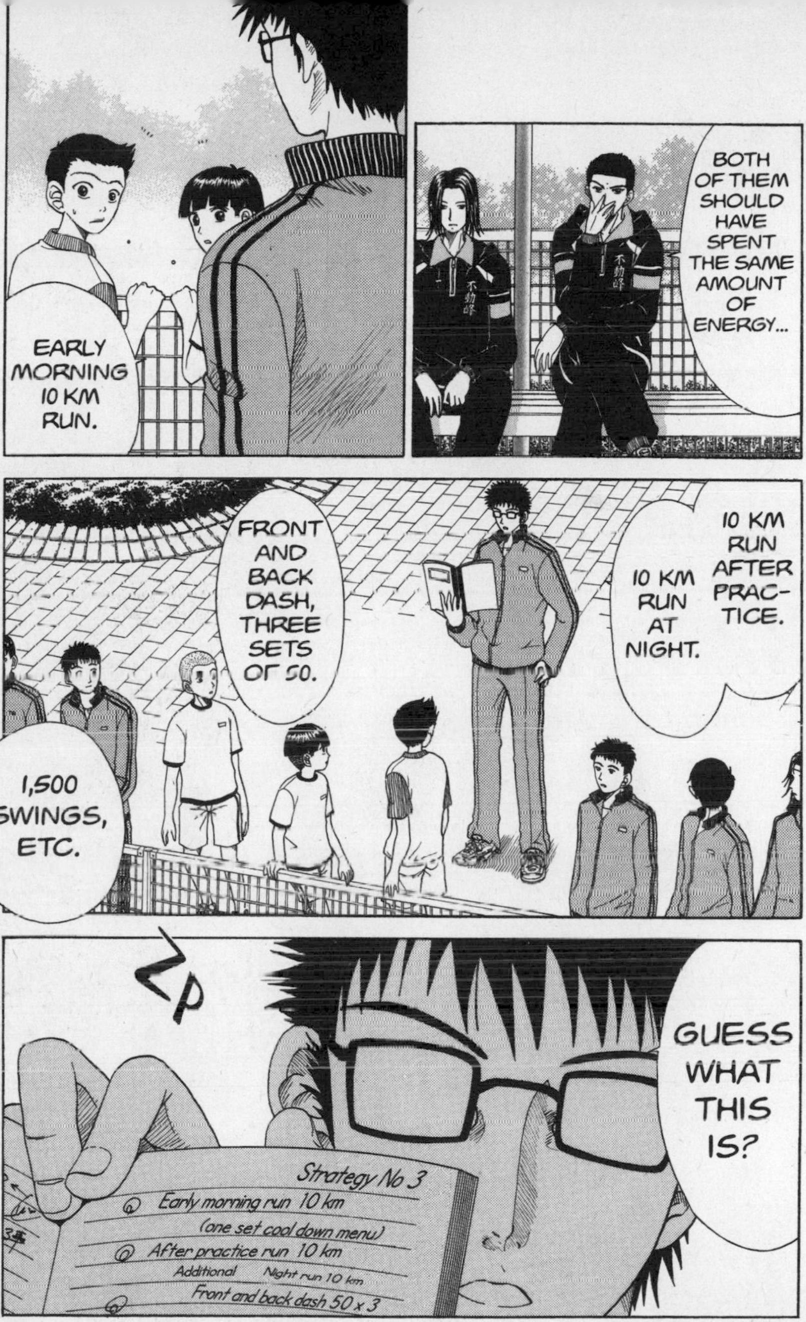
BOTH OF THEM SHOULD HAVE SPENT THE SAME AMOUNT OF ENERGY...
EARLY MORNING 10 KM RUN.
10 KM RUN AFTER PRAC-TICE.
10 KM RUN AT NIGHT.
FRONT AND BACK DASH, THREE SETS OF 50.
1,500 SWINGS, ETC.
GUESS WHAT THIS IS?
Zp
Strategy No 3
Early morning run 10 km
(one set cool down menu)
After practice run 10 km
Additional Night run 10 km
Front and back dash 50 x 3

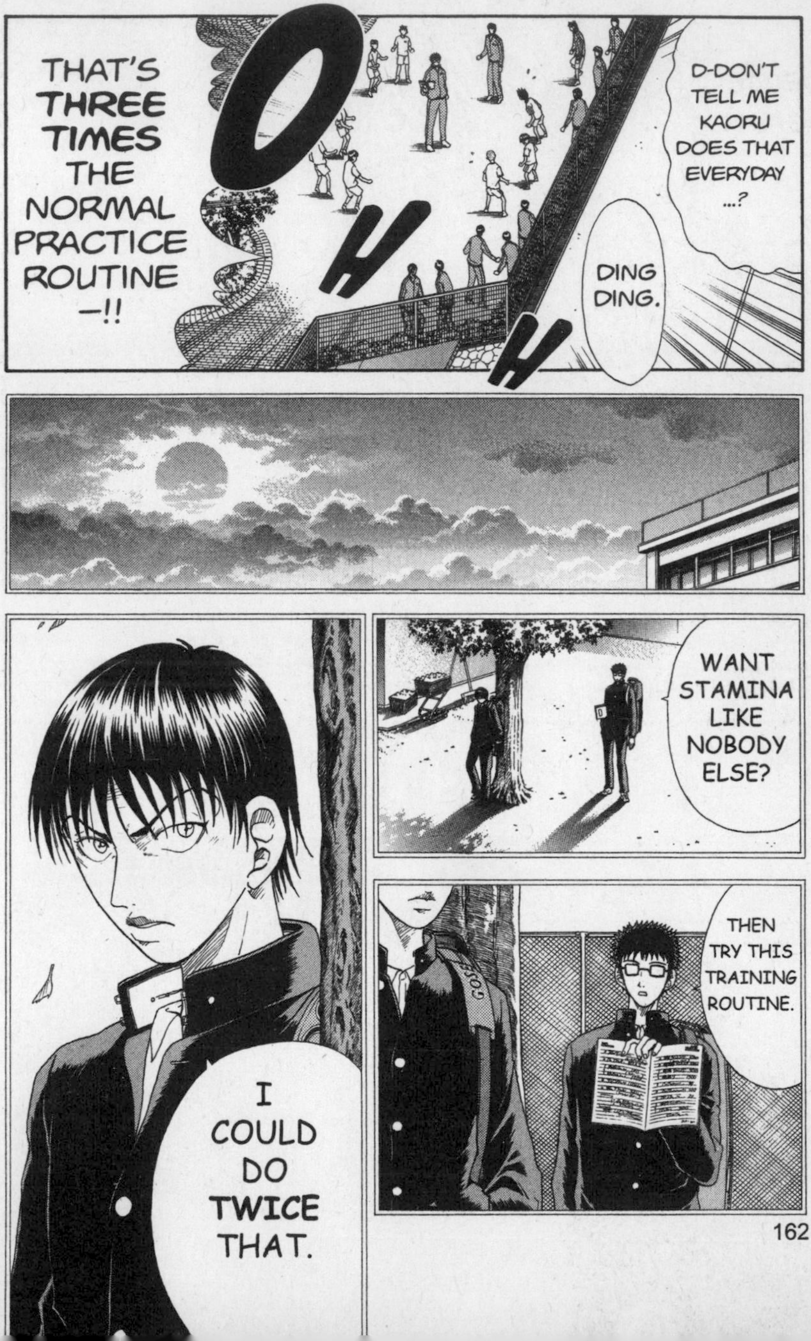
D-DON'T TELL ME KAORU DOES THAT EVERYDAY ...?
DING DING.
OHH
THAT'S THREE TIMES THE NORMAL PRACTICE ROUTINE—!!
WANT STAMINA LIKE NOBODY ELSE?
THEN TRY THIS TRAINING ROUTINE.
I COULD DO TWICE THAT.

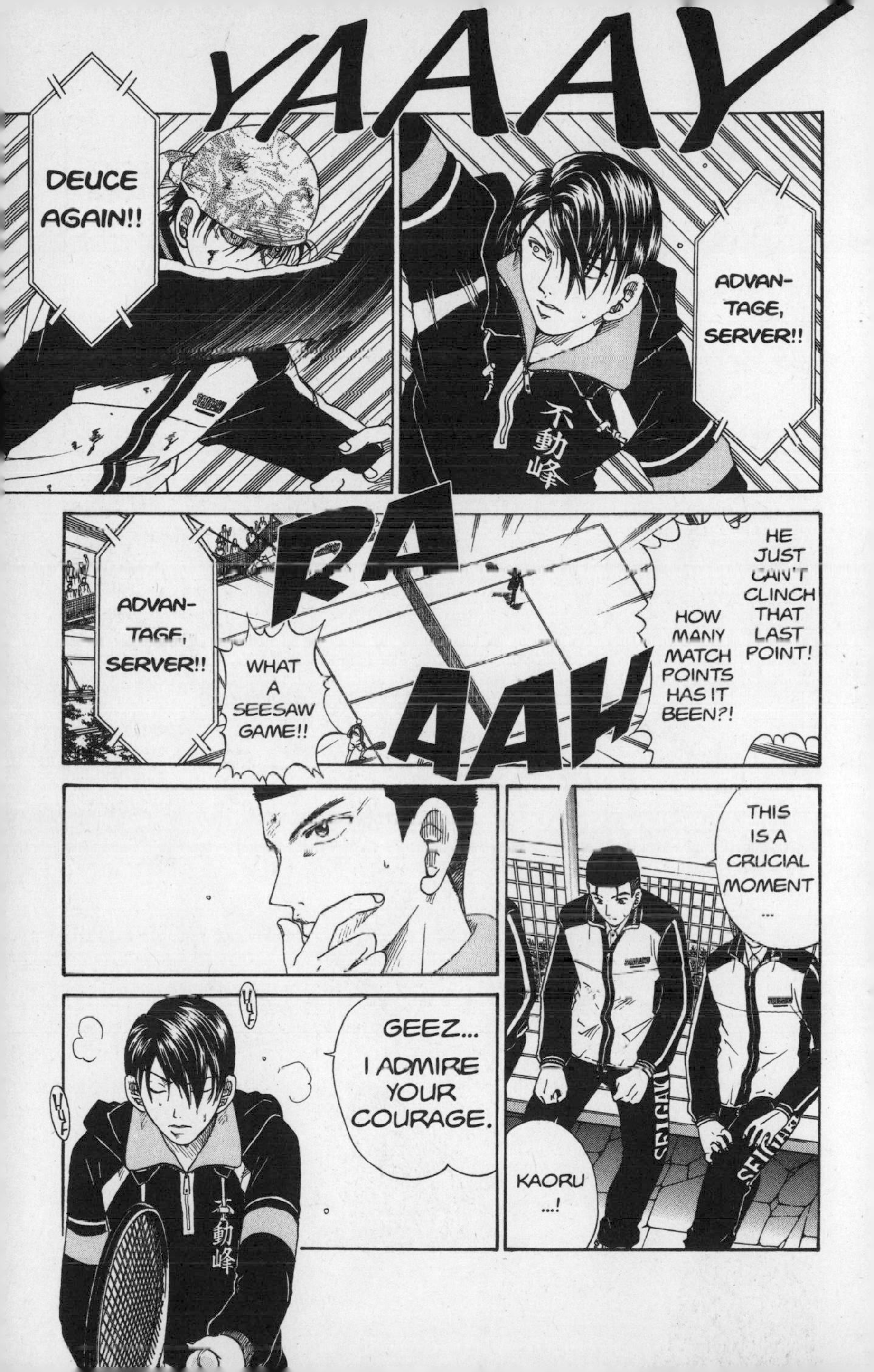
YAAAY
ADVAN-TAGE, SERVER!!
DEUCE AGAIN!!
RA AAH
HE JUST CAN'T CLINCH THAT LAST POINT!
HOW MANY MATCH POINTS HAS IT BEEN?!
WHAT A SEESAW GAME!!
ADVAN-TAGE, SERVER!!
THIS IS A CRUCIAL MOMENT ...
KAORU ...!
GEEZ... I ADMIRE YOUR COURAGE.

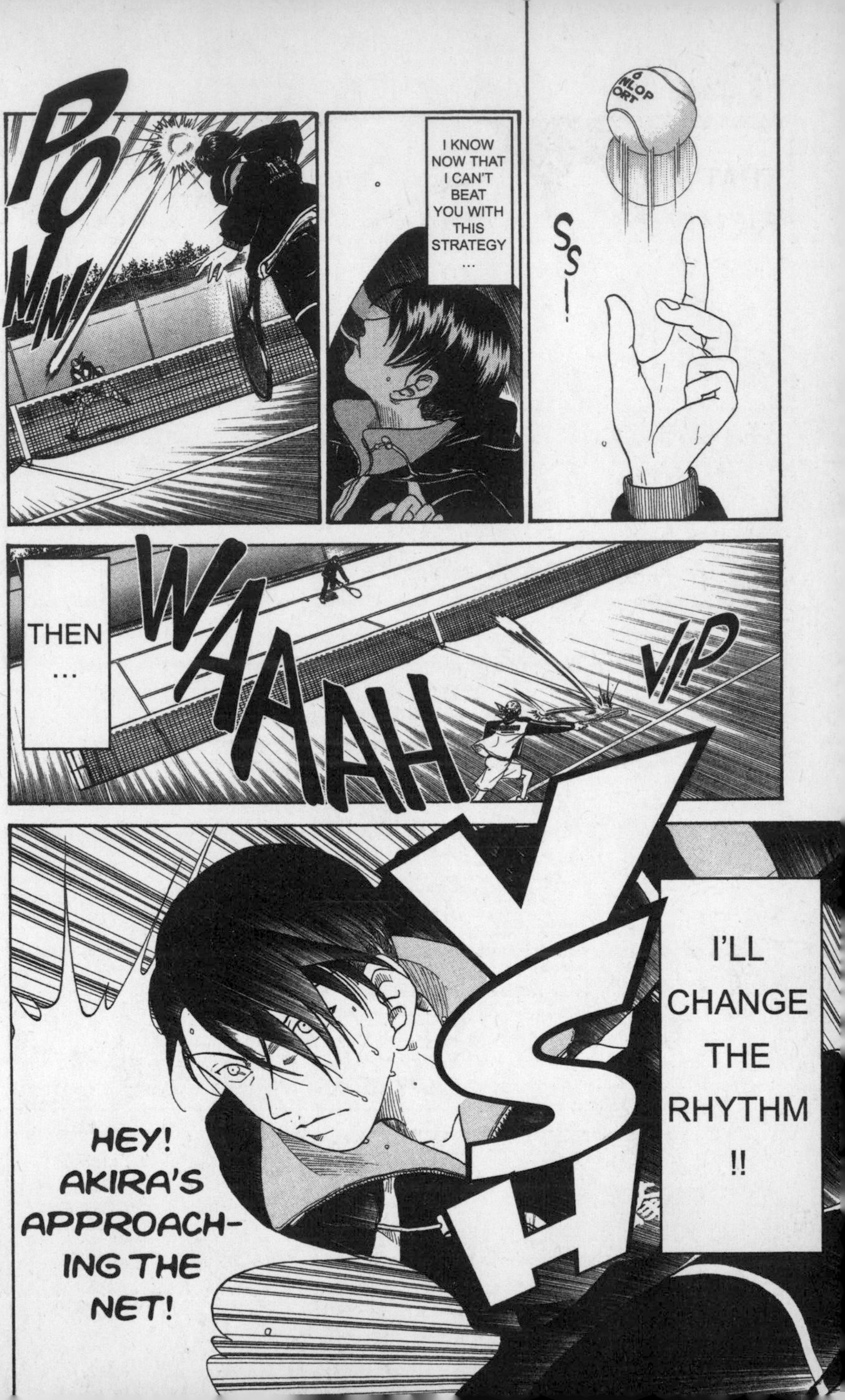
SS!
I KNOW NOW THAT I CAN'T BEAT YOU WITH THIS STRATEGY …
POMMM
VIP
WAAAH
THEN …
I'LL CHANGE THE RHYTHM !!
VSH
HEY! AKIRA'S APPROACH-ING THE NET!

READ THIS WAY

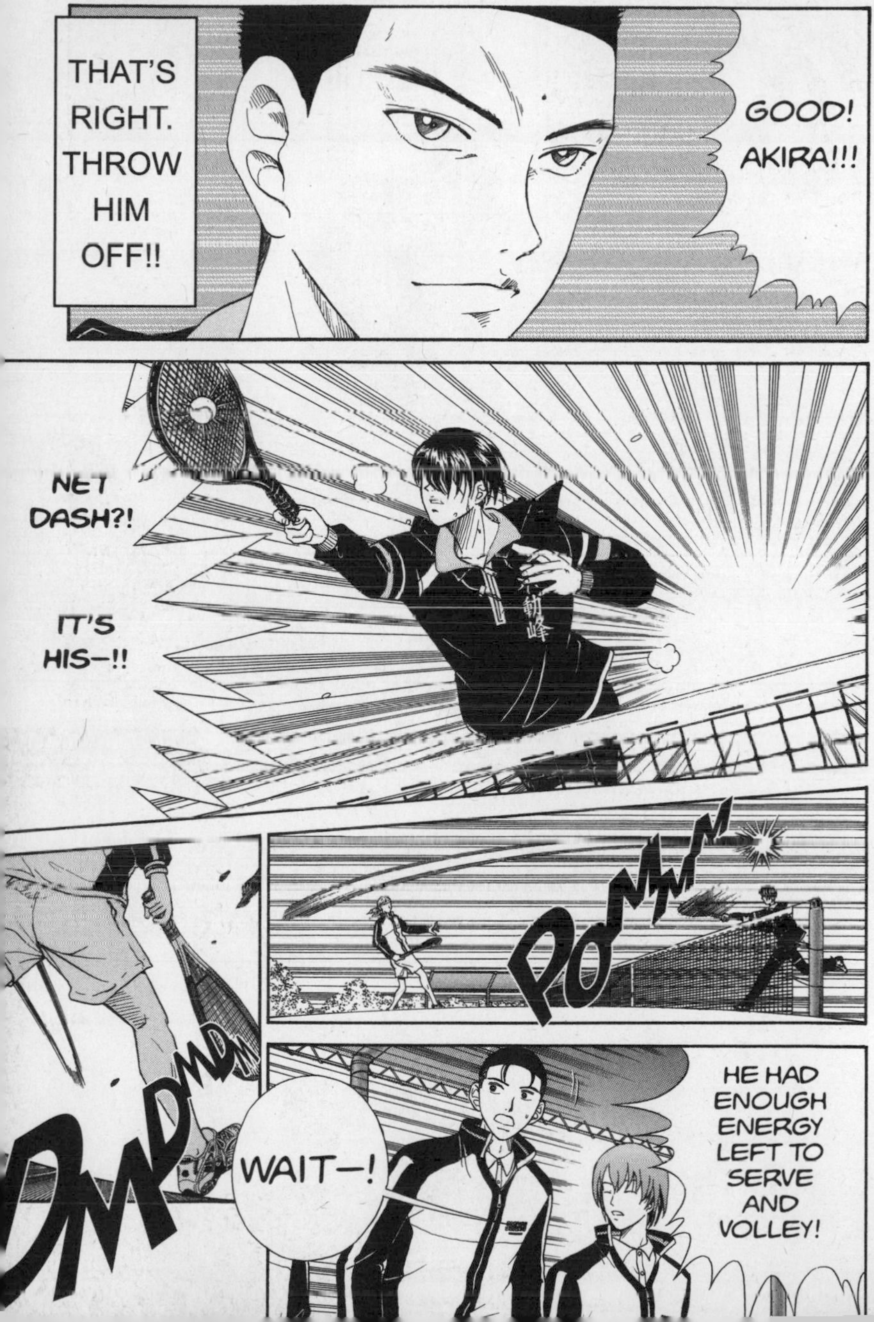
GOOD! AKIRA!!!
THAT'S RIGHT. THROW HIM OFF!!
NET DASH?!
IT'S HIS-!!
POMMM
HE HAD ENOUGH ENERGY LEFT TO SERVE AND VOLLEY!
WAIT-!
DMDMDM

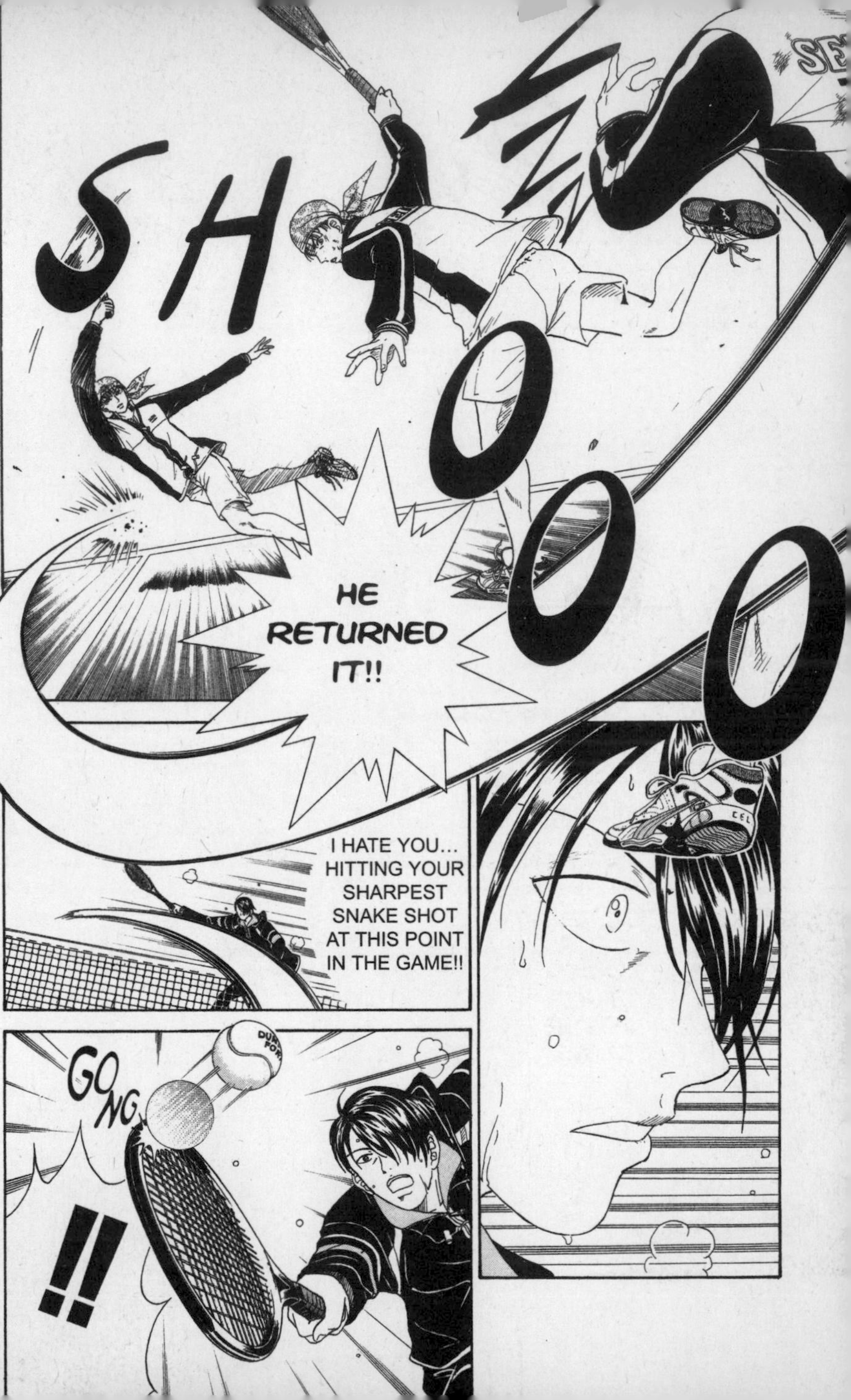
SHOOOOO
HE RETURNED IT!!
I HATE YOU… HITTING YOUR SHARPEST SNAKE SHOT AT THIS POINT IN THE GAME!!
GONG
!!

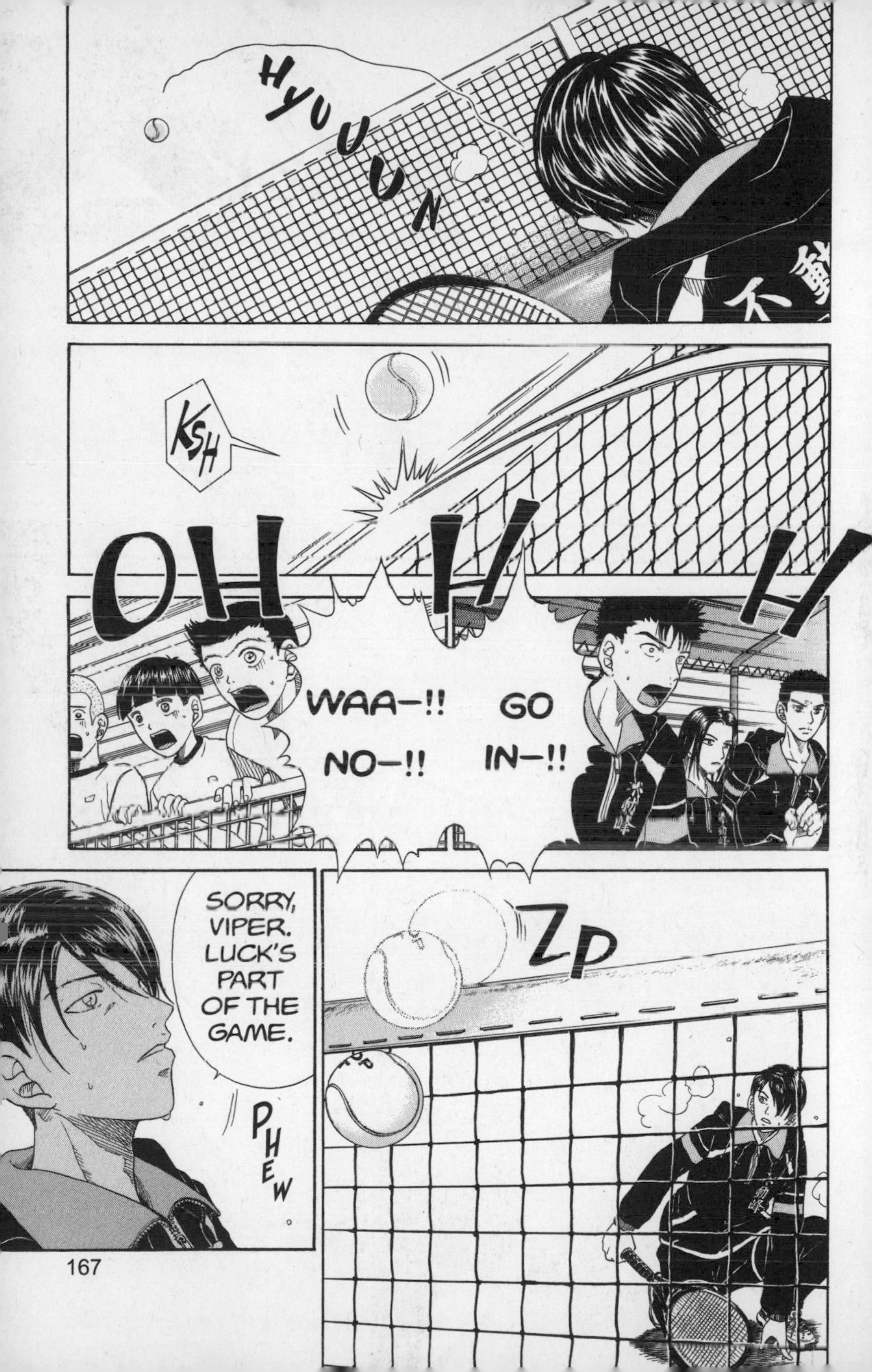
HYUUUN
KSH
OH!!!!
GO IN-!!
WAA-!! NO-!!
ZP
SORRY, VIPER. LUCK'S PART OF THE GAME.
PHEW

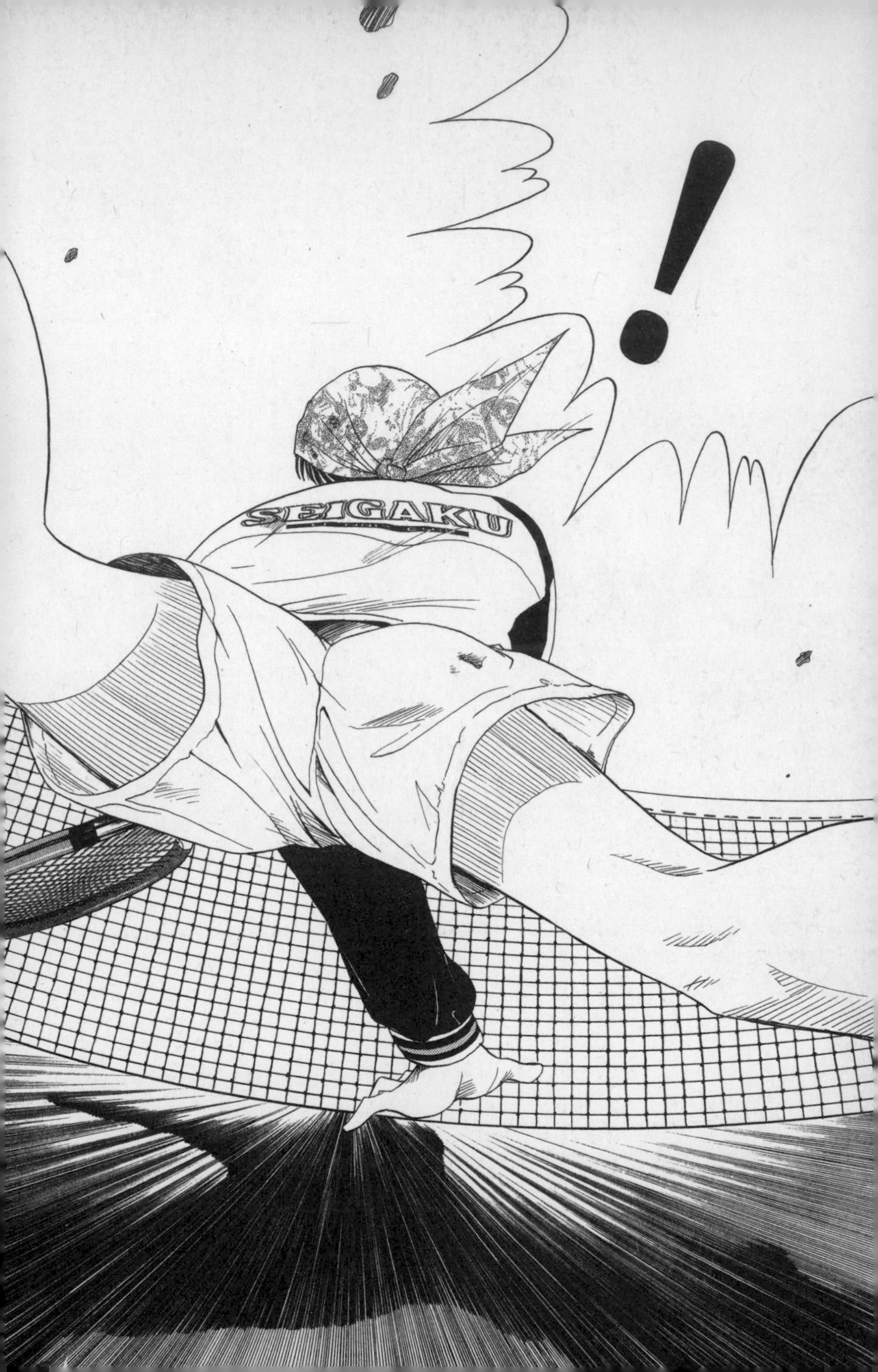
!
SEIGAKU

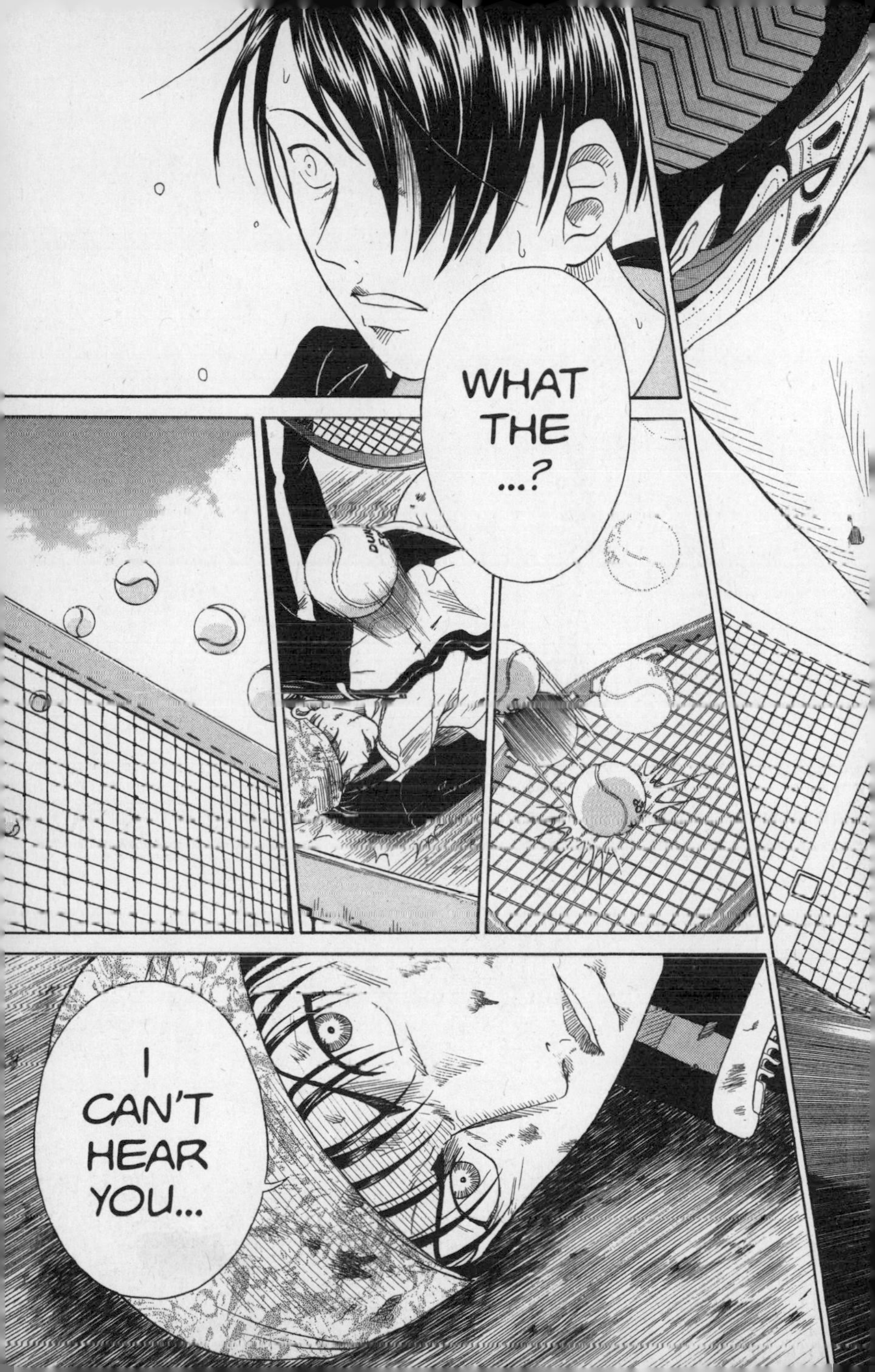
WHAT THE ...?
I CAN'T HEAR YOU...

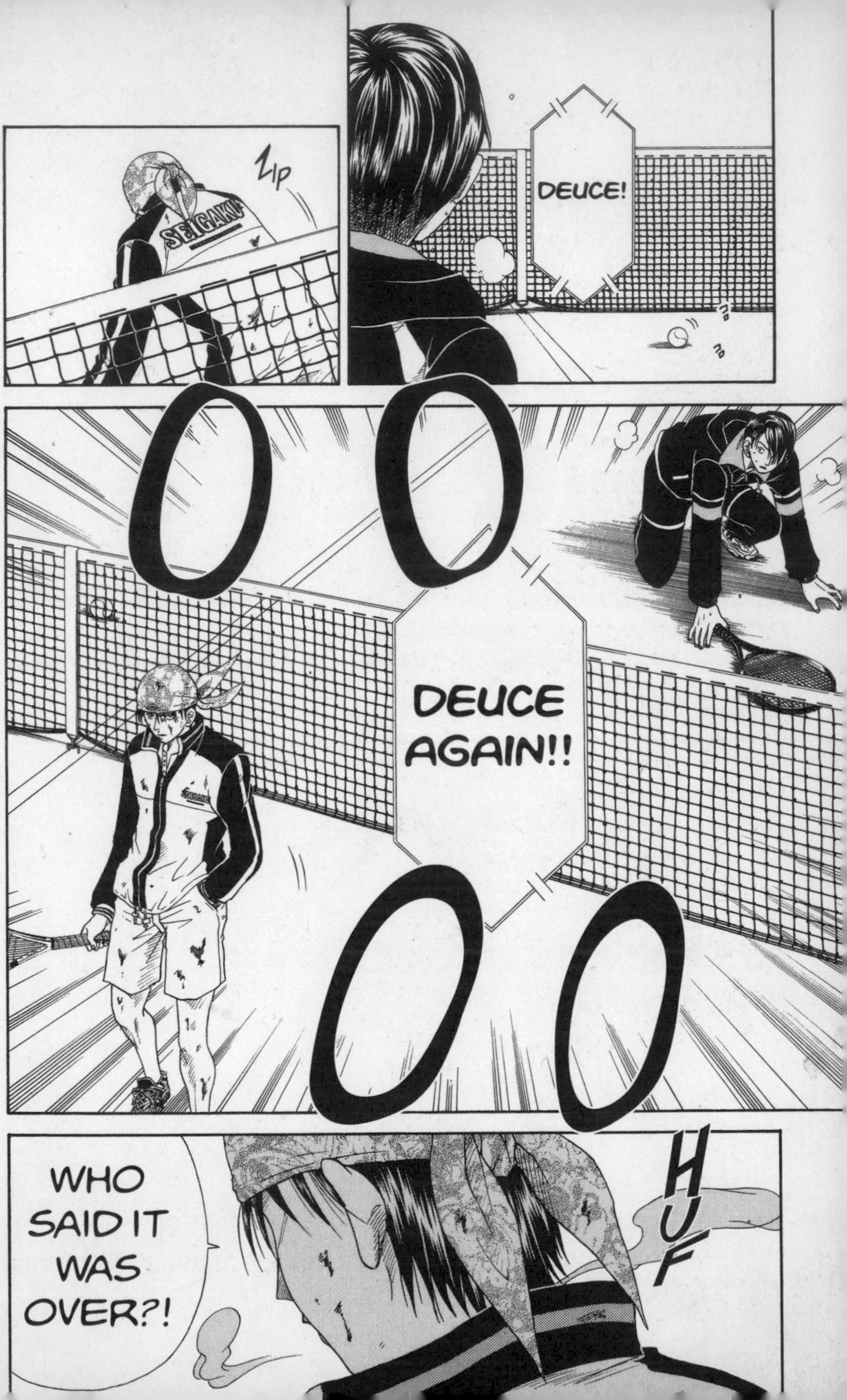
DEUCE!
ZIP
OO
DEUCE AGAIN!!
OO
HUF
WHO SAID IT WAS OVER?!

READ THIS WAY

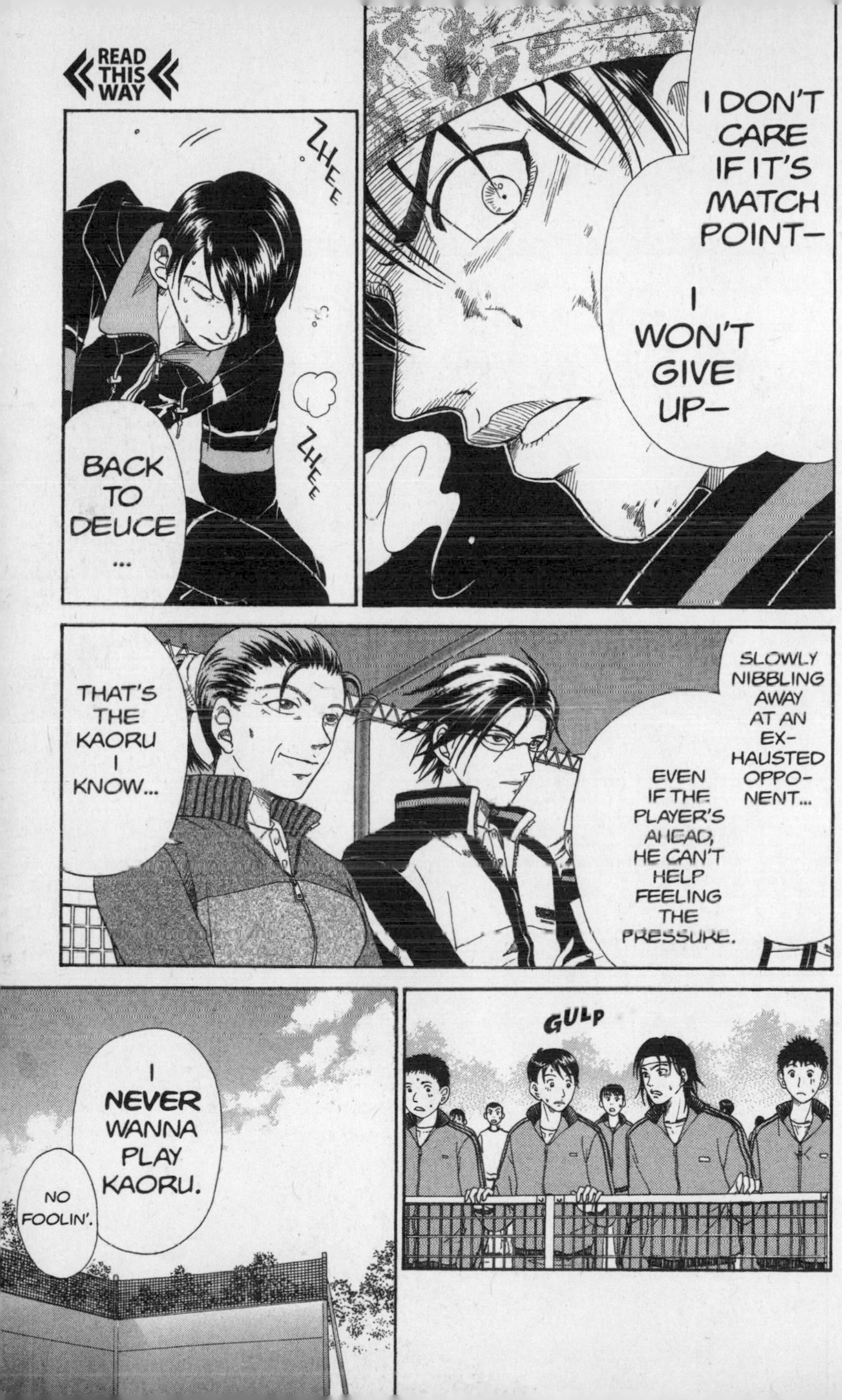
I DON'T CARE IF IT'S MATCH POINT—
I WON'T GIVE UP—
ZHEE
ZHEE
BACK TO DEUCE...
SLOWLY NIBBLING AWAY AT AN EX-HAUSTED OPPO-NENT...
EVEN IF THE PLAYER'S AHEAD, HE CAN'T HELP FEELING THE PRESSURE.
THAT'S THE KAORU I KNOW...
GULP
I NEVER WANNA PLAY KAORU.
NO FOOLIN'.

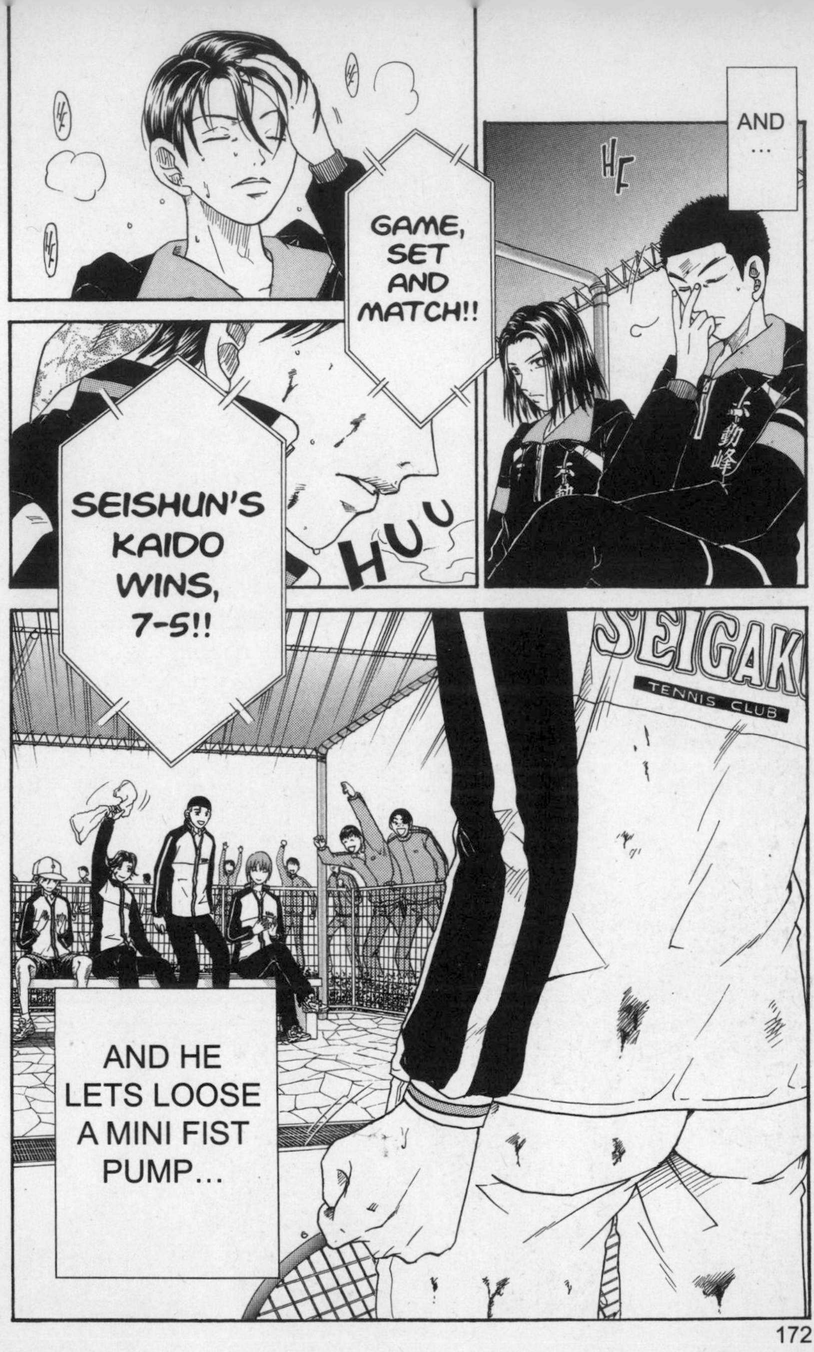
AND …
HF
GAME, SET AND MATCH!!
SEISHUN'S KAIDO WINS, 7-5!!
HUU
SEIGAKU
TENNIS CLUB
AND HE LETS LOOSE A MINI FIST PUMP…

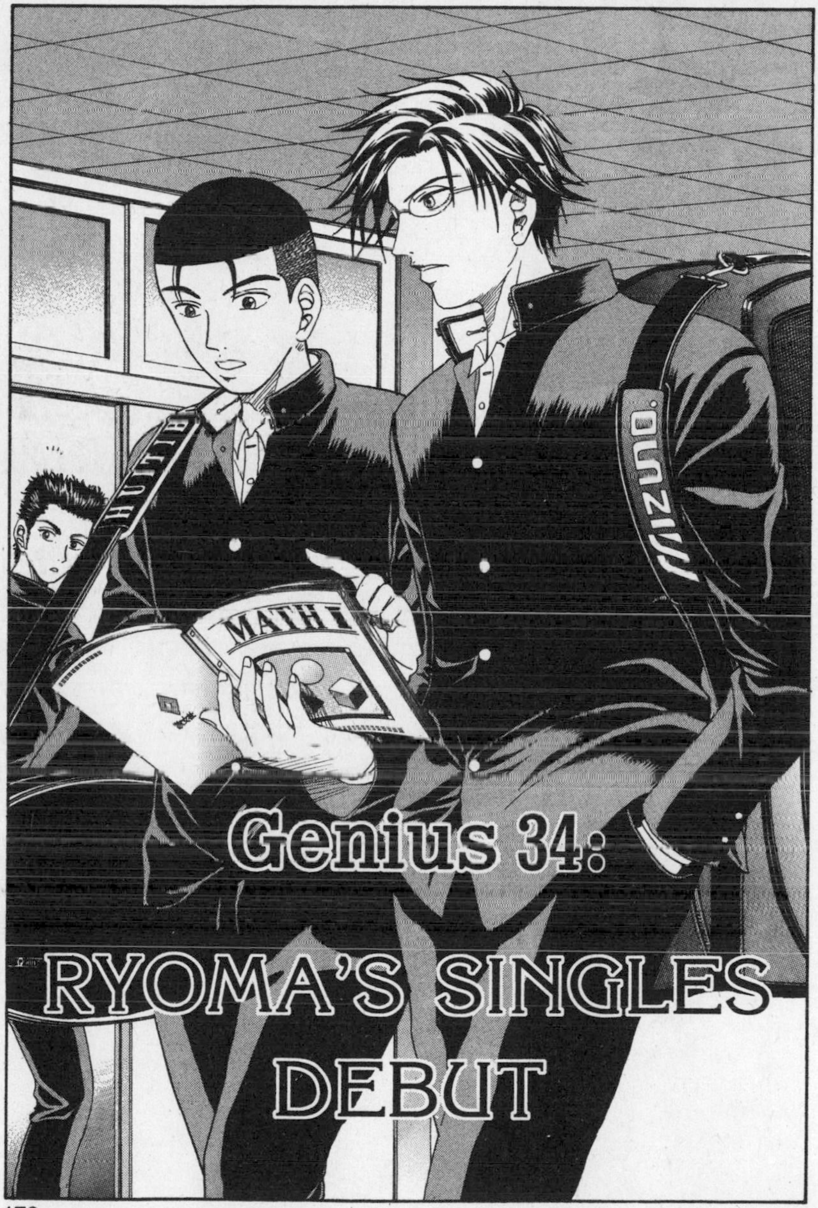
MATH I
Genius 34:
RYOMA'S SINGLES
DEBUT

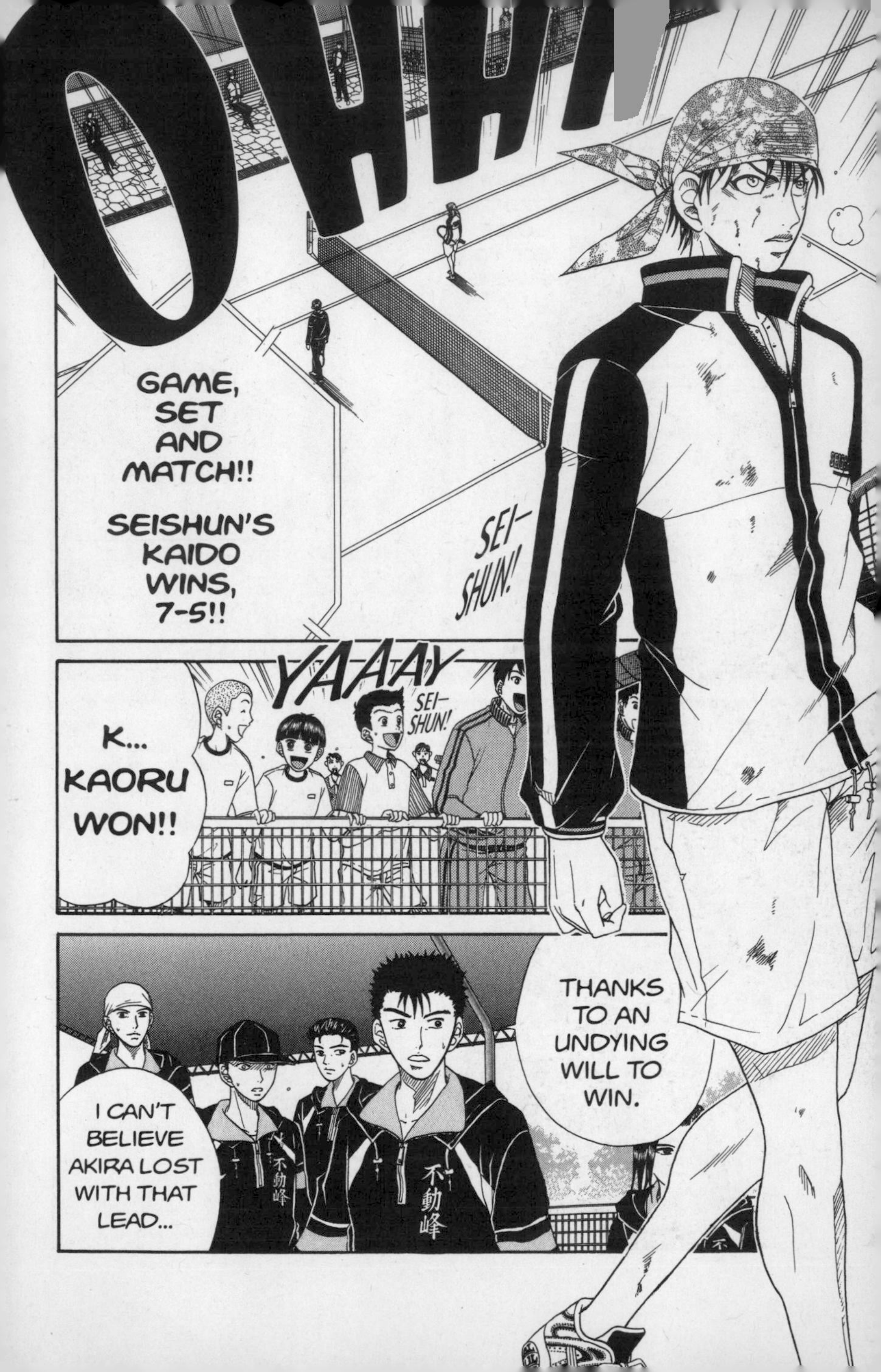

OHH!
SEI-SHUN!
GAME, SET AND MATCH!!
SEISHUN'S KAIDO WINS, 7-5!!
YAAAY
SEI-SHUN!
K... KAORU WON!!
THANKS TO AN UNDYING WILL TO WIN.
I CAN'T BELIEVE AKIRA LOST WITH THAT LEAD...
不動峰
不動峰

READ THIS WAY

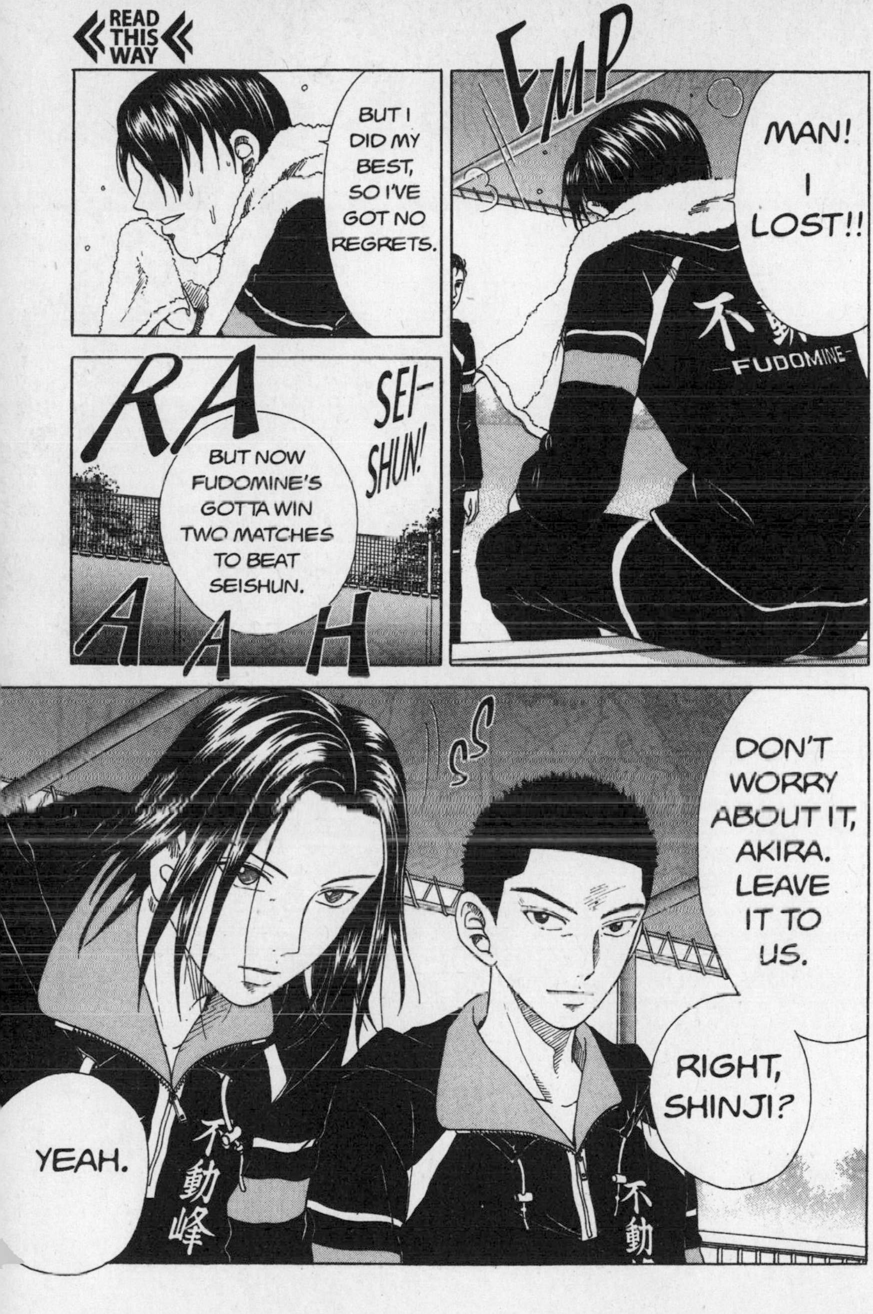
EMP
MAN! I LOST!!
FUDOMINE
BUT I DID MY BEST, SO I'VE GOT NO REGRETS.
SEI-SHUN!
RA AAH
BUT NOW FUDOMINE'S GOTTA WIN TWO MATCHES TO BEAT SEISHUN.
DON'T WORRY ABOUT IT, AKIRA. LEAVE IT TO US.
RIGHT, SHINJI?
YEAH.

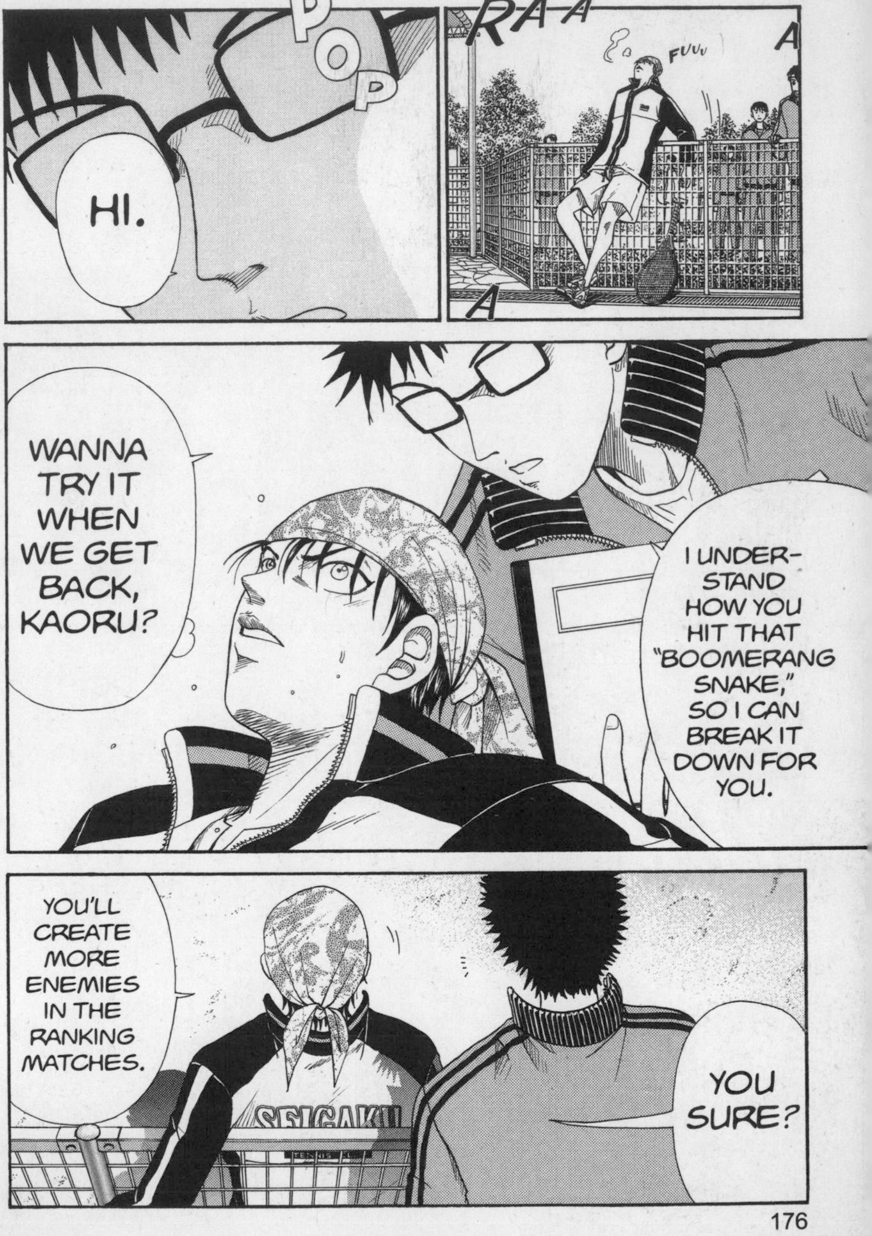
RAAAA
FUUU
POP
HI.
I UNDERSTAND HOW YOU HIT THAT "BOOMERANG SNAKE," SO I CAN BREAK IT DOWN FOR YOU.
WANNA TRY IT WHEN WE GET BACK, KAORU?
YOU'LL CREATE MORE ENEMIES IN THE RANKING MATCHES.
YOU SURE?
SEIGAKU

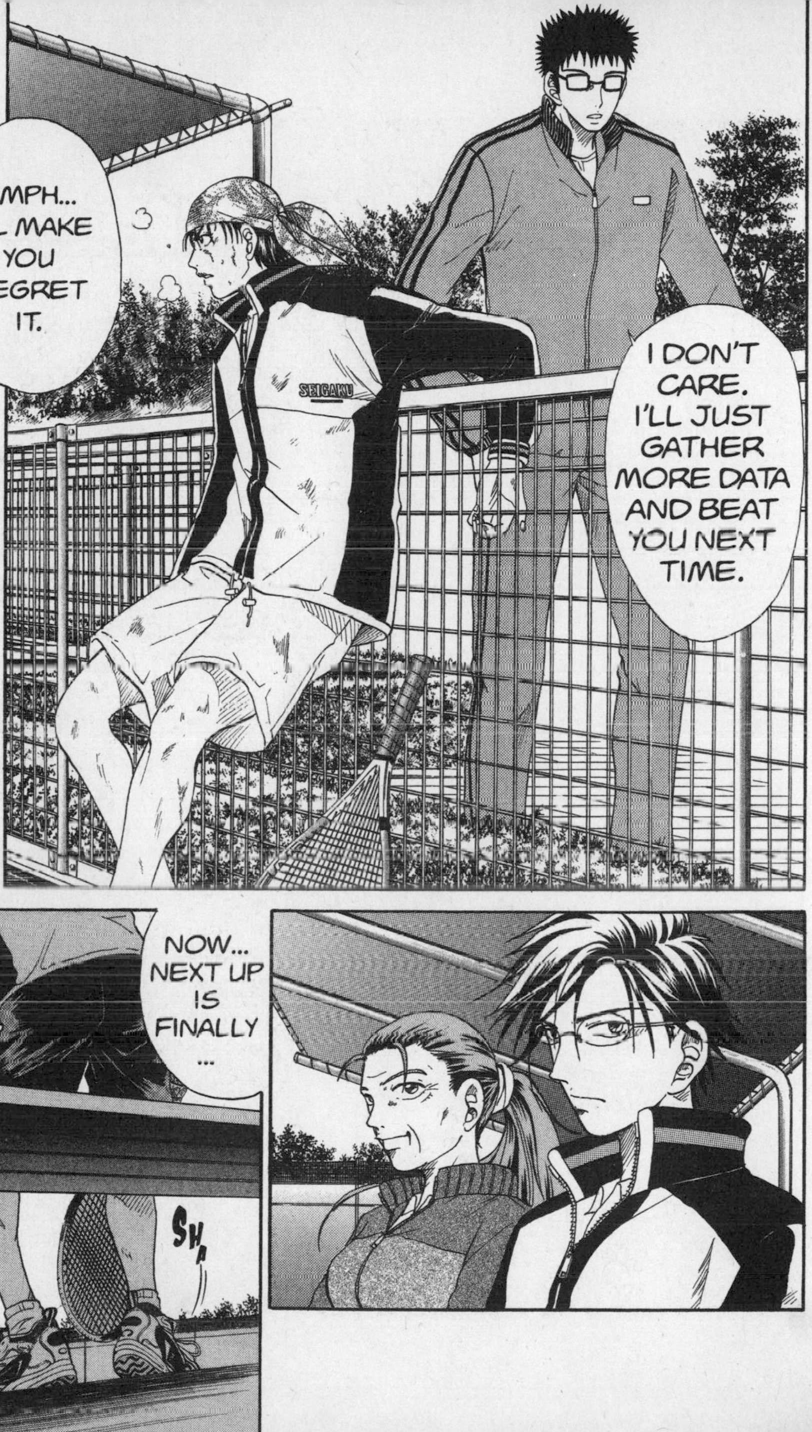
HMPH... I'LL MAKE YOU REGRET IT.
I DON'T CARE. I'LL JUST GATHER MORE DATA AND BEAT YOU NEXT TIME.
SEIGAKU
NOW... NEXT UP IS FINALLY ...
SHA

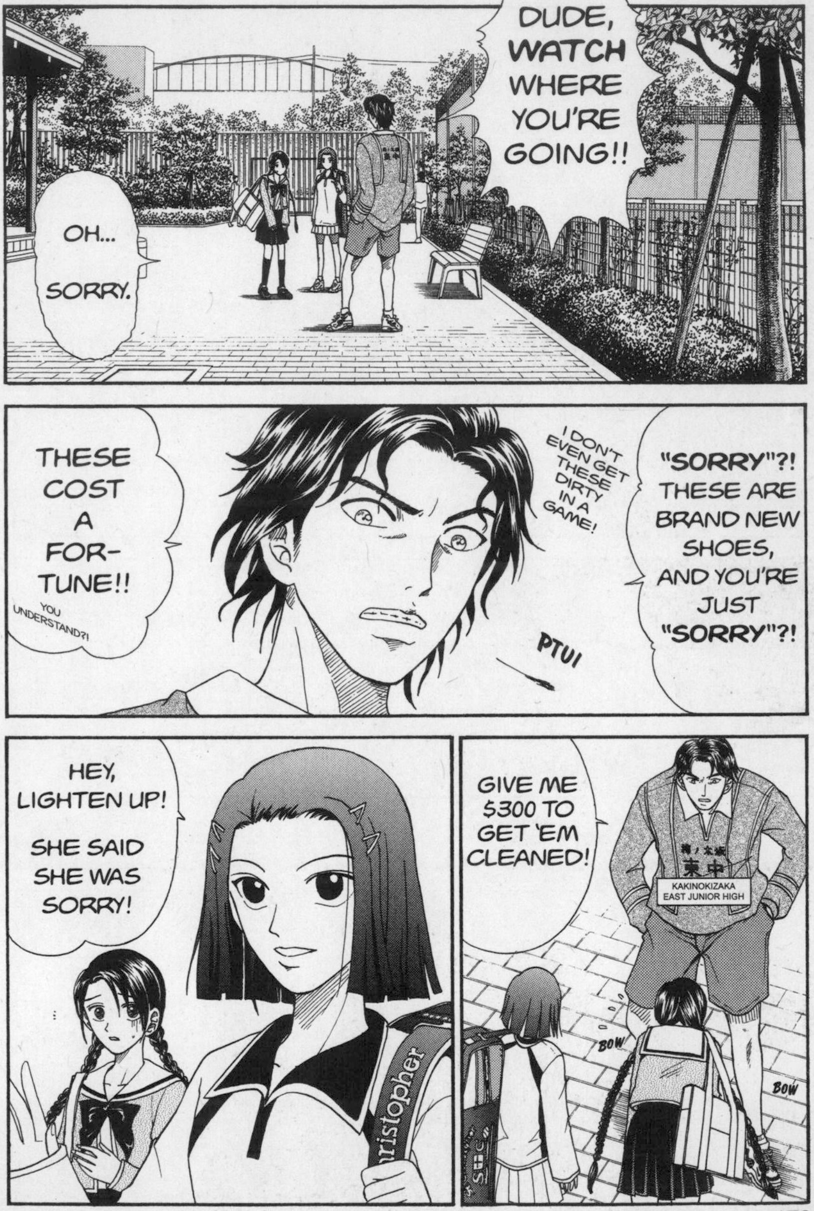
DUDE, WATCH WHERE YOU'RE GOING!!
OH... SORRY.
"SORRY"?! THESE ARE BRAND NEW SHOES, AND YOU'RE JUST "SORRY"?!
I DON'T EVEN GET THESE DIRTY IN A GAME!
PTUI
THESE COST A FOR-TUNE!!
YOU UNDERSTAND?!
GIVE ME $300 TO GET 'EM CLEANED!
KAKINOKIZAKA EAST JUNIOR HIGH
BOW
BOW
HEY, LIGHTEN UP!
SHE SAID SHE WAS SORRY!

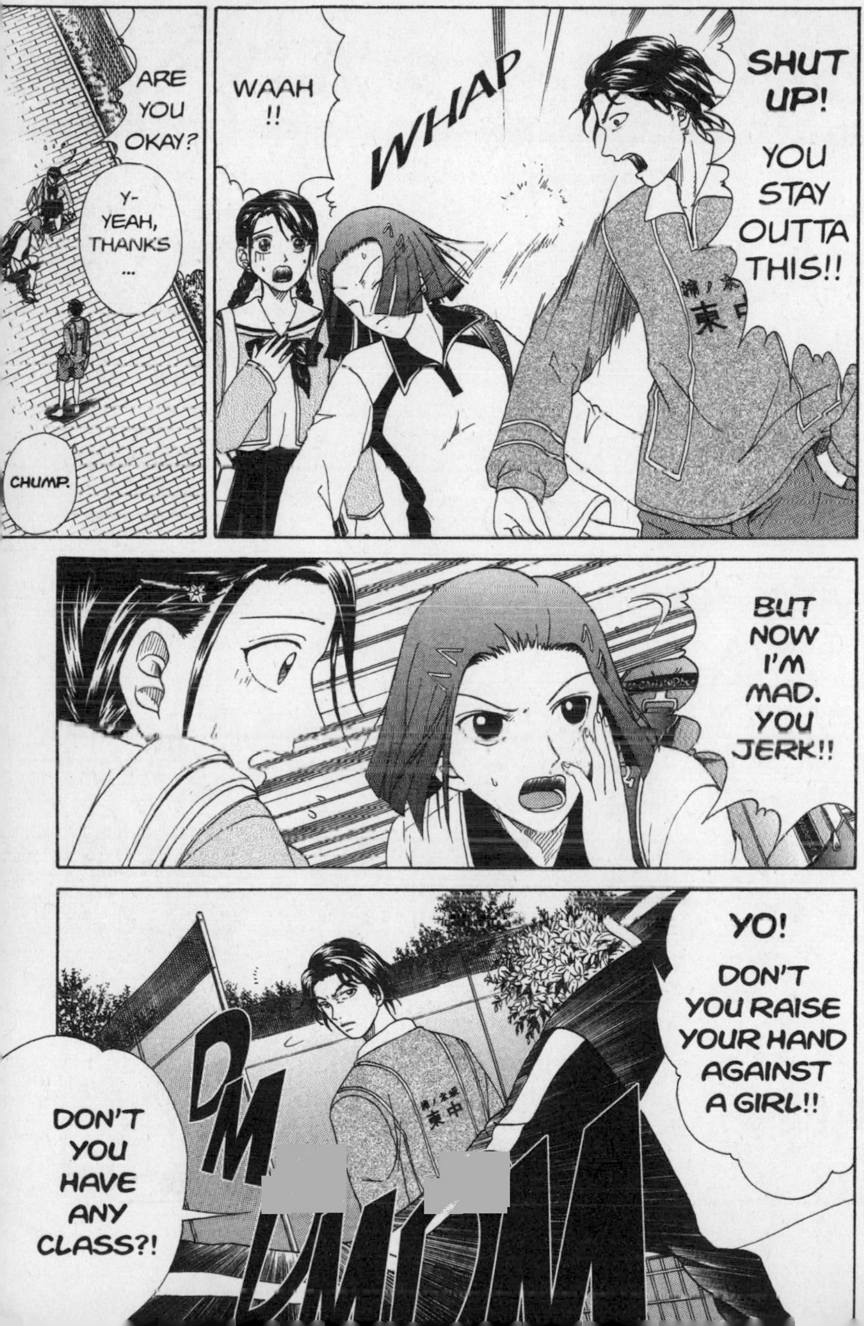
SHUT UP!
YOU STAY OUTTA THIS!!
WHAP
WAAH !!
ARE YOU OKAY?
Y-YEAH, THANKS ...
CHUMP.
BUT NOW I'M MAD. YOU JERK!!
YO!
DON'T YOU RAISE YOUR HAND AGAINST A GIRL!!
DON'T YOU HAVE ANY CLASS?!

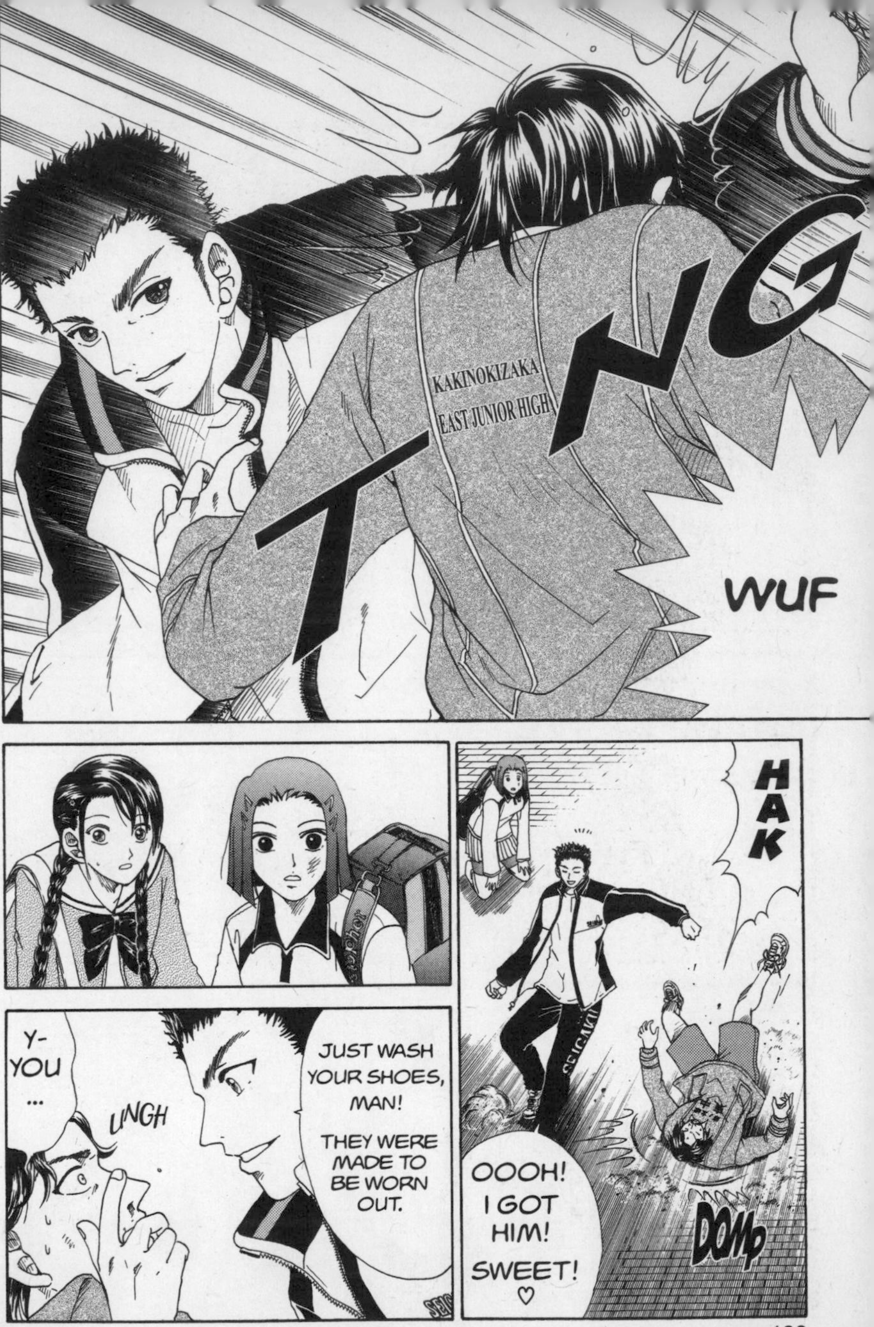
KAKINOKIZAKA
EAST JUNIOR HIGH
THG
WUF
HAK
OOOH! I GOT HIM! SWEET! ♡
DOMP
JUST WASH YOUR SHOES, MAN!
THEY WERE MADE TO BE WORN OUT.
UNGH
Y-YOU ...

READ THIS WAY

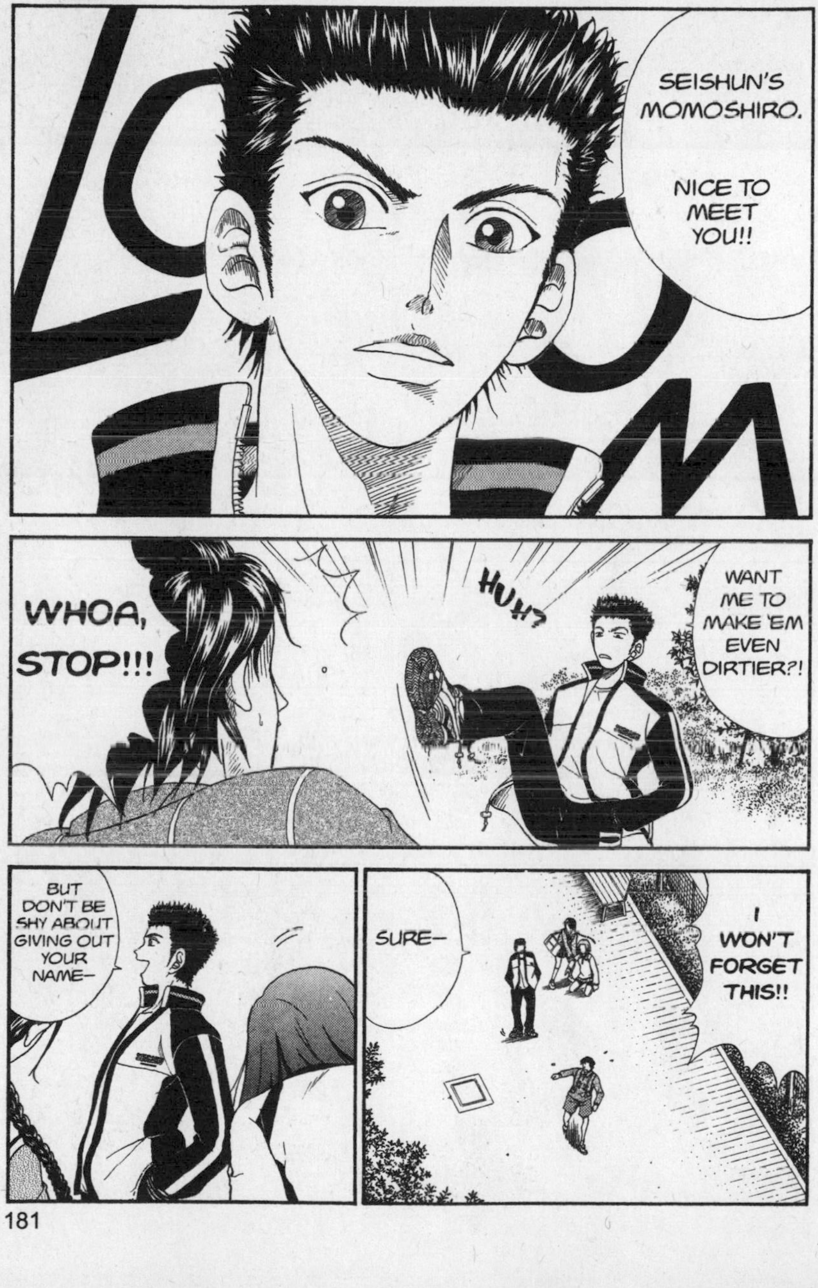
SEISHUN'S MOMOSHIRO.
NICE TO MEET YOU!!
WANT ME TO MAKE 'EM EVEN DIRTIER?!
HUH!?
WHOA, STOP!!!
I WON'T FORGET THIS!!
SURE–
BUT DON'T BE SHY ABOUT GIVING OUT YOUR NAME–

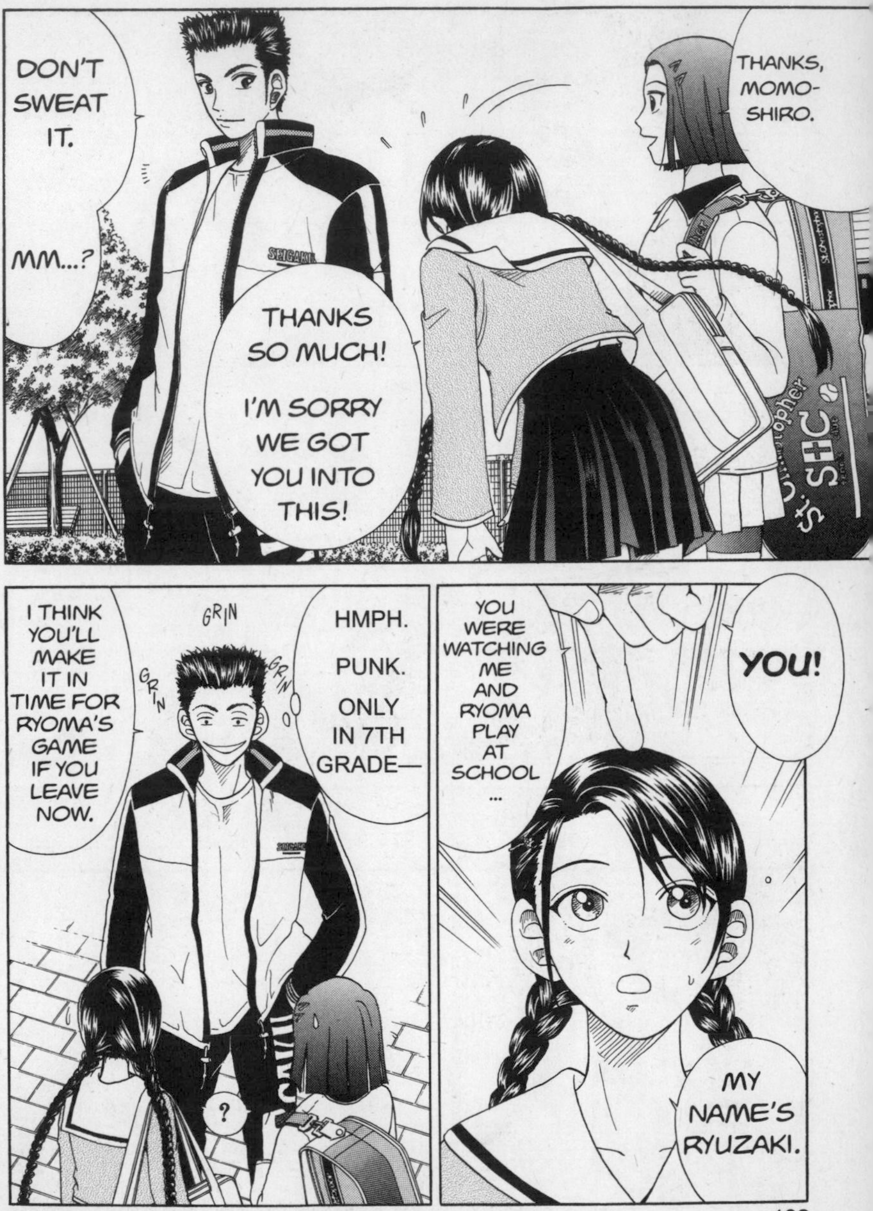
THANKS, MOMO-SHIRO.
THANKS SO MUCH!
I'M SORRY WE GOT YOU INTO THIS!
DON'T SWEAT IT.
MM...?
YOU!
YOU WERE WATCHING ME AND RYOMA PLAY AT SCHOOL ...
MY NAME'S RYUZAKI.
HMPH.
PUNK.
ONLY IN 7TH GRADE—
GRIN
GRIN
GRIN
I THINK YOU'LL MAKE IT IN TIME FOR RYOMA'S GAME IF YOU LEAVE NOW.
?

READ THIS WAY

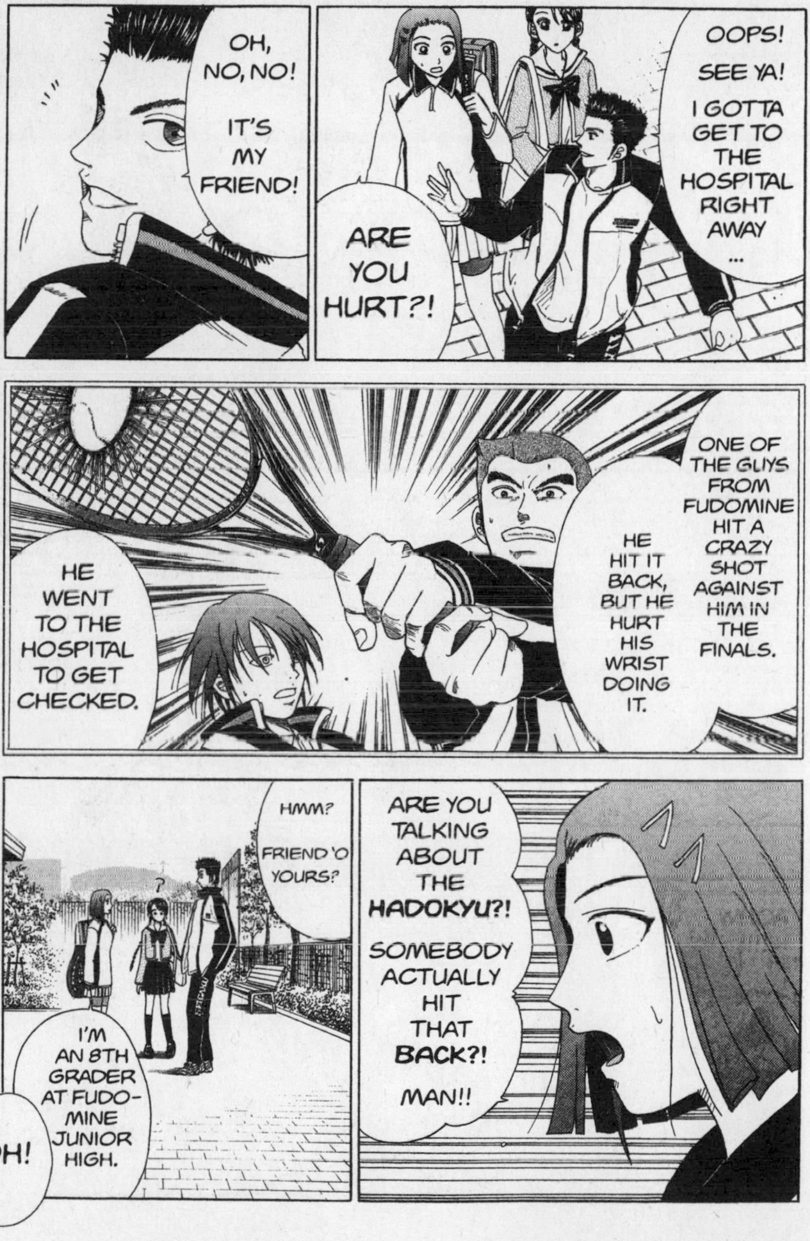
OOPS! SEE YA! I GOTTA GET TO THE HOSPITAL RIGHT AWAY ...
ARE YOU HURT?!
OH, NO, NO! IT'S MY FRIEND!
ONE OF THE GUYS FROM FUDOMINE HIT A CRAZY SHOT AGAINST HIM IN THE FINALS.
HE HIT IT BACK, BUT HE HURT HIS WRIST DOING IT.
HE WENT TO THE HOSPITAL TO GET CHECKED.
ARE YOU TALKING ABOUT THE HADOKYU?! SOMEBODY ACTUALLY HIT THAT BACK?! MAN!!
HMM? FRIEND 'O YOURS?
I'M AN 8TH GRADER AT FUDO-MINE JUNIOR HIGH.
OH!

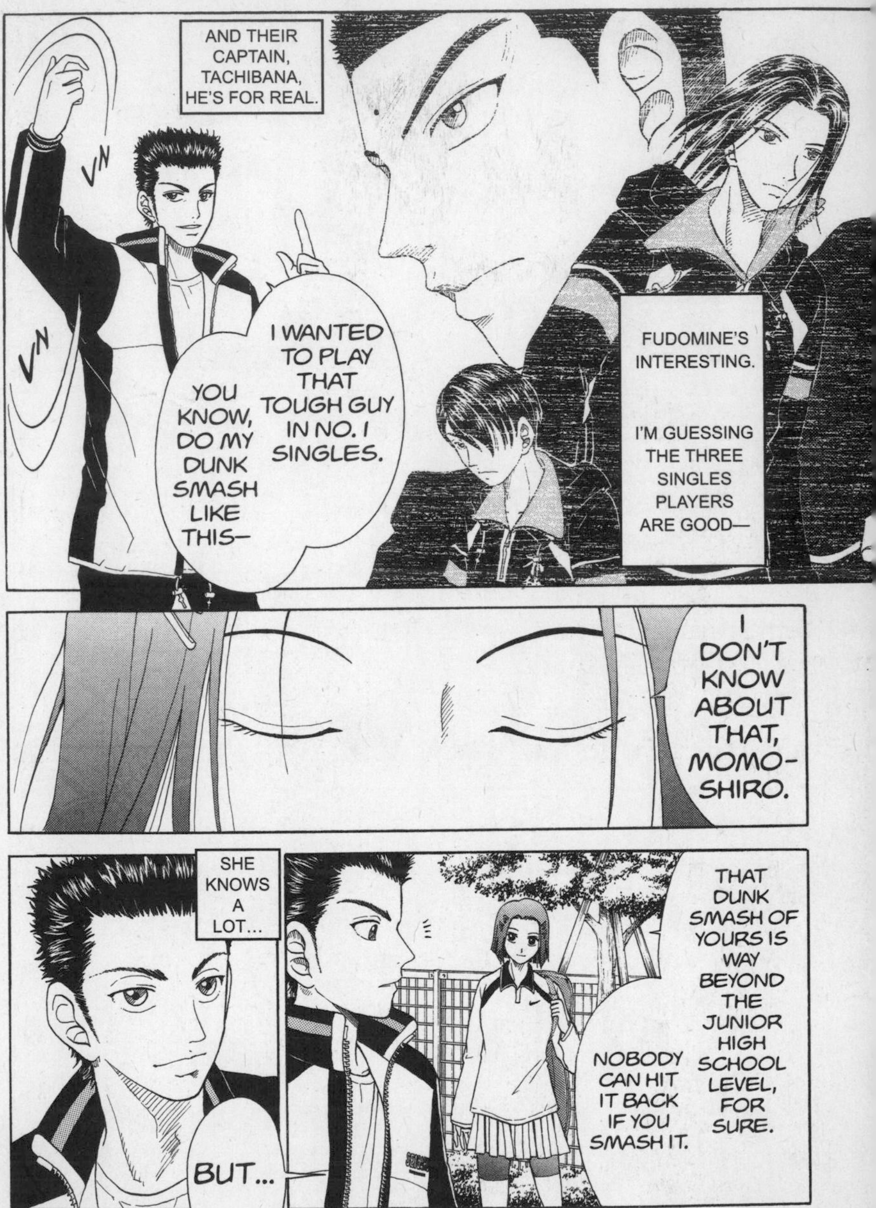
FUDOMINE'S INTERESTING.
I'M GUESSING THE THREE SINGLES PLAYERS ARE GOOD—
AND THEIR CAPTAIN, TACHIBANA, HE'S FOR REAL.
I WANTED TO PLAY THAT TOUGH GUY IN NO. 1 SINGLES.
YOU KNOW, DO MY DUNK SMASH LIKE THIS—
VN
VN
I DON'T KNOW ABOUT THAT, MOMOSHIRO.
THAT DUNK SMASH OF YOURS IS WAY BEYOND THE JUNIOR HIGH SCHOOL LEVEL, FOR SURE.
NOBODY CAN HIT IT BACK IF YOU SMASH IT.
BUT...
SHE KNOWS A LOT...

READ THIS WAY

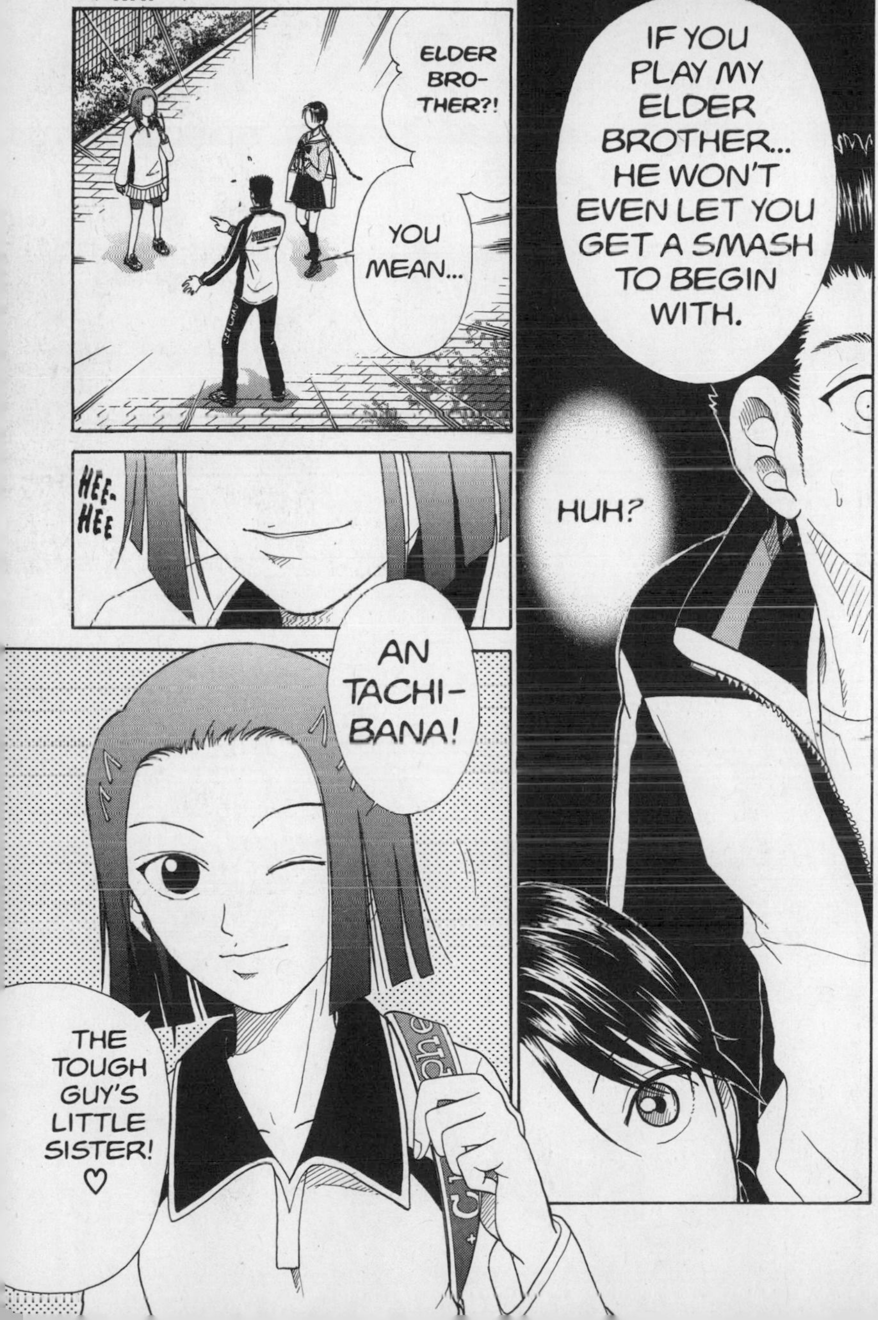
IF YOU PLAY MY ELDER BROTHER... HE WON'T EVEN LET YOU GET A SMASH TO BEGIN WITH.
HUH?
ELDER BRO-THER?!
YOU MEAN...
HEE-HEE
AN TACHI-BANA!
THE TOUGH GUY'S LITTLE SISTER! ♡

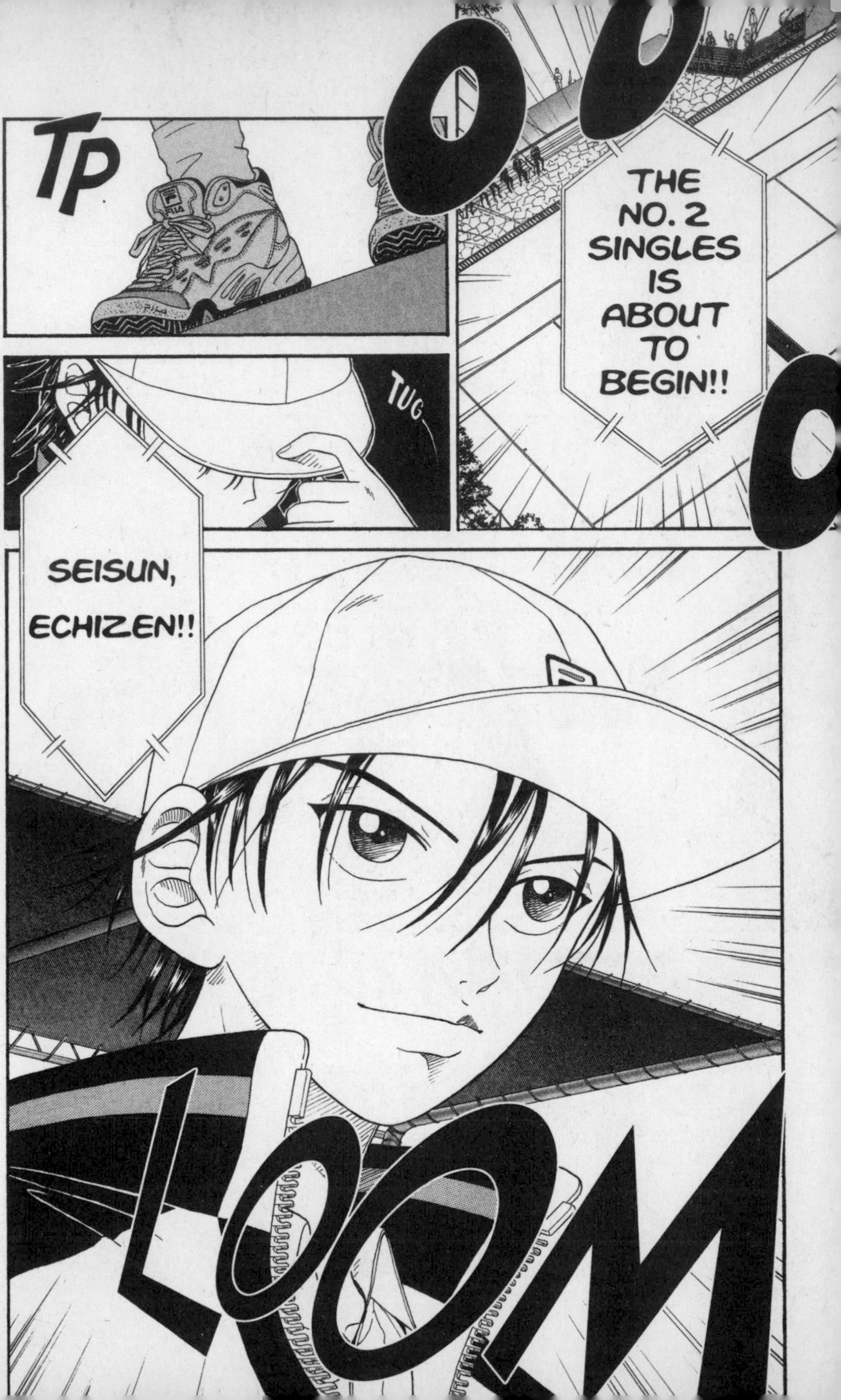
THE NO. 2 SINGLES IS ABOUT TO BEGIN!!
TP
TUG
SEISUN, ECHIZEN!!
LOOM

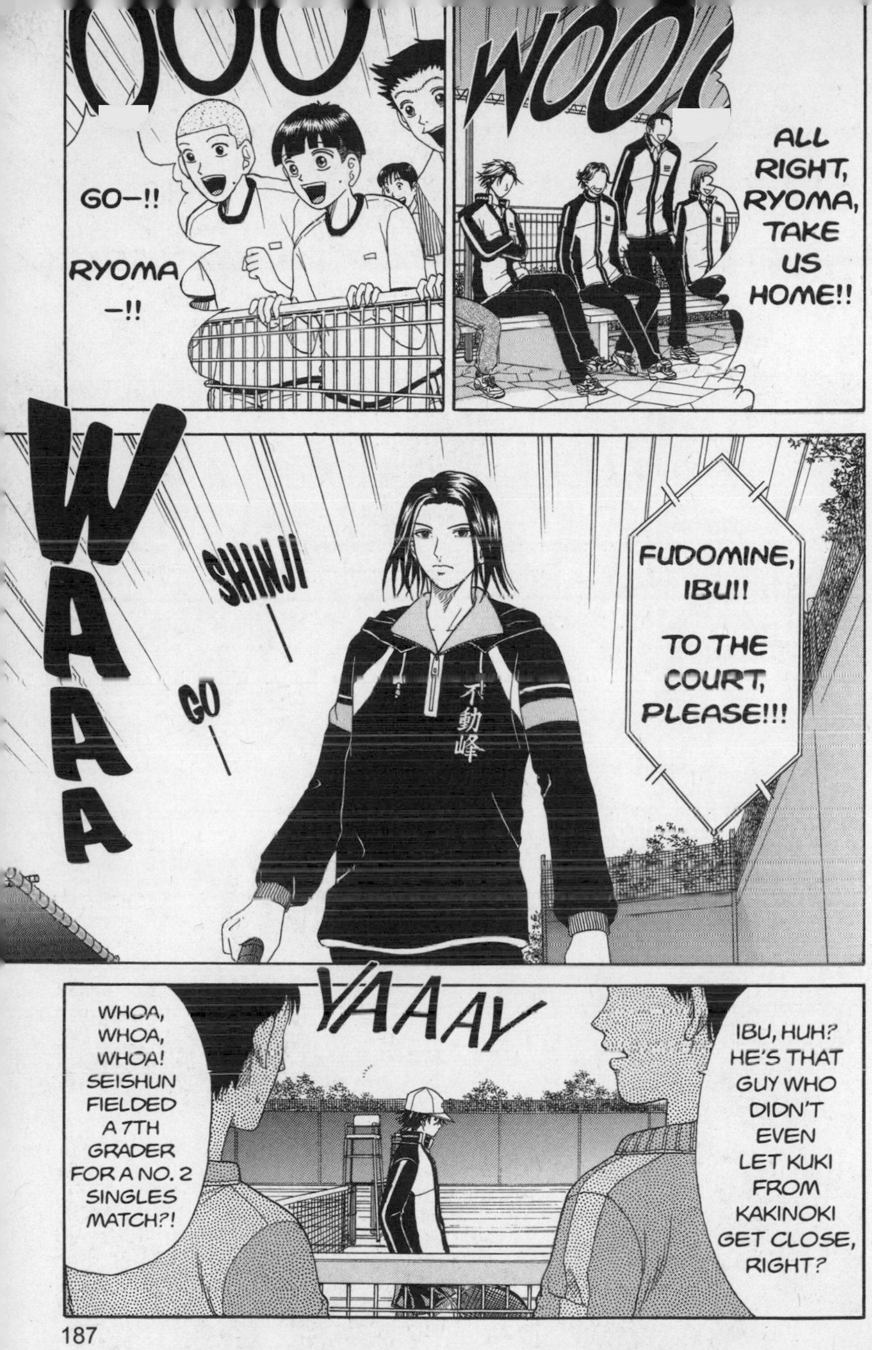
WOOO
ALL RIGHT, RYOMA, TAKE US HOME!!
OOO
GO—!!
RYOMA—!!
FUDOMINE, IBU!!
TO THE COURT, PLEASE!!!
SHINJI—
GO—
WAAAA
IBU, HUH? HE'S THAT GUY WHO DIDN'T EVEN LET KUKI FROM KAKINOKI GET CLOSE, RIGHT?
YAAAY
WHOA, WHOA, WHOA! SEISHUN FIELDED A 7TH GRADER FOR A NO. 2 SINGLES MATCH?!

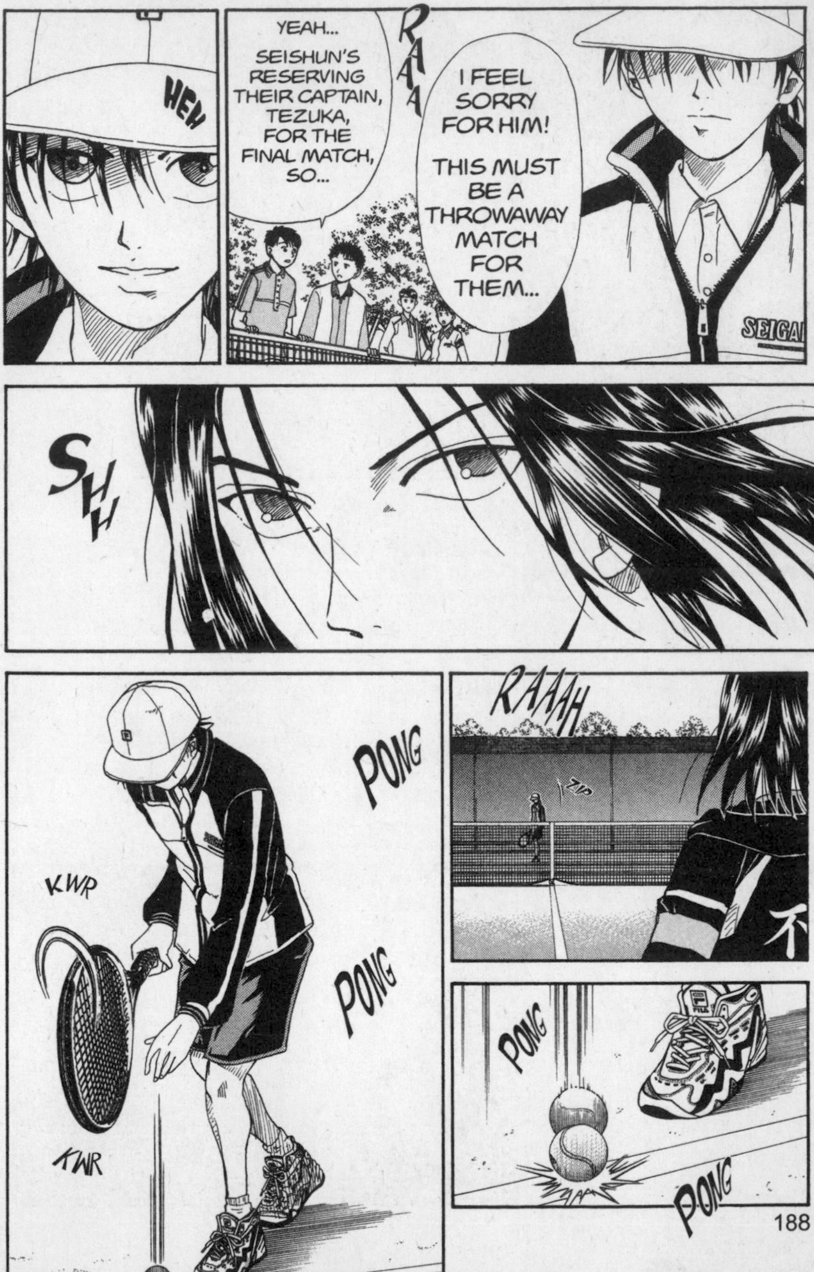
RAAA
I FEEL SORRY FOR HIM!
THIS MUST BE A THROWAWAY MATCH FOR THEM...
YEAH... SEISHUN'S RESERVING THEIR CAPTAIN, TEZUKA, FOR THE FINAL MATCH, SO...
SEIGA
HEH
SHH
RAAAH
ZIP
PONG
PONG
PONG
PONG
KWR
KWR

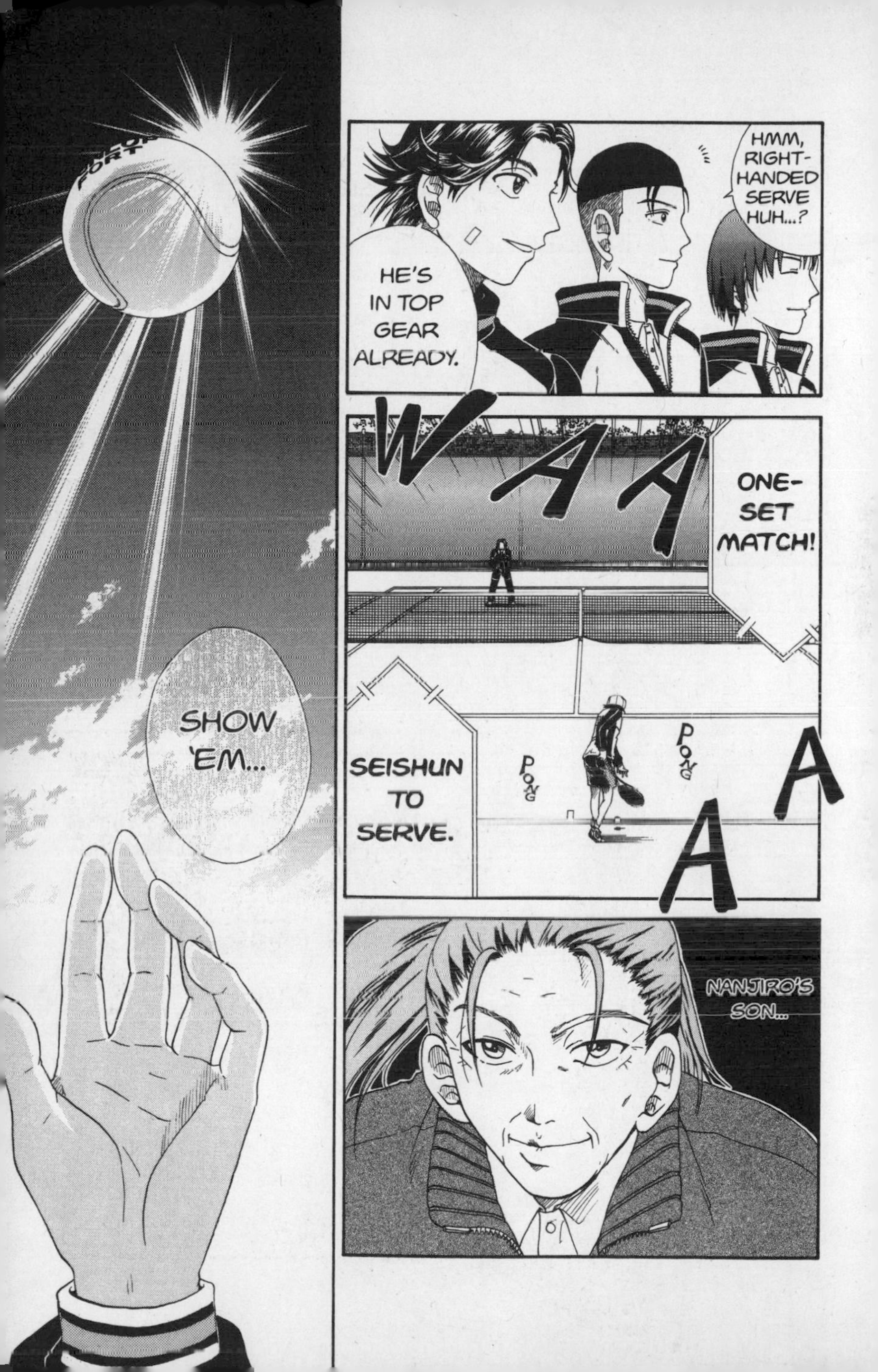
HMM, RIGHT-HANDED SERVE HUH...?
HE'S IN TOP GEAR ALREADY.
WAA
ONE-SET MATCH!
SEISHUN TO SERVE.
PONG
PONG
AA
NANJIRO'S SON...
SHOW 'EM...

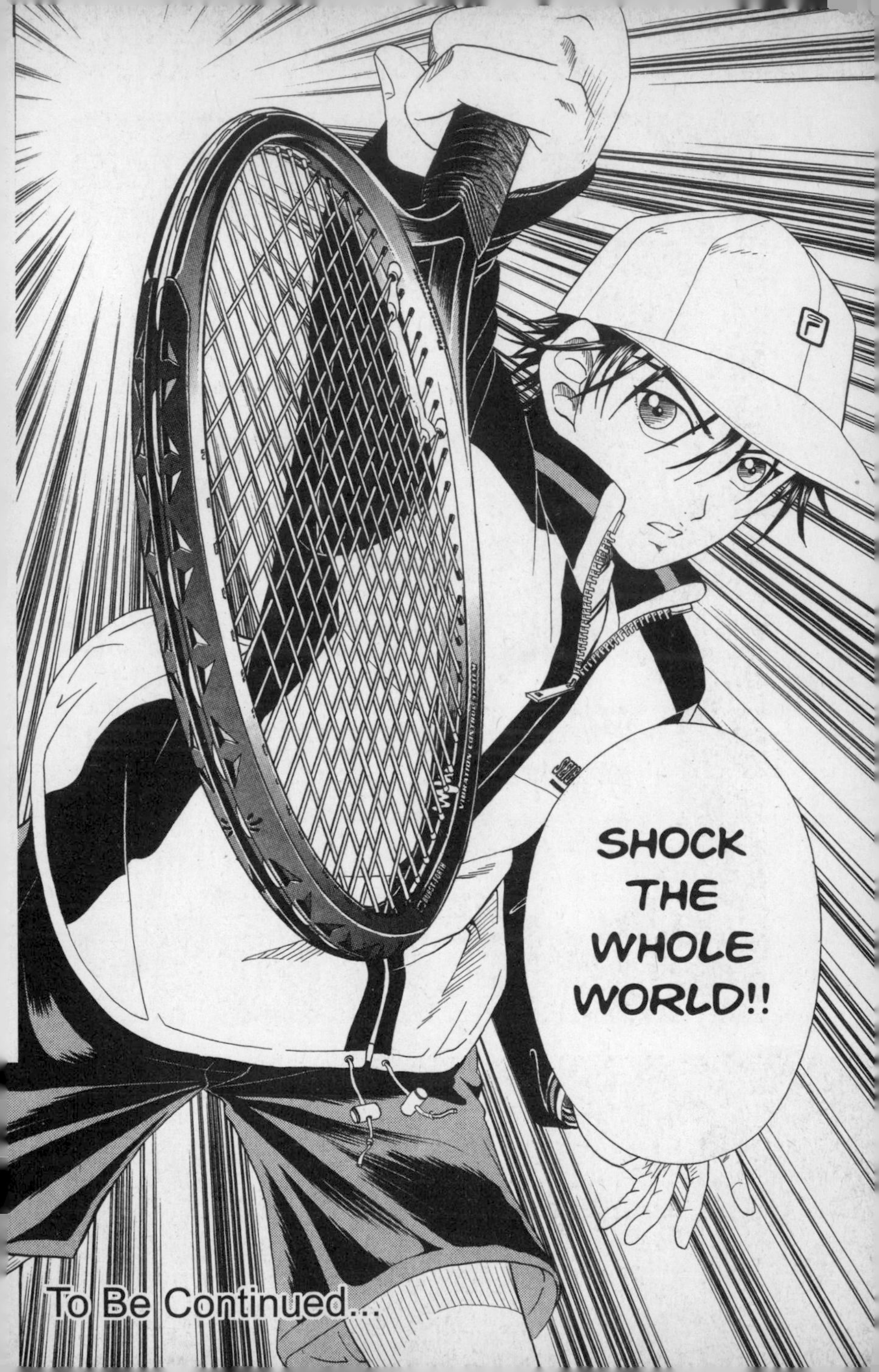
SHOCK THE WHOLE WORLD!!
To Be Continued...

In The Next Volume

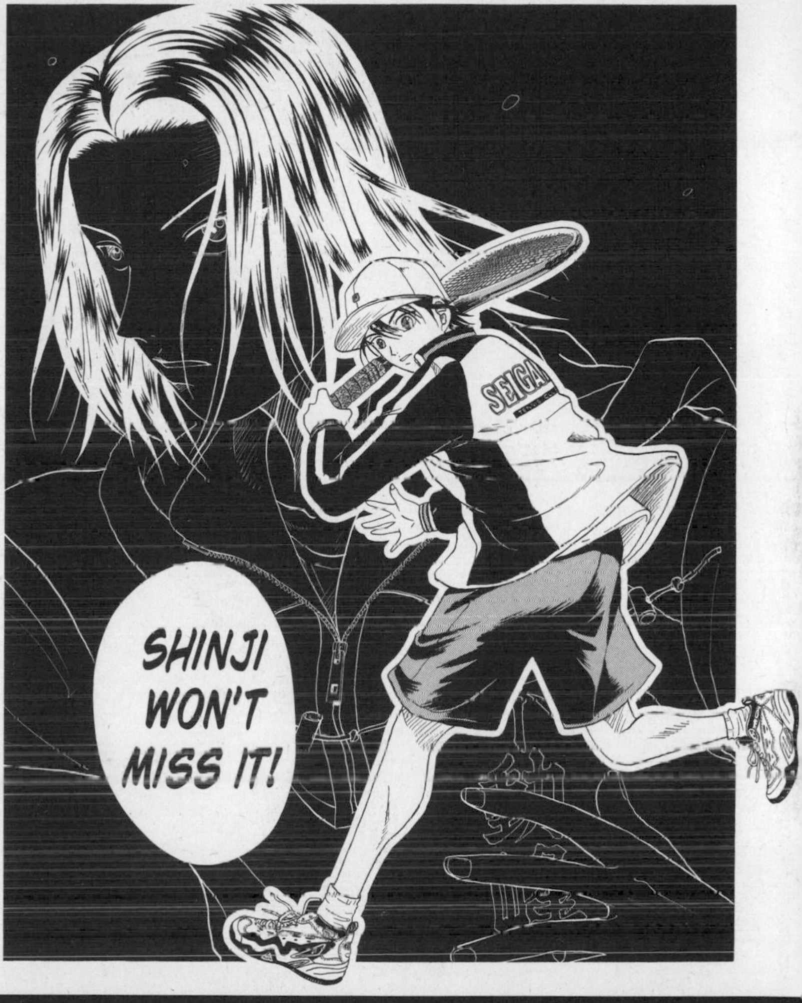
SEIGAKU
SHINJI WON'T MISS IT!

With only one victory away from advancing to the City tournament, Seishun Academy pits The Prince of Tennis Ryoma Echizen against the mysterious and mumbling Shinji of Fudomine.

Available Now!

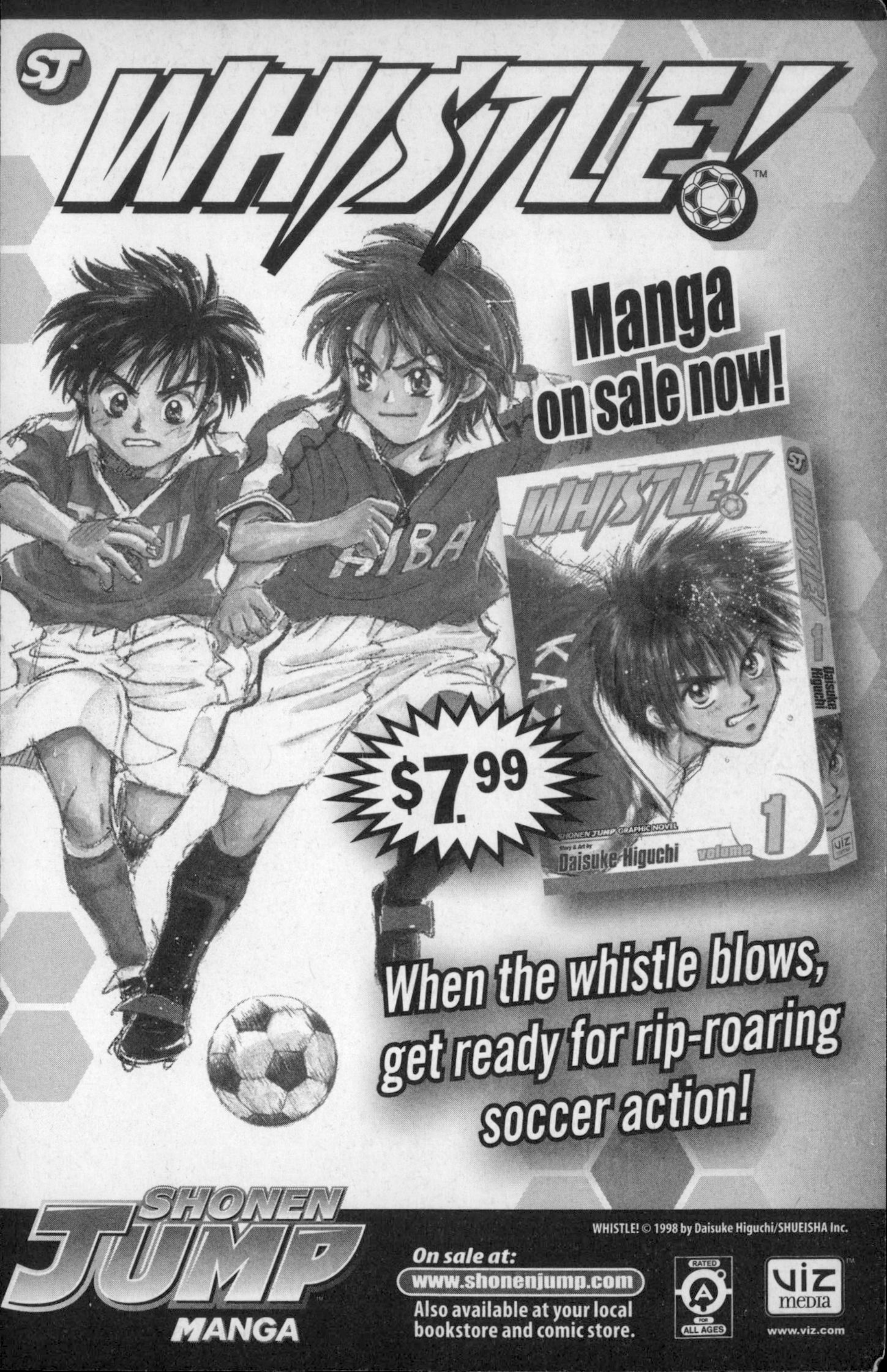

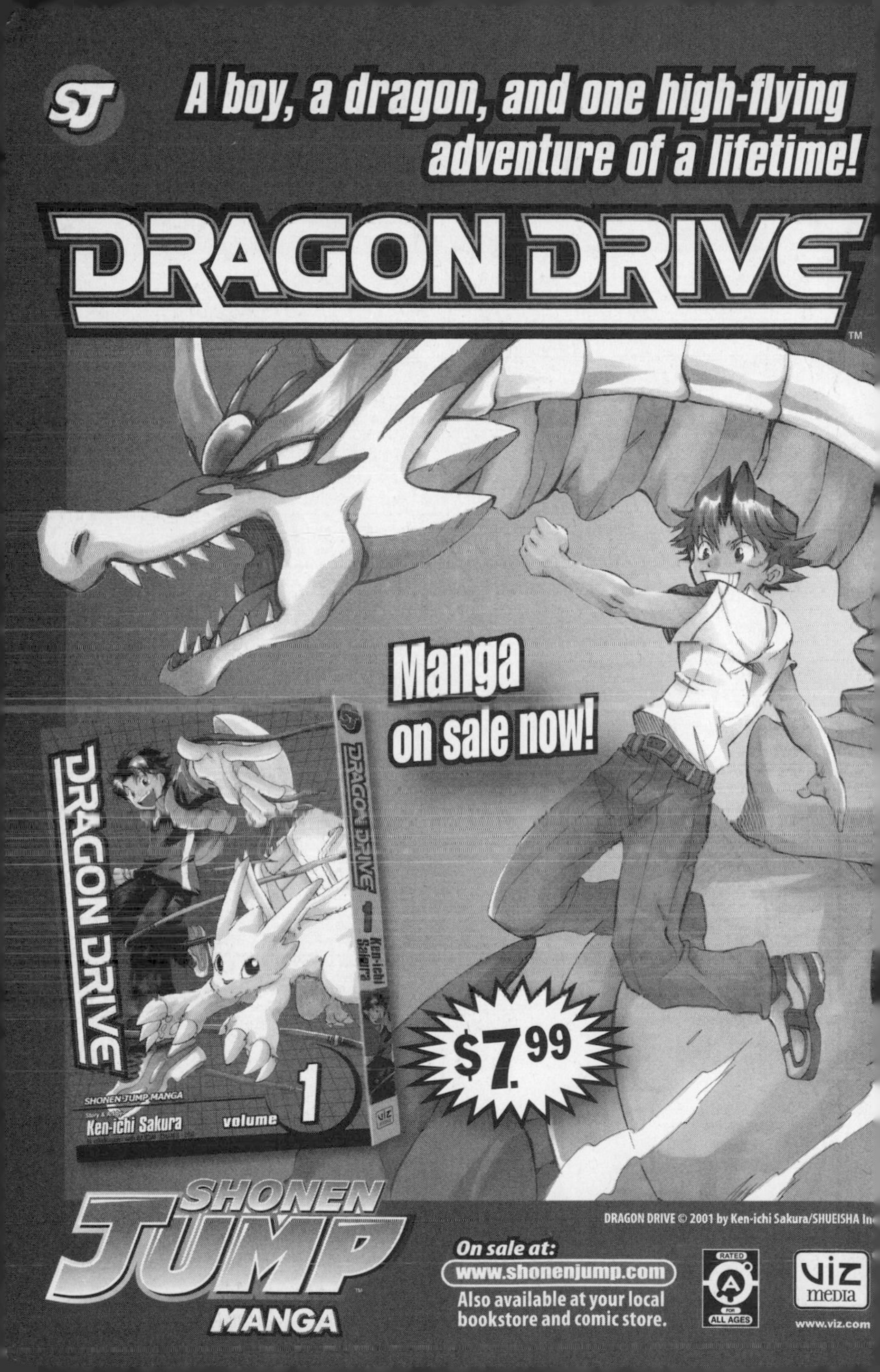
SJ
A boy, a dragon, and one high-flying adventure of a lifetime!
DRAGON DRIVE
TM
Manga on sale now!
DRAGON DRIVE
SHONEN JUMP MANGA
Ken-ichi Sakura
volume 1
DRAGON DRIVE
1
Ken-ichi Sakura
$7.99
SHONEN JUMP MANGA
DRAGON DRIVE © 2001 by Ken-ichi Sakura/SHUEISHA Inc
On sale at:
www.shonenjump.com
Also available at your local bookstore and comic store.
RATED A FOR ALL AGES
VIZ media
www.viz.com

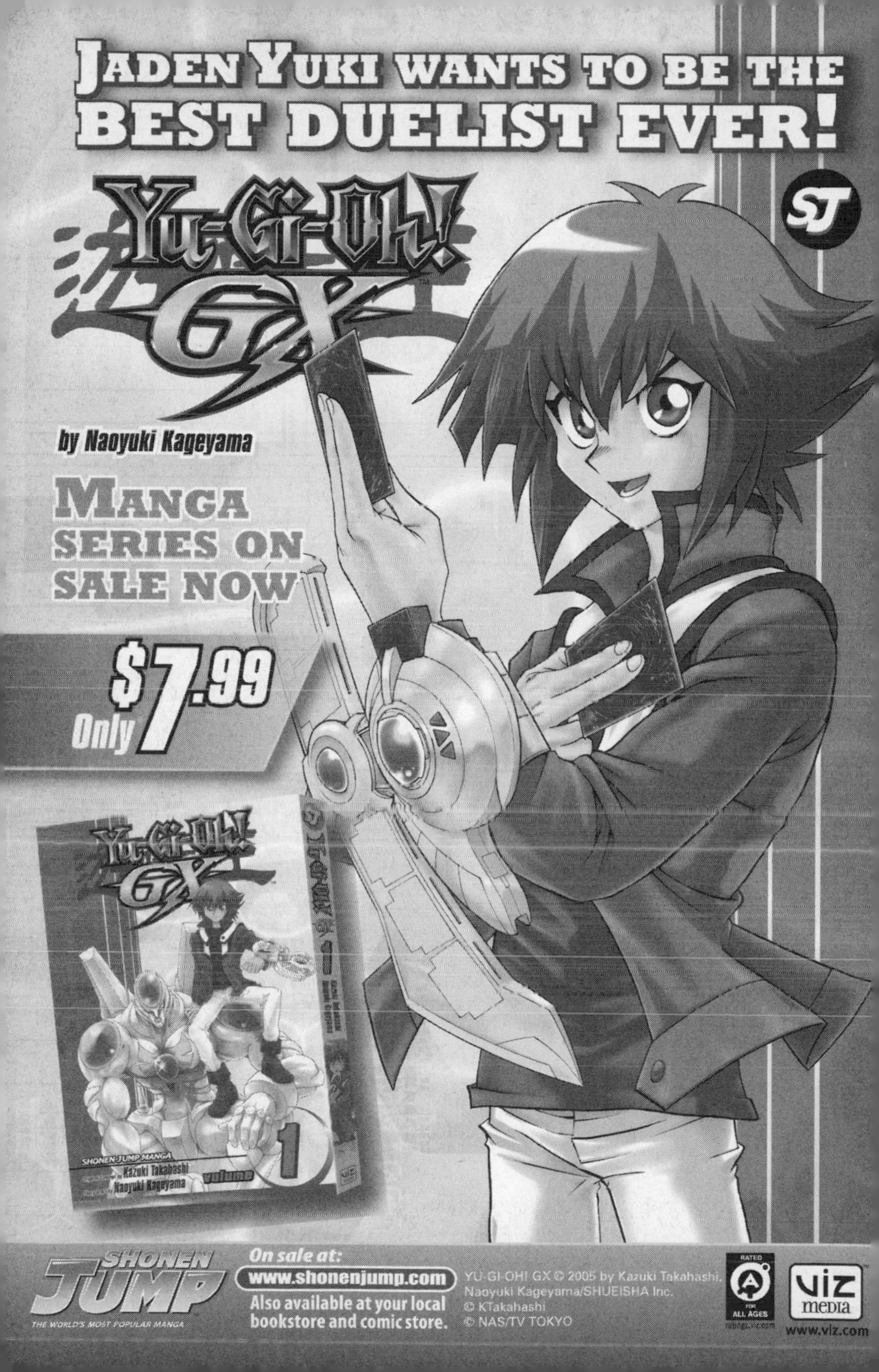

JADEN YUKI WANTS TO BE THE BEST DUELIST EVER!
SJ
YU-GI-OH! GX
by Naoyuki Kageyama
MANGA SERIES ON SALE NOW
Only $7.99
YU-GI-OH! GX
SHONEN JUMP MANGA
Kazuki Takahashi
Naoyuki Kageyama
volume 1
SHONEN JUMP
THE WORLD'S MOST POPULAR MANGA
On sale at:
www.shonenjump.com
Also available at your local bookstore and comic store.
YU-GI-OH! GX © 2005 by Kazuki Takahashi, Naoyuki Kageyama/SHUEISHA Inc.
© KTakahashi
© NAS/TV TOKYO
RATED A FOR ALL AGES
VIZ media
www.viz.com

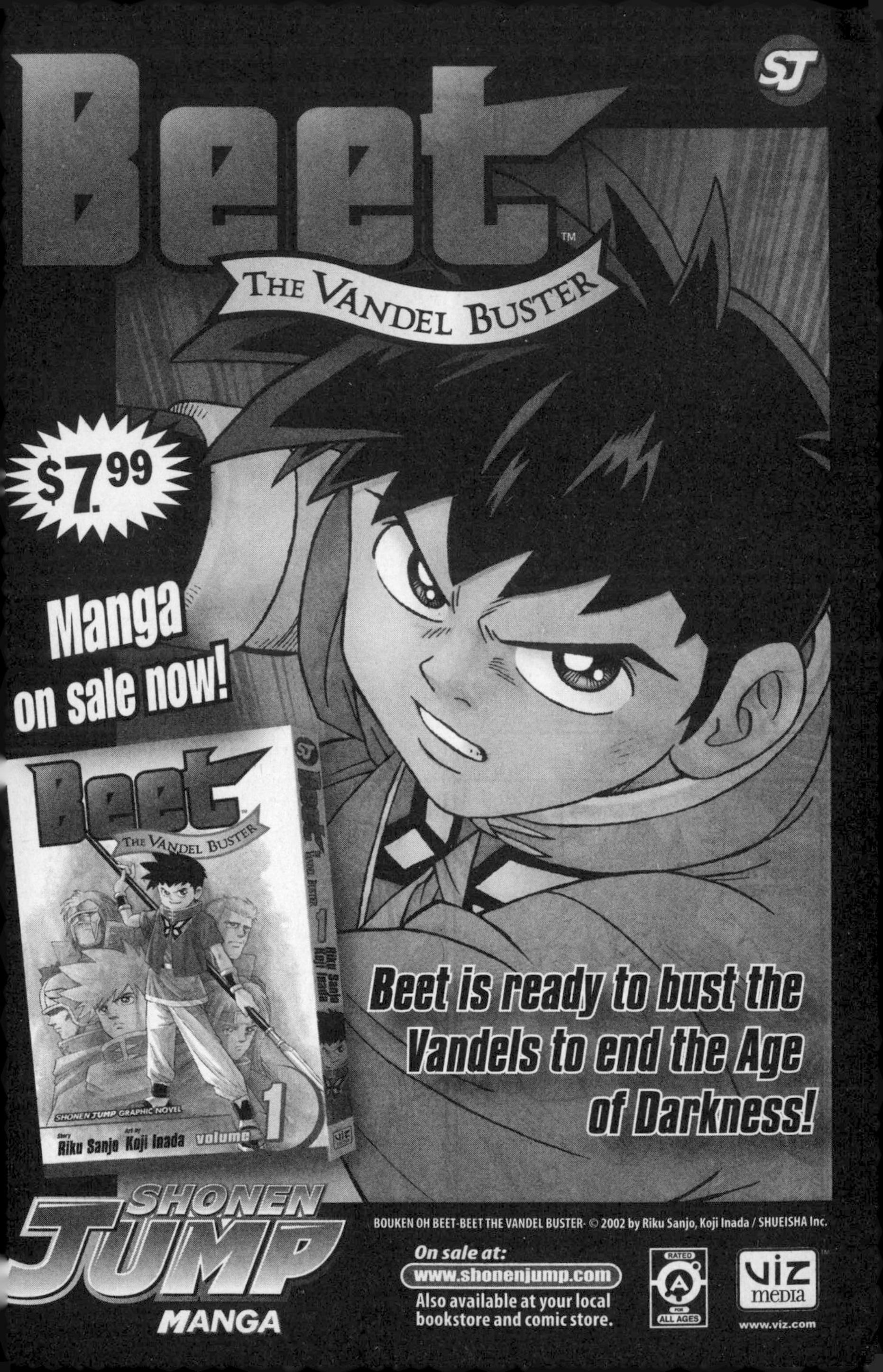
SJ
Beet™
THE VANDEL BUSTER
$7.99
Manga on sale now!
Beet
THE VANDEL BUSTER
SHONEN JUMP GRAPHIC NOVEL
Story Riku Sanjo Art by Koji Inada
volume 1
Beet is ready to bust the Vandels to end the Age of Darkness!
SHONEN JUMP MANGA
BOUKEN OH BEET-BEET THE VANDEL BUSTER- © 2002 by Riku Sanjo, Koji Inada / SHUEISHA Inc.
On sale at:
www.shonenjump.com
Also available at your local bookstore and comic store.
RATED A FOR ALL AGES
VIZ media
www.viz.com

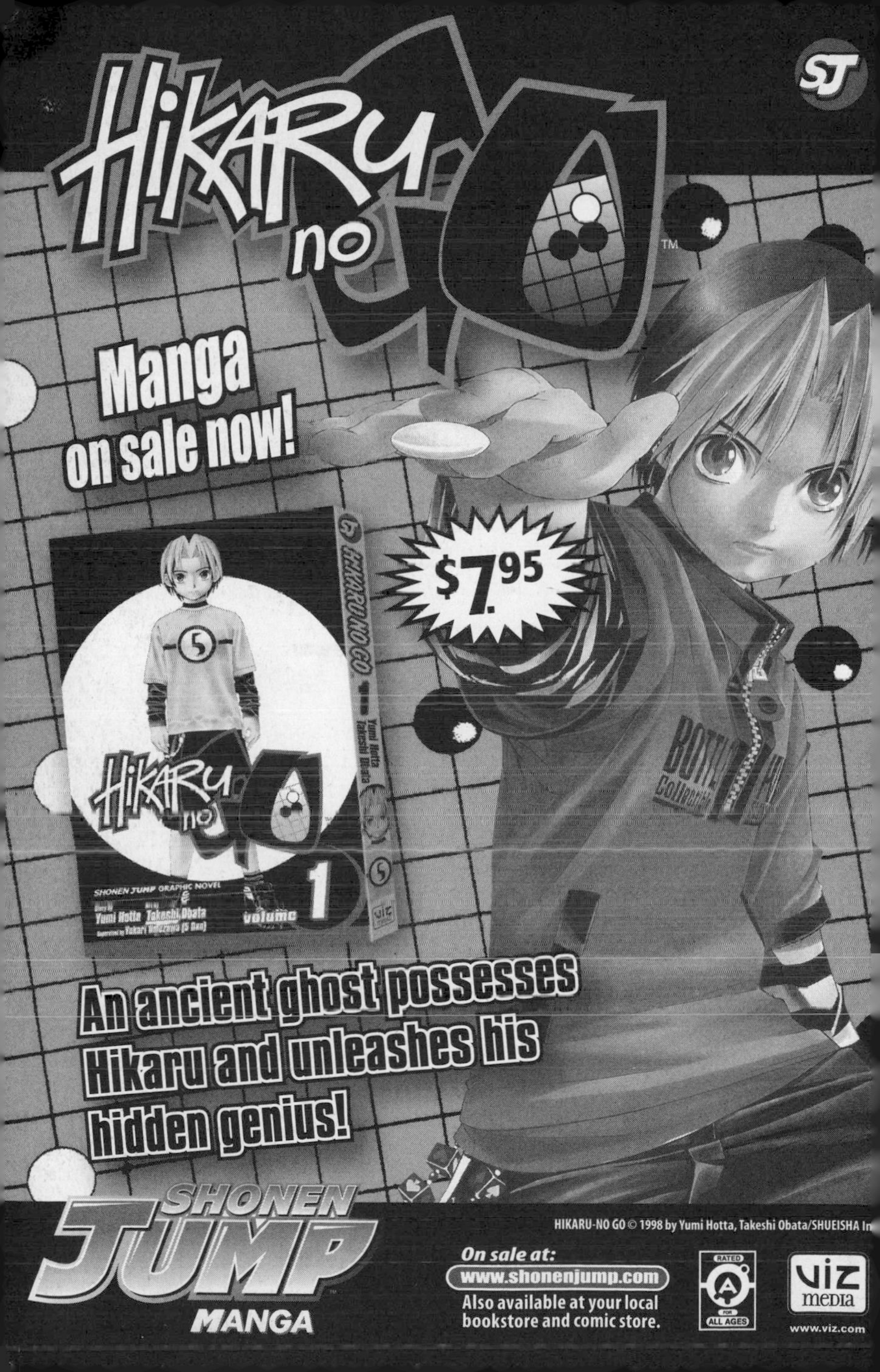
SJ
HIKARU no GO™
Manga on sale now!
$7.95
SHONEN JUMP GRAPHIC NOVEL
Yumi Hotta Takeshi Obata
volume 1
An ancient ghost possesses Hikaru and unleashes his hidden genius!
SHONEN JUMP MANGA
HIKARU-NO GO © 1998 by Yumi Hotta, Takeshi Obata/SHUEISHA In
On sale at:
www.shonenjump.com
Also available at your local bookstore and comic store.
RATED A FOR ALL AGES
VIZ media
www.viz.com